Can there be a post-modern hermeneutic of the Scriptures which does full justice to the text? Jim De Young and Sarah Hurty say Yes. They center the hermeneutic spiral on a renewed spirituality, giving emphasis to the Holy Spirit as the interpreter of both the Word and history, validated by the community of faith. Bible students who have felt that earlier methods of interpreting the Bible, while orthodox and secure, result in rather unfaithful "abstract meaning" will find exciting and challenging ideas in *Beyond the Obvious*.

Stephen A. Hayner
President, InterVarsity
Christian Fellowship

If the Church is to "do" and "live" her theology as she should, it must be based upon an accurate understanding of the seed-bed from which that theology comes. While there are many creative (and even questionable) ideas in their book, De Young and Hurty have as their larger goal a system that will aid us in our interpretive task. Not satisfied with the status quo, they offer new insights that will challenge our thinking and hopefully make us more exacting in our study of the Word of God. Read to your benefit; critique them to their benefit; and the Church will be the stronger as a result.

W. Robert Cook
Professor of Biblical Theology
Emeritus
Western Seminary

The authors offer a timely and vigorous challenge to the hermeneutical status quo among Evangelicals. Their daring proposal places the Bible in the center of the community of faith under the power of the Holy Spirit. I hope *Beyond the Obvious* receives a hearing. The book will greatly clarify the issues in the current hermeneutical debate.

David Fisher, Senior Minister
Park Street Church
Boston, Massachussetts

There is much food for thought in this use of the Old Testament in the New Testament. What is said here could be combined with discussions elsewhere to help form a solid basis for a discussion of this issue by evangelicals.

Darrell Bock
Professor of New Testament Studies
Dallas Theological Seminary

This is a noteworthy and valuable effort for recognizing the implications of culture in hermeneutics. By making the Kingdom of God central, a whole-Bible view of mission develops from this hermeneutic, deepening and broadening our understanding of God at work in the world.

Donald K. Smith, Chairman, Division of
Intercultural Studies, Western Seminary
Founder of Daystar University
Nairobi, Kenya

Beyond The Obvious

Discover the Deeper Meaning of Scripture

James DeYoung, Th.D.
Sarah Hurty, Th.M.

VISION HOUSE
PUBLISHING, INC.

Gresham, Oregon

BEYOND THE OBVIOUS
© 1995 by Vision House Publishing, Inc.

Published by James DeYoung, Th. D.
and Sarah Hurty, Th. M.
1217 NE Burnside, Suite 403
Gresham, Oregon 97030

Printed in the United States of America

International Standard Book Number: 1-885305-14-1

95 96 97 98 99 00 01 02 03 04 - 10 9 8 7 6 5 4 3 2 1

Dedication

To Patricia
my companion on life's journey

and

To our children
James David, Rebecca Ann, Rachel Inez, Ruth Ann

Joint Heirs All

To Wayne,
my brother-husband-friend.

*I am delighted
that our God has made us life companions
on this pilgrimage of faith.*

Contents

Acknowledgements

No book can come into print without help from a number of people—at least ours certainly didn't! While all the faults of this book our entirely ours, we wish to express our thanks to a few of those who helped us in some way to complete it or to make it better than it would have been.

First, we thank Dr. Robert Cook. In spite of his disagreement with us on several tenets of this book, he has been our most enthusiastic encourager and willing and careful thinking partner over the last three years.

We are grateful to those who have seen something worthwhile in our book and have endorsed it. What an encouragement you have been.

We have benefitted from the input of various students, and especially, Tom Hauff, graduate fellow in New Testament. We also appreciate our publisher and long-time friend, John Van Diest, and our patient editor, Steve Halliday, for their encouragement, and faculty at Multnomah College of the Bible and Biblical Seminary and the faculty here at Western Seminary for vigorous and stimulating discussion.

Writing a book is an all-consuming project that demands the most from our families. The greatest debt I, Jim, owe is to my wife, Patricia, and to my children, James, Rebecca, Rachel, and Ruth. They sacrificed much to allow me to write this book.

I, Sarah, am grateful to my husband, Wayne. Without

his support, I could not do all that I do. He believes in me when I doubt and sacrifices his comfort for my sake. I am also thankful to my sisters Robin and Rachel, whose help with some of the housework keeps me sane when deadlines press by giving me order in chaos and more time to write.

Forward

Here is a stimulating, thoroughly evangelical and orthodox, challenge to the dominant evangelical paradigm of biblical interpretation known as the single meaning, authorial intent approach. These authors argue that just as we ought to learn from Scripture itself about the Bible's own nature and inspiration, so we need a method of interpretation that likewise is derived from the Bible itself and not imposed on it from outside. This method is discovered by studying carefully how the New Testament authors understand and use the Old Testament. While not denying the validity and necessity of finding the literal, grammatical-historical sense of the Old Testament, this sense is not enough. Since the Holy Spirit, not the human authors, is the ultimate Author of Scripture, meanings of the text unknown and unintended by the human authors are possible to discover through the continuing direct revelatory work of the Holy Spirit to believers both in their reading of the Bible and apart from Scripture. This way of understanding the Bible is the apostles' method, but it is not limited to the first century. It is also available today for us. This proposal puts the Spirit back into evangelical interpretation.

Furthermore, the authors argue for the "kingdom of God" as the center of biblical theology and the "essential" core of all biblical revelation which provides control for all further deeper meaning revealed by the Spirit. The Christian community also provides the context where all deeper meaning is tested over against the normative revelation given by the

Holy Spirit through the original authors of Scripture. No "deeper meaning" of the Bible can be accepted which is contradictory to the literal, grammatical-historical sense of Scripture or which is dissonant with the "kingdom of God" center of all the Bible.

Finally, their proposal requires that any theory of interpretation must be able to show how it integrates into a total world and life view. Practice of the Christian virtues which lead to union with God (a modified Reformed view of sanctification) must go hand in hand with understanding the outward authorial sense and the inward, deeper Authorial intent of Scripture. Part of this process is the working out of the progress of theological formulation in the Church and part is the discernment of God's revelatory acts within secular history.

All of this is offered as a proposal in the spirit of vulnerability and dialogue which is intended to lead to revision and further dialogue. The proposal provides a viable alternative for non-Pentecostal evangelicals to restore the Spirit to interpretation without succumbing to the historical excesses of "enthusiasm." By their careful and thorough unpacking of the central thesis, the authors have earned a serious hearing. The piece is well researched in all the modern hermeneutical literature and it is especially interactive with evangelical discussions to date.

Hasty connections of these ideas with Pietism, charismaticism, allegorism, feminism and fears of weakening biblical authority are unwarranted. Such objections are red herrings. The proposal will stand or fall on other grounds such as its ability to explain consistently the varied biblical phenomena and to show that it can guide effectively the Church today in response to the varied challenges that it faces.

I believe the book is an impressive and convincing corrective to the one-sided emphasis of some evangelicals on single-meaning authorial intent hermeneutics. For some time I have wondered about the same problem of the "what it meant, what it means" in terms of an authoritative Word from the Lord for today. This proposal has excited me in terms of what it might mean for a new paradigm for evangelical ethics. I hope it will get a fair and wide hearing in the evangelical community.

Alan F. Johnson, Professor of
New Testament and Christian Ethics
Wheaton College

Introduction Vignette

A Conversation Overheard
in Berea, A.D. 51

Paul, Silas, and Timothy arrived a bit past six. The evening meal was ready, but Pyrrhus and Damaris and their family could hardly eat, what with all the excitement. They had just become new believers of the Way upon hearing Paul preach in the synagogue the wonderful message of Jesus. Paul had presented the Gospel persuasively, finding Jesus and His saving work in surprising places in their very own Scripture—the Law, Prophets, and Writings. And Pyrrhus and Damaris and their fellow Berean Jews had examined Scripture every day for two weeks to see if what Paul said was true. Most of the discussion centered on finding Jesus as the fulfillment of prophecy all across their Torah! Many Jews believed, along with Greek women and men, even as persecution from others began to mount. It was a tense but exhilarating atmosphere.

Near the end of the meal, Sopater, the twenty-year-old son of Pyrrhus and Damaris, could restrain himself no longer. He suddenly blurted out, "Paul, I want to go with you and teach others that Jesus is Messiah. Please instruct me how to interpret Scripture like you do. I think it's amazing to find Jesus where Moses, Isaiah, David, and others did not know they were speaking of Him, but God was. This can only be proof that Jesus is God's Messiah. Please show me how I can do this!"

Paul's answer was totally unexpected. "I'm so sorry, Sopater, but only I, as one of the apostles, can interpret Scripture this way. You see, we are inspired by the Holy Spirit, and you are not. Of course, I have taught Silas and Timothy to open Scripture this way, but you cannot. We are following the example and instruction of Jesus Himself on this matter. I'm sorry, my son."

"But do we not have the Holy Spirit to lead us into all Truth, to teach us also?" Sopater asked in desperation.

"Yes," Paul answered, "but Jesus promised that He would send the Spirit only to us to guide us in this special way. You can only repeat our words, only go as far as we've gone. Your

interpretation of Scripture must be limited to what the human authors intended. I admit that I've compromised this a bit by instructing Aquila and Priscilla, Apollos, and my companions here, Timothy and Silas, but you are not of this enlarged apostolic circle. Don't be discouraged, though. There is much to be done everywhere."

"But Paul, we have examined Scripture daily to test the truthfulness of what you say," replied Damaris on behalf of her son. "Do you mean that we can't follow your method of interpretation, when that's how you showed us that Jesus is the Messiah? We used your approach to examine Scripture to see if what you said is true, and on that basis, we believed!"

"I'm sorry, but that's the way it is."

"But sir, you said that we should put into practice whatever we have learned or received or heard from you or seen in you. Doesn't this apply to your method of interpreting holy Scripture, as well? If not, it calls into question the integrity of what we have believed. Where does the cut-off point come, when your converts can't do what you've done?" Such was the bluntness of Pyrrhus.

Before Paul could respond, visitors at the door alerted the apostle that Jews from Thessalonica were approaching and seeking his life once again. Paul departed for Athens at once, leaving instructions for Silas and Timothy to catch up with him.

Pyrrhus' questions went unanswered.

Reading Scripture:
What's All the Fuss About?

A Conversation Overheard in Berea, A.D. 51

This fictional conversation (based on Acts 17:10-12) is a tongue-in-cheek look at one of the most hotly debated topics in the evangelical church today—how to read the Bible. In order to protect the Bible from the abuse of interpreters making it say anything they want it to, strict rules have been laid down for what the Bible can mean.

The problem is that the biblical writers themselves did not always follow these rules. And it is often the experience of everyday believers that not even the Spirit follows these rules when He speaks to them in the Word. So are these rules right? Are we being biblical in the way we read the Bible? We want to be free to discover all that the Spirit means to communicate in and through Scripture, and at the same time, be secure that what we have discovered is true.

It's All a Matter of Interpretation

Recently a seventeen-year-old asked me why I believe the Bible. "Wasn't it written thousands of years ago," he asked, "to different people in a different culture? Then how can it apply to us today? Isn't any application you make just your own interpretation...a matter of your own opinion?"

His questions startled me. It is not because I didn't have any answers (although the answers aren't easy to explain to someone who doesn't necessarily want to get into a deep discussion). I was startled because these sorts of questions were coming from a rather ordinary seventeen-year-old who still had a year left in high school and who could not ever remember attending a church service! I wondered with amazement if he had any idea how deeply philosophical his questions were. I read and ponder such "philosophical" questions regularly as part of my studies, but he had unconsciously soaked up from the culture around him a certain philosophy or way of looking at the world that made believing the Bible seem to be a ridiculous and even impossible thing to do.

Not even Christians are immune to this idea. Have you ever been in a home Bible study where the group has gone around the circle and everyone has explained "what this passage means to me"? Soon you begin to wonder if there is one right meaning, and if so, how do you know if you have it? You know that you have presuppositions and that your family, your culture, and the teachings of the churches you have attended all have colored how you read a passage. How can you be one hundred percent certain that you are right? Even when you are certain you stand on solid ground, see what response you get when you try to comment on a misguided notion held by a brother or sister! Dare to discuss such differences as though there might be a *right* way of viewing a passage, and quite often you will hear the retort, "Well, that's *your* interpretation!"

But we can't succumb to this subjectivism so easily, or it will prove deadly. How we do interpretation identifies us, instructs us, determines what we find meaningful and satisfying. How we do interpretation enables us to know what is real, learn how to know the truth, and do the right thing. It reveals God. In our postmodern world, it may be the only way to hold on to ultimates.

The Need for Good Hermeneutics

These examples point to the need for *principles on how to understand the Bible;* this is *hermeneutics.* In the early 1990s a number of new textbooks on hermeneutics have been published. It is a hot topic right now, and for several good reasons.

1. We are living through a major paradigm shift, a complete change in the way we think about the world, the core ideas of which are dubbed *postmodernism*. Whereas both premodernism and modernism affirmed an objective reality that could be discovered and talked about, postmodernism in its extreme form claims there is no such thing. This means that there is no truth, but only our subjective interpretations of our experiences.

There is an important distinction to be made here. Postmodernism claims not merely that we will never *know* truth perfectly because of our experiences and presuppositions, but that there *is* no truth to know. And since there is no truth or objective reality, language ultimately doesn't refer to anything. With no truth or reality to be talked about, words refer only to more words; there is no objective or "correct" meaning in any use of language. The meaning of any (written or spoken) message is not determined by what the author or speaker intended to convey, or even by what a written text says, but instead is created by the reader or hearer. Since each reader comes with a different background, each one creates his own meaning and every meaning is equally valid. Interpretation, then, is no more than interpretations of interpretations. The implications of such a philosophy for understanding the Bible as the Word of God are obvious: there is no definitive Word of God. (If the rise of postmodernism is news to you, you may want to see Appendix A to become familiar with the basic ideas of premodern, modern, and postmodern thought, which form part of the background of the discussion in this book.)

2. We are acutely aware of the need to bridge the gap between the world in which the Bible was written and the world in which we all live today. Postmodernism has done us some favors in again bringing this to our attention. In contrast to historical-critical methodology which sought only to discover what the Bible meant in its own context, postmodernism's emphasis is on the meaning for the person reading the text. While we differ with postmodernism on the implications of vastly different worlds for the communication of meaning, we benefit nevertheless from its exploration of the

problems. We hope the days of the solitary preacher who merely expounds the historical meaning of a text and leaves it at that (as though God's meaning is automatically clear and that the mere proclamation of truth magically cures all personal and social ills) will soon be gone. How to understand the meaning of God's Word for today is a primary interest of contemporary hermeneutics.

3. The Church has grown rapidly in other parts of the world. Believers from Latin America, Africa, and Asia now far outnumber those from the United States and Western Europe. Areas which once were mission fields are now sending out missionaries. This incredible cultural diversity has impressed upon us two things:

a) We need to contextualize the message to communicate it effectively to whatever culture we find ourselves in.

b) We, in all parts of the Church, need to listen to each other so that we can remove the cultural biases and discover truth together.

Doing theology is the task of the worldwide Church, not only of the Western white male. The world stage is set for a theological revolution that may surpass even that of the Reformation.

4. The veritable explosion of understanding in such diverse fields as linguistics, philosophy, psychology, and sociology has had a major impact on our understanding of hermeneutics. New texts on the topic are necessary as we enter the dialogue in such fields, learn the good things from them, and revise our approach to understanding the Bible.

What Is the *Plain* Sense?

Some readers may be new to this discussion. If you are, you may be saying, "If only people would pay attention to the plain sense of Scripture, we wouldn't have these problems." In one sense, we couldn't agree more. When I took a hermeneutics course in seminary, I was a little indignant that I was paying several hundred dollars to be taught how to read properly. I recognized many of the concepts from my undergraduate courses on how to teach reading to elementary school children! Most of the time, we all manage to read and listen to others' use of language so that meaning is effectively shared—we "get" what each other "means" and the world goes 'round.

On the other hand, this isn't as simple as it seems. Just try learning another language (and the whole cultural world view of the people who speak it) well enough to speak like a native! We unconsciously and automatically process all the myriad linguistic and nonverbal rules and elements of shared history or world view that go into understanding each other, but the seeming ease with which we do so belies its incredible complexity...and the potential for mistakes! How many times a day do we in various ways ask, "What do you mean?"

The difficulty in understanding is increased when the form of communication is less familiar to us. Not many people understand poetry these days, and the problem is even worse if the poetry is giving some vague prophecy of the future! It is a learned skill. Having read little else than newspaper or magazine articles and school textbooks, many of us have trouble enjoying the depth of meaning even in a well-crafted story.

The difficulty in understanding is increased exponentially when the authors are from backgrounds drastically different from their readers. The Bible is full of stories, poetry, parables, and such things, written by peoples from different times in different languages, with different customs, values, literary styles, and ways of viewing the world—and we can't ask them if we have understood what they meant! So while the basic skills we use without thinking are good enough that we can get the basic message of the Bible, there is still plenty of room for error. Combine all this with our natural propensity to read into the Bible our own experiences and presuppositions, along with our sinful bent toward distorting God's truth so that we don't have to obey it, and we can be sure of one thing—we do make errors!

That's why the idea that the meaning of Scripture is found in the plain sense is a bit deceiving. To this some might reasonably respond, "Just because the task is difficult, it doesn't mean that the meaning isn't found in the plain sense. When you follow the rules for reading the particular kind of literature, and when you understand the text from the perspective of the person writing (i.e., his cultural and historical context and purpose for writing), then the meaning of Scripture is indeed found in the plain sense." This is called the *literal* or *grammatical-historical* hermeneutic. It is good common sense, and it is the method usually used to understand any literature.

Doing It *Their* Way

After more than twenty years of teaching the grammatical-historical hermeneutic, I can see only one problem with it: it doesn't appear to be the way the biblical writers always did it!

When we examine how the biblical writers used previously written Scripture, we see that they seemed to "discover" meaning there that, judged by its original context, can hardly be imagined to have been in the mind of the original author. This problem is especially evident in the way the New Testament authors used Old Testament passages to prove that Jesus Christ fulfilled prophecy (or to make some theological point).

So where did they get this additional or "deeper" meaning? Was it put there by God and did they merely discover it later? Or is it something the original authors did indeed know and intend so that it is not really additional meaning? If it is additional meaning, did later writers create it or did they find it? And if they found it, how did they find it? What principles guided them so that they discovered truth and not merely something they wanted to see? Can we practice their hermeneutic? Why or why not? Of what benefit could it be?

These questions have vexed the Church since the writing of the New Testament. Many approaches have been tried and abandoned and many solutions offered, but sixteen hundred years after the close of the Canon, we still haven't agreed on our hermeneutic! The fact that the questions are still hanging over our heads attests to how vital they are.

The answers should help us to know how better to understand the meaning of Scripture and how to apply it to our own situations, even as the biblical writers applied previously written Scripture to theirs. How the New Testament uses Old Testament passages can also give us insight into the theological relationship of the testaments, with major ramifications for our theology, and thus for our living. This will help us to understand such important things as how the Old Testament law applies to the believer and what we should expect in the end times. Better understanding of these things helps us to answer very practical questions of everyday life:

- What is the Sabbath, and if we are bound to keep it, how?

- Can married Christians have sex while the wife is menstruating?

- Should we use corporal punishment in law enforcement, or even capital punishment for that matter?

- What can women do in ministry?

- Is the Christian Coalition a valid biblical expression of Christian political involvement?

- Should we seek some political expression of the Kingdom of God on earth, or even its priniciples?

- Why can't we kill abortion providers?

- Does God hide His face when we step into the bathroom or the bedroom?

Ultimately, the question of additional meaning in Scripture affects a myriad of such things.

Our Purpose and Plan

Most of the new textbooks on hermeneutics have been general works designed to teach all the basics about how to read the Bible. As such, they deal with the questions about deeper meaning only indirectly. The purpose of this book is to explore more comprehensively the question of deeper meaning in Scripture. It is more about *metahermeneutics*, the theory of doing interpretation, rather than detailed instructions for its practice.

In the first part of the book, we illustrate the problem and present and evaluate various historical and contemporary solutions to the matter. Then we present and explain our own special solution. In the second part of the book, we explore some corollaries of the solution we suggest. Here we develop more thoroughly the theology of certain important things usually mentioned only in passing by other texts, such as the role of the Holy Spirit in helping us understand the Bible, a model of spirituality and its part in knowing God who Himself is love and truth, God's design for learning in community (including the Church worldwide), and even how we should think of history. The hermeneutic of Scripture also helps us to interpret history so we can make sense of our world.

By the end of this book, typical readers will gain two things:

1) A better understanding of how to read and apply Scripture in order to intimately know God the Author.

2) A deeper insight into and appreciation of the crucial role that they personally play in the Church's never-ending task of listening to the Spirit in His Word and in His action in history (including the everyday experiences of each of our lives).

These things together empower us to take our part in actualizing God's Kingdom on earth in our own day, in the moments of our individual lives, and together as the Church impacting the world for God's glory.

Tipping Our Hand

Before we begin, we want to tip our hand regarding the solution we will offer to the problem of deeper meaning in Scripture. We believe that we can and should practice the hermeneutic of the biblical authors, and we have what we think is a promising idea about how to do it. One of the unique aspects of our solution is how we tie together a biblical center and a hermeneutical method. We have been working on this idea for some time now, and until recently, our proposal seemed radical. We have read the most recent hermeneutics texts, however, and have discovered that most of them claim there is deeper meaning in Scripture and that we should be able to practice the biblical hermeneutic. The solutions these texts offer are sometimes advances over past attempts, but we feel they are still subject to the same criticisms usually made in more recent discussions. Nevertheless, within them we have heard echoes of different parts of our own idea, which we hope proves to be the leading of the Spirit in all of us as He guides individuals and small groups in disparate places simultaneously to the discovery of His truth.

If we make some small contribution to this discussion, we will be fulfilled. We think we have an idea that might work. In some ways it is quite similar to other historical and contemporary attempts, as it should be, if indeed God is slowly teaching us His truth throughout history.

We invite your input as part of the Spirit-led Body of Christ, but we don't expect that you will necessarily agree. A surprising number of those with whom we have had serious discussions have affirmed the potential of our idea, but a few others have opposed the notion of deeper meaning or of practicing a hermeneutic that can find it. If our solution proves plausible, then we have our work cut out for us because our explorations indicate that it suggests nothing less than a complete world view with impact for every aspect of theology and life.

In the glad humility that comes from knowing that we are all one growing together through time, and that until Christ comes again, no formulation is final (and ours isn't even close), we welcome any who would like to respond as we put forward this idea.

One final word. We have tried to keep the book plain enough so that interested readers who are fairly new to the topic can still follow along with understanding and enjoyment. For this reason, we have reserved more technical or in-depth discussion and research information for the endnotes under "For the Curious and the Careful." Nevertheless, some parts of the topic are naturally more challenging than others. Uninitiated readers can still gain much and enjoy the book even if they don't understand it all the first time they read it. Perseverance through the more difficult parts will pay off.

However, if you are tempted to skip parts, let us make a recommendation. Chapter 1 is very helpful because it sets up the problem that the rest of the book discusses. Chapters 2 and 3 discuss historical and contemporary attempts to find deeper meaning. They can be skipped if the study of history bores you or if you already know it so well you don't want a review. However, since they are helpful for greater understanding of the issue, you may choose to come back to them later. Chapters 4 through 9 explain our proposal for a hermeneutic, the role of the Holy Spirit in interpretation, and how to understand spiritual life, community, and God's work in history in relation to understanding Scripture.

At the beginning of each chapter, you will find a vignette, like the one at the beginning of this introduction. They are all historical fiction—a mixture of created story and real biblical people and events. While some are more serious, others are playful, obviously importing questions from our day into the first century. Occasionally this helps us to see in a new way. Each of the stories is designed to give an idea of what the following chapter is about.

We believe it is entirely possible to read this book on hermeneutics and have your spirit renewed, your life with God revitalized, and your sense of participation in God's Kingdom mission deepened and empowered. At least, we sincerely hope this proves true for you and your faith community. We invite you to join us and hope you enjoy the discussion.

Did the Prophets Write Better Than They Knew?

Silas' fingers were growing numb from the cold and the meticulous work of taking Peter's dictation. He had to take a break.

"Peter, do you mind if we take a rest here for a few minutes? You speak faster than I can write, especially when I need to correct some of your phrases to make sense out of them."

"I really do need to hear back what you've written. The thoughts come to my mind so fast and furious I can hardly contain myself. The suffering of Jesus as our Messiah brings hope and comfort for all of us as we face persecution for our faith. I'm so anxious to have our brothers and sisters scattered all over Galatia and Asia and elsewhere, hold fast in faith and not let their trials overwhelm them. There is no telling what Nero may blame us Christians for next."

"How about it if I read it back to you in a minute? I've been thinking about what you said regarding Jesus' fulfilling prophecy from our Scripture—what our prophets, especially Isaiah and David, have said about the suffering and glory of Messiah in their writings. This is the same thing Paul claimed when I wrote for him at Corinth.

"But I have a question about this which keeps bugging me, Peter. You said that as the prophets tried to discover the time and circumstances of Christ's death and following glory, the Spirit of Christ revealed to them that they were actually serving us and not themselves when they foretold the things now preached in the gospel. Do you mean to go that far? I mean, this implies that the prophets themselves did not understand what they were writing, but that the Spirit did, and that he reveals to us additional meaning in the words they wrote. I'm really concerned. How can the Spirit intend a meaning beyond what the writer intends to mean?"

"Silas, you just answered your own question! While Scripture is the word of human writers it is even more so the Word of God Himself. At times God means more than the human writers could grasp. This is a witness to the very special

nature of Scripture—it's supernatural, just as Moses told us. Is it such a strange thing to think that at times our God's meaning exceeds man's meaning? And don't you remember what I've often told you that our Lord Himself read Scripture this way and promised to lead us into all truth? This is part of the fulfillment of His promise."

"I see, I see. Since there are two authors to all Scripture, we must read Scripture on two levels. One level gives us meaning suited to the author's particular situation. The other level gives us the larger perspective of God Himself. I'd like to search all of Scripture to find Jesus as much as possible. It will be a wonderful way to convince our unbelieving Jewish friends that Jesus is not only Messiah but also God Himself in human flesh. I have a feeling that this is an almost inexhaustible search and discovery."

"Indeed, it is, Silas. But let's get back to work and read what you have written. You have a wonderful way with words. Perhaps God will guide you to write your own epistle along these lines some day. It might convince more of our Jewish people to put their faith in Jesus as the promised Messiah."

"And to think that we ourselves are part of this process of divine revelation. Maybe I'll write an anonymous word of encouragement to our people. It's not nearly as important that people hear what we say. Rather they must hear the voice of God."

When they read Scripture, did the biblical writers discover meaning beyond what the original authors intended? What examples in the Bible give us reason to think that they did? And if they did do this, can and should we try to do the same? Why or why not?

Chapter One

Interpretation
The Biblical Writers Do It Differently

"So as the Holy Spirit says" (Hebrews 3:7).

The only motivation for writing this book is to shed additional light on a problem that has challenged the Church for almost two thousand years. The problem is: How do we interpret the Bible so that it continues to speak to each new generation?

This problem uncovers another one that must first be answered. How do later writers of Scripture interpret earlier ones? This is usually stated in this way: By what method did Jesus and the apostles interpret the Old Testament? If we are to avoid imposing on the Bible every whim of interpretation in our goal of making the Bible relevant, we must know the Bible's own way of interpreting itself. *To have any authority, any lasting persuasion, our method of interpretation ought to be the same as the Bible's.* If we are going to choose not to practice the Bible's own method of interpreting itself, we had better have a good reason for not doing so. Yet, surprisingly, most do not interpret the Bible the way that it appears to interpret itself.

So we come to the question, How do biblical writers use previously written Scripture? By *use* we mean everything from making obvious quotations to making less specific allusions and borrowing terminology. The usual response to such a question is that the biblical writers use the meanings of the previous texts as found by following the grammatical-historical (literal) method. But there are many examples which suggest this answer may not be adequate. The purpose of this chapter is to illustrate this contention. To do this we will first review what the literal method is. Then we will consider quickly several examples from many parts of the New Testament that just don't seem to fit, and finally we'll take an in-depth look at an instance of Jesus' use of Scripture.

THE GRAMMATICAL-HISTORICAL HERMENEUTIC

What do we mean by the literal method of interpretation? While this is continually being discussed and refined, there is general consensus that a strict, literal interpretation is the method of interpreting the Bible according to the grammatical and historical background of the original situation. Literal interpretation affirms that the author has a single intention in what he writes. It is this meaning which we are to discover and explain by study of the grammar, history, and context of the author. In other words, it is the plain, normal sense of words.[1]

To help bring more precision to this matter, we should distinguish among some concepts.[2] Within the confines of the grammatical-historical hermeneutic, *meaning* refers to the fixed, single intention or assertion of the author. *Significance*, on the other hand, is the import of a passage for us. This is always changing and pertains to us, not the author. *Application* is the practical working out of the significance of a passage in our lives.

To illustrate these differences let's consider the sentence, "God so loved the world." John's *intent* or *meaning* is to affirm that God loved all mankind in a particular way. The *significance* is that you and I are part of mankind, so God loved us. The *application* is that I believe this and respond to His love, accepting eternal life (just as the rest of John 3:16 says).

We try to interpret virtually all literature by this method. According to many who use the literal method to interpret

Scripture, the fact that Scripture has a divine Author as well as a human author does not change this approach, although we seek the guidance of the Holy Spirit in interpreting. Both the human authors and the divine Author had the same intended meaning as they wrote Scripture.

SCRIPTURE'S USE OF SCRIPTURE

The literal hermeneutic makes good sense and helps to prevent people from interpreting the Bible whatever way they wish. The problem is that often it is not the hermeneutic of the biblical authors. Following are several of the most difficult and perplexing examples of how the New Testament authors interpreted Old Testament Scripture. While some of these may, with difficulty, be explained by the literal method, some of them simply cannot (and many others could be added).[3]

Examples from Hebrews

Hardly any other book pays such rich dividends on the use of the Old Testament by the New as does the Book of Hebrews. We give but a few examples—and they all challenge literal interpretation.

1. No other passage from the Psalms is used so frequently in the New as is Psalm 110:1.

The LORD says to my Lord: "Sit at my right hand until
I make your enemies a footstool for your feet."

Jesus was the first to cite this psalm. He used it to point to His status as David's Lord or Master, even though the prevailing opinion among the Jews was that Messiah was to be merely David's son (Matthew 22:41-45; Acts 2:33-35). Implicit is Jesus' own preexistence and deity. So this enthronement oracle, which seems to present Messiah as David's and/or Solomon's son, actually presents Him as David's Lord, namely, deity. And this is how this passage is used everywhere else in the New Testament (to refer to Jesus as Lord), especially in Hebrews (1:3, 13; 8:1; 10:12; 12:2).

2. Again from Psalm 110, verse 4 is quoted, indeed exegeted or interpreted in detail, several times in Hebrews. Particularly in chapter 7 the author takes great pains to say that Christ fulfills it.

The LORD has sworn and will not change his mind:
"You are a priest forever, in the order of Melchizedek."

This verse reminds us that not only will David's Lord be King (v. 1), He will also be Priest—but a special kind of priest, unknown (or at least not mentioned) since Genesis 14:17-21. The fact that Jesus fulfilled this psalm is not all that the author claims. He goes further by asserting that Melchizedek of Genesis 14 is himself prophetic of Jesus, even in the smallest of details such as: his name (Melchizedek, king of righteousness), his place (Salem, he will be king of peace), and even what is *absent* in Genesis 14 (lack of mention of genealogy, birth, and death are prophetic of Jesus' being a priest forever). Literal interpretation is utterly incapable of discovering this meaning for Jesus from Genesis 14. And neither did David discover by literal interpretation of Genesis 14 that Melchizedek's order was to be Messiah's, that Messiah should be both King (v. 1) and Priest (v. 4).

3. In Hebrews 1:10-12 the author says that the words of Psalm 102:25-27 were spoken by God to (or, of)[4] Jesus. Yet the psalmist was speaking to Yahweh, God the Father, as the Creator of the universe. Thereby Hebrews asserts that God identifies Jesus as Creator of the universe, who will endure eternally. How can Hebrews change the authorial intention of the psalmist?

4. The author of Hebrews takes statements regarding David's son Solomon and claims that they are spoken of Jesus. In Hebrews 1:5-6 the author takes Yahweh's words in 2 Samuel 7:14 ("I will be his father, and he will be my son") as His words about Jesus' sonship. Again, in 1:8-9, the words in Psalm 45:6-7 regarding Solomon ("Your throne, O God, will last for ever and ever") are said to be spoken actually of Jesus the Son to demonstrate His deity.[5]

5. In Hebrews 2:6-8 the author quotes Psalm 8 which extols man ("the son of man") as God's creature crowned with glory and honor, with everything in subjection under His feet. Obviously David is reflecting on the nobility of man per the creation account of Genesis 1:26-27 and chapter 2. Then the author observes that "we do not yet see all things put in subjection under him" but we see Jesus who, as man, is already crowned because He suffered death (2:9). The implication is that Jesus is the son of man in Psalm 8. But did David have Jesus in mind, as Hebrews implies? Also David spoke of the present era, whereas Hebrews refers to the "age to come."[6]

6. Finally, Hebrews 10:5-7 quotes Psalm 40:6-8 and says that David's words were spoken by Christ when He came into the world. He came to do God's will perfectly with His entire being and so sanctified all His people. Yet did David intend these words to describe Messiah, or himself? This is especially sticky, for part of the psalm makes confession of sins (Psalm 40:12). This psalm also becomes the basis of the Servant passages of Isaiah (e.g., 42:1-9; 44:1-5; 49:1-7; 52:13-53:12).

Examples from the Gospels and Acts

Another challenge to literal interpretation occurs in Matthew's gospel. He asserts that when Joseph and Mary took the Christ child to Egypt to escape the slaughter of Herod (Matthew 2:14-15), they fulfilled Hosea 11:1, "Out of Egypt I called my son." How can Matthew take words spoken with reference to Israel and say they were fulfilled over a thousand years after the Exodus by Joseph and Mary? This is just one of several examples of Matthew's use of the Old Testament in which he considerably expands the meaning of the original passage.

A few examples from Acts will show that other apostles followed this practice.

1. Peter says that the miracles of Pentecost (2:1-4) fulfilled what Joel (2:28-32) foretold about the Day of the

Lord. Yet Joel predicted not just the coming of the Holy Spirit, but catastrophic events in the heavens. Did Joel intend his words to refer to the first or the second coming of Christ, or both?

2. In 2:22-36 Peter says that David spoke of the resurrection of Christ in Psalm 16:8-11. Yet this hardly seems in accord with literal interpretation of the psalm, which would refer the words to David himself (note such phrases as "I saw the Lord always before me" and "you will not abandon me to the grave").[7] Peter also claims that Psalm 110:1 (which we discussed above) speaks of Jesus, not David. In both cases Peter seems constrained to correct a common understanding that these psalms referred to David (2:29-32, 34).

3. In 4:24-30 Peter claims that what Herod, Pilate, the Gentiles, and the Jews did to Jesus fulfilled what the Holy Spirit spoke through David in Psalm 2, and that this was determined beforehand by God (v. 28). Yet Psalm 2 speaks of the enthronement of Messiah: "I have installed my King on Zion, my holy hill" (v. 6)—words more appropriate of the second coming of Christ than the first.

4. Similarly to Peter, Paul cites three passages as pointing to the resurrection of Jesus (13:32-39), two of which are the same as Peter's: Psalm 2:7, Isaiah 55:3, and Psalm 16:10. Indeed, Paul defends his and Barnabas' whole ministry to the Gentiles by saying that the Lord has commanded them (v. 47) to do such by the words of Isaiah 49:6: "I will also make you a light for the Gentiles, that you may bring my salvation to the ends of the earth." Yet in the first half of verse 6, Isaiah's words are intended of the Servant of the LORD who will restore the tribes of Judah and before whom kings will bow down (v. 7). Has not Paul found meaning here that Isaiah never thought of? How can Paul's meaning be reconciled with Isaiah's? Surely not by literal interpretation!

Examples from Paul

Next we consider some troubling examples from Paul.

1. In 1 Timothy 5:17-18 and 1 Corinthians 9:9-12 Paul cites the same passage (Deuteronomy 25:4) to defend the

right of apostles to be paid for their labor. Yet Paul does not just quote, "Do not muzzle an ox while it is treading out the grain." He goes further and asks: "Surely he (i.e., God probably, rather than Moses) says this for us, doesn't he? Yes, this was written for us." How can Paul make such a claim about the divine intention? What did the human author, Moses, intend?

2. In 1 Corinthians 10 Paul cites several experiences of Israel in the wilderness. One of these is the nation's drinking from the spiritual rock which followed them (vv. 1-5), and he says, "That rock was Christ." He claims that these events happened as examples (i.e., as types) for us as believers (vv. 6-10), that these things "were written down as warnings for us, on whom the fulfillment of the ages has come" (v. 11). Were we in Moses' intention when he composed the record of these events? What does He mean to say that we live in the era of fulfillment?

3. In the only passage which is explicitly identified as "being spoken allegorically" (Galatians 4:24-31; NIV has v. 24 as, "These things may be taken figuratively"), Paul seems to find additional meaning or significance beyond the grammatical-historical meaning.[8] Hagar represents the covenant of Moses, Mount Sinai, Ishmael and slaves, and present Jerusalem. Sarah represents the Jerusalem above, and if we carry out the contrasts, Isaac, the new covenant, and perhaps Mount Zion. Surely Moses did not intend this understanding. He did not know of the heavenly Jerusalem nor of the new covenant. What method of interpretation is comprehensive enough to allow this? On what basis does Paul have liberty to interpret Hagar and Sarah this way? May we do as Paul and engage in this kind of interpretation at other places in the Old and New Testaments?

4. Finally, Paul says almost explicitly that earlier scripture has deeper meaning beyond that known by the human author and now revealed in the gospel. He says in Galatians 3:8: "The *Scripture foresaw* that God would justify the Gentiles by faith, and *announced the gospel in advance* to Abraham: 'All nations will be blessed through you.'"

PROBLEM OF MALACHI 3:1 AND 4:5 IN MATTHEW 11:10

It is fitting that we focus more in-depth on Jesus and His hermeneutic, for all Scripture bears witness to Him. He taught His approach to His disciples and they have instructed us. For this reason we will look more closely at Jesus' use of Malachi 3:1 and 4:5 in Matthew 11:10 and 14. Interpreters of the Bible often discuss this instance, with its unique characteristics of form and content, when trying to understand Jesus' hermeneutic.[9]

New Testament Context

In the context of Matthew 11, John the Baptist sends his disciples (because he himself is in prison) to ask Jesus if He is the coming one, the Messiah,[10] or should he look for someone else. This provides the opportunity for Jesus to vindicate John's ministry and show its relationship to the Kingdom (11:2-19). Jesus first answers John by pointing to the works which validate him (11:2-6).[11] Then Jesus eliminates all speculation as to John's identity (11:7-15) by affirming that John is a prophet but that this description falls short. Jesus mysteriously affirms that John is much more than a prophet.

> This is the one about whom it is written: "I will send my messenger ahead of you, who will prepare your way before you" (11:10).

Here Jesus quotes Malachi 3:1 to claim that Malachi was prophesying directly about John as a messenger—not just any prophet—and a messenger of none other than Messiah Himself. John will prepare Messiah's way. The implication is that Messiah is present and the time of messianic fulfillment is at hand.

So great is John's position that Jesus claims He speaks the truth when He affirms that John the Baptist is the greatest person (not just prophet) ever born (v. 11a). Then, paradoxically, Jesus immediately adds, "Yet he who is least in the kingdom of heaven is greater than he" (v. 11b).

Somehow the presence of the Kingdom radically alters values.[12]

Jesus' assessment of John's greatness is based upon three other things: the advancing of the Kingdom (v. 12); the fact that "all the Prophets and the Law prophesied until John" (v. 13) (i.e., John belongs to two eras, ending one and beginning another,[13] and this implies the finality of John's ministry); and that if the people are willing to accept it, he is "the Elijah who was to come" (v. 14).

In this last sentence, Jesus seems to be saying that the scope of John's ministry is limited only by the people's response: if they are willing to receive this prophecy about John, the Kingdom would fully come and John would become Elijah.[14] The reference to Elijah's coming derives from Malachi 4:5. This passage is tied to Malachi 3:1 since they both make reference to the era of Messiah and the coming day of unprecedented judgment.

So now Jesus has cited Malachi twice and made two claims of fulfillment regarding John.[15] He is the messenger before Messiah and he is also Elijah. How can John be both? Why must Elijah come? Is this what Malachi the prophet means? Jesus invites us to listen carefully (v. 15): "He who has ears, let him hear." This may be an invitation, if you will, to consider with spiritual sensitivity a meaning which is below the surface or obvious meaning.

It is clear that the Kingdom is emphasized in the context of Matthew 11. This observation is important for reasons shown above and because the method of interpretation which we will introduce is anchored to a proper understanding of the Kingdom.

Old Testament Context

Now let's take a look at what these two quotes from Malachi were talking about in their original context.

"See, I will send my messenger, who will prepare the way before me. Then suddenly the Lord you are seeking will come to his temple; the messenger of the covenant, whom you desire, will come," says the LORD Almighty (Malachi 3:1).

"See, I will send you the prophet Elijah before that great and dreadful day of the LORD comes" (Malachi 4:5).

Malachi serves as God's call to Israel to return to the God who has loved her. A prophecy is given in 3:1-4:6 (which includes both of our quotes) about the coming Day of the Lord, when He comes in judgment. This prophecy is intended to answer the evil attitude of Israel that Yahweh rewards the evil as good and that the God of justice does not exist (2:17). God is wearied by such talk and will not tolerate it. No one can endure the day when the messenger and the LORD come to refine Judah (3:2-5). Indeed, the day of judgment is coming to punish the wicked and reward the righteous (4:1-4). Yahweh's way is prepared by His messenger (3:1), and He is preceded by the appearance of the prophet Elijah (4:5). The LORD is a great King and His name is to be feared among the nations (1:14).

The two verses above are pivotal in Malachi. Actually, 3:1 takes up earlier promises of God's presence and deliverance by way of an angel (Exodus 23:20-24) and His coming as ruler-redeemer (Isaiah 40:3).[16] Our two verses promise that Yahweh the King (1:14) will come as Priest to His temple (3:1)[17] to judge and make restoration as He brings in His Kingdom. He will be duly heralded by a messenger, Elijah. God will thus be vindicated.

Minor Changes That Make Major Differences

Jesus makes several small changes when He quotes these passages (when we examine them in the original languages) that don't make any difference, so we won't look at them here.[18] A few changes that Jesus makes in His use of Malachi, however, do suggest major significance for interpretation and theology. These concern His triple use of the second person personal pronoun in Matthew 11:10: *you, your,* and *you;* and

His mention of Elijah in 11:14. To understand these changes, let's look at the quotes again side by side.

"I will send my messenger ahead of *you*, who will prepare *your* way before *you*" (Matthew 11:10).

"See, I will send my messenger, who will prepare the way before *me*" (Malachi 3:1).

Of the three pronouns in Matthew 11:10, the first two are added by Jesus[19] and have little significance by themselves. The last word, however, represents a change from the Old Testament's *me*. In this third change, Jesus alters the text of Malachi from an address by Yahweh *about Himself* ("before me") into an address from Yahweh *about Messiah* ("before you"). So *me* becomes *you*. By adding the other two pronouns (*you* and *your*), Jesus makes it a point of emphasis. In so doing He identifies Himself, the Messiah, with Yahweh.

The other matter to note is that Jesus identifies John with Elijah in 11:14 by bringing together the two passages of Malachi 3:1 and 4:5. He reinforces this after the events that occurred on the Mount of Transfiguration where Moses and Elijah appeared with Jesus as He was transfigured. This event is associated with the final words of Matthew 16, which speak of the "Son of Man coming in his kingdom." Jesus tells the three apostles that "Elijah has already come" (Matthew 17:12). The disciples "understood that he was talking to them about John the Baptist" (17:13). Yet, clearly, John did not see himself as Elijah. According to John's gospel, when directly asked if he was Elijah, John said no (John 1:21). The Pharisees believed his statement (1:25).[20]

Did Malachi believe an actual Elijah would return before the day of judgment? Did he have in mind John the Baptist—or anyone at all—who should come prior to the first coming of Messiah and not just the day of judgment? Did the Kingdom arrive in the coming of Jesus, and did the day of judgment come with Him?

Since Jesus claimed that Malachi prophesied about John, did Jesus change the meaning of Malachi? On what basis did Jesus find this additional meaning and for what reason or purpose? Does Jesus violate Malachi's meaning in the sense of contradicting him, or does He simply show additional or *deeper meaning?* Do Jesus' words, "He who has ears, let him hear," in verse 15 help here?

While we have raised many questions,[21] there are just two major problems.[22] First, why does Jesus make the changes from the first person pronoun in Malachi 3:1 to the second person pronouns in Matthew 11:10? Second, why does He identify the messenger with John the Baptist? The first question concerns Jesus' identification; the second concerns John's. These are also "how" questions: How or on what basis does Jesus do this? All of this is in the context of the Kingdom and its meaning. What is the importance of the Kingdom in Jesus' life and ministry and its impact upon how He understood Scripture?

DOING IT *THEIR* WAY?

Few would dispute that we should go to Jesus to find the model for living a life committed to God. He is our example of trust, obedience, and of the overcoming life. Paul exhorted believers to imitate Christ and himself (1 Corinthians 4:16; 11:1; Philippians 3:17; 4:9; 1 Thessalonians 1:6-7). Now, if we should imitate Jesus in spiritual growth, it would seem that He should be our example in how to interpret Scripture as well. He was such to His disciples, as Luke 24 shows.

Yet it may come as a surprise to most Christians that the traditional view is that we cannot follow Jesus and His disciples in their method of interpreting Scripture. This is so because they find meaning which we cannot or should not find by a literal interpretation.

The argument seems pretty simple to us: If Jesus and His disciples are models for us in ethics and theology, why are they not models for how we are to interpret Scripture?

The Options

There are only four possibilities:

(1) The New Testament practices a hermeneutic which finds only one meaning, the literal meaning, in the text of previous Scripture, and we can follow this practice.

(2) The New Testament practices a hermeneutic which finds additional meaning beyond the human author's intention, but we cannot follow this because they were inspired and we are not.

(3) We can practice or follow the hermeneutic of the New Testament even when it finds additional meaning, but cannot claim normativity for our interpretation because we are not inspired and the Canon is closed.

(4) We can practice the hermeneutic of the New Testament even when it finds additional meaning, and claim normativity for our interpretation because the Canon is not closed and the Spirit leads us authoritatively.[23]

Those who favor (1) do so with conviction, yet cannot explain by literal interpretation the uses of the Old Testament as explored in our discussion. We will also show that this, in its strictest form, is not the view of the Church throughout its history. (2) is a safer view than (3) and holds that since God inspired the writers of Scripture, their hermeneutic is qualitatively (or essentially) different from ours. The problem is that there is no command against our reproducing their hermeneutic. In fact, it seems that they set an example for us and encourage us to do so. Further, promises regarding the ongoing ministry of the Spirit in teaching and leading into all truth seem to assume it. And the Church is built not only on the apostles, but also on the prophets and their prophesying.

Besides, can we really accept Paul's message while simultaneously rejecting his interpretive methods that bring and sustain it? Can we so cleanly separate the apostolic faith and doctrine from apostolic exegesis? As has been pointed out, the "substructure of all Christian theology" arises from the apostolic patterns used to interpret the Old Testament.[24] This is why we began our study with a survey of the way the New Testament quotes and otherwise uses the Old Testament. View (2) is safe, but it has difficulty answering these questions and may be under an illusion regarding how we actually read Scripture.[25]

So we favor (3). Since the Canon is closed,[26] we do not embrace view (4). Therefore, we cannot claim normativity for our interpretations.

When we say that we cannot claim normativity, we mean that in the sense that we cannot write new Scripture. However, deeper meaning intended by God in a text is normative. Therefore, any accurate interpretation of this meaning is normative (just as the apostles' similar interpretations were). But since we have no way of knowing with absolute certainty if any of our interpretations (whether literal or deeper meanings) are entirely correct, we cannot claim normativity for any of our interpretations. We live as though many of them are normative because they have stood the test of the centuries as accurate. But in theory, only Scripture itself is normative, and our interpretations are always subject to testing.

We are explaining this because some people wonder about the nature of those interpretations which find deeper meaning. They ask if such interpretations are not less authoritative than literal ones. Such people are bothered that we cannot maintain the illusion that deeper meanings are found "scientifically" according to the rules of grammar and history. But if they accurately reveal meanings intended by God, then they are just as normative as literal ones.

Others ask: "It seems difficult to have meanings revealed by the Spirit which are then not just as normative as Scripture. Does this not compromise the closing of the Canon and the special nature of Scripture?" These people function under the illusion that we understand grammatical-historical meanings in full, apart from the aid of the Spirit, and that His work in revealing deeper meaning is somehow different. These and many related questions regarding the work of the Spirit are discussed in chapters 5, 6, 8, and 9.

Our Infallible Guides

Certainly Jesus Himself leaves us with the impression that we are to do as He did in interpreting His Bible, the Old Testament. Both by His ministry and words, as recorded in the Gospels, we find Him setting this model. Before He died, He claimed that Moses wrote of Him and that his witness is to be believed (John 5:46-47; see also Hebrews 11:26). Jesus said to the Jews in this context: "You search the Scriptures because you think that in them you have eternal life; and it is these that bear witness of Me"[27] (John 5:39, NASB). After the resurrection, on the road to Emmaus, He reproved two of His followers for not finding Him in all the Scriptures. "Beginning with Moses and all the Prophets, he explained to them what was said in all the Scriptures concerning himself" (Luke 24:27). He is the subject of the entire Jewish canon (the Law of Moses, the Prophets, and the Psalms), and He had said this during His ministry (24:44). He had to open both their hearts and their minds in order for them to understand this (24:25, 45).

The disciples learned well from Jesus.[28] The cases cited in this chapter clearly witness to the endeavor of the apostles to find Jesus throughout their Scriptures, even where we would probably not find Him.[29] So strong is this conviction of the pervasiveness of the Scriptures' witness to Jesus that John the Apostle could write in the Apocalypse that "the testimony of Jesus is the spirit of prophecy" (Revelation 19:10). With their model, why should we ourselves do any less than pursue this objective?

There is another strong indication within Scripture itself that ordinary Christians are to follow the hermeneutical practice of the apostles. Luke writes that the Bereans of Acts 17:10-12 "were of more noble character than the Thessalonians, for they received the message with great eagerness and examined the Scriptures every day to see if what Paul said was true."

Note how significant this is. From the context we know

Paul was reasoning in the Jewish synagogue that Jesus was the fulfiller of prophecy and other Scripture (the Old Testament; cf. 13:17-41, 47; 17:1-3, 10-12). These passages show that Paul found Jesus in places the Jews did not suspect Him. The Berean Jews searched the Scriptures to see if what Paul said was true. Paul used the same hermeneutic with them for reading Scripture as he did in his epistles. In order to check to see if what he said was true, these ordinary, devout Jews had to be able to use the same method. On the basis of what they found, they believed. So when the Berean Jews tested Paul's interpretation, they approved implicitly both the content and the method by which he found it. This seems to lead us to the almost unavoidable conclusion that Paul's method is normative and to be emulated by believers universally.

This incident from Acts extends the hermeneutical practice of the New Testament from Jesus and the apostles to the ordinary Christian! And it is further implied wherever later Scripture, intended for a Jewish audience (such as Hebrews), uses earlier Scripture.

Yet some will object that when the New Testament asserts that certain things fulfill Old Testament passages, the word *fulfill* can mean "illustrate" or something else, so that the Old Testament does not actually mean this deeper meaning. The problem with this objection is that the writers are often citing such passages for *validation* of their theological assertions; fulfilled prophecies are given as proofs. Old Testament citations cannot validate the biblical writers' message unless the passages in some way mean what the writers say the Spirit meant in writing them.

It is true that the biblical authors/apostles make their appeals on other bases as well: eyewitness testimony of Jesus' life, death, and resurrection; apostolic authority and divine revelation; and miracles authenticating their authority and message. But let's return to the example of the Bereans. They did not accept Paul's testimony on these bases alone. They searched the Scriptures to see if what he said was true. They were seeking validation.

This brings up another objection that some have against practicing the hermeneutic of the biblical authors. They believe that having sufficient controls on meanings found are not enough—we need methods to validate these deeper meanings. We need some way of telling which of the possible interpretations is/are positively the right one(s). Again, the Bereans' testing of Paul's message was for the purpose of validation. Therefore, their criteria for validation must have been different from ours. Should we impose twentieth century ideas of validation back on the text and dismiss their hermeneutical practice because it doesn't measure up—or should we seek to understand what their criteria for validation were?

Having said all this, we want to affirm that many modern day interpreters are at least somewhat open to the possibility of practicing the hermeneutic of the biblical writers. Take the practice of typology, for instance. Virtually every interpreter and every textbook on hermeneutics admits or affirms that typology is outside or beyond grammatical-historical interpretation (see chapter 3 endnotes). Yet nearly all suggest that with controls we can practice this method! Finding additional types is going beyond a grammatical-historical approach. But typology cannot explain all of the instances where the biblical authors found deeper meaning. The hermeneutic we will suggest is a broader approach that accounts for typology and other incidents of deeper meaning. Those who do not object to finding additional types may find our suggestion helpful.

And there is a growing number of noted evangelicals and others who advocate that we can practice the hermeneutic of the biblical writers—even when it goes beyond the grammatical-historical approach. This number includes people such as M. Silva, S. L. Johnson, C. Blomberg, D. Moo, and nearly all of the most recent books on hermeneutics. We refer you to the appendix on reproducing the hermeneutic of the biblical writers for information on this topic.

So What?

It becomes increasingly clear the more we pursue this issue that there are several instances where the New

Testament interprets the Old in strange and varied ways, and surely not in a literal way. Is there some other way to explain them all? It seems odd for the Church to approach the Scriptures with a method of interpretation learned outside Scripture, rather than discover and use Scripture's own method of interpretation. Scripture's method will explain such uses of Scripture as discussed above.

But why should we seek to understand and perhaps emulate the Bible's own hermeneutic? First, the Bible is the source of our theology and our ethics, and without a very good reason against it, the Bible should also be the source of our hermeneutic. Second, if we use a different hermeneutic from that of the biblical authors, then we may well be unable to understand Scripture as they did or to find meaning in it for our individual and community lives as they did. Without the proper hermeneutic, we may lack understanding and actually discover one day that we zealously worked *against* the Kingdom! Third, we may well undermine the faith if we accept the theology of the Bible but reject the hermeneutic which discovers it in earlier writing. We sever the link between the time of Scripture and our own.[30]

In the following chapters we will trace the past interpretation of the Church in its struggle over literal and deeper meaning, as well as present current trends. Only then will we lay out our approach. We follow this path to gain historical perspective on biblical interpretation. These chapters will help to validate a more adequate approach.

Philo and Paul:
A Clash of World Views

*Already Saul had been in Damascus for over a year. During
this time God had transformed the young zealot from a rabid
persecutor of the Church of Christ to a committed disciple of
Jesus the Messiah. The changes were monumental for the one
who was so steeped in Judaism that he had earned the title "the
Destroyer." And his zeal found its match in his training. It had
been vigorous, impeccable, and without equal. No one could
claim a better preparation, except perhaps one, the renowned
Philo himself. But on a cold winter day even Philo would meet
his match in Saul.*

*Philo was now over fifty. Born to a rich and influential
family, Philo enjoyed power and prestige. His brother Alexander
was one of the richest men of his day. Philo was devoted to public service, even enjoying membership in the embassy to Gaius
(Caligula) in the year 39.*

*His real love, however, was contemplation and philosophy. In
earnest pursuit of the latest learning, he linked the Stoic idea of the
logos with the Platonic world of ideas to explain how God creates
and sustains the world and reveals Himself to His creatures. With
missionary zeal he tried to show that the Gentile quest for religion
and philosophy found its true goal in the God of Scripture. To this
end he employed the allegorical interpretation of the Greeks to
interpret Jewish Scripture. In the process he reinterpreted history
and miracles and other "embarrassments."*

*Then something happened which deeply impacted his life. His
nephew, Tiberius Alexander, apostatized from the Jewish faith and
eventually became Procurator of Judea and Prefect of Egypt. Philo
was stunned. How could such an embarrassing thing happen in
such a famous Jewish family? In his search for answers, Philo
heard that another well known Jew, Saul of Tarsus, had also abandoned Judaism. He now embraced the Way of Jesus as Messiah
and was calling for faith in His name. Philo had to learn more.*

*Philo found Saul on one of his fasts in the desert. Having been
graciously admitted into Saul's tent, Philo got right to the point.*

*"Saul, why would you, a young Jewish Pharisee with the
finest training available under Gamaliel, forsake it all for Jesus*

Christ? What made the difference? What does Jesus have to offer that Judaism doesn't?"

"Everything in the universe is centered in Jesus as the Messiah of Israel. Yet He is more. He is God. He is the true Logos you have been searching for, Philo, and He can be found everywhere in our Scripture. Even His death and resurrection were foretold."

"Saul, you can't be serious. Why, all of my training says that you can't read Scripture that way. What I've learned from reading Plato and the Stoics makes this ludicrous. Scripture has to be read differently from ordinary literature. Like the Greek classics, it must be read allegorically. The historical meaning of miracles and prophecy is secondary. Jesus can't fulfill prophecy. Unless you keep up with the current philosophy, you and Christianity will soon fade into irrelevancy."

"Philo, I've read much of your writings. I sense in them a genuine longing to know God. But we cannot know the true God apart from what He has been doing in the world. I've discovered that reality is knowing God in the name of His incarnate Son, Jesus.

"I agree that Scripture is different from all other books; it has human authors and a divine Author who wants to reveal Himself to you if you will believe. But in our search for the eternal Truth in Scripture spoken by God, we cannot deny His work in history. His promises for the future are fulfilled in Jesus who alone is worthy to bear the divine name."

"I am sorry, Saul, but I cannot accept your interpretation. We know with our advanced learning today that such things do not happen. God used these stories in order to communicate deeper truths so we have to read them allegorically to make proper sense of Scripture. Besides, how would another apostate go over in the family? No, I have a reputation to maintain."

"I'm sorry to hear this. I hope your decision isn't final."

In the pages that follow we show how world views have impacted the interpretation of Scripture throughout history. Jews like Philo, Christians like Augustine and Calvin, and modern interpreters like Bultmann all have one thing in common—in lesser or greater ways they harnessed Scripture to a foreign world view, and this brought distortion. We are still in danger of doing so today in our attempts to understand meaning and to make Scripture relevant.

Chapter Two

Back to the Future

Historical Search for Deeper Meaning

"Remember the former things, those of long ago"

(Isaiah 46:9).

I n the last chapter we discovered that New Testament writers often use Old Testament Scripture in surprising ways. They seem to find meanings which go beyond the intention of the human author—beyond so-called literal meaning. This is both perplexing and intriguing.

How or why do they do this? What bounds or limitations did they follow? Could they find just any meaning? Does their practice affect the authority of Scripture? Is there a central concern to their approach to interpretation? Is there a "big picture" that guides their thinking which we could rediscover and come to own as ours as well?

To many, this discovery that Scripture has an additional or deeper meaning sounds novel and threatening. We want to show in this chapter that pursuit of such a meaning, under various names, has a long history. We will include only those matters which affect additional levels of mean-ing as found among the Jews or in the Church, past and present. We will take up the concerns regarding subjectivity in a later chapter.

First, a quick word about history may be necessary for those who care little about it.[1] We must make this trip back for several reasons. Our whole approach calls for community evaluation of truth, as a later chapter will explain. This is not only the contemporary community, but the whole Body—past, present, and future. To be true to our approach, we must listen to history.

Next, this trip back is His story—a history which itself reveals truth. Interpreting the past reveals more about God, ourselves, and His truth and ways. A later chapter will help us better understand the nature of this history.

Finally, we just may learn something new. Even we who have taught many years have discovered this to be true. So stick with us in our journey on a trail of twists and turns. We hope that you will come to see that the landscape we are about to sketch actually invites us to consider doing hermeneutics a new way! We must engage the future, and by going back we will be better fitted to do so.

Jewish Interpretation Searches for Relevance

We begin with the time before the New Testament existed.[2] God had not spoken for four hundred years. How could the old text still have relevance? The Jews created oral teaching to interpret the Old Testament text for contemporary Jews. This Aramaic interpretation (known as the *Targums*) became as authoritative as the sacred text itself.

At the time of Christ, the Jews experimented further with various levels of meaning in the text. They came to distinguish between the clear, plain (literal) meaning of the biblical text (the *peshat*) and the hidden sense of the text (the *remaz*). They also distinguished between the allegorical sense (*derush*), from which the "exegesis" (*midrash*) was derived, and the mystical (Cabalistic, esoteric) sense (the *sod*) of the text. When they engaged in exegesis or interpretation, they produced two forms: that which was historical, illustrative, practical and allegorical (*haggadic midrash*), and that which dealt with legal matters and applied the text to cases not prescribed in the Mosaic law (*halakic midrash*).[3]

Subsequently in the first century, the Jews began codifying their oral tradition (the *Mishnah*) which had been added to the law. To this Hebrew document they later added a commentary (the *Gemara*) in Aramaic, and the combination of these two came to be known as the *Talmud*.

The rabbis created various rules for interpreting these texts, just as we do today. The first to do this was Hillel, who sought to discover the clear or plain sense of the text. Many of these rules are still helpful for understanding Scripture.[4] As other rabbis concocted more sets of rules, there was a gradual departure from this plain sense.

Another source for digging into how the Jews interpreted the biblical text comes from the caves of the Qumran community, which gave us the Dead Sea Scrolls (discovered in 1947-48). Members of this community went overboard to contemporize everything in the Old Testament in their interpretation (called the *pesher*) while ignoring altogether the historical sense. For example, the Babylonians of Habakkuk 1:6 were made into the Roman Empire as the oppressors of Israel.

Finally, the Jews of Alexandria, Egypt, led by the example of Philo, delved into allegorical interpretation for those biblical texts which seemed to present absurdities, vulgarities, or other embarrassing things (including miracles!) to the Greek mind and its world view. To make the biblical text palatable, these Jews used the approach of Plato the Greek who divided the world into the two spheres of the visible (hence literal, corresponding to the body) and the invisible (the deeper meaning, or the *hyponoia*, corresponding to the soul). The historical or literal sense was viewed as an obstacle to the allegorical sense. So began the practice of tailoring an interpretation to fit a world view, of making the Bible relevant by allegorizing it.

In summary, we find that the Jews sought in differing ways to make the biblical text relevant, both by interpreting the literal meaning of the text and by finding meaning beyond the literal meaning.[5] In finding the deeper meaning, they often disregarded or contradicted the literal sense. Thus their interpretation had few constraints. By their detailed application to the smallest details of life, the rabbis made the biblical message burdensome for the Jews.

Yet some Jewish techniques are inviting. It has become popular for many today to use the Jews' *midrash, pesher,* and allegory as keys to understanding the deeper or additional meaning of the New Testament writers when they depart from the literal meaning.[6] After all, Jesus and the apostles were first century Jews. In the next chapter we will evaluate the merits of these approaches.

The Deeper Meaning Comes of Age

Very early, the interpretative method of the Church was represented by Clement of Rome in 1 Clement (ca. A.D. 95) and Ignatius (d. 110) in his epistles to various churches. These two "apostolic fathers" view the Old Testament as preparing for Jesus Christ and usually treat it rather literally. Later, Justin Martyr (d. ca. 165) often engaged in fanciful exegesis in his attempts to find Christ in the Old Testament, yet respected the historical events in the original context. Irenaeus (d. ca. 200) helped to encourage the typological approach (the practice of finding types in the Old Testament later fulfilled in Christ and the New Testament)[7] and respect for the clarity of Scripture. These early interpreters began to set the trends for interpretation.

For the following years of the Christian Church, historians commonly divide interpretation into three main schools or methods. First, the *Alexandrian* school is represented by Clement of Alexandria (d. 215). Enamored with the method of Philo, he sought to interpret all Scripture allegorically. His disciple, Origen (185-253/54), a noted theologian and the Church's first great textual critic, also adopted Philo's method. But he went further than Philo. Origen expanded the senses of Scripture to three: the body or fleshly (the literal), the soul or soulish (the psychical relating to the will), and the spirit or spiritual (speaking of Christ). To demonstrate his growing maturity, the interpreter was to make an "ascent" (*anagoge*) of the soul upward from the level of the flesh to the level of the spirit. Origen bequeathed this method to his successors, including Gregory Thaumaturgus, Pamphilus, Eusebius of Caesarea, and Gregory of Nyssa (ca. 335-394). Scripture, if not all of life, is allegorical and descriptive of spiritual or heavenly things. By this approach, every earthly thing corresponds to a spiritual or heavenly counterpart.

The second main school, the *Antiochian*, is associated with the literal method. It is represented by Lucian of Samosata, Diodorus (ca. 290), Theodore of Mopsuestia (d. 430), and John Chrysostom (d. 407). The key word for this school is *theoria*, coming from a Greek word meaning "to see." Yet the spiritual sense was not overlooked by these interpreters; indeed, they wished to avoid an overly literalistic approach. They believed the meaning of a text was both literal and spiritual, historical and typological. The biblical writers perceived spiritual truth at the heart of the historical event.[8] In other words, the historical event is the vehicle for the spiritual and theological truth. As one observer notes, this school saw the Christian meaning "as a 'higher sense' beyond the literal meaning, and their differences from the dominant Alexandrian approach must not be overemphasized."[9] This is significant, for it is popular to cite this school in support of only a very narrow view of the literal sense. We believe that we should have a greater appreciation for the twofold sense of this school.

The third main school of interpretation in the early Church is the *Western* school, and is represented by Hilary, Ambrose, Jerome, Augustine, and Cyril. This eclectic ("pick and choose") school incorporated features from both of the other schools and added the authority of tradition in interpreting the text. While Augustine stressed the need for the literal sense as the basis for the allegorical meaning, he enlarged the senses of Scripture to four.[10] Eventually, four terms were popularly used in the Western church: the literal, allegorical, tropological (or moral), and anagogical (mystical or eschatological). By way of illustration, Jerusalem is literally a city of Israel; allegorically it is the

Church; tropologically it is the faithful soul; and anagogically it is the center of the new creation.

The major point to be gleaned from this brief overview of interpretation in the early Church is that all schools of interpretation found a spiritual meaning in the text of Scripture. Whether or not Christians understood this as a separate sense or meaning, they at least recognized it. They considered the literal sense—what we understand as grammatical and historical—as insufficient. We believe that the idea of the anagogical (eschatological) sense is especially worthy of renewed consideration as we grapple with explaining the deeper meaning.

The Fourfold Sense Prevails

The fourfold sense of interpretation prevailed throughout the Middle Ages. Yet some sought to correct or modify the accepted method of interpretation. Scholars such as Hugo of St. Victor (1096?-1141) and his disciple Andrew, along with the major influence of Thomas Aquinas (1225-1274), stressed the literal sense as the basis for all other senses. Yet this is the sense intended by the author, and for Aquinas, this author is God, not the human prophet or writer.[11] Nicholas of Lyra (1270-1340) insisted on the literal sense as the only adequate basis of doctrine. Yet because the literal sense is the meaning which the author intended, and Scripture has two authors, there is a double literal sense. In certain instances the literal-prophetic sense takes precedence over the literal-historic.[12] On the other hand, others, such as Stephen Langton (1150-1228), who divided our Bible into chapters, preferred the spiritual meaning over the literal.

The Literal Meaning Gains Supremacy

The influence of the Reformation on biblical interpretation can hardly be overstated. The Reformers made the literal meaning supreme and laid the foundation for grammatical-historical interpretation.

Just prior to the Reformation there was a new emphasis in biblical interpretation based on grammatical, historical, and philological study. The names of J. Reuchlin, D. Erasmus, and J. Colet belong here. These influenced Martin Luther both in his condemnation of allegory and in his insistence that the literal or historical meaning is the only legitimate basis for interpretation.[13] Luther also focused on Christ as the true spiritual sense of Scripture communicated by the historical sense. Luther embraced the twofold literal (literal-historic and literal-prophetic) sense so that Scripture is both a history of what God has done and also what He is going to do.[14]

John Calvin similarly defended the literal sense, and argued that all doctrine should be based, not in the tradition of the Church, but in the text of Scripture alone. He particularly developed the role of the Holy Spirit in interpreting and applying the truth.[15] The Spirit gives both the conviction of the truth of Scripture and gives understanding through gifted interpreters, but He does not directly aid everyone in understanding. The authority of Scripture comes by the inner witness of the Spirit, not by reasoned proofs.[16]

Both Luther and Calvin believed that the interpretation of the Word must also be accompanied by its application in the life of the believer.[17] This helped to give balance to their concern for objectivity. Others with this view of interpretation include Melanchthon, Zwingli, Bucer, Beza, and William Tyndale.[18]

Yet did the Reformers, in defending literal meaning to this extent, overreact to abuses in the previous approach of the Middle Ages? There is reason to believe that they did. Prior to his break with Rome in 1517, Luther believed that God could speak in both external and internal (immediate ways), through the Holy Spirit (although the position of the Church as ultimate interpreter of Scripture prevailed). But when Lutheranism became somewhat established, Luther reacted against teachers such as the Anabaptists who wanted to follow the inner witness of the Holy Spirit. Luther put the external working of God through the Word and the sacraments ahead of the internal witness of the Spirit. One receives faith or the Spirit only through the

Word written and preached.[19] The idea of God speaking immediately was frowned upon and obscured by exposition of the written Word.

Similarly, Calvin, in spite of his emphasis on the guidance and inner witness of the Holy Spirit, apparently denied to others what he had allowed for himself. He so feared the subjectivism of Anabaptists "driven by the Holy Spirit" that he even frowned on private Bible study and advocated that people listen in church to the authorized exposition of Scripture through the minister of the Word. For Calvin, this took "the place of prophecy in the Christian Church: the Holy Spirit speaks to and guides believers through preaching."[20] Unfortunately, this position greatly enhanced the place of the preacher and tended to separate laity and clergy—a consequence still evident today.[21]

We can be grateful to God for His work in the Reformers to bring us back to the primacy of literal interpretation. Yet they seem to have left a heritage that denies the possibility of immediate communication with the Spirit regarding the interpretation of Scripture and the discovery of additional meaning. Reflecting their world view with its emphasis on rational and cognitive learning, they tended to make the literal meaning the only meaning, and in so doing ruled out the possibility of God speaking anew.

Interpretation Comes Under Attack

The post-Reformation era in interpretation began with the dual impact of pietism and rationalism in the seventeenth and eighteenth centuries. Pietism stressed personal experience in holiness in the interpretation of Scripture, and is represented by P. Spener, John Wesley, and Jonathan Edwards. Listening for the voice of God in Scripture with a commitment to obey it made possible greater understanding of its message. Rationalism, on the other hand, stressed human reason as supreme over the interpretation of Scripture and is represented by T. Hobbes, J. Locke, and B. Spinoza. René Descartes, called the father of the modern era, divided the cosmos into the domains of matter (pertaining to science) and of mind or spirit (pertaining to theology).[22] This division brought to Western thinking a horizontal dualism, separating the two realms. Immanuel Kant (1724-1804), similarly holding to the sovereignty of reason, sought to separate the realm of universals, God, and immortality (the "noumenal realm"), from the realm of sense experience (the "phenomenal realm"). Taken together, these influences make all knowledge subjective. Since reason is made the final criterion for truth,[23] the final consequence is to deny the possibility of truth. Ultimate realities cannot be discovered—only believed.[24] This has had a lasting impact on interpretation.

During the eighteenth and nineteenth centuries, through the influence of such men as Schleiermacher, Ritschl, and von Harnack, concern for interpretation waned. Instead, liberal theology pursued rationalistic and critical concerns about the Bible's sources and history.[25] It was Friedrich Schleiermacher who did the most to place the study of Scripture on a credible par with the study of other literature as he sought to integrate Christian faith and "modern" thinking. He laid the "methodological groundwork" for today's widely practiced grammatical-historical exegesis.[26] He showed that interpretation is a twofold task, consisting of a historical-critical study and a theological-believing study which seeks to integrate the text with the world view of the interpreter.[27] Once again, interpretation of the biblical text became tied to a world view, this time embodying the grammatical-historical method. The new method of interpretation was not the result of refining the method or of discoveries of new resources for the method, but the result of a new world with its commitment to the historical-critical method, the principle of evolution, and the idea of progress.[28]

Rudolf Bultmann became the most influential biblical interpreter of this century. He was able to wed the existential philosophy of Heidegger to hermeneutics. Adopting Kahler's distinction between critical, scientific history (*Historie*) and true, real, transcendent history (*Geschichte*), Bultmann sharply distinguished between historical study and the faith. Thus interpretation is not just explaining the original meaning of the text, but interpreting "the event of Jesus Himself *into* the existential framework of the contemporary believer" (italics theirs).[29] This makes meaning totally subjective.

In his revolutionary commentary on Romans, Karl Barth emphasized the authority of Scripture, and reflecting the influence of Kierkegaard, the need for a personal encounter with God. We mention Barth with Bultmann because their works led to a revolution in interpreting the Bible and doing theology called neo-orthodoxy (or dialectical theology).[30] Their existentialist approach means that the Bible doesn't become God's Word until we have an encounter with Him. An existential world view was imposed on the text. The results of this are still evident today in the rejection of Scripture as objective revelation normative for the Christian.

Bultmann and others were both heirs to and developers of their own critical literary approaches for the interpretation of Scripture. The attempt to find the literary sources of the Gospels (source criticism) had preceded them. Building on this critical study, Bultmann made the major contribution to the study of how early Christians developed (and even created) oral traditions about Jesus to meet some felt need which later was recorded in the Gospels. This study was called *form criticism*. Subsequently, critics attempted to discover the theological motives which guided the early redactors in choosing their oral tradition about Jesus (redaction criticism).

The major effect of all these approaches was to denigrate inspired Scripture to the level of ordinary literature. Interpretation became a wholly natural pursuit. The great mistake of Bultmann and others was to assume that the biblical writers had interposed their ancient, contemporary world view into the very heart of the gospel. They believed this had to be removed, be "demythologized," by modern man with his world view.

The only problem is that one world view and philosophy replaces another. Bultmann seemingly failed to consider whether the biblical world view might derive from God and not from the culture in which the authors wrote. Also important to our own study is Bultmann's radical denial of the true relevance to the Christian of the Old Testament. He thereby shut the door to the concept of a biblical center or world view which encompasses both testaments, and the relationship that such a biblical center might have to hermeneutics.[31]

The Author Dies and the Reader Takes Over

Coinciding with the various literary approaches sketched above, new discoveries in the area of language and semantics have affected how we do interpretation. The study of language involves the distinction between historical matters pertaining to the author (called diachrony) and contemporaneous matters pertaining to the reader (called synchrony). Using this distinction, most critics totally reject the author's intended meaning in their interpretation of terms and the biblical world view.[32] The result is that the text says what the reader, not the author, wants it to say. In addition, scholars pursuing the meaning of meaning applied the distinction between sense (what is said) and reference (the thing spoken about) to focus on the crucial matters of the context and the intention of the author.[33] Yet the net effect of this pursuit is to place the reader once again in a position of preeminence over the author.

Discoveries in semantics (the study of meaning) have had a great impact on biblical interpretation, especially on deeper meaning. The so-called *new hermeneutic* represents a new view of language so that the biblical text now interprets the reader, not vice-versa. The object of concern is not the text, but the reader. Whereas in the past the focus had been on the author and his text, now the center of attention shifted to the self. Scholars turned from developing a method for interpreting the text to studying the structure of understanding itself.[34] This again puts the emphasis on the reader.

We can trace, step by step, how this shift of focus developed. In essence, each form of study arose after the other because scholars neglected a particular aspect. While this is a complex study, we can give the general outline.

Form and redaction criticism, with their emphasis on historical matters associated with the authors/redactors (diachrony), failed to deal with the significance of the literary form and plot development (synchrony) of the text. So a new approach, structuralism, sought to uncover the structures—not the meaning—behind the author's thought and to reorder his experience and reality in terms of a deeper meaning. Structuralism brings the focus to what the text means in the present with no concern for the author's intended meaning. Meaning is never fixed.[35] Gadamer's view of language prepared the way by fusing the two horizons—the text and the interpreter—so that the past and the present merge. But merging past and present according to the interpreter's determination leads to the denial of history and the loss of human freedom. This brought the reaction of poststructuralism. Various contemporary world views are used to examine the text and an infinite variety of meanings result so that we are even further removed from the author and text.[36] Indeed, the author is dead. Reader-response criticism arose to go even further and to posit "not only the autonomy of the text but the veritable union between text and reader at the moment of response."[37] The original text and meaning now disappear as the reader, as part of a community in dialogue with the text, creates meaning.

Because the reader and his meaning are everything and the author and text nothing, extreme reader-response criticism makes it impossible to communicate. Such an approach allows you, the reader, to read these sentences with any meaning you desire, or with no meaning at all! Such a negative development brought about deconstruction, seemingly to "correct" reader-response criticism by challenging "the communicative power of language itself." It deconstructs all previous meaning as it attempts to free the interpreter from the false constraints of Western patterns of thinking which have produced meaning.[38]

In this way we have come to an almost intolerable state of interpretation. Such matters as the relationship of the testaments as a determiner of meaning (for the New adopts the world view of the Old) have been largely neglected.

Both the Author and the Reader Are Essential

Today the pendulum is swinging back to restore balance in interpretation. The two approaches, one emphasizing the author (diachrony) and the other emphasizing the reader (synchony), are not mutually exclusive, but complementary and interdependent. Both are necessary.[39] This has led to mediating positions whereby all three elements of author, text, and reader play a role. For example, canonical criticism has risen in recognition of the need to give more place, alongside the place of the reader, to the text and to its canonical framework.[40] Although it gives less place to authorial intention, it has attracted the support of evangelicals (as the next chapter will show). Others (including supporters of literalism) seek to recover and restore the author's intended meaning or the text's intended meaning. However, even with this counterswing of the pendulum, much concern and skepticism are directed toward a search for interpretation that honors the original authors and Author of Scripture.

SO WHAT?

The revolution in hermeneutics just traced reflects the need and ongoing search for a balanced and relevant hermeneutic. We now stand on the brink of another revolution, namely the rejection of modernism (the modern world view) and the rise of deconstructive postmodernism. The new way asserts that there is no longer one unifying center or basis of meaning. There is no truth, only interpretations of interpretations.

The times are challenging for all of us, but perhaps no more so than they were for Luther and Calvin five hundred years ago. At that time they set the trajectories of Christian interpretation. We must answer some questions.

- Can we recover the Reformers' zeal for a redemptive center of Scripture—but find a better center?

- Can we recapture the place they gave to the Holy Spirit—but enlarge it to include His immediate communication?

- Can we embrace their principle of the analogy of faith (Scripture interprets Scripture)—but discover and practice the Bible's own method of interpretation?

- Can we emulate their diligence in fashioning a grammatical-historical hermeneutic—but pursue a method which incorporates the supernatural world view of the Bible?

As the Reformers met their times, we are called to meet ours. We go back but to a new future. For the first time in its history, most of the Church is located in Africa, Latin America, and the Far East—areas which have never known the theological and cultural impact (the world view) of the Reformation. The Church there has nothing to go back to.

Can we find a new approach to interpretation, a new paradigm of hermeneutics, which will suit these new times?[41] Is there a more holistic way of conceiving reality in a world view which may answer the despair and disillusionment of deconstructive postmodernism? Can we discover the Bible's world view as a key to interpretation?[42]

A new hermeneutic must address both the transcendent and experienced realms and meet postmodern people's needs, yet maintain the truth of Scripture.[43] Our next chapter surveys the contemporary pursuit for a hermeneutic which would explain the deeper or additional meaning which the New Testament discovers in the Old, and sets the stage for how our approach fits into this.

How Do We Explain
Deeper Meaning?

*It was dark and dingy beyond description. The beating made
the prison even more inhospitable. No one had stood with Paul
at trial this time, and it had gone badly, from a human perspective. Paul felt so lonely...again. Even Timothy had delayed coming so that he and Luke had been without food and drink for two
days. Luke, beloved physician, friend, and fellow prisoner, had
done his best to relieve Paul's suffering, but now the wounds on
his back had become infected. Paul knew it was only a matter of
time. Still there was so much to do. He had sent his companions
in the gospel to several places to see that the work continued. If
he was to die he wanted to do all he could to keep the flame
alive. He still had so much to learn. He was eager for Timothy
to bring his scrolls of Scripture.*

*Paul continued to muse over his circumstances. It was espe-
cially hurtful to have Demas forsake him at this critical juncture.
It made Timothy's presence more urgent than ever. How could
Demas have done this? Just three years before he had stayed with
him and Luke in his earlier imprisonment. He had undergone
persecution. So when release had come, Demas took special joy
in having remained loyal. Perhaps that was the problem. Perhaps
Demas was loyal to him rather than to Jesus Himself. So now
this second imprisonment just proved to be too much.*

*Questions kept bothering Paul. Was Demas a believer? What
was it in the world that captured his love and drew him away?*

*Demas had been so promising. He brought to the ministry not
only a quick mind for learning the deep things of God, but also
training in letters and the philosophy of the day. Like Apollos he
could reason with the best of the Jews and Gentiles. But on more
than one occasion Paul had noticed that Demas made claim to
secret knowledge. He thought that deeper meaning in Scripture
could be discovered by a favored few who had access to a hidden
gnosis in special revelation. For Paul, this synthesizing of Christ
and the pagan mystery religions was fatal, even blasphemous.
Perhaps his rebuke had been too harsh—but what else could Paul*

have done? Demas' compromise stabbed at the very heart of the gospel!

Paul remembered an especially sharp argument with Demas. Paul had used allegory to interpret the circumstances of Sarah and Hagar to find additional meaning that Moses was unaware of. Demas accused Paul of expounding a special knowledge and being hypocritical in condemning Demas for doing so. Paul had tried to point out that all believers possess the Spirit and the mystery of Christ, and so have everything they need to grow in the knowledge of the truth. But Demas seemed more interested in faulting the apostle than learning truth.

Demas was gone, but perhaps not forever, Paul hoped. He would receive Demas back just as he had Mark. For himself, he knew above all else that his hope was not in men but in God alone. The Lord was standing by him, strengthening him, opening Scripture to him. This was enough. The message would continue to go out, enlarging the circle of believers ever more. Until the time appointed, he was invincible. And then his Lord would bring him safely to His heavenly Kingdom.

Throughout history, many possibilities have been explored for explaining how the biblical writers read deeper meaning in Scripture. Within evangelicalism today, several ideas are being discussed. We review questions about the adequacy of the single-authorial intention hermeneutic, and briefly survey and evaluate today's suggestions of structural methods and theological motifs for explaining how the biblical writers read Scripture.

Chapter Three

The Future
Is Here

Contemporary Pursuit of
Deeper Meaning

"We have a word of prophecy made more certain"

(2 Peter 1:19).

In the previous chapter we traced how Jews and Christians struggled in their interpretation of Scripture as they tried to make the Bible relevant and yet retain its original message. They sought to relate the literal meaning to an additional or deeper meaning. Between these two the pendulum has swung back and forth from age to age, and a world view has often been imposed on the Bible. All of this has shaped the present discussion.

As we face the hermeneutical challenges of a future where all truth and reality are rejected, we must wholeheartedly pursue a satisfactory way of relating the two meanings. We now show why both literal interpretation and the other explanations of the biblical hermeneutic are inadequate. In subsequent chapters we will put forth our own method.[1]

Struggling with the Literal Method

New findings in language and interpretation have sharpened our awareness of the need to better understand various concepts such as meaning and intention. Literal interpretation, sometimes known as the plain, normal meaning of words,[2] distinguishes among meaning, significance, and application.[3] Meaning is found only in the single meaning, original intention.[4] Meaning pertains to the assertion of the author and is "fixed and unchanging; significance is never fixed and always changing."[5] Significance pertains to the relation between what is said and our own situation. We, the readers, determine the significance. Finally, application is the practical working out of the passage for our instruction and response.[6] So when we interpret according to the literal sense (the grammatical-historical sense), we mean that a writer has a single intention in what he writes and it is this that we seek to discover and explain by study of the grammar, history, and context of the writer.

For the most part, these distinctions are helpful for interpreting literature. They prevent total subjectivity by the reader and preserve the author's intention and his text. But the approach still runs into problems. Meaning and intentionality are far more complex than the method admits. How does an author speak to our present situation? How do we apply his words? These questions are compounded when we come to dual-authored Scripture. Traditional literalists insist that the divine Author and the human author have the same intention, that the Holy Spirit inspired biblical writers to interpret earlier Scripture by a literal approach, and that He guides our interpretation by this same approach. They insist there is no difference in method between how we interpret Scripture and any other literature.[7] It is grammatical-historical. According to some, for us to depart from this sense and method raises questions regarding authority and inerrancy.[8]

Yet in our first chapter we have shown that the literal approach is not adequate to explain Scripture's own use of Scripture. In our major test case, Malachi prophesies about a messenger and Elijah; Jesus said He spoke of John the Baptist; and John said he was not Elijah. Did Malachi intend John the Baptist as his single intention, or didn't he? Was Jesus wrong in finding John in Malachi? And did Malachi intend Jesus Himself as the revealer of Yahweh, the Lord who is to come to His temple as the "messenger of the covenant"? The literal approach appears inadequate here and in the many other cases we briefly discussed.[9] And if the literal hermeneutic is inadequate to explain Scripture's own use of Scripture, then departing from the literal hermeneutic can hardly threaten the authority and inerrancy of Scripture that traditional literalists believe the biblical writers teach. There must be another answer.

One way to deal with deeper meaning in prophecy such as this is to appeal to a generic sense. Originally called generic prediction[10] and recently popularized by Walt Kaiser as generic promise,[11] this method seeks to uphold literal meaning with its distinction between the original, intentional meaning of the author, and the later significance of an utterance.[12] According to generic promise, prophecy has one meaning which is of a generic or corporate nature.[13] So a prophet may have in mind multiple fulfillments of a single, broad, generic sense—not one specific person, but a generic one. Thus Malachi has in mind not one specific person, such as John the Baptist, but a generic messenger who comes in the spirit and power of Elijah (cf. Luke 1:17, 76-79) throughout time.

But, we ask, does a prophet have as his authorial intent a whole string of generic "fulfillments"? Or does this method simply redefine authorial intent in order to protect a literal hermeneutic and to reject dual authorship (contra 1 Peter 1:10-12) as an explanation for additional meaning?[14] Yet the later human authors of Scripture emphasize divine intention (authorship) over human intention in the prophecy they quote.[15]

Some appear to seek relief from the inadequacies of literal interpretation by redefining meaning, while yet staying with the literal approach. Even Kaiser seems to have tried this. In his latest work, he broadened the concept of meaning to include such concepts as sense (which is the single thing being said about the referent or referents), referent (what is spoken about—may be multiple as intended by the author), intention (which determines the referent or referents a word is to have), and significance (which relates the meaning to some person or circumstance and is ever changing).[16] But this is really only a semantic change from Hirsch's distinction between meaning and significance. Kaiser maintains the same distinctions, but calls them *meaning-as-sense/intention and meanings-as-significance*.[17]

Millard Erickson advocates erasing the distinction between meaning and significance. He suggests that the meaning of a text encompasses two aspects: the original signification (both referents and principles) and the later significance (application of principles). The idea of *intention* is broadened to "affirmation" or "assertion" to focus on the product of the intention rather than the process, and to include both original and future persons and situations.[18] Other writers go further and place the divine, fuller meaning within the original meaning because meaning is multidimensional. It even includes application.[19]

While we believe these have made some significant and lasting suggestions, we wonder whether this is still literal interpretation. Did Malachi have in mind these later applications as his single meaning original intention?

Kaiser himself appears unclear here in his recent work. He points out that the intention determines the referent or referents, and that the divine and human intentions are equal. Yet he then quickly adds that "this is not to say that the divinely intended referents were limited to those that the author saw or meant."[20] This seems contradictory. Kaiser's co-author takes a different position which allows for additional meaning.[21] So defense of a purely literal interpretation seems increasingly more difficult to explain.[22]

There is a substantial number of interpreters, past and present, who find in varying degrees that a strictly literal (grammatical-historical) interpretation is inadequate to explain citations of prophecy and other interpretation within Scripture. They support a deeper meaning in terms of a theological "plus" to grammatical-historical interpretation. They are not voiding the literal meaning, but finding a meaning that goes beyond it. They come to a deeper meaning, or some sort of additional meaning, on the basis of new discoveries in the meaning of meaning (semantics), as traced above; or because of the special dual nature of Scripture as both human and divine (the Holy Spirit is at work); or because of a combination of these. These interpreters, to name a few, include F. F. Bruce, B. Waltke, E. E. Ellis, W. LaSor, R. Longenecker, C. F. H. Henry, D. Hagner, S. L. Johnson, E. Johnson, B. Westcott, F. Delitzcsh, J. I. Packer, V. Poythress, D. Bock, M. Erickson, and J. Calvin.[23]

But even more important is the witness of Scripture itself. The Bible indicates that human authors often did not understand their writings. Several passages make this clear (Daniel 8:27; 12:6-9; John 11:44-52; 1 Peter 1:10-12).[24] The verb for *fulfill* used in many places where the Old Testament is cited may be rendered "to fill again," "to fill completely" (see Matthew 13:14 citing Isaiah 6:9-10).[25] In addition, the apostles and other writers of Scripture consciously recognized that both their writings and earlier biblical writings were of a divine nature. Scripture is the product of both the divine Author and the human author (cf. Deuteronomy 5:22-33; Acts 1:16; 2 Peter 1:20-21), and Scripture places emphasis on the divine Author, as the book of Hebrews illustrates well.[26] This implies that meaning cannot be limited to the authorial intent of the human author.[27] Passages such as Luke 24:25-27, 32, 45 and John 3:10-13 show that Jesus assumed a deeper meaning and had to open both the hearts and minds of the apostles to understand Scripture. His practice in using the Old Testament became theirs. At times the apostles show significant freedom regarding original intention.[28] They fulfill what Jesus affirms in Matthew 13:52 that a scribe of the Kingdom would bring out of his treasure things old and new (cf. Romans 11:25-27). For example, Luke 1:68-79 is expanded in Luke 19:44; Acts 13:47; 15:14; 26:16-23.[29]

The rest of this chapter takes up the major alternatives to literal interpretation. It will build a case for our new approach and will hint of its features. We first discuss major structural approaches, and then turn to more narrow theological motifs used to explain deeper meaning in Scripture.[30]

Just a word before we begin. It is important to realize that all of this is an "in house" discussion. All evangelicals espouse some form of the grammatical-historical hermeneutic. What we and others are arguing against is a strict version of it which reduces all meaning to the simple intention of the human author. Those who recognize the complexity of meaning are struggling to find a reformulation of the grammatical-historical hermeneutic to accommodate this, so we can express in theory more accurately what we (often unconsciously) do in practice. This new theory will be like the grammatical-historical hermeneutic in that it will espouse objective meaning according to the author's intention. But it will be unlike the grammatical-historical hermeneutic in that it will espouse valid meaning that cannot be reduced to the single intention of the human author—which is the central, defining element of the grammatical-historical hermeneutic. So our suggested hermeneutic is basically a *reformulation* of the grammatical-historical hermeneutic that does not agree with the latter's central element as it is currently defined.

Structural Explanations of Deeper Meaning

Already we have introduced such major approaches as allegory, *midrash*, and *pesher* as employed by the Jews in their attempt to interpret the Old Testament. Some want to identify them as methods practiced within the New Testament as well. Allegory became predominant among Christians for a thousand years during the middle ages.

Pesher. The *pesher* method comes from the Qumran community of the Dead Sea Scrolls. These Jews applied the Old Testament to contemporary events by claiming a "this is that" fulfillment between the text and the event. As we showed in Chapter 2, they displayed little respect for the original intention of the author in contextualizing

Scripture. This approach centers on apocalyptic (end time) events and claims a special revelation of the mystery or key to the interpretation.[31] Everything becomes an end time event. According to its supporters, *pesher* is not extensive in Paul,[32] but is utilized by Matthew,[33] and is the most frequent way by which Jesus cited His Bible.[34] Hence when Jesus said, "This is that..." (Matthew 11:10) in making John the messenger, many think that He was using *pesher*.

Yet it is not clear how widespread this Qumranian method was in the first century. It is doubtful that Jesus or any New Testament author had such a disregard for the original historical context.[35] *Pesher* fails to provide any guidelines for using non-literal interpretation and cannot explain Malachi's own non-literal meaning, since he wrote hundreds of years before Qumran. It does not appear possible or wise for us to practice this method today.

Midrash. This is probably the central concept in rabbinic exegesis. The Hebrew word means to *seek, study, interpret,* and denotes an *interpretive exposition.*[36] As a good summary, we can say that *midrash* seeks to go deeper than the literal sense and explain "the hidden meaning contained therein by means of agreed upon hermeneutical rules in order to contemporize the revelation of God for the people of God.[37] It is characterized by "that has relevance to this" (cf. *pesher* above) and occurs, it is claimed, in Paul and Jesus.[38]

While there may be parallels between rabbinic methods and the New Testament,[39] many of the devices employed, such as decoding hidden meanings and citing isolated proof texts, are simply not present in the New Testament.[40] Jesus does not follow the atomizing literalism of the rabbis, picking apart words and phrases, engaging in *ghematria* (deciphering meaning from numbers), and other schemes. He gives a straightforward claim to fulfillment without trying to take Malachi apart piecemeal. He is conscious of context (note his allusions to the Old Testament in 11:5-8). Like *pesher* above, this approach fails to respect the historical meaning and provides little control for the new or deeper meaning. In fact, Jesus and the Apostles warned against the interpretive gymnastics of the rabbis and Pharisees. Their method does not seem reproducible for us today.

Allegory. The allegory of Philo and other Jews led them to find spiritual truths divorced from history while rigidly attached to the very letter of the text. Yet the biblical author is concerned with facts, the historical sense.[41] The instances cited by some interpreters (such as Galatians 4:21-31; Hebrews 7:1-10; and 1 Corinthians 9:9-10) do not show the antihistorical nature of allegory. In Matthew 11 Jesus believes that the messenger and Elijah of Malachi find fulfillment in another person, not an idea or concept or truth.

Typology. This method is a genuine approach widely practiced in the New Testament. For example, the furniture of the tabernacle and other matters associated with it and the temple (the altar and sacrifices, the veil, the golden cover of the ark of the covenant) are all types of Christ and of the heavenly realm (see Hebrews 9).

When we come to typology, we must avoid being too broad or too narrow in our interpretation.[42] We can be too broad if we find typology everywhere. We can be too narrow if we reject typology as an exegetical method on the basis of the claim that it is not consistent with a literal meaning which embraces one meaning, found by means of grammatical-historical study.[43] Since typology, some say, embraces significance not intended by the author, it is disqualified from being an exegetical method.[44]

Yet, we believe that typology is not to be divorced from exegesis, even though it cannot be fully "regulated hermeneutically, but takes place in the freedom of the Holy Spirit."[45] It very much involves a deeper meaning and was readily practiced by the Bible in its exegetical method (see 1 Corinthians 10; Romans 5).

Thus, by typology, the messenger of Malachi 3:1 and Elijah of 4:5 typify John the Baptist. Even Malachi himself may do so. Yet Jesus seems to go beyond typology when He asserts that John *is* Elijah and *fulfills* Malachi 3:1 (Matthew 11:10, 14; 17:12-13). Indeed, future fulfillments are yet to come (Matthew 11:11) and perhaps the actual Elijah before the day of judgment (Malachi 4:5). Typology does not seem to be broad enough in scope to serve as an all-encompassing hermeneutical method for significant portions of Scripture, such as wisdom and apocalyptic and legal literature, or any discourse not oriented toward historical event. Its exact content and scope cannot be defined.[46] Even though we believe that we should find additional types,[47] we have no guiding center for their discovery. Typology is a subset of a broader method that encompasses literature that typology cannot. In addition, typology alone tends to depreciate Old Testament history as nothing more than a "copious picturebook."[48]

Analogous Fulfillment. Several attempt to explain the hermeneutic of Scripture as that of analogous fulfillment. As an overarching model, it would include several of the above methods. The model is based on the observation that there is "both a similarity and a difference between one object, event, or idea and another object, event, or idea." This approach rests on the fact that "fulfillments are normally analogical and only occasionally literal. Even literal fulfillments are analogous due to differences of space and time."[49] However, while this method provides a major explanation for the fulfillment of the Old Testament in the New, the method fails to explain why the analogue of Elijah and John exists. It seems to fail to take the original promise as expecting an actual fulfillment. In effect, it denies a deeper meaning altogether. It also fails to equip us so that we may discover with some confidence other analogies to contextualize the message for our own era.

THEOLOGICAL EXPLANATIONS OF DEEPER MEANING

Because the purely structural relationships above have proven inadequate, interpreters have posited various theological ideas or motifs to explain deeper meaning. It is here that the discussion about biblical hermeneutics is particularly focused.

The Purpose of God. This motif means that the New Testament declares that the plan of God has been brought to fulfillment. History, then, is the working out of the divine purpose. This motif may be represented in prophecy by double or multiple fulfillment or sense. This view means that several successive persons or events fulfill a given prophecy. This motif is a plausible solution to the use of the Old Testament in the New. In this way, John the Baptist may fulfill Malachi, as well as several other messengers yet to come. Yet this approach lacks specificity. We need to know what is this purpose in order to use it to discover the full meaning of such texts.

Christology. The significance of Christology as a link between the Testaments can hardly be overestimated. The living presence of Christ is a determining factor in all New Testament exegesis and the Old Testament is to be interpreted christocentrically. It is one of the four major exegetical presuppositions of the earliest Christian use of the Old Testament.[50] Clearly, Christ is prophesied as the "messenger of the covenant" in Malachi 3:1. However, this motif or concept is inadequate by itself.[51] Christology is part of a broader concept and is the means of achieving this larger purpose, answering the question, "Why the Christ?" Further, the Christological approach has been faulted for spiritualizing or allegorizing the Old Testament and thus demeaning the value of the Hebrew religious experience in its own right (and history along with it).

Heilsgeschichte. *Heilsgeschichte* is the history of God's saving acts, culminating in and encompassed by the Christ-event. God is sovereign over history and works His purposes in it to accomplish His goals. This concept brings coherence and consistency to all that takes place. We can say that both Malachi and Matthew represent a salvation history—God's special dealings with His people. However, this is inadequate to explain detailed fulfillments and it is doubtful that all Scripture has this as its basic theme.[52] Salvation history is not broad enough. The concept itself does not seem to arise from the biblical text.[53] More significantly, in the view of Pannenberg, *Heilsgeschichte* depreciates history (*Historie*) by separating actual history from salvation (or redemptive) history.[54] It produces a suprahistory as God's realm of working.

Promise-fulfillment. The concept of promise-fulfillment is another way to link the Testaments and to explain deeper meaning.[55] This concept shows the proper preparatory nature of the Old Testament. It is essential to progressive history and our concept of God.[56] It is implicit as well as explicit in Scripture (e.g., Jeremiah 33:14; Hebrews 11). Depending on whether we support dispensationalism or covenant theology, we can find the fulfillment either to be literal (as the promise is), or to be spiritual (unlike the promise).

Yet does Jesus exhaust the promise of a messenger's coming? There appears to be no way to know beforehand what fulfills the promise. While this motif may be a helpful way of viewing the Testaments in relationship to each other and specific passages which are clearly promise-oriented, it is too narrow or limited and fails as a hermeneutic for the rest of Scripture[57] (especially in a genre such as wisdom literature).

Sensus Plenior. Many writers, especially Roman Catholics but also evangelicals, appeal to a hidden meaning called *sensus plenior.*[58] It is that fuller, deeper, spiritual sense which lies below or beyond the literal sense and is unknown to the human author.[59] In its better form a relationship exists between the literal sense and the fuller sense. As applied to Malachi 3:1 and 4:5, it means that the fulfillment of Elijah in John the Baptist is a meaning not consciously intended by the human author (Malachi), but is a meaning intended by God and integral to the text and later discerned by Jesus.[60]

While *sensus plenior* is helpful, we need to be more certain as to the parameters of control. Considerable subjectivity in identifying the additional meaning in Malachi remains. It seems difficult to practice today with the needed sense of assurance or authority that the deeper sense is normative. *Sensus plenior* really does not resolve the difficulty,[61] for it fails to delineate what is the relationship of the senses and how one gets from the literal to the deeper meaning and why one should do so.

Canonical Approach. Out of concern over the subjectivity of a sensus plenior approach, many are turning attention to a canonical approach to explain the deeper meaning. The ultimate canonical context, the whole Bible, provides the basis for a "fuller" sense to Scripture and human intention.

There are several advantages to this approach.[62] For some, the chief one is that it avoids dual meaning: God did not intend or implant additional meaning necessarily hidden from the human author at the point of inspiration, though He knew in His providence that greater meaning would be unfolded as the Canon grew.[63]

On the other hand, others appear to support dual meaning. J. I. Packer writes that

> though God may have more to say to us from each text than its human writer had in mind, God's meaning is never less than his....God's further meaning, as revealed when the text is exegeted in its canonical context, in relation to all that went before and came after, is simply extension, development, and application of what the writer was consciously expressing.[64]

Packer calls for teaching the Bible as a whole to provide the framework for interpreting each particular passage. Hence interpretation involves the three steps of exegesis, integration with the rest of Scripture, and then application.[65]

Faulting both the allegorical and literal approaches, B. Waltke and others support a *canonical process* approach for interpreting the Psalms. Waltke believes that progressive perception of meaning paralleled the growth of the Canon and its progressive history through four stages. Yet the "original authorial intention was not changed in the progressive development of the canon but deepened and clarified."[66] As a result Waltke, as Augustine and Bonhoeffer before him, finds Jesus Christ in all the Psalms.[67] In regard to prophecy, Waltke believes that it "should be interpreted as having an invisible, spiritual fulfillment."[68]

Hence, our understanding of what Malachi 3:1 and 4:5 mean is derived from their use in Matthew 11 and 17, and elsewhere in the Canon. The messenger is John the Baptist and he heralds Jesus as the "Lord to come to His Temple."

This approach, while having an advantage over *sensus plenior*, cannot tell us how or why the passages are linked;[69] that is, what principles or conceptual center guided Jesus as He unfolded the meaning of Malachi from within His Canon. Consequently, we cannot pattern our hermeneutic after His in order to discover anything beyond what He (or His disciples) has explicitly unfolded. This and other approaches raise the issue of how prophecy will be fulfilled. Does the deeper meaning lead to spiritual fulfillment?[70]

Restrained Reader-response Interpretation. A final form of theological exegesis used to justify additional or new meaning never envisioned in the original context is that of reader-response. In this postmodern approach, different communities of believers generate new meanings. The reader is everything. The most legitimate form of reader-response interpretation appears to be like that of Klein and his co-authors, who, as others above, cite the precedent of the use of the Old Testament in the New. The emphasis is on understanding a text in its literary context instead of the author's intended meaning. The new or fresh meaning which Jesus finds beyond the original, historical intention of Malachi is possible, yet the historical meaning of the text remains primary.[71] This approach avoids the usual subjectivity of reader-response criticism while acknowledging the "creative enterprise" of understanding a biblical text. Yet this approach really fares little better than the two preceding. It gives no objective criteria from within Scripture for determining the particulars in the creative enterprise.

In summary, all the attempts to explain deeper meaning in Scripture, and particularly, Jesus' use of Malachi, fall short in one of two ways. First, the larger structural methods (*pesher, midrash*, allegory, typology, analogous fulfillment), while giving some explanation for Jesus' claim of fulfillment in Matthew 11:10, fail to explain adequately why the structures exist, and fail to give parameters for interpreting the meaning in the structures. This led to the search for a theological center. Second, all the theological centers or methods fail to provide specific enough guidance for discovering and/or interpreting the additional meaning in Malachi and texts representing other genres. They also fail to be broad enough to encompass or include other motifs. So while some of these approaches may explain Jesus' use of Malachi, they fail to explain all such uses. And these approaches provide no means to reproduce the hermeneutic of Scripture, or at least they do not claim to.

SO WHAT?

So what does all this have to do with interpretation? In this chapter we have discovered three chief reasons for the pursuit of a deeper meaning in addition to the literal meaning. First, and foremost, we have the example of Scripture. When Scripture uses Scripture, we cannot limit meaning or signification to the single intention of the human author—the grammatical-historical (literal) meaning. We often discover additional or deeper meaning. While we do not want to draw too strong a dichotomy between the divine Author and the human author, citations in the New place the emphasis on God as author over human authorship, and implicitly this means God's intention over a human's.

Second, modern discoveries in the field of semantics or meaning will not allow us to ignore the accretions or additions that texts acquire through time as interpreters in the Church grapple with the meaning of texts.

Third, there is a growing sense among evangelicals that so-called scientific exegesis or the grammatical-historical method is inadequate to interpret a dual-authored, supernatural book. We are too rationalistic if we overlook or shirk the dynamic of the Holy Spirit to continue to communicate in and interpret His Word. This concern is the modern counterpart of a two-thousand-year search to find the deeper meaning of this dual-authored book.

What Is the Kingdom?

Salome waited patiently for her turn to speak. Although she still had her doubts, it was now or never. Her opportunity may never come again. She had to ask Jesus.

As she stood there waiting for Him, her thoughts raced back over the last three years. How their lives had changed since Jesus had come! He had chosen her sons, James and John, to be among the Twelve. On many occasions she had delighted in waiting on Him in her home, listening to Jesus answering their questions.

Jesus had preached that the Kingdom had arrived, and from the beginning Salome had believed. She was convinced that He was the promised Messiah sent to deliver Israel from its Gentile oppressors. His miracles and teaching, to say nothing of His lineage from David, validated His claims. She and Zebedee had carefully instructed their family in the messianic hope, and now that hope was materializing before their very eyes. The prospects for her family and nation consumed her imagination. The masses were ready for Him and so was Salome. She did all she could to promote Him.

Her sons had taken up her convictions with enthusiasm. They had abandoned everything to follow Him through thick and thin. Throughout the cities of Israel they proclaimed that the Kingdom was at hand. With Jesus' authority they dispensed peace and judgment, healed, and even forgave sins. Sometimes they went too far, such as when her "Sons of Thunder" wanted to call down fire from heaven.

Yet the meaning of the Kingdom was not as clear as Salome would have liked. It was a hotly contested issue. Some Jews—the Essenes living near the Sea of Salt—tried to find all the messianic promises fulfilled in their own leaders and community, with the Romans as their enemy. The Zealots even went so far as to assassinate Roman soldiers. The Jews in Alexandria were using Greek philosophy to allegorize everything and deny history, miracle, and prophecy. For them there was no real kingdom. Others resorted to unbridled typology. Most destructive of all were the Pharisees. They rejected the reign of any Messiah, including Jesus, except in some intangible, ethereal way. Many of their rules of interpretation obscured the obvious meaning of Moses, David, Isaiah, and the rest. She wondered how she could ever understand Scripture apart from a Pharisaic education. For a Jew of the land it was a time that tried her faith in the promises.

Salome recalled the episode when John the Baptist wondered why Jesus did not reveal Himself as Messiah, assume His reign, and deliver Israel. Why did He leave John to die in prison? Salome wondered. Zebedee seemed to be bitterly disappointed. "Maybe the Pharisees are right after all," he said. Yet Salome reminded her husband that the Pharisaic approach was not the answer. There was little place left for God and for faith.

Salome had struggled with her own doubts. Jesus Himself did little to relieve her concerns. At times He spoke of His reign over Israel and the whole world, then He would speak of it as already among them, and yet not of this world! She believed that somehow all of this was true even if she couldn't understand everything.

When Salome first heard of plots to destroy Jesus, she began to think the unthinkable. Messiah Jesus might die! But even this must fulfill some divine purpose. John had encouraged her with His promise that He would rise from the dead. Perhaps then He would reign.

The jostling of the crowd brought Salome back to the present. Jesus was approaching! She could bear the doubts and ambiguity no longer. Her last opportunity to assert her faith had come. She believed and she would lay claim to her stake in the Kingdom to come.

As His eyes caught hers she said, "Master, I ask You a favor. In Your Kingdom, grant that my sons may sit at Your right and left hand."

It was a simple request, but Jesus saw it as an expression of profound faith and commitment—even to death, and He told her so. The other ten misunderstood. But Jesus had affirmed her faith and the real essence of rulership—to be a servant of all. Salome was content. She would continue to believe, to hope, and to serve. The Kingdom had begun!

The search for the central message of Scripture still goes on. In the following pages we set forth the idea that a Kingdom reading of Scripture meets the concerns of a central theme and makes a coherent story of history. To resolve the ambiguity and uncertainty of the concept we define Kingdom in a particular way.

Chapter Four

The Kingdom Center

What in the World Is God Doing?

"The kingdom of God is at hand"

(Matthew 4:17).

I n the preceding chapters we explained that the biblical writers found deeper meaning in Scripture, which the grammatical-historical hermeneutic cannot account for, and we described historical and contemporary attempts to grapple with this. Now we are ready to put forward our own suggestion. In this chapter we explore the central theme and world view of the Bible. We believe that this is the key to understanding how the biblical writers found deeper meaning in Scripture and will describe this hermeneutical approach in the next chapter. Then the following four chapters will explore certain very important corollaries of this hermeneutic: the work of the Holy Spirit; an attendant model of spirituality; the role of community in discovering and discerning truth; and the way God reveals Himself to us in history. For now, let's take a look at what the Bible is all about.

All the world is a stage, it has been said. In no sense is this more true than in the great drama being played out which we might call the "Conflict of the Ages." The plot in Scripture and history reveals a cosmic war between two kingdoms in which we are all playing a part according to God's plan. It is against this backdrop of God's Kingdom purpose in history that biblical writers have both written and interpreted Scripture.[1]

THE KINGDOM CENTER

The curtain rises. In the beginning, God created the heavens and the earth. His highest and most exalted angel, Lucifer, had become proud and committed high treason against the God of the Universe. He was cast from heaven for plotting, "I will be like the Most High." The kingdom of darkness and rebellion was born (Isaiah 14; Ezekiel 28). Chaos reigned. All was dark and gloomy. The curtain comes down.

The Spirit of God hovered over the formless, empty earth. Then God said, "Let there be light," and there was light. He dispelled the darkness and formed and filled the earth.[2] And God saw that it was good (Genesis 1:2-25).

Then God created man in[3] His own image, in the image of God He created him; male and female He created them. God blessed them and commissioned them to multiply, and fill the earth, and subdue it. All creation was in union with God, in harmony with His nature. Order reigned. And God saw all that He had made, and behold, it was very good (Genesis 1:27-31).

God's plan was to establish His Kingdom through the praise and obedience of humankind. Man and woman were to be His companions in His offensive war against Satan and the ominous chaos caused by sin. The earth was to be His Kingdom, and as His representatives, they were given authority to rule. They were His vice-regents;[4] He shared His rule with them and He pursued intimacy with them.

God had created humanity innocent, without sin. But He loved humankind enough to create a race of people with wills of their own, to choose freely to whom they would give their allegiance. In all creation He forbade them only one thing, to eat of the fruit of the Tree of the Knowledge of Good and Evil in the middle of the Garden. Satan, disguised as a serpent, tempted Eve to join him in rebellion against God, enticing her with the promise, "You will be like God." She ate, and Adam with her, and sin entered God's good creation (Genesis 3:1-7). Seemingly, the hope of God's Kingdom upon the earth was dashed. The curtain falls again.

Adam and Eve had freely chosen to side with Satan. God's creation was no longer in union with Him. It did not conform to His nature. Earthly and spiritual authority was rent asunder as the earth came under the dominion of sin. The image of God in humankind was distorted. Sin separated humanity from God. Humankind were now isolated, alone in their sin, out of union with God. To symbolize this, He drove them from the Garden of Eden (Genesis 3:22-24), unfit for His presence.

But God's plan was gracious. Even as He announced the curse of sin, He promised the victory of humanity over Satan through the seed of the woman (Genesis 3:14-15). God still wanted to establish His Kingdom, and to do it through humankind, but now humanity needed to be saved.

Humanity continued in rebellion against God, so much so that God deemed it necessary to destroy the whole world in a flood. He chose a remnant, eight persons, through whom He would establish His Kingdom. When Noah and his family disembarked from the ark, God renewed His commission to them to multiply on the earth. But this time He did not restate their full authority over it; instead, the animals would fear them (Genesis 9:1-17).

Humanity continued in rebellion against God. But God, by His grace, chose from among them Abraham, with whom He made a covenant to bless him and his descendants and to bless the whole world through his seed (Genesis 12:1-3). God chose Isaac, the son He promised to Abraham, who inherited his covenant, with the promised land and seed. Then God chose Isaac's son Jacob, whose children would become the people Israel.

God chose Israel to be His Kingdom, visibly manifested upon the earth, over whom He Himself would be King. He began to fulfill in them His promise of land and seed. He made His covenant with them and gave them the Law. He would be their God, and they would be His people. In them earthly and spiritual authority would be reunited as they obeyed God in fulfillment of the covenant. David and Solomon led the people into one of the most glorious kingdoms on earth.

But God's purposes were not for Israel alone. He desired the whole world to come to salvation and rule (Isaiah 49:6). The nation of Israel was to act as a priest for God (Exodus 19), spreading the knowledge of God among the Gentiles in fulfillment of His Word to Abraham, "In you all the families of the earth shall be blessed" (Genesis 12:3).[5]

But Israel also rebelled against God, and He rejected her from her position as priest (Hosea 4:6-7).[6] The curtain comes down once more.

So God Himself entered the world of humankind as the man Jesus Christ. He was the promised Son, the seed of the woman (Genesis 3:15-16), the seed of Abraham (Galatians 3:16), and the seed of David (Romans 1:3). Jesus resisted Satan's temptation to circumvent the cross and gain all authority by worshiping him (Matthew 4:1-11; Luke 4:1-13). Jesus did what Adam had failed to do—obey God fully (Hebrews 10:5-8). Christ, the sinless New Adam, God Himself, died for the sin of humanity and was raised from the dead so that through union with Him, humankind might be redeemed. He tore the curtain in two!

Christ is the Messiah, the promised One, who would come in the last days to establish the Kingdom of God upon the earth. With His blood, He inaugurated the promised New Covenant, a time when sins are forgiven, God's Spirit dwells within humankind, and righteousness reigns upon the earth (Jeremiah 31:31ff). By His resurrection, He ushered in the long awaited Kingdom of God. He has ascended to the right hand of God and all rule and authority are His. The Kingdom is *here*. The last days are *now*.

But not entirely. The Kingdom of God is here, but not everyone is a citizen of it. God does reign, but Satan, his demons, and unredeemed humanity are all in rebellion against Him. All earthly and spiritual authority are not yet united. Satan still rules his domain of darkness and he seeks to destroy the Kingdom of God. The Church is the visible manifestation of God's spiritual Kingdom upon the earth. As the people of the earth become part of the Kingdom of God, His Kingdom invades the kingdoms of the world. He will build His Church, and the gates of hell shall not prevail against it (Matthew 16:18). The Kingdom is forcefully advancing (Matthew 11:12).

Those who accept His gracious gift of salvation by faith in Christ are delivered from the domain of darkness and trans-ferred to the Kingdom of His beloved Son (Colossians 1:13). They become part of His Kingdom, His people, who are prophets, priests, and kings to a world that desperately needs the salvation of God through Jesus Christ (1 Peter 2:9-10). To them Jesus has renewed God's commission to humankind, "Go into all the world and tell the gospel to all creation and make disciples of all the nations" (Mark 16:15; Matthew 28:18-20). Through their union with Christ, redeemed humanity has regained their authority (Matthew 28:18; Acts 1:8) to participate in God's war against Satan's kingdom of sin and darkness. Their task is to tell the world about Jesus, until Jesus comes again and reigns physically upon the earth as King over His Kingdom, when all spiritual and earthly authority are reunited. Through the power of Christ, the ruler of this world shall be cast out (John 12:31). The victory of God's Kingdom and His people is sure, for as He promised in the beginning, God will crush Satan under the feet of redeemed humanity (Romans 16:20). Thus, faith is the vic-tory that overcomes the world (1 John 5:4).

It is God's purpose to glorify Himself by establishing His Kingdom through the redemption of humankind. From the beginning, we have had an evangelical commission from God. We have repeatedly rebelled against God's Kingdom and His purposes for us. But God graciously redeems us and restores us to our former role of participation in His cosmic mission of establishing His Kingdom of truth and love upon the earth. Yet, in the process, God goes further than restoring what was lost. He gives to us—in our re-creation in the image of Christ—a greater degree of intimacy and nobility than we would ever have experienced in our original creation, had we not rebelled (see Romans 5). Such is the gracious way of God to be glorified in all ways!

A QUESTION OF CENTERS

The biblical authors were writing from God's perspective on what He is doing in history. God's perspective provides the grid for understanding all that He is doing, including the history that is recorded in the Bible.[7] The all-encompassing cosmic story of the universe is a world view.[8] In a sense, this can be called God's world view. A world view includes what we believe to be real, how we know . . . truth, and what is moral or good. It explains our understanding of reality.[9] It includes all that exists, both seen and unseen, whether in time or beyond time. This biblical world view of God's Kingdom mission is the Bible's main theme.

Why is the discovery of a biblical center important? Perhaps an illustration from the realm of science will help. For many years, scientists have dreamed and searched for a GUT, *Grand Unifying Theorem*, that in one equation will explain all that there is, including gravitation, electromagnetism, and strong and weak nuclear forces. While Einstein's general theory of relativity went far to explain the relationship of energy to mass, light, space, and time, the GUT—if it can be found—has the potential to bring explanation and unity to what for now seems to be unreachable, diverse, and disjunctive. It will make sense of the physical universe.

The Kingdom center can serve as the GUT, not just of the Bible, but of all we do, think, and are—indeed, of all existence and of all the universe. It will thereby include the scientists' own GUT.

But is the Kingdom the center of all Scripture? Many

centers have been suggested. How can we defend our center as best? This is a crucial matter, for if we are wrong here, we not only affect our own ability to practice the hermeneutic we are suggesting, but the interpretation of the biblical text as well. Now we need to examine other suggested centers and why we believe they are inadequate.[10]

We already looked at a few of the possible centers in Chapter 3. Our concern there was to evaluate certain theological themes that have been used to explain how the biblical writers found deeper meaning in Scripture. We especially noticed this deeper meaning in the way the writers of the New Testament use the Old Testament. So, behind the question of deeper meaning in Scripture is a more foundational issue: What is the relationship between the Testaments? This is the question which theological centers are really attempting to answer.

While all theological centers try to explain the relationship between the Testaments, only some attempt to explain the phenomenon of deeper meaning as well. We looked at a few of these suggested centers in chapter 3, including Christ, salvation history, and promise-fulfillment. Now we will take a look at other theological centers suggested as the main theme of the Bible and the relationship between the Testaments.

Covenant

The motif of the covenant acts as an integrating theme of Scripture.[11] It is pervasive, ranging from the agreement made with Adam and Eve to that made with Noah, Israel, and David. It includes the actualizing of the New Covenant during the present age. Nevertheless, covenant fails to encompass all biblical motifs and types of literature. As far as a central theme is concerned, covenant fails to include transcendence in its emphasis on communion. Covenant is the means of securing another end, the Kingdom, and is not the end itself.

The Kingdom of God

Some have presented the transcendence of God as King as a biblical center, which immediately has been charged with lacking the emphasis of *immanence* (nearness) found in the concept of covenant or communion. This is a serious concern, for God is not only King, but also He who makes agreement with man as His partner and seeks relationship with him. This tension has led others to suggest that there is a dual center, such as both the rule of God and communion between God and man. Yet this seems a bit disjunctive and limited. How is the rule of God related to the limited idea of communion? There is a broader concept which will relate these in a more satisfactory way.

God

Others go one better and suggest that God, or Yahweh, is the center of Scripture. While God is certainly pervasive in and out of Scripture, we ask at once, what is it about God that the Bible and history affirm? We need a verb to add to the noun or subject.

Multiplex Approach

Others suggest that the center is unsolvable if we try to narrow it to one idea or concept, so they support a multiplex approach involving the above and other concepts such as the holiness of God, the election of Israel, promise and fulfillment, and the glory of God.[12] Yet do we have to resign ourselves to this broad position of disparate centers? Can we try again to find a solution to the center?

KINGDOM AS RULE AND RELATIONSHIP

Let's return to the concept of Kingdom. This is the center that we have chosen in spite of the objections made to it. We are not using Kingdom as it is usually thought of, emphasizing God's transcendent greatness over His immanence, His nearness, and goodness. There is a more accurate understanding of the Kingdom which answers the typical objections. We understand Kingdom as having a dual significance: God rules over His creation in a transcendent way (remote, separated, distant; He is God) and relates to them in an immanent way (near, intimate, close; He is Father and Brother). God's Kingdom is both rulership and relationship.[13]

The Kingdom must have this dual significance because God by nature is such and so relates to His creation.[14] This is in accord with the biblical teaching of God's Kingdom existing in two senses: a broader sense of all under His sovereign control whether in blessing or in judgment; and a narrower sense of those in the favored relationship of eternal life. Those who are in relationship are then ruled in willing submission from within their hearts. Beginning with shadows of this relationship in Genesis and "ending" with the eternal state and its bold intimacy, God seeks to be one with His people, in the closest communion with them.[15] We reach our highest nobility when we deliberately give up ourselves to Jesus in sovereign preference.[16] So, as all humankind is brought into relationship with God, He rules over all His creation as willing subjects. His Kingdom is actualized on the earth.

We can illustrate these two aspects of the Kingdom this way:

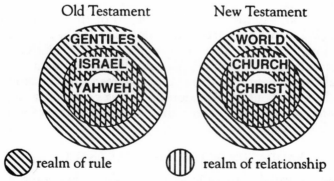

Old Testament   New Testament

GENTILES   WORLD
ISRAEL   CHURCH
YAHWEH   CHRIST

realm of rule   realm of relationship

In the Old Testament, God (Yahweh) rules over all the earth. The Kingdom in this broadest sense is the largest circle. God is in the center. The inner circle represents all those in relationship with Him. Ideally, this is all of the ethnic group/political nation of Israel, as God's people and His Kingdom on the earth. God reigns in their hearts and they bring the light to the Gentiles who are unknowingly under the rule of God but not yet in relationship with Him. Though there is the general distinction between Israel as the ones who know God and the Gentiles who don't, in reality, not all of those who were Israel according to the flesh were the true Israel, and some Gentiles knew God. The major addition to this that the New Testament supplies is that Jesus Christ is Yahweh.[17] Those who are in relationship with Him are part of the multi-ethnic, invisible Church (rather than some political expression of the Kingdom) charged with the commission to spread the Kingdom by bringing others into relationship with Christ the King.

In the Kingdom center we are able to bring together God's rule and glory and holiness, on the one hand, with covenant, communion, and salvation on the other. Even salvation (in the highly regarded center, salvation history, or *Heilsgeschichte*) is part of the larger purpose of Kingdom and not sufficient in itself. Our tracing of the Kingdom center above shows that the Kingdom extends farther back in time and farther forward in time, and includes salvation within it. Also, not everyone is saved but everyone is reconciled to God, whether through salvation or through judgment (2 Corinthians 5:18-19; Colossians 1:20-22). The Kingdom center is able to encompass both of these emphases because it itself is both radically transcendent and radically immanent.[18] In this manner we meet the concerns voiced above about the Kingdom and other centers.[19] It also seems to meet well the criteria that various writers set forth for such a center.[20]

VALIDATION OF THE KINGDOM CENTER

How are we able to validate such a Kingdom center as the biblical world view? In one sense we can't. Entire books are written on just one aspect of such a monumental task, so we can make only cursory comments here. A most fundamental way to validate the Kingdom center is to see if it works. Does it make sense of all of reality, fit the facts of Scripture and life and the world around us, and meet our deepest needs?

We can also take a look at the witnesses that Scripture itself uses. In 1 John 5:6-10, John cites several witnesses to

Jesus Christ: the water and blood, which is the witness of history; the Holy Spirit, which is the witness of God; and the believer's witness and that of mankind, which is the witness of the community.[21] First, we can cite the support for the Kingdom center which the Christian community has made prior to us—a consideration which is absolutely essential in the process of interpretation. Second, we can let the testimony of God in the Bible itself tell us what the center is. Third, we can weigh the witness of history.

The Witness of the Community

There is broad support for the Kingdom center. In regard to the preaching of Jesus, "Modern scholarship is quite unanimous in the opinion that the Kingdom of God was the central message of Jesus."[22] The Kingdom is the heart of Jesus' mission—it's what He came for.[23] Again, many point to the nature of the Kingdom as, in some real sense, both present and future: it is here but not yet.[24] And the Kingdom is nothing new in Jesus' teaching. It goes back to the prophets, and the entire Old Testament.

This is not all. Many acknowledge that the Kingdom is the theme also of history and not only of Scripture.[25] It is the focal concept for understanding the purpose and plan of God within history. The present age is the beginning of the fulfillment of the eschatological promises.[26]

The Kingdom theme is a theme greater than that of redemption or salvation. The Reformers made salvation the center of the Bible, and the modern counterpart of this is salvation history, *Heilsgeschichte*. Yet this is too limited. The purpose of salvation is to restore man to his nobility to rule and enjoy God so that God's Kingdom is actualized on the earth. Kingdom history (*Reichsgeschichte?*) is the better concept, as we discuss in chapter 9.

The Witness of Scripture

While the Bible does not explicitly say that the Kingdom is its center, it almost does. Writers have pointed this out, tracing the witness of Scripture, from Genesis to

Revelation, to its Kingdom center.[27] In an appendix we have collected additional passages which speak of both aspects—rule and relationship—in close proximity. A few extended displays of this dual nature belonging to Kingdom will show its significance.

For detailed elaboration of the Kingdom center with its dual aspects, Psalm 145 can hardly be surpassed. Here the opening words are addressed to "my God the King." David first extols the transcendence of God, "Great is the LORD and most worthy of praise; his greatness no one can fathom." David rehearses God's works, mighty acts, splendor, majesty, deeds, and abundant goodness (vv. 3-7). He then speaks of His immanent greatness, "The LORD is gracious and compassionate, slow to anger and rich in love" [one of the most frequently quoted passages in the Old Testament, derived from God's self-revelation in Exodus 34:6]; "The LORD is good to all"(vv. 8-10).

In this acrostic psalm, the middle verses (vv. 11ff.) begin to describe God's transcendent Kingdom. It is characterized by glory, might, glorious splendor, and eternality. He tells of its endurance (v. 13). "Your kingdom is an everlasting kingdom, and your dominion endures through all generations." Then David extols God's providence toward His creation as he describes God's immanence (vv. 13b). "The LORD is faithful to all his promises, and loving toward all he has made." He is the one who supports, sustains, and satisfies the desires of every living thing (vv. 14-17). God's hand is open to all (v. 16).

More intimate yet is His relationship to His saints who extol Him (first introduced in v. 10). He is loving toward them, near them, fulfills their desires, hears their cry, saves them, and watches over all who love Him (vv. 17-20). How could God be more intimate than this?

As it began, the psalm concludes with praise (vv. 21). David joins his personal witness to that of all creation, and invites us to join him. "My mouth will speak in praise of the LORD. Let every creature praise his holy name for ever and ever." This psalm beautifully portrays the Kingdom center and its dual nature.

Another rewarding example comes from Isaiah 40. Here Isaiah intermingles God's transcendent reign with His immanence. Following the proclamation in verse 9, "Here is your God!" comes the summary in verses 10-11 of what the entire chapter is about, explaining what God is like. Verse 10 speaks of His power and rule in judgment and verse 11 of His intimate and tender care of His people. Unpacking verse 10, verses 12-26 extol God's greatness. He created all that is and reigns over everything. Nations are a drop in the bucket—as dust; people are as grasshoppers and chaff.

Then come verses 27-31. Following immediately after a display of God's awesome transcendence, these verses unpack verse 11 to say, "And this great God is for you!" He carries His people close to His heart as a shepherd his lambs. They who wait upon Him renew their strength: they walk, they run, they fly.

The New Testament enhances the pattern of the Old where God is revealed as King over all the earth and as Yahweh in covenant love with His people. Jesus intimately brings the Kingdom of God to all who believe in Him. The new birth accomplishes this (John 3:3, 5). In Jesus the Kingdom is present (Luke 17:21) and we reign (Romans 5:17).

One particular passage deserves special mention, for it places the Old Testament in continuity with the arrival of the Kingdom of heaven. After giving the parables of the Kingdom (Matthew 13), Jesus concludes by saying, "Every teacher of the law who has been instructed about the kingdom of heaven is like the owner of a house who brings out of his storeroom new treasures as well as old."[28]

The Kingdom is the summation of all of Paul's preaching and teaching, according to Luke (Acts 19:8; 20:24-25; 28:23, 31; cf. Colossians 1:13; 4:11; 2 Timothy 4:18). The Kingdom idea is behind his sarcasm in 1 Corinthians 4:8.

Indeed, so pervasive is the Kingdom in Scripture that theologies have been written entirely around the Kingdom theme. We should read Scripture primarily as a narrative of

God's Kingdom manifest in rule and relationship. Scripture is a story about the Kingdom. It is this that illuminates an earlier, uncomprehended unity.

The Witness of History

Another witness to the Kingdom theme is that of history. If history also is revelatory, it must witness as well to the Kingdom theme (a later chapter and appendix expand on history as revelatory). Is the Kingdom being actualized in our experience today? In the light of world wars and ethnic cleansing in the twentieth century, in the face of abortion, genetic engineering, euthanasia, and drugs are the principles and values of the Kingdom being realized more and more?

We reply, first of all, what would the world be like if Jesus had not come? Would not the world already have been destroyed, as in Genesis 6-8, had not the truth and love found in Jesus been revealed?

Since history has to be interpreted, we can really understand it only from the perspective of its end. We know this end beforehand in the resurrection of Jesus, which we take by faith. Paradox is also involved, for Scripture itself says that alongside the growth of the Kingdom is the growth of the wicked.[29] The parables of the weeds and the net (Matthew 13) illustrate this well. Perhaps part of the explanation is realizing that we do not recognize sin apart from the light; that sin is a perversion of light. As Jesus' Kingdom advances, the forces of evil will only intensify their futile attempts to destroy it. Ultimately, we must take the growth of the Kingdom by faith. It takes eyes of faith touched by His rule and relationship, by His sovereignty and love, to see the Kingdom.[30]

The Greatest Witness

Yet there is another witness in history—that of the Incarnation itself. In actuality, it is part of the Kingdom witness of all the preceding: the witnesses of the community, Scripture, and history. Defying all explanation, this mystery pointedly trumpets the dual nature of Kingdom. For God the King chose to actualize His Kingdom by His becoming human so that He might accomplish His rule on earth through relationship. God's realm is being actualized in this world. Jesus could say that the Kingdom is here because it is present in His person and His people.

As biblical realists, we go forward to make disciples of all nations, knowing that He has given us all authority. The evil age has been assaulted by the Kingdom which is here but not yet totally. The King is present. The Snow Queen's winter is yielding to the thaw of Aslan the Lion.[31] Satan is defeated and bound. Death is conquered. Sin is broken. We hasten His return (2 Peter 3:12).[32] Maranatha—may the Lord and His Kingdom come!

So What?

What does the Kingdom center have to do with a biblical hermeneutic? Simply this: *The Kingdom is the center from which biblical writers think and write and in turn interpret others before them.* This is how they find deeper or additional meaning. They are conscious of a greater purpose[33] God is accomplishing, often behind the scenes but occasionally up front and center stage.

Why do the biblical writers do this? Because the Kingdom center is the divine world view, the perspective from which all reality can be known and defined. And it is ever advancing, being actualized or realized more and more by the person of Christ in and through His Church. The world view fits life and prepares us for life—it is a world-and-life view.[34]

In the preceding chapters, the explanations of deeper meaning all fail to be linked satisfactorily to the central theme of Scripture. That is, none of the suggestions linked the internal method of interpretation—which includes the literal and the deeper meaning—with the Bible's central theme or center. Even though all of us give much attention to context, *few have seen the significance of using the largest context of all—the biblical world view—to get to the biblical hermeneutic.* The Kingdom center provides the largest biblical context or grid for interpreting Scripture and history.

Because this center is biblically sourced, we know implicitly that this biblical world view transcends our own modern one or those of the ancients. It is universal and transtemporal and thus avoids being time-bound. We avoid that which has plagued the Church through the ages—formulating a hermeneutical method on the basis of a contemporary philosophy or world view.[35] From the beginning this has been done by Jews and Christians with their allegorization, by modernists such as Bultmann and Barth with their existentialism, by language specialists with their linguistic theories of reader tyranny and total subjectivity, and to a lesser degree, by the Reformers with their emphasis on salvation and a basically rationalistic approach. All of these imported a world view into the Bible from outside of it. This is not what the biblical writers did. They did not succumb to the known pagan world view, but rejected it and sought to supplant it.

We seek to discover Scripture's own world view and let it speak for itself. *We deliberately affirm that this Kingdom world view must become our hermeneutical key to the interpretation of Scripture.* The next chapter shows how this can be done.

Reaching for Reality

In dead silence *Priscilla and Aquila* listened to the Roman her-
ald. *Emperor Claudius* had just issued an edict that all Jews and
Christians were to be expelled from Rome at once!

"What are we going to do? Where are we going to go?"
Priscilla asked her husband.

Aquila understood his wife's desperation. The edict meant that
absolutely nothing could be taken from the city except the clothes
on their back. "Let's not fear," he said. "God is loving and in
control of everything—our goods, family, even our lives." His
words were partially helpful.

The edict was not totally unexpected. For the last several
months he and his family had suffered one abuse after another.
Tentmaking jobs had become more and more scarce ever since he
had been ejected from the guild on charges that he refused to contribute to the support of the guild's deity. As a faithful Jew, he
never had done this, but until recently this had been overlooked.
Now with the frenzy of fundamentalist idolatry, no compromise
was permitted. His family were made a public spectacle and suffered the humiliation of being charged as disloyal Roman citizens.
When they went to the market they could hardly buy enough
food since every seller branded them as revolutionaries of the
state. It was impossible to find a tutor for their four children.
Their fellow Jews despised them for embracing Jesus as the
Messiah, and their parents had totally disowned them. Priscilla
was even criticized by some in the assembly for instructing men.
Everything seemed to be going badly.

"You know, this turn of events is an opportunity for blessing.
After all, did not Jesus Himself tell us that our life did not consist
of the abundance of possessions? We should joyfully accept the
taking of our property because we have better and lasting possessions. Our citizenship is in heaven, not in Rome. We belong to
His Kingdom.

"The Romans live and die by the material things of life. They
build bigger homes, seek the best education for their children, add
more servants, acquire animals, pamper their pets, and invest in
land and commodities. Yet look at the decadence that has come
with it! They indulge in adultery, drugs, homosexuality, and

abortion. Imagine, they kill their own children! And then they die of sexual disease, gluttony, exposure, and suicide. What a life—what an empty, unfulfilled existence!"

Priscilla could not help but reflect on her past ministry of teaching the other women, and on occasion, the men. She had known such freedom and acceptance. She and Aquila had experienced such joy in ministry together.

They had also reached out to help others. When Andronicus and Junias, Paul's relatives, had been jailed, Aquila and especially Priscilla had taken care of them. Aquila recalled the time they had risked their lives for Paul, to shield him from angry Jews bent on stoning him. In the process they rescued the precious scrolls Paul had dictated for the churches of Galatia and Thessalonica.

At dawn, Aquila and Priscilla, with their children and others from the assembly, left Rome. Singing hymns from the Psalter, they felt like Abraham, seeking a heavenly city. Looking over her shoulder, Priscilla saw hundreds of burning homes throwing up dense, black smoke. "There go our tents," she said.

"Remember how Paul taught us to look beyond the present, temporal world? We are to fix our eyes on the eternal, what is invisible, not the visible. All of our sufferings are light in comparison to Messiah's, and momentary. They are actually achieving for us eternal consequences of glory that far outweigh them all," Priscilla recounted.

Still she wondered how any future ministry at Corinth, their chosen destination, could possibly surpass what they enjoyed at Rome. Little did she know how greatly their lives would touch the churches of Corinth and Ephesus, and such powerful leaders as Apollos. They would team up with Paul, Timothy, Silas, Titus, Sosthenes, and many others. All the churches of the Gentiles, Paul would later say, had reason to be grateful for them. They had given their lives for others.

We call the temporary and eternal realms in which we live the existential and essential realities. Tied to the Kingdom center, they form the world view of Scripture. When properly applied, this world view of reality explains how later writers understood additional meaning when they read Scripture. It is the key to biblical interpretation.

Chapter Five

Kingdom Reality

Making the Best of Both Worlds

"The things which are seen are temporal;
but the things which are not seen are eternal"
(2 Corinthians 4:18).

A t last we get to explain our proposal for a hermeneutic that will help us understand how the biblical writers found deeper meaning in Scripture. The Kingdom center is the key to interpretation. As the central theme, it helps us to understand all the smaller parts of Scripture. More than this, though, it is the "world view" from which Scripture was written. It has within it a particular view of reality that is reflected not only in what Scripture says explicitly, but how the biblical writers found deeper meaning in Scripture. This means that the Kingdom center is intrinsically related to a specific hermeneutic.

As far as we are aware, this is the first time that a hermeneutic for interpreting Scripture has been based upon a particular biblical center.[1] Our purpose in this chapter is to present the paradigm of reality inherent in the Kingdom center, show biblical support for it, and explain how it can be used as a hermeneutic in interpreting the Old and New Testaments.

PARADIGM OF REALITY

By its demand of faith, Christian theology requires belief in at least two dimensions of reality. One dimension is seen and understood through sense experience, while another dimension—the spiritual—is unseen. "Now faith is the assurance of things hoped for, the conviction of things not seen" (Hebrews 11:1). This verse could be construed as referring not to spiritual things that exist unseen, but to past or future events that are believed by faith. In the larger context, though, we know that the author of Hebrews assumes belief in the spiritual realm, for he writes of the tabernacle and other institutions on earth as shadows or copies of their realities in heaven (Hebrews 9:23-24). Paul also writes of "things visible and invisible" (Colossians 2:16) and of the shadow versus the reality (2:17). The Lord's prayer assumes two realms or "places" when it says, "Your Kingdom come; your will be done on earth as it is in heaven." Belief in the spiritual realm is absolutely fundamental to our faith. We rehearse this truth now in order to organize its parts into a paradigm of reality that will help us in reading Scripture.

Description of the Paradigm

There are three aspects to this paradigm of reality.[2] The first part is the realm of reality that includes all that we can perceive with our senses regarding the material world in creation, and all that we experience in relationships and the social and political structures of our society, including family and governments. We will call this dimension of reality *existential reality* because it includes those things that we automatically experience in our bodily existence. This reality is changeable and transitory.

The Christian faith, by its very nature, demands belief in another reality, an unchangeable constant, an absolute that is the ground of our existential reality. We will call this reality *essential reality*, the realm of God Himself. It is those things in the spiritual realm that will be true forever. First and foremost, this is God. He Himself is Reality. All that is exists in Him or by His sustenance. God is the only being who exists in Himself; all others exist because He gives them existence. Absolutes, such as love and truth and holiness, exist forever because they are part of God's character. We call this reality essential reality because when you boil everything down, this is the essence of reality. Everything else exists in relation to it, and it is the perspective from which all things are to be viewed. Thus, essential reality is God Himself and everything that He makes to be forever true. This includes such things as our union with Christ, our justification before God, our being His children, our relationship to each other as brothers and sisters in Christ, and the defeat of all the dark powers in the universe. This reality abides forever.

This understanding of reality is another way of describing aspects of the Kingdom center we discussed in the last chapter. Essential reality and existential reality roughly correspond to the Kingdom of God and the kingdom of Satan. The kingdom of Satan is "the world," as Scripture calls it, sinful man and his societies and institutions oriented away from God. The Kingdom of God is the reality and presence of God Himself and all those things of love and truth which characterize Him, along with His Church (as the Kingdom is now expressed)—all those who have believed in Him, have been born again, and now live for Him.

We cannot emphasize the following point enough. Existential reality in itself is not the kingdom of Satan, as though existential reality is intrinsically evil. Rather, it roughly corresponds to sinful humanity and all its institutions *oriented away from God*. Scripture calls Satan the "god of this world" (2 Corinthians 4:4). Nor does this paradigm imply that there is some dualism of spiritual and physical realities, in which matter is less than holy.[3] The truth is that this physical reality is temporary and transitory, as Paul and Peter remind us; but a new physical reality is coming. God's purpose is to bring the physical reality and all earthly institutions and powers, into conformity with His nature. Thus, matter, though it is changed, is affirmed as such.[4] For now, essential reality is higher than existential reality only because it is more true, meaning that it is more perfectly conformed to God Himself. As soon as essential reality is entirely actualized in existential reality, one will not be better than the other because they will be one and the same.

This brings us to the third aspect of the paradigm, which is *actualization*. It is God's purpose to actualize His Kingdom on earth, or in other words, to actualize essential reality in existential reality. The world as we now find it is filled with sin and every destructive force. Two thirds of the world is economically oppressed. Mindless prejudice and racism fan the flames of bitter, violent hate. Society's moral fabric is disintegrating, families are rent apart, children are emotionally and spiritually orphaned and even killed—all in the name of individual rights and freedom, a freedom which Scripture declares is slavery to sin. As awful as this is, it is tame compared to the brutal, soul-withering starvation, rape, and murder carried out in countless civil wars and oppressive regimes throughout the world.

God intends to make all this right, to come to earth and dwell here among His people.[5] By His death and resurrection, Christ inaugurated the new age. The end has come. God's Kingdom has dawned. He is here now in His Church, which is the Body of Christ, mediating the presence of the living God upon the earth. His purpose for the Church is to extend this Kingdom by spreading the gospel of Jesus Christ for the salvation of every person so that those who are saved become part of the Kingdom of God. This salvation is no mere "spiritual" event that secures heaven for an individual on some vague, distant day after death. This salvation is meant to right the wrong and reorient the world toward God through the one saved. Thus the Church, and the Christians comprising her, are saved for a purpose, called to participate in God's mission to glorify Himself by actualizing His Kingdom upon the earth.

Implication of the Paradigm

For the present, the Church is the Kingdom of God, the presence of Christ upon the earth. Every Christian is a citizen of this Kingdom, not of the world, and Christ is his King. The Christian belongs to a new order under His reign, living according to His law of love. According to essential reality, this means that the Christian is free from obedience to every earthly institution. Yet, he is to use this freedom, not to rebel, but to submit to all social institutions as the roles are then currently defined, disobeying only when those roles require immoral conduct. He is even to submit to the discipline of the institution when he must disobey that institution in order to obey God. This suffering for his faith is both judgment and grace for purging from sin and progress in sanctification, and for the privilege of following in the steps of Christ, eventually to share also in His glory.

This means that the Bible's exhortations to submit within social institutions are not based upon essential reality (what is true for all time) but upon existential reality (the standards for those institutions in that historical moment). As both Peter and Paul strongly indicate, this is so that the gospel will not be put to shame, but that others within those institutions may be won by the believers' good conduct. In a sense, this good conduct is defined by society rather than by God, for though believers are part of a new order, they are to give up their rights of the eschatological order (essential reality) to submit to the world order for the purpose of winning some. Those Christians who find themselves in relationship with each other within these institutions will progressively work out the standards of the new order within their relationship. They are exhorted to view each other as brothers and sisters, one in Christ, joint heirs of grace. The ruling principles of the Kingdom are love and truth. The truth of God is to be actualized first in the Church and then throughout society, but it is to be done slowly, prayerfully, for reasons of love and by means of love, sacrificing one's own rights and freedom for the good of God and others.

Slavery is the most ready example (1 Corinthians 7:17-24; Colossians 3:24ff). Slaves are exhorted to obey their masters and to be willing to suffer the consequences if they must disobey in order to obey God. They are to submit to existential reality, while keeping in mind essential reality. It is Christ they serve, and should it be that their master is a

Christian, then they are to serve him all the better, for they are serving a brother and so are working for the Kingdom. Masters, on the other hand, are pointed toward essential reality for the basis of their conduct. While they are not told to release their slaves—even though essentially no person owns another—they are told to modify their behavior in light of the fact that before God, they and their slaves stand equal, and He judges impartially (Galatians 3:28; Ephesians 6:5-9). So Paul exhorts Philemon to accept back Onesimus, not only as a slave, but as much more than a slave—as a brother. Similarly, he said that slaves are to submit, but if they can become free (doing so within the constraints of the social order), then this is better (1 Corinthians 7:21).

Truth slowly changes relationships within the Christian community, and to the degree that the Christian community is coextensive with the larger society, relationships are changed within that society. The gospel has the power to reorder all of society according to essential reality—though God states that this will not occur in entirety before the second advent of Christ and the establishment of His millennial Kingdom. Then, as He promised, all wars will cease and the meek will inherit the earth. In this way, the Kingdom of God is realized upon the earth in fulfillment of the prayer Jesus taught His disciples, "Our Father in heaven, hallowed be your name, your kingdom come, your will be done on earth as it is in heaven."

The Paradigm in the Bible

In one sense, the most thorough biblical support for this paradigm of reality is the Kingdom center itself (discussed in the preceding chapter). Nevertheless, there are some passages that reflect it explicitly. One of the clearest examples is 2 Corinthians 4:16-18.

Therefore we do not lose heart. Though outwardly we are wasting away, yet inwardly we are being renewed day by day. For our light and momentary troubles are achieving for us an eternal glory that far outweighs them all. So we fix our eyes not on what is seen, but on what is unseen. For what is seen is temporary, but what is unseen is eternal.

In this passage the ideas of *outwardly, troubles* and *what is seen* reflect existential reality; the words *inwardly, glory* and *what is unseen* reflect essential reality; and the phrases *wasting away, being renewed, is achieving* and *we fix our eyes* reflect the process involved in actualizing essential reality in existential reality. Note that the examples in the last group are all verbal ideas in the present tense; a process is underway, taking Paul the apostle (and all believers) from one reality to another reality.

Paul writes regarding that process even more directly in 2 Corinthians 3:17-18.

Now the Lord is the Spirit, and where the Spirit of the Lord is, there is freedom. And we, who with unveiled faces all reflect the Lord's glory, are being transformed into his likeness with ever-increasing glory, which comes from the Lord, who is the Spirit.

Paul's words in Romans 8:18-25 present three successive examples which illustrate well the concepts of the paradigm. Paul begins in verse 18:

I consider that our present sufferings are not worth comparing with the glory that will be revealed in us. (19) The creation waits in eager expectation for the sons of God to be revealed. (20) For the creation was subjected to frustration, not by its own choice, but by the will of the one who subjected it, in hope (21) that the creation itself will be liberated from its bondage to decay and brought into the glorious freedom of the children of God.

(22) We know that the whole creation has been groaning as in the pains of childbirth right up to the present time. (23) Not only so, but we ourselves, who have the firstfruits of the Spirit, groan inwardly as we wait eagerly for our adoption as sons, the redemption of our bodies. (24) For in this hope we were saved. But hope that is seen is no hope at all. Who hopes for what he

already has? (25) But if we hope for what we do not yet have, we wait for it patiently.

In Romans 8:18-23, the existential reality is that evil abounds and affects us deeply. The essential reality is that glory is to be revealed to us (v. 18) and we have the first fruits of the Spirit (v. 23); finally, we are already adopted as sons (cf. Galatians 4:5-6). The process of actualization is that we experience the sufferings of the present time (v. 18), we groan within ourselves (v. 23), and we wait eagerly for our adoption as sons, the redemption of our body (v. 23).

In Romans 8:19-22, the existential reality is that creation has been subjected to futility unwillingly (v. 20) and enslaved to corruption (v. 21). The essential reality is that creation is set free into the freedom of the glory of the children of God (v. 21); it is already reconciled by Christ (Colossians 1:20). The process of actualizing essential reality is that creation is longing (v. 19), groaning and suffering childbirth pains (v. 22) as it waits eagerly for the revealing of the sons of God (v. 19) in hope (v. 20).

In Romans 8:24-25 the existential reality is that we do not yet have in full our ultimate salvation (v. 24); we do not see it (v. 25). The essential reality is that the hope of our adoption, namely the resurrection of our bodies, has been secured (v. 23). So the process of actualization is that we groan within ourselves and hope as we wait eagerly with perseverance for it (vv. 23-25).

In all three of these examples of redemption of the body, creation's deliverance, and realization of hope, there is suffering and an attitude of eager waiting for actualization. The verb *eagerly await* is used most frequently of awaiting eagerly the return of Christ (1 Corinthians 1:7; Philippians 3:20; Hebrews 9:28; in 1 Peter 3:20 it is used of God's forbearance), when all that we wait for will be ours in full. The matters of essential reality in the paradigm are already in some measure being realized. They have been secured and assured by Christ's death and resurrection. They await full actualization.[6]

One final way to determine if the paradigm is biblical is to see if using it as a hermeneutic helps us to understand the Bible. Then it is biblically supported not only by the Kingdom center and a few explicit passages, but also because it helps us to make sense of all of Scripture, including the passages where biblical writers seem to find deeper meaning in prior Scripture. To see how it helps us to understand some specific, difficult issues in the New Testament, look at the Appendix D, "Kingdom Light on Difficult Issues." For now we will explore how to use the paradigm as a hermeneutic in general.

USING THE PARADIGM AS A HERMENEUTIC

The Meaning of *Deeper Meaning*

If this paradigm is the view from which Scripture was written, then it may also hold the key to how the biblical writers found deeper meaning in previously written Scripture. Let's take a moment now to explain more thoroughly what we mean by "deeper meaning."

The primary meaning of this phrase so far has been "a fuller meaning in Scripture intended by the divine Author, related to the human author's meaning but unknown to him." But we have deliberately used the phrase *deeper meaning* instead of "*a* deeper meaning" or "*the* deeper meaning" in order to accommodate another meaning we have for this phrase. Another way we can think of deeper meaning in Scripture is, what does it mean *for me?*[7] How can we find meaning in Scripture for our own lives and for the world around us? This gets into the areas normally called *application* and *contextualization*. How we apply the truth of Scripture to our own lives and contextualize its message to different audiences is, by its very nature, variable. In this case we can't speak of "*a* deeper meaning" or "*the* deeper meaning" as though it is objective because the meaning for each receiver will be different. This may sound a lot like the error of postmodernism, but there is one big difference. How we find deeper meaning in Scripture for ourselves and the world around us is related to *the* deeper meaning put there by God.[8] The paradigm of reality can be used as a hermeneutic to find both the deeper meaning in Scripture and deeper meaning for applying and contextualizing Scripture's message.

IN THE OLD TESTAMENT

The Essential Meaning of a Text

The way this is done is by distinguishing between the existential reality and the essential reality of a biblical passage.[9] The existential reality of a text is the meaning that it had for the original writer. This includes the historical persons and events referred to and the significance that the writer intended in writing about them. For an example, let's go back to our problem of how Jesus interpreted Malachi 3:1 and 4:5. The existential reality of the passages is that the prophet Elijah will come and that a messenger will go before Yahweh and prepare His way when He comes in judgment in the eschatological Day of the Lord.

The essential reality of any passage is that meaning which is *tied* to the existential reality, but which *transcends* these details in such a way that if the details change, the essential meaning remains unchanged.[10] Returning to our example again, the essential reality of the passages in Malachi is that a messenger in the Spirit and power of Elijah will prepare the way of Yahweh when He comes in the Day of the Lord. It does not matter that His coming would be in two parts, or that the Day of the Lord would last millennia, or that He would come as a man, or that the messenger preparing His way would not be the actual prophet Elijah. These details did not change the essential meaning of Malachi's prophecy. The kinds of things that would not have fit his essential meaning would be calling Judas the prophet Elijah or having John the Baptist prepare the way of someone who was not Yahweh (because while another person could come in the spirit and power of Elijah, it is difficult for someone to "sort of" be God).

This essential meaning is the single sense of the biblical text. The existential reality referred to in the text is the historical *particularization* of that single sense (essential meaning). Many historical particularizations of that one broad sense are possible. As the most obvious example, this is how prophecies can have multiple fulfillments in history. Those who espouse a strict grammatical-historical hermeneutic would likely agree with this so far. Where we differ is this: we affirm that there are examples where it seems that the biblical writers could only have understood or affirmed the historical particularization of which they wrote and were not aware of the broader sense that, nevertheless, God intended in their writing. Sometimes they only intended the existential meaning, not the essential meaning, and when this happens, we call this *deeper meaning*. No matter how many historical particularizations there are, there is really only one sense of that passage, whether or not the human author was aware of that sense.

It is important to note that the human author often intends the essential meaning of the text. For instance, Moses attached greater significance (as did God in participating) to his description of the events of Abraham sacrificing Isaac than the mere details of the story. The essential meaning of this story is likely the same as what Moses intended. It is even conceivably possible that Malachi did intend through some sort of "generic prophecy" more than the existential meaning of Elijah going before Yahweh when He comes to judge in the Day of the Lord. But this seems unlikely. He writes in specific terms, not in vague, generic descriptions, and he gives no other indication that he intends the details metaphorically. A generic meaning seems foreign to the context. In any case, he certainly did not foresee John the Baptist as Elijah, Yahweh in the flesh, His coming twice, or an agelong Day of the Lord.

As we tried to show in chapter 1, the human author is often unaware of the essential meaning of what he is writing. Since prophecy by its very nature is somewhat mysterious, let's move away from it to a narrative passage for another example of what we mean.

In Galatians, Paul "allegorized" Hagar and Sarah and Jerusalem and the New Jerusalem in order to contrast the way of the Law and promise. Now Moses was a deeply spiritual man, more in tune with God and His purpose than most of us, and he quite naturally understood symbolism. He may well have seen in Sarah and Hagar a contrast of two ways in general that may be called the way of God and the way of the world, a contrast that can be seen throughout the Old Testament, including people like Abel (and Seth) and Cain, and Jacob and Esau. But in writing about Sarah and Hagar, Moses, as the one through whom the Law came, simply could not have seen in these two women a contrast between the way of promise and the Law.

Further, Paul is drawing from more than just Moses. Moses himself knew nothing about the significance of Jerusalem to his people, since it was just a foreign city in his time. So when Paul finds deeper meaning in these events, he is actually not finding deeper meaning of a particular text, but of a significant portion of the Old Testament, and ultimately of the history that it relates. And who is the only Author who transcends all this? God intended in these very real, historical, dust-and-glory people, places, and events, a contrast of two ways. They are not mere metaphors; yet without violating the integrity and reality of their personal experience, their lives have deeper meaning intended for us.

So the deeper meaning of any passage can be found by distinguishing between the essential reality and the existential reality in it. Since the existential meaning includes both the things the writer refers to and the significance he intends for his words, this sometimes includes the essential reality of that passage. Not always was the essential meaning unknown to the writer. In fact, since the essential meaning is inextricably related to the existential meaning, the human writer may have known the essential meaning most of the time.

Essential Meaning Related to the Kingdom Center

A question arises, though, about passages in which the deeper meaning is unknown to the human author. How do we know if the essential meaning we believe we have found there is correct? We know that it has to be tied to the existential meaning (which can be found through the grammatical-historical hermeneutic), but there is surely room for more than one plausible idea, especially if we engage in the freer type of interpretation that Paul occasionally did.

The answer is that any suggested essential meaning of a text must be related to Scripture's central theme, which is the actualization of God's Kingdom. This means that we need to understand this theme and the nature of God and His Kingdom very well. This is the broadest context for understanding any Scripture passage. This is the perspective from which God understands any biblical passage and what He was doing at that particular point in history as He worked out His plan. We have dubbed this viewpoint the perspective of *Kingdom reality*. Reading the Bible from the view of Kingdom reality will keep us from bizarre ideas for deeper meaning that have nothing to do with God's purposes (which is what true allegorization often did, using the Bible to support a contemporary philosophy).[11] It will also keep us from falling a step or two short of finding the timeless meaning of a passage so that we end up applying biblical commands to ourselves which God did not intend for our time and cultural context.

Applying the Essential Meaning to Life

It is the essential meaning of a passage that helps us to apply Scripture to our own lives. This is the meaning that transcends time and culture. This is the meaning that is related to God and how He is working out His Kingdom. We take this meaning and ask the Spirit's help in working it out in our own culture and particular life circumstances. It is important to note at this point that we can't merely take a Scripture passage in isolation and look for the essential reality of the text because we may fall short of finding its essential meaning. We need to look for its essential meaning in light of God's entire revelation.

For instance, if we were to look for the essential meaning of the command to keep the Sabbath, we would discover that it is based upon God resting on the seventh day after creating the universe. This sounds like a permanent reason for keeping the Sabbath so why don't we observe this commandment today (as do the Seventh Day Adventists)?

The reason is that Jesus, in the New Testament, taught that the Sabbath itself was to be for man's pleasure. In that light the early Church no longer kept the Sabbath, and Resurrection Sunday replaced Sabbath Saturday as the regular day of worship. In essential reality, all days are the same so that we are not *required* to keep any day (Colossians 2:16-17). God's Kingdom rest has come, though not entirely (Hebrews 3-4). Every day is filled with worship, every day a Sabbath Saturday and a Resurrection Sunday.

But because we recognize our own weakness and our need in this in-between period for a particular time set aside, we choose to keep a regular day of worship and certain holidays in order to rehearse and celebrate the truths of our faith. Most of us need to set aside these times (including daily quiet time) in order to carry through the reality of the truth in every moment of every day. So, many of us choose to take a Sabbath rest to pray and to play on Sunday. But we do not keep it legalistically, and we may choose to do some small task that day. And if God brings circumstances into our lives so that we can't worship on Sunday (as in the case of working Sundays for a necessary job), or even so that it is impossible for a time to take a significant part of any day for a Sabbath rest, we do not need to feel guilty as though we are breaking some command of Scripture.

This is but one small example of how we could fall short of understanding a passage for our own day. Entire denominations are built on such differences. How true it is that everything in life eventually boils down to hermeneutics!

One final word before we move on to how this hermeneutic is used in the New Testament. The line between finding the deeper meaning of a passage (an objective meaning placed there by God) and finding deeper meaning *in* a passage (subjective meaning for our own lives) is often fuzzy. The prophets of Israel are an example of this. They applied Scripture to their own time in calling God's people to return to the God of their fathers. These same events in their own time also served as the occasion for receiving revelation by the Spirit of deeper meaning of their Scripture, unknown to the human author, which they then applied to their time. In everyday life, these become entwined for us as well. There may not be clear lines between applications of biblical truth we make to our own circumstances and deeper meaning (unknown to the human author) that we discover by the Holy Spirit.

IN THE NEW TESTAMENT

Many of us feel fairly comfortable with finding deeper meaning in the Old Testament because we believe we have the climax of revelation in the New Testament which provides the interpretive norm or controls necessary for finding that deeper meaning. The question is, how are we to apply this paradigm as a hermeneutic for reading the New Testament? Are we to look for deeper meaning there, intended by the divine Author and unknown to the human one, just as we can in the Old Testament?

To be honest, we haven't decided on our own answer yet. We're still too early in the process of testing this paradigm to feel comfortable in making definitive pronouncements, and we invite you to explore this with us if you are interested. We have given it some thought, though, and want to describe for you some tentative conclusions. To organize these thoughts, we are going to ask and answer the two questions above separately.

Understanding the New Testament Author's Meaning

Can we apply this paradigm as a hermeneutic for the New Testament? And if so, how? Our answer to the first part of this question is a definite yes! The first thing we need to do is to realize that this Kingdom center (and, we believe, the paradigm along with it) is the world view from which the New Testament authors wrote. They knew that the Kingdom had come and that they belonged to a totally different order, citizens of the Kingdom and not of this world, headed for a celestial city. Until they arrived, they were to be missionaries, engaging the world to win some, using their Christian freedom to adopt the practices of the now foreign culture in which they found themselves so that they would cause no unnecessary offense as they brought the truth to the lost.[12]

The second thing we need to do is to realize that the New Testament authors were not presenting a finished theology in their writings, but, especially in the Epistles, were working out this theology in the context of the world. They knew that though the end had come, the Kingdom was still in the process of being actualized. This means that the New Testament is a case study for how we are to advance God's Kingdom on earth. In the text, then, is the essential reality of the Kingdom, the existential reality of the situations they were facing, and the process and strategies they were to use to seek the actualization of the Kingdom on earth. Out of love they were to give up all of their rights in order not to bring unnecessary offense to the gospel, to spread the gospel for the salvation of individual souls, and then to aid them in slowly working out in their communities all the truth embryonic in the gospel.

This leads us to the third thing we need to do. We must understand the nature of this Kingdom and the means we are to use to actualize it on earth. We can discover the nature of the Kingdom by studying direct descriptions of it. We can also learn about it in the statements and commands found especially in the Epistles. The statements tell us what is true about God or about us within the Kingdom. The commands tell us how we are to behave, which will reveal to us what it is like to be in this Kingdom. We can also learn what the Kingdom is like by examining the means we are to use to actualize it because the means must reflect the nature of the Kingdom. The Kingdom cannot be accomplished except by Kingdom means.

Doing these three things will enable us to discern just what New Testament writers are telling us to do and why they are telling us to do it. They are telling us to do some things because they are in keeping with God's character. These things, such as meeting the needs of the poor and maintaining sexual purity, do not change according to time and place (although they may look different in different contexts). Other commands are given in order to advance the gospel in the social circumstances of the original recipients. Let's return to the example of slavery again.

Most of us believe that slavery is wrong because it violates the image of God in humanity, but this is difficult to prove from a surface reading of the Bible. If it is wrong, then why do Paul and Peter tell Christian slaves to submit to their masters? They do so because slaves acting on the essential reality of their freedom in Christ and leaving their masters would bring upheaval in the society and recrimination against the gospel so that its progress would be blocked. Instead, they were to be especially honest and diligent slaves so that they could win their masters and others to the gospel. Even though they were truly free, their part in the advancement of the gospel was to give up their freedom and spend their entire lives as slaves if they could not become free through socially approved means.

Understanding the difference between essential reality, existential reality, and the process of actualizing essential reality in existential reality will keep us from making the same error that many sincere Christians in the South did. They mistook biblical commands regarding the *means* of advancing the gospel as the *end*, and then justified slavery by pointing to these commands in Scripture.

Finally, we need to realize that God is forever in the process of actualizing His Kingdom on earth. In essence, the end has come, but it still needs to be fully realized. This will help us to apply Scripture to what is happening in our own time. For example, John says that the spirit of the antichrist is whatever denies that Jesus Christ came in the flesh. (From other parts of Scripture we know also that the antichrist will be incredibly evil and will set himself up as God, cf. Revelation 13.) Then John says, "Dear children, this is the last hour; and as you have heard that the antichrist is coming, even now many antichrists have come" (1 John 2:18). Though there will be one who is the ultimate fulfillment of the antichrist, the end is now here and the spirit of the antichrist is here also, manifest in many people and institutions until the completion of the end.

Returning again to our example of Jesus' use of Malachi, this may help us to understand His enigmatic statement that even though John the Baptist is the greatest of all born of women, the least in the Kingdom is greater than he. Jesus' death and resurrection and the coming of the Spirit at Pentecost accomplished the Kingdom in essence. Perhaps, in a sense, Jesus' statement means that we are all John the Baptists performing the same basic function. We are greater than he because the Kingdom has come. Now, we all, with the power of the Spirit in this Kingdom age, act as prophets in preparing the way of Yahweh in Jesus Christ for His coming again in the completion of the end. When we understand that God is always actualizing His Kingdom, we are able to discern what in our time is a manifestation of evil and the Kingdom; which efforts are using Kingdom means to accomplish God's good; and which are misguided.

Deeper Meaning Unknown to New Testament Authors?

Now for the second part of our question. Are we to find deeper meaning in the New Testament that was unknown to the human authors like we can in the Old Testament? Our tentative answer is no. The reason for this is that the end has come in the death and resurrection of Jesus Christ. In this we have the definitive interpretation of history. The New Testament provides the final, normative revelation explaining this end and its relation to all things so that it provides the interpretive norm for all that goes before (Scripture and history) and all that goes after (theology—or tradition—and history). Because of this we may say that there is no deeper meaning left to be unfolded.

This needs to be carefully explained. Obviously, the deeper meaning remains to be unfolded in the sense that we are waiting to see it happen in history as the end comes to completion. But because the end has come and the New Testament writers are explaining this end as the interpretation of everything, it is unlikely that there is *essential* meaning in their writings that remains for us to discover. What about the book of Revelation? Surely John didn't know the details of how all that is going to work out in history? This is true, but notice what it is that he didn't know: he didn't know the details of the existential reality that his prophecies foretold, and neither do we. This is veiled in symbolic language. But deeper meaning is *essential* meaning unknown to the human author.[13] The fact is, essential reality is just about all that John describes in his highly symbolic language (except perhaps his letters to the churches in chapters two and three).[14] It is so "essential" instead of concrete that there is much dispute over whether the millennium lasts a thousand literal years, or even whether Christ's reign on earth is physical.

The discovery in time of the missing existential details is not an unfolding of essential reality. Deeper meaning is discovered only if an essential meaning unknown to the author is later uncovered. Because the whole point of the New Testament seems to be an explanation of the occurrence and the essence of the end, we think it unlikely that there is deeper meaning in the New Testament unknown to its writers.

Still, our answer is only a tentative no because of one caveat. Paul says,

> We know in part and we prophesy in part, but when perfection comes, the imperfect disappears....Now we see but a poor reflection; then we shall see face to face. Now I know in part; then I shall know fully, even as I am fully known (1 Corinthians 13:9,10,12).

Does what we come to know more "fully" pertain to existential reality only? Or might it be that deeper understanding of essential reality is further unfolded? This seems even more likely when we read what John says: "Dear friends, now we are children of God, and what we will be has not yet been made known. But we know that when he appears, we shall be like him, for we shall see him as he is" (1 John 3:2). We see here that we know *some*—that is, that we will be like Him—but also that there is more that has not yet been made known. This "more" seems to pertain to essential reality. After all, how can heaven be anything but growing in understanding of essential reality as we encounter God directly for all eternity?

If all this is true, then can we rule out the *possibility* that this dark glass through which Paul looked is getting lighter and lighter as the processes of history help us to understand truth better? (We will discuss this idea of history in Chapter 9.) Or is more of essential reality unfolded only when He comes again? There remains the possibility that we can come to a greater understanding of essential reality corporately through time, perhaps even through a deeper meaning in the text unknown to the human authors.[15]

Three Final Questions

In closing, we should briefly address three questions. (We discuss these questions more thoroughly in chapter 10.) First, how does our hermeneutic relate to the grammatical-historical hermeneutic? The grammatical-historical hermeneutic goes a long way toward helping us to understand the meaning consciously intended by the human author. This meaning roughly corresponds to the existential reality in a biblical text. Where the essential reality is not known/intended by the human author, this literal hermeneutic is insufficient. So the paradigm incorporates within it the grammatical-historical hermeneutic, yet goes beyond it. Nevertheless, the essential meaning it discovers in a passage is intrinsically and inextricably related to the literal meaning.

Second, are we saying that this paradigm is the hermeneutic that the biblical writers used? We do not contend that the biblical writers *consciously* went through the process of distinguishing the essential reality and existential reality of a passage. Rather, they were steeped in the world view of the Bible, and the Spirit used this perspective to help them find deeper meaning. The paradigm simply codifies this process.

Third, can we practice the hermeneutic of the biblical writers in finding deeper meaning? By codifying the hermeneutical process of the biblical writers, the paradigm empowers us to practice their hermeneutic with a sense of freedom and security. One of the goals of a postmodern approach to reading is to allow us to find meaning directly in reading the text without going through some philosophical system.[16] The paradigm seems very much to be a sort of philosophical system. We are not saying that we have to go through this system for the Spirit to reveal valid meaning to us. We know from experience that this is not so. The paradigm can be used to do so, however, and it can also provide a means of checking the validity of ideas for meaning.

So What?

Using the paradigm as a hermeneutic empowers us in the following ways:

1. We have an objective, hermeneutical guide for discerning the authenticity of the Spirit's leading in what the deeper meaning (unknown to the human author) of any biblical text might be.

2. We have a viewpoint from which to read Scripture (which in a sense is God's world view) that will help us to discover the essential meaning of a passage, whether or not that essential meaning was known to the human author. This will help us to keep from stopping a step or two short of this meaning and making an absolute command out of something that God meant only as a temporary contextualization. Because the paradigm is tied to the biblical world view, it also keeps us from reading in our own world view and reinterpreting the Bible according to contemporary philosophy.

3. Essential meaning is what we are to apply to our lives and work to actualize in the world, and what we are to use to interpret what is going on around us. This may help us to understand such things as whether we should join efforts such as the Christian Coalition, which seem to politicize the Kingdom. This will also help us to develop theology based in truth that is deliberately formulated to address the varied questions and needs of secular humanity.

4. We have a general guide for checking the validity of our impressions of what the Spirit is leading us to do. We can also evaluate whether we should participate in various efforts to work for God's will. He will not lead us to accomplish the Kingdom except through Kingdom means, as revealed in the New Testament. This may shed light on if and how we should participate in civil disobedience on such issues as abortion.

Cool It
But Don't Kill It

"Will you please sit down and be quiet!" Stephanas had lost
his patience. His wife had a prophecy but several deacons were
all speaking in tongues at the same time and her voice could not
be heard.

Stephanas appreciated the exuberance and freedom of worship
at Corinth, but for several months chaos had overwhelmed all
semblance of order. Believers were choosing sides behind leaders
such as Paul, Apollos, Peter, Sosthenes, even Christ Himself to
bolster their views of spiritual gifts. Some even wanted to ban the
special gifts of the Spirit altogether, claiming that they were too
disruptive and for the immature. Some women made Priscilla of
Ephesus their role model and were involved in praying and prophesying. But many men were wary of this new-found freedom of
worship for the women, and some husbands were making it tough
going for their wives at home. The troubles in worship were
spilling over and even bringing slander to the gospel. Some unbelievers were openly ridiculing believers as mad and scoffing at the
power of Christ to change lives.

Paul had promised to give detailed instructions in a letter, but so
far it had not arrived. So Stephanas was delighted when Phoebe,
the deacon from nearby Cenchrea, arrived. With Paul's authority,
she would mediate things and inform him by letter to Ephesus of
the situation. Immediately she sought out Chloe and Stephanas
who were respected leaders and among the first converts.

*"Tell me, my sister and my brother. What is at the root of all
the bickering and quarreling?"*

"Well, it has many faces." Chloe tried to organize her thoughts.
*"We know that all this dissension and disorder cannot please God.
Yet we don't want to quench the Spirit either. We need to find balance. I think the central problem concerns what authority the new
revelation from the Spirit has. Is it just for an individual among us,
for our whole church, or for the Body of Christ everywhere for all
time?"*

Stephanas disagreed. *"I think the core issue is the gift of
prophecy. If the Spirit moves someone, even a woman such as
my wife, to prophesy, it cannot have error. It should simply be*

obeyed. And this is so whether the word be about the future or for edification. But my wife can't be heard."

"But how do we know it is the Holy Spirit, and not some other spirit, who is communicating?" asked Phoebe. "I've heard the Apostle John warn the Ephesians about false spirits. He gave them various tests for discerning them. Yet he also encouraged us with promises that the Spirit in His unction would continue to teach us all truth. Does this not agree with the two tests of a prophet that Moses told us about?"

"But I wonder," Stephanas pondered, "who should do the testing, the discerning? Other prophets? The whole community of faith? Probably it should be as broad as possible."

Phoebe invited Chloe to list the other points of controversy.

"Well, I can think of several. How do we know when a message from the Spirit is universally authoritative or only locally so? How is the human prophet involved in the process? Is every Christian a prophet, as well as a priest and king?"

"Well, those are important questions. I suggest we deal with the dissension by adopting some guidelines for the exercise of the gifts such as tongues and prophecy. You know the saying, we should 'cool it but not kill it.' I suppose Paul will put it differently in his letter but I think he will go along with these suggestions when I write to him." Phoebe knew Paul hated legalism and wanted believers to experience as fully as possible their freedom in Christ when gathered together.

Phoebe concluded by saying, "One day I suppose that believers will have to debate these matters all over again, since we can't claim that the Spirit is leading us today to adopt these particular rules of worship for them. Their circumstances will no doubt differ from ours, although I can't imagine how. Uh, does that qualify me or disqualify me from being a prophetess?" she grinned.

In keeping with the issues above, we answer three critical questions about the Spirit's role in interpretation, clarify the gift of prophecy, and explain how all of this works out practically.

Chapter Six

The Holy Spirit

Listening to the Divine Exegete

"The Spirit teaches us all things"

(1 John 2:27).

PUTTING THE "SUPER" BACK INTO THE SUPERNATURAL

All across America there is a hunger for reality, for finding the spiritual dimension of life. You can browse any secular bookstore and find books on angels, the after-life, on spirituality, and the occult. Talk shows on radio and television serve up a regular fare of interviews with spiritual "leaders" or personalities on spiritual themes. Our technological age stresses communication, information, inventions, and efficiency, while at the same time removing us ever further from that which can satisfy the heart and soul. We all feel it. We want to pause, to reflect, to wait, to contemplate. We are part of a growing stirring of the Spirit for reality.

We have spent years teaching Bible and methods of interpreting the Bible, even from the original text. Yet we can miss the central focus of our existence and calling—to know God and to help others to know Him. We can be trained in hermeneutical theory but never practice Spirit-led interpretation. We are challenged by sermons to live for God, yet rarely are encouraged to live as Jesus lived, to be His disciples. We are called to commitment and renewal, but our approach to spirituality fails to tell us how to listen to God's voice afresh. We memorize the Bible and teach it incessantly, yet we never discover the key to God's heart. We seek independence and autonomy—we want to do our own thing. Yet we can hardly stand our success. We thirst for intimacy, for someone who cares, for doing God's thing.

That is, until a friend comes along who has discovered it.

So she shares it with us and we begin to see again, for the first time. Our crisis provides the occasion for new birth, for renewal, and it is so simple we wonder how we missed it for so long. We are eager to be in the midst of others who have found it, who experience freedom and deliverance from common trifles, whose walk with God is a child-like trust. Prayer changes. We embrace the exhilarating life of delighting in God and find that He more than reciprocates in delighting in us. We are overwhelmed at the thought that we can bring joy to the heart of God—real, spontaneous attending to Him. His Word becomes, among other things, a letter of endearment. And the Spirit never disappoints.

Yet when it comes to scholarly methods of interpreting the Bible, the Holy Spirit may as well be dead.

Before you have a heart attack, let us explain. While we believe that the Holy Spirit is alive and active and we welcome His work,[1] our method of interpretation has no concrete role for Him.[2] This is true for two reasons. First, the grammatical-historical hermeneutic treats the Bible just like any other book. Its divine authorship makes no difference in how we are to understand it. By discovering the human author's intention, we believe we have exhausted its meaning. Second, the role of the Holy Spirit is usually confined to convicting us of the truth of what Scripture says and applying it to our lives.[3] He does not help us to understand the meaning of the text (which even an unbeliever can do through the grammatical-historical hermeneutic), and He certainly does not lead us in finding deeper or essential meaning that He placed there, unknown to the human author and not explicitly cited in the New Testament.

Let's take a closer look at the two reasons why we have no concrete role for the Holy Spirit in biblical interpretation.

We treat the Bible as any other book because in a sense, it is like any other book. It is great literature. A grammatical-historical approach commends the historically-based nature of our faith. God acted in our history and spoke our language. There must be common ground with the unbeliever to convince him of the truth. And if God is the God of everything, then He must make sense in our world. The Incarnation is the ultimate example of God accommodating Himself to us.

We also find ourselves emotionally attached to grammatical-historical interpretation because it won out after a thousand-year struggle with methods that abused the text and detracted from its credibility. It fits our western and modern world view embracing rational and empirical evidence. We find comfort in an approach that promises to explain Scripture's mystery, paradox, enigma, and just plain problems!

On the other hand, with its divine Author guiding people to write it, it is unlike any other book. Can we avoid the implications of its supernaturality? Do human methods of interpretation reach the heart of God? To fail to acknowledge the Spirit as the Bible's source and interpreter will leave us perpetuating another kind of imbalance that preceded the grammatical-historical method during the Middle Ages.

If we do acknowledge the Spirit's presence in the interpretational process, we usually limit Him to the end of the method, applying the truth received from Scripture, rather than communicating truth directly to us throughout the process. We think that only apostles are promised special power to understand meaning. We reason that if the Bible is human history in human language, we shouldn't need the Spirit's help to understand meaning. Also, any new communication regarding meaning seems to challenge normativity and orthodoxy, opening the door for sects and heresy. We fear the subjectivity of His helping us to understand Scripture, including those very passages which touch upon His role in interpretation. We know all too well that some will claim a special revelation and insist that it is normative for all the church. Fearing the abuse of prophecy by date setting and novel, autonomous interpretations, we eschew it altogether and bury the greatest gift.[4]

Three Crucial Questions

What we believe the role of the Holy Spirit to be in interpretation depends largely on how we interpret several key Scripture passages. But how we interpret these passages is greatly influenced by the faith tradition in which we have grown up. Evangelical biblical scholarship is dominated by the Reformation heritage. In response to Roman Catholicism, the Reformation emphasized the perspicuity of Scripture, the idea that the Bible is clear and plain in its meaning and can be understood by the everyday believer apart from the church (in contrast to mysterious, spiritual meanings which only church leaders could understand). In itself this is very good, but along with it came a quashing of the role of the Holy Spirit in understanding the Bible. The Holy Spirit was denied a place in understanding/interpreting in order to keep in check the disagreeable sects who were claiming the leading of the Spirit.[5]

Therefore the Spirit is confined to illumination, an illumination which only makes the reader willing to receive the message. There is a tendency toward considering His more spectacular gifts to have ceased, such as prophecy. Yet we believe that if we take a careful look at the pertinent passages, we will see that the Holy Spirit helps us to *understand truth*, not just receive it, and that He has an ongoing ministry in revealing truth to us.

In this section we seek to answer three questions as we consider Scripture's witness to the Spirit's role as Exegete.[6]

Our first question is: Does the Spirit aid us only in receiving the Word, to convict us to receive it? Or does He actually assist us in understanding it, giving us insight into it? The first alternative concerns our response, or the significance of a passage to us; the second concerns our understanding of the meaning.[7] If the Holy Spirit helps us only in receiving the truth, then an unbeliever can understand the meaning of Scripture as well as the believer; his only problem is that he will not yield his will to or welcome the interpretation.[8] The second option permits the possibility of discovering a deeper, essential meaning due to the divine Author.

The second question is related to the first. Does the Holy Spirit continue to speak to us directly, or does He speak only mediately, through Scripture? The former concerns additional revelation; the latter limits the role of the Spirit to Scripture. Those who support the first option of immediate communication believe that the Spirit also speaks mediately through Scripture. It is probable that the first option is the more popular, the second option the more scholarly.[9]

The third question flows from the second one. If the Spirit continues to speak today, does He still reveal new truth? Were the promises of the Spirit leading into new truth for the apostles only, or are they also for us today?

We will take a look at some key Scripture passages to answer these questions. Then we will explore how our answers affect our understanding of the gifts of the Spirit for today, especially the gift of prophecy.

Paul: The Spirit Speaks Beyond the Text

1. *1 Corinthians 2:12-14.* This is probably the most crucial passage for us to consider in understanding the Spirit's role in interpretation. Here Paul deals with the relationship of the Holy Spirit to believers in general and to his own ministry in particular. He describes all believers as having the Spirit within (vv. 10-12), speaks of the ministry of himself and others (v. 13), and returns to all believers again (vv. 14-16).[10] Let's look at the three crucial verses (12-14).

We have not received the spirit of the world but the Spirit who is from God, that we may understand what God has freely given us. (13) This is what we speak, not in words taught us by human wisdom but in words taught by the Spirit, expressing spiritual truths in spiritual words. (14) The man without the Spirit does not accept the things that come from the Spirit of God, for they are foolishness to him, and he cannot understand them because they are spiritually discerned.

It is clear that both verses 12 and 14 refer to the Spirit's aid in *understanding* or *interpreting the meaning*.[11] While the first half of verse 14 refers to significance, it does not seem possible to restrict the Spirit's role only to helping people accept the message as true because the second half talks about understanding. So the first crucial question is answered thus: this passage supports the role of the Spirit in helping us to understand the spiritual message, not just to receive it. He helps us first to understand and then to receive—opening both our minds and our hearts, as Jesus did on the road to Emmaus (Luke 24). We give further scriptural support for our view near the end of this chapter.

We gain the answer to the second crucial question from verse 13. Paul says that his and others' speaking is "not in words taught us by human wisdom but in words taught by the Spirit, expressing spiritual truths in spiritual words" (or, as the margin of the NIV reads: "interpreting spiritual truths to spiritual men").

We struggle to understand the last words of this verse. They are rendered differently in various translations. We view them as expanding Paul's claim in the middle of the verse that he speaks words taught by the Spirit (13b). He is saying (in 13c) that the things of the Spirit (the "things freely given us by God," v.12) have to be explained or expressed by means of, or with, the words taught by the Spirit.[12] Thus Paul in the very last words of the verse is simply saying that his interpreting or expressing the things of the Spirit has to be "in language appropriate to the message, not with human wisdom."[13] A spiritual message has to be communicated by spiritual (although also human) words from the Spirit. In other words, Paul adapts or accommodates his words to the subject.[14] Since the subject matter comes from the Spirit, his words to express it have to come from the Spirit.[15] This has significant implications for how we interpret Scripture. For any message, whether directly from the Spirit, or indirectly, such as through the written Word, must be expressed (and interpreted) by words taught by the Spirit.[16]

But to what does Paul refer? Many appeal to this verse to define the doctrine of illumination, that it is the Spirit's role to clarify the written text, that He does not reveal additional truth beyond it.[17] Yet this is not the case, as we are about to show. Others see inspiration of Scripture here and not revelation in general. They affirm (as do we) a closed Canon, and ongoing revelation seems to threaten this. Yet this fear arises from the failure to distinguish what is normative (authoritative for all for all time), and what isn't. Revelation from God is always authoritative but not necessarily normative.

The crucial point to note is that Paul is dealing with his preaching ministry. The context has nothing to do with the written Word,[18] but with the preaching of the gospel, the spoken word (1:17-22; 2:1-7, 13), and the message of wisdom which has been revealed by the Spirit (v. 10).[19] This message may come by way of apostles, prophets, or any gifted person in the assembly, whether later inscripturated or not. So the passage deals with oral revelation (v. 10) and interpretation (vv. 11-16, although v. 13 is probably revelation again) through any gifted person, not just an apostle.[20] This seems confirmed by 14:26 (each one has a teaching, has a revelation, has a tongue, has an interpretation) where again both ideas of revelation and interpretation by all believers are brought together in one verse. Although by extension or application we may find the significance of the verse to include the written text (for Paul also communicated the written Word by the same spiritual means), it is not the primary meaning.

In summary, we can affirm the following from verses 12-14, if not more.[21]

(1) Paul and others received revelation from the Spirit directly.

(2) Paul expressed this revelation in forms given by the Spirit.

(3) Paul expects his readers to understand revelation by the Spirit.

So with regard to the second crucial question, this passage (and others)[22] supports the idea that the Spirit has an ongoing role of directly revealing (vv. 10, 13) and interpreting (vv. 11-16) truth to us, apart from the written text.[23] This is in accord with the gift of prophecy exercised at Corinth, which gift Paul encourages, especially over tongues (11:1-16; 12:10; 13:8-9; 14:1-5—which point is also supported by the passages from John's writings discussed below).

2. *2 Corinthians 3-4.* When we turn to 2 Corinthians, we find that the *minds* of the Jews are veiled or made dull (3:14) and a veil covers their *hearts* (3:15). Only in Christ is the veil removed (3:12-18). In chapter four Paul asserts that the god of this world has blinded the mind of the unbeliever or natural person (4:4); he cannot see the light of the gospel. In contrast, the believer has had the light shine in his heart (4:6). This change has come about by the Spirit of the new covenant who conveys life (3:6) and freedom (3:17). The new covenant was inaugurated by Jesus just before His death, so all of us in the Body of Christ have this veil removed. This passage reinforces our view that the Spirit empowers believers to understand the meaning of Scripture, and not just convince them of its significance.[24] The Spirit affects both mind and heart; the two cannot be separated.

John: The Holy Spirit Teaches New Truth

We see three views possible regarding the impact of John's writings on interpretation or illumination.

(1) They support the ongoing ministry of the Spirit to illumine and teach new truth to all Christians in the church.

(2) They support only the ministry of the Spirit to the apostles, the writers of Scripture.[25]

(3) They support both ideas.

We believe the last alternative is best.

1. *John 14-17.* As Jesus' last discourse to His apostles in the upper room before His crucifixion, it appears at first that this passage is addressed initially to the apostles alone. Yet clearly some of the discourse is also intended to be an ongoing promise to you and us in the Church. For example, in 17:20ff., Jesus prays also for those who will believe through the apostles' message, that all may be one, just as He is in the Father. This prayer for oneness gives future focus to His entire discourse (cf. 14:11, 20; 15:4-10). It may properly be argued that all of 17:20-26 includes future believers, such as us today. It is more certain that Jesus' expression that He *will continue to make known* the Father to them (v. 26) supports an ongoing witness of the Spirit in light of the context. There is also the Spirit's ongoing ministry of convicting the world (16:7-11).

What about the rest of the discourse? John 14:26 reads:

But the Counselor, the Holy Spirit, whom the Father will send in my name, will teach you all things and will remind you of everything I have said to you.

The verse seems to refer only to the apostles, for Jesus had been with them (14:26). Only they could be reminded of previous teaching. Yet several teachings here (14:1-7; 15:1-17) parallel teaching elsewhere, including the work of the Spirit in leading believers into the truth (1 Thessalonians 1:5; 2:13; Ephesians 3:14-19).[26] The same verse (14:26) also promises that the Spirit *will teach you all things*. This goes beyond *reminding* and parallels the promise of 1 John 2:27 (see below) which refers to ongoing ministry. So while John 14:26 assures us today that the subsequent revelation through the apostles is historically and theologically trustworthy,[27] it does more. In light of the larger context of John's and Paul's writings, we may conclude that Jesus had us in mind in His words of John 14.

John 15:26-27 seems to parallel the apostles' witness with the future witness of the Spirit, which may go beyond that of the apostles'.

> When the Counselor comes, whom I will send to you from the Father, the Spirit of truth who goes out from the Father, he will testify about me; (27) but you also must testify, for you have been with me from the beginning.

While the witness of the Spirit may now include primarily the written Word, the sense in John's writings speaks of his internal witness (cf. 1 John 5:7-11).[28]

In 16:13-14, Jesus says that the Spirit of truth will come.

> He will guide you into all truth. He will not speak on his own; he will speak only what he hears, and he will tell you what is yet to come. He will bring glory to me by taking from what is mine and making it known to you.

This passage basically parallels that of chapter 14. The words describe the Spirit in the role of an exegete by "taking from what is mine and making it known" *to you*. This work then sets forth a model of what the human exegete does. It is without question that new truth is in view here, at least for the apostles. The promise of His guiding into all truth is not retrospective only (regarding what Jesus has already said) but also prospective (leading them into new truth that expands or develops what they already know).[29] In part, it has come to pass. We know that Jesus communicated new or additional truth between His resurrection and ascension (e.g., see Acts 1:3-5). When we consider the Epistles, it is clear that new revelation is also communicated through the apostles, such as Paul (e.g., Galatians 1; 1 Corinthians 1-2; etc.). In addition, as we have already shown, the New Testament quotation of the Old Testament conveys new truth not formerly revealed. Finally, the gifts of prophecy (on occasion), tongues, revelation, messages of knowledge, imply the revealing of new truth. The important question then becomes how normative this truth is for the whole Body.

2. *1 John 2:27.* When we read John's first epistle, we are especially convinced that he teaches that the Spirit continues to reveal truth to all believers. In 1 John 2:20, John affirms that his readers have the anointing of the Holy Spirit and all of them know the truth.[30] Then he asserts even more in verse 27.

As for you, the anointing you received from him remains in you, and you do not need anyone to teach you. But as his anointing teaches you about all things and as that anointing is real, not counterfeit—just as it has taught you, remain in him.

Note that John says all have this anointing (which is the Holy Spirit, and perhaps also the Word); that He continues to teach (present tense) about all things (parallel to John 14:26—not just reminds about former truth); and that the new teaching will be in accord with what He has already taught (past tense; it cannot contradict former truth). Some assert that this promise is limited to remaining in Christ,[31] but clearly it concerns *all things* and the *truth* (vv. 20-21). And the words cannot be limited to subjective interpretation.[32]

While it is difficult to understand precisely what 1 John 2:27 means, it is clear what it does not mean. The promise is not limited to the apostles (note *you*); it is not limited to abiding (note *all things*); it is not limited to the past (note the present *teaches*); and it is not limited to Scripture or mediated revelation (his [the Spirit's] *anointing teaches you*).

None of these passages from Paul and John can be limited to illuminating the biblical text, for most of the New Testament was unwritten at the time of 1 and 2 Corinthians (A.D. 55 and 57). If John's writing is the latest (near the end of the first century), then much of the writing of the text already has been completed; but the promises in John 14 and 16 and especially 1 John seem to suggest that truth and teaching was yet to be revealed! In other words, according to the logic of some interpreters, we should have had 1 Corinthians written near the end of the first century (to refer to the biblical text or Canon) and John and 1 John written in the early fifties (to promise future teaching in the form of the Canon).

Should some interpreters suggest that with the closing of the Canon we can limit the interpretation of these passages to the written, biblical text, this would only prove our view of what they mean or teach. Since there is no mention in these passages of the written message, we would have to ascribe such an interpretation to the work of the Spirit to continue to illumine interpreters of His church with additional insight or truth beyond the biblical text. So the Spirit speaks beyond Scripture.

The Spirit Bestows the Gift of Prophecy

We have answered the three major questions raised at the beginning. The Spirit helps us to understand the meaning of Scripture; He speaks to us directly, Spirit to spirit; and He leads us into new truth. So how does the ongoing ministry of the Spirit to speak directly affect our view of spiritual gifts, especially that of prophecy?[33] We answer that all the gifts are operative in the Body, due to the very nature of the community of faith as an organic whole, knowing no temporal or geographical boundaries. As most important among the gifts, we need to reinvigorate prophecy and the prophetic office in our interpretation of Scripture and discovery of new truth. As we explore this, we need to keep in mind that the prophetic gift pertains not just to foretelling, but to proclaiming God's truth (forthtelling). Paul associates various ideas or manifestations with the gift of prophecy,[34] including (at least) all of the following: understanding or interpretation, knowledge, edification, exhortation, and consolation (1 Corinthians 14).[35] He also elaborates it as knowing all mysteries and all knowledge (13:2).

In his message on the day of Pentecost, Peter affirms the universality of prophecy as he interprets Joel, who in turn had taken up Moses' desire that all become prophets: "I wish that all the LORD's people were prophets and that the LORD would put his Spirit on them" (Numbers 11:29). Thus, it is not surprising that Peter says (Acts 2:17-21):

"In the last days," God says, "I will pour out my Spirit on all people. Your sons and daughters will prophesy, your young men will see visions, your old men will dream dreams. Even on my servants, both men and women, I will pour out my Spirit in those days, and they will prophesy" (vv. 17-18).

Here the possession of the Spirit seems virtually equivalent to prophesying.[36] This helps identify what it means to have the Spirit by virtue of the New Covenant and having God's law on our hearts and all knowing Him (Hebrews 8:10-11). Prophecy is one of the results.

Paul exalts the gift of prophecy and expects every believer to exercise it in some measure. A cursory overview of 1 Corinthians 11-15 supports this.[37] Even though there are extraordinary instances of prophecy,[38] there can be little doubt that, at least in its forthtelling aspect, all may exercise this gift.

In addition, it is appropriate that all believers fulfill the office of prophet, along with that of priest and king. Our prophetic office is based on our identity in Christ, the witness of Scripture, and the mandate of creation.[39]

So why are we making so much of the gift of prophecy in our study? If our paradigm of reality as a hermeneutic assumes that the biblical authors find an essential meaning, and that we can follow their example, then it is vital that the gift of prophecy for interpretation and communication be within the reach of every believer. In addition to finding essential meaning, prophets contextualize the message for their own day and interpret the times by the leading of the Spirit. Prophecy is also necessary to do theology.

While some may possess this gift in special measure it is to be exercised by all just as is the gift of faith or giving. We are to seek the gift of prophecy or discernment for the common good (1 Corinthians 12:7). While gifts are given sovereignly, as the Spirit determines (1 Corinthians 12:11, 18, 28), we also are to desire eagerly the greater gifts (12:31), especially prophecy (14:1, 5, 39), and pray for such gifts (14:13). Paul would have all believers prophesy (14:5, 12, 24, 29-32). The imperative for us today is that we should make a concerted effort to pray for and seek the gift of prophecy, that we might interpret the voice of God afresh as He reveals His truth.

Understandably, this idea scares some people. They want things to be certain and under control, and they definitely don't want the truth to be corrupted, which is a valid concern. Such concern goes overboard, though, when it is the primary reason that we decide these gifts cannot be for today. We are acting presumptuously when we quash the working of the Spirit in the interest of safeguarding the truth, as if He cannot take care of that Himself as He works in the community in the exercise of His gifts.

Part of the ministry of the Spirit in protecting the truth from error is His gift of discernment. As various people exercise the gift of prophecy, as described above, Scripture teaches that others in community, including other prophets (1 Corinthians 14:32), should exercise discernment by comparing it with the truth, the faith already revealed (the principle of the analogy of faith: Romans 12:6; so also 1 Thessalonians 5:20-21; 1 John 2:27; 4:1-3).[40] In addition, Paul sets forth several rules for prophesying (1 Corinthians 14:29-33).[41]

LET'S GET PRACTICAL

We have attempted to demonstrate that the Holy Spirit helps us to understand the meaning of Scripture, that He speaks to us directly, that He teaches new truth, and that all of this is protected and provided for in a number of the Spirit's gifts to the community, especially that of prophecy. For those of us who are new to such ideas, let alone the practice of them, there are many questions about how this works out in real life. Let's explore for a bit some of the questions and implications that extend from our answers to the three crucial questions we investigated above.

What Meaning Does the Holy Spirit Help Us to Understand?

If we say that the Holy Spirit helps us to understand the meaning of Scripture, not merely to accept its truth, then there are some troubling questions to answer. Just what meaning does He help us to understand? Does the fact that the Spirit helps us to understand it mean that unbelievers can't understand Scripture? Why can't unbelievers understand the same meaning? Is it not written in logical, propositional statements, in human language? If we say that unbelievers can't understand Scripture, haven't we fallen into Kant's error of divorcing the spiritual world from the sensory world so that they have nothing to do with each other?

Tough questions. Neither one of us is a linguist or psychologist, so understanding the intricacies of meaning is outside of our training. We will do our best to answer these questions from Scripture.[42]

An unbeliever can understand some level of meaning. Both Scripture and the preaching of the gospel (within Scripture and today) assume this. For example, Paul in Athens (Acts 17) found common ground with his hearers. He assumes their partial understanding of a biblical world view, a biblical history, and their own poet's writing where it concurred with biblical truth or was evident in general revelation (17:28).

In addition, Romans 10:14 affirms that belief can occur only when there is someone to be heard. Paul then asserts that belief or faith comes by hearing the message and "the message is heard through the word of Christ" (v. 17); and that all Israel, as part of the world, did hear (v. 18) and Israel did understand (v. 19). Yet all did not hearken to or accept the gospel (v. 16). Hence they did not hear and understand fully.[43]

With this concur the words of Jesus regarding one purpose of parables (Matthew 13). They are spoken because knowledge of the secrets of the Kingdom is given to the disciples but not to the people (v. 11; note the assumption of the sovereign work of God in this statement). For the unbelieving, the purpose of parables is to hide truth. Though the people see, they do not see; though they hear (v. 13), they do not hear or understand. This paradox fulfills the prophecy of Isaiah (6:9-10) that Israel will be ever hearing but never understanding, ever seeing but never perceiving (14). Their heart has become calloused, affecting their hearing and seeing (v. 15). Isaiah concludes:

> Otherwise they might see with their eyes, hear with their ears, understand with their hearts and turn, and I would heal them.

It seems as though the heart is the seat of the problem. In an unbeliever, it keeps her not only from turning to God (being converted), but from fully seeing, hearing, and understanding. The total person is involved. Since the text is talking about meaning and not just significance (in Hirsch's terms), the unbeliever can neither understand fully nor respond.[44]

Returning to Matthew 13 again, we find that the explanation of the parable of the sower (vv. 18-23) expands on the ideas of hearing and understanding. The first soil symbolizes the person who hears the message about the Kingdom but does not understand it, even though it is sown in his heart. The second and third also apparently do not understand it (the second receives it with joy but fails to last, and the third has the Word choked and is unfruitful) and for one reason or another fail to continue. The fourth, it is specifically said, "hears the word and understands it," and because he bears fruit, he is good.[45] All four soils produce an appearance of fruition.

Here then lies the answer to our dilemma. It is possible for the unbeliever to hear and to know truth, whether in general revelation or in the special revelation of Scripture. God has acted in human history, interpreted Himself in human language, and designed the sensory world to reflect Him in whom we are to believe; therefore the unbeliever can understand at some level. Yet this is not full hearing or full understanding. Sin infects the very core of every person and impairs not only the will to accept and submit to the truth, but even the ability to understand it. We are unitary beings and what affects one part affects the whole. The mind, will, emotions, body—the total person—is affected by sin.[46] The texts specifically speak of inability to understand. Whatever way we try to describe what degree of understanding unbelievers do have, it is a degree which is insufficient.[47] Only the Holy Spirit can supply this level of understanding.[48] It is this level of meaning that the Holy Spirit leads us into, and each level deeper, as we progress in the truth.[49]

What Does the Spirit Communicate to Us?

The things that the Spirit communicates to us can be divided into two general categories. The first category includes those things that do not seem to relate directly to truth. The Spirit communicates directly to us such things as specific, personal instructions and personal applications of Scripture for our guidance. For example, the Spirit may give us specific directions regarding our life mate, our place of employment, our pursuit of education, the size of our family. He may communicate, Spirit-to-spirit, particular words of love, grace, and conviction that are found generally in Scripture. He may tell us a specific problem in our lives to address, or ask us to do a particular act of love for a specific person. In a larger perspective, He may give a church instructions regarding its ministry outreaches, problems within the church, the kind of discipline to apply, or the shape of collective worship experiences. He may also give a prophetic word to an individual or to the community about what is going to happen in such things as these.

The second category of things that He communicates to us relate more directly to truth. He helps us to solve exegetical questions and create new theological constructs. He helps us to discover deeper meaning in Scripture, to make connections between Kingdom reality and the surface meaning of the text. He may even lead the whole Body to a new formulation of orthodoxy, such as we find in the Nicean Creed and Apostle's Creed.[50]

The grammatical-historical interpretation is sufficient for the most basic understanding of Scripture. But by practice, we have all had the experience of finding meaning which goes beyond the grammatical-historical meaning (if we even know what this is), perhaps when doing devotional reading.[51] We find deeper meaning both by our tradition and by direct communication which the Holy Spirit initiates despite our blindness to His presence. Our hermeneutic of Kingdom reality (representing a divine world view) is closer to what we actually do.

How New Is the Truth That the Spirit Reveals?

The idea that the Holy Spirit continues to teach new truth immediately raises alarm. Certain important questions must be answered. What do we mean by *new* truth? How does it relate to Scripture? Is this new truth authoritative? Is it normative? Can more Scripture be written?

The communication or revelation of the Spirit takes different forms. Many things that the Spirit communicates to us would not be considered truth per se, such as instructions to the person or the community regarding direction in decision-making or specific application of Scripture truth. Other things He communicates, though, can be considered to be truth. It may be things like the essential meaning of a passage, a new theological idea, or the creed of a denomination or of the whole church. Should we call this new truth? Jonathan Edwards is typical of a truncated view when he asserts that the Holy Spirit does not add new words, propositions, or doctrines to the Scriptures. Rather, He "drives home in the heart what the mind grasps. He gives only a due apprehension of those things that are taught in the word of God."[52]

So why do we call this new truth? The first reason is, as we saw above, the truth that the Spirit is to lead us into includes things that have not yet been revealed (John 14-17), and the Spirit still teaches us today (1 John 2:27).

Jesus' words in Matthew 13:52 support this idea. After telling several parables about the Kingdom, He says that a teacher of the law who has been instructed about the Kingdom of heaven brings out of his storeroom treasures old and new. This suggests that new things would be discovered in Scripture by reading it after having been instructed regarding the Kingdom, and that new truth is yet to be revealed during the time of the Kingdom of heaven (which has begun).

The second reason is that our experience indicates that it *is* new truth. Our collective understanding of the truth has developed through time as we have continued to formulate theology. For example, we understand better today the doctrine of the Trinity and how Christ is both man and God.

There are two reasons why many do not consider such theological formulation to be new truth. First, they believe that the apostles understood everything that we do today, and that we are only uncovering what they knew but never explained or developed fully in Scripture. We need to disabuse ourselves of the notion that the apostles were walking deposits of complete, fully developed knowledge of God and His truth. God did give them all the essential, core revelation, but they, too, were people of their time. Their understanding of this truth developed slowly throughout their lives as they reflected on it and processed their personal and communal experiences. We can actually trace the development of an apostle's theology in Scripture. So while they received all the core truth, they did not develop it all.

This leads us to the second reason that theological formulation is usually not considered to be new truth. Many people contend that it is not new because it is simply an unfolding of what the apostles have in bits and pieces in the Scripture. If the apostles had lived long enough and thought about the same revelation from other viewpoints (such as the Greek mindset that asks questions about *being* rather than *doing*, which helped us to develop the doctrine of the Trinity and the relationship of the two natures of Christ), they would have developed the same theology.

This is true—but it doesn't mean it is not new! It is new in that it is something that we corporately did not understand before (although sometimes it is recovery of something lost, as in the case of *justification by faith* in the Reformation). Yet it is not new in the sense that it is something radically different and contradictory to the revelation from the Spirit in the Bible.

Perhaps the illustration of two Greek words for the ideas of "other" and "another" will help. In Galatians 1, Paul distinguishes a message which is a gospel of a qualitatively *different* kind from that which is a gospel of the qualitatively *same* kind. It is similar to distinguishing the Book of Mormon as another, different kind of bible, and not another translation of the same kind, such as the NIV and NASV are.[53] So the truth revealed to the believer is of the (qualitatively) same kind as that already revealed in Christ in the Canon.[54]

So, if it is new truth, is it authoritative?

All communication from the Spirit, whether dealing with specific personal and community concerns or things we consider truth, is authoritative. If it is an authentic word from the Spirit, it is true and authoritative. After all, He is God! The *extent* of its authority depends on the scope of the revelation. It may be fully authoritative for me or you as an individual, perhaps for a whole local church. If it is doctrine that becomes authoritative for the universal church, we pronounce it orthodox, but not canonical. Paul illustrates the first category: he often had direct, authoritative revelation for himself (e.g., Galatians 1; Acts 22-23). Acts 13 illustrates the second category: the church at Antioch obeyed the Spirit in sending out Paul and Barnabas. The Jerusalem council of Acts 15 illustrates the third category: apostles, elders, and the whole church fashioned an orthodox statement affirming that Gentiles did not have to be circumcised to become Christians. No biblical verse could be cited by them, but it "seemed" good to them and the Holy Spirit to decide this way (15:28). The existence of the Canon also represents the third category outside Scripture. After three hundred years, the church universal came to agree almost unanimously on the Canon.[55]

This last level of authority is illustrated by other decisions of church councils. The Spirit has given new truth to the church in the form of those decisions which hammered out the Canon, the nature of Christ, the nature of the Holy Spirit, and others. They use language which went beyond the words of Scripture. They are almost as authoritative as the words of Scripture itself.[56] Yet the test of their authority is always Scripture—what the Spirit has already revealed (1 John 2:27). The Spirit, being God, cannot reveal something contrary to what He has already revealed and yet remain God.

But if this truth is authoritative, is it also normative, true for the whole church for all time? Can it be made part of Scripture? Why or why not?

The difficulty in answering these questions is one of the most compelling forces behind the view that limits the work of the Holy Spirit to the text of Scripture. One of the biggest reasons some people deny that the Spirit leads into new truth is that this is the only way they can see to protect Scripture. They know that the Canon is closed and that no more Scripture will be written. So how can we have the Holy Spirit revealing new truth that is not put in Scripture? How can we have authoritative revelation that is not also normative?

One reason that it can be authoritative without being normative is that it applies only to a subset of the church and not the whole church. It is too particular. But these things are not usually considered to be truth per se. What about the things that we are calling truth, like orthodox theology? If the Spirit reveals such things, why can they not be put in the Canon? Is there any basis for claiming that the canon of Scripture is closed beyond asserting that the Spirit now works only through Scripture?

The answer is yes. The Canon is closed because the end of history has been revealed in the death and resurrection of Jesus Christ. The revelation interpreting the meaning of these events was given to the eyewitnesses of the events and to those who recorded it in Scripture during the eyewitnesses' lifetimes. This end of history in Christ is the interpretive norm for all that comes after it, since all that follows is the unfolding of the essence of this end. For this reason, the Canon is closed and acts as the standard to test all subsequent claims to truth to see if they are indeed from the Spirit. This is why we do not need to limit the Spirit's work in order to protect His Word!

GOD IS NOT THE BIBLE ANSWER MAN

Now, having said all this about God communicating with us directly about details of our lives and helping us to understand Scripture in various ways, we also need to say that God is not the Bible Answer Man. He will not rush to our side and whisper the right answer in our ear every time we have a question or have to make a decision. It's the same thing in prayer. God is not a vending machine. We can't blithely put in a few coins and push the right buttons and expect that what we want will come tumbling down. While for a time God may answer prayers right and left, eventually He will no longer jump at our every request.

One reason He often stays quiet is so that we can grow up and become more independent. *Independent?* You thought you were supposed to be absolutely *dependent* on God! Right? The answer is yes and no. Yes, we are absolutely dependent upon God because ultimately everything comes from Him. But we should not be dependent upon Him to make decisions and do things for us that He has empowered us to do for ourselves. This does not honor God. He may choose to tell us exactly what we should do when we face a particularly difficult decision, and maybe even tell us why we are to do it. But if a similar dilemma arises that requires the same wisdom principles to answer, we should not expect that He will tell us what to do again. His purpose is to mature us and empower us to decide and act for ourselves, and there would be something wrong with Him if He didn't. It's perfectly fine for a parent to spoon feed an infant and tie her shoes for her, but if this parent is still doing this for a normal ten-year-old, there is something wrong.

Does this mean that we can outgrow God? Of course not!

While we become independent in those things that He has already taught us, we never outgrow our need for Him. Ultimately, we are dependent upon Him for everything. We are also forever facing new challenges, being stretched as obstacles come our way and we engage the world for God and His Kingdom. There is a sense in which we should always be living on the edge, getting ever more deeply involved in God's Kingdom mission, fighting dark powers within ourselves, our communities, in others' empty, broken lives, coming again and again to the end of ourselves and discovering that we are inadequate to face it alone. This is when the Spirit steps in once more and works in marvelous ways. This process continues forever because God is infinite, and so seems our capacity to know Him and grow.

God is not interested in giving us snap answers to all our biblical questions. We learn in the struggling. We learn that the most important thing is to know God, not answers. Occasionally He will, for our personal good or for the good of the Kingdom, give us a specific solution to an exegetical problem, a new theological idea, or an insight into the deeper meaning of a passage. Most of the time, though, He lets us live in the question and slowly grow into the answer.

He does the same thing regarding personal life decisions. Once in awhile He may want us to make one specific choice and not another. Between two perfectly good job options, for instance, He may have a reason that He wants us at a particular one. But most of the time we are free to choose whatever we please within the bounds of what is morally sound, practicing the discipline of decision in the way of wisdom. And we don't need to fret about missing His will! God does not play hide and seek and then ruin our lives when we fail to find Him. We simply need to ask Him and keep a listening spirit for whatever He may tell us directly or through other people and circumstances. If we truly want to hear (which means also to obey), then He will not let us miss His word to us. The rest of the time, we are His will,[57] and our decisions are His decrees, since He works quietly in and through all things, even when He is not giving specific directions, Spirit to spirit.

This goes for understanding the Bible, too. We need to ask Him and listen for His voice as we practice such disciplines as prayer and meditation. But if He doesn't give us a specific answer, the conclusion we come to in all sincerity is fine with Him for the time being, even if eternity proves it to be less than accurate. He is at work in all our study and our thinking before Him, and the result is His will for the moment.

So how do we tell the difference between His voice and our own ideas? Our answer may not be welcome. We learn to tell the difference mostly through practice. As we keep a tender spirit, over time we learn to discern His voice as we grow to know Him, listen to others, proceed humbly and cautiously to follow our best understanding, and take an honest and balanced look at the results. Sometimes He may speak with such startling clarity and fill us with such confidence and confirm His word with such results that we have no doubt. Other times He may teach us how to discern His voice or He may bolster our faith by giving us specific, predictive words of prophecy which subsequently come true. Sometimes He speaks as clearly as if He used a human voice. The rest of the time, we can be comfortable trusting in the quiet work of the Spirit in all things, even if it smudges the line of certainty and clear distinction between the Spirit's work and ours.

Community plays an important part in training our discernment. Other people can check our interpretations and test our ideas against clearly known truth and their more mature understanding of the way God works. This checking of the community is especially important for one who is recognized by the community as one to whom God speaks reliably. There is never room for a dictatorial spirit which refuses to be subject to scrutiny by the community.

This does not mean that the community is always right. There may be a tension between our personal understanding and that of the community, since He may be using us to change the community (in a loving manner). Appeal to church authority is not an easy out from the responsibility and the seeming insecurity of personally discovering truth. For our good, God often leaves us to live with the ambiguity. This drives us to grow in knowing God, to live in community, and to walk in faith and humility.

In our espousing the Spirit's speaking, we do not want to encourage a sort of esoteric "treasure hunting" approach to reading Scripture, which will be the tendency of some no matter what we say. (These are the same type of people, struck with apocalyptic fever, who might engage in date-setting and games with numbers and letters.) What we mean to encourage is a new way of seeing, if you will, reading from another perspective, the biblical world view, led by the Spirit. Scripture will unfold more clearly in many ways: exegetical and theological tangles will unravel; contemporary meaning will come more readily and certainly; new truth will be discovered in the development of theology as we ask new questions; and yes, so-called deeper meaning (like that which the biblical authors saw) may be found, though this will likely be the least significant result of all of these.

We also wish to avoid any form of spiritual elitism. God works in everything we do when we are submissive to Him. So one who truly loves and seeks God need not be consciously discerning the Spirit's work to receive the benefits of it. While we do believe that the Spirit does speak to us discernibly and that through practice we can grow in our ability to hear Him, we cannot absolutize this for everyone at all times. Spiritual classics through the centuries attest, and common experience affirms, that most people go through seasons when sometimes God speaks clearly and sometimes He is silent. But even when He is silent, He is always working. While a great number of believers receive relatively rare experiences of the Spirit in which they are absolutely certain of His speaking, most are not so certain most of the time. Many quite spiritually mature believers may never be certain of His speaking, whether because they are cautious or because of the way God chooses to relate to them. We have to remember that it is God who chooses how He relates to each of us, according to what is best for us, so one way is not better than another. Our disposition of heart is what matters. We also want to affirm, though, that those who attend to the reality of God at work in all things, however He relates to them, experience a dimension of the spiritual life that others do not. And we want to encourage those who have never been open to the idea that God speaks to them directly to explore this possibility.

What we are striving for in understanding the work of the Spirit is balance. We are attempting to avoid both extremes: on the one hand, those skeptical persons who believe that the Spirit never speaks directly and only works in natural human processes, and on the other, those unreasoning persons who claim every idea and feeling as a direct revelation of the Spirit. We have put forth our understanding of pertinent Scripture passages, but it must be said that other readings are both possible and reasonable, or they would not have survived this long. They survive rather tenaciously because they best account for the personality and the experience of individuals and communities.

We are convinced, though, that to avoid a parochial theology that fits only the faith experience of our own communities, we need to account for the spiritual life of the whole church. It is definitely true that much fraud and abuse occur in the more charismatic spiritualities. But unless we are prepared to say that *every* single experience of tongues or prophecy or word from the Lord is faked, socially taught, or demonically inspired, we must read Scripture and formulate theology in such a way that accounts for them. (This is one reason why we have difficulty believing that any of the gifts have ceased, even though they may not be practiced in our communities.)

It is also true that less charismatic spiritualities are often powerless and lifeless (just as many, more charismatic ones are really weak below the surface). Nevertheless, unless we are prepared to say that the spiritual lives of less charismatic people are categorically less deep, authentic in experience, and transforming of individuals and the world, we must read Scripture and formulate our theology in such a way that fully respects their spirituality as God-designed and more than just a plateau on the way to some higher plane.

It will help the church tremendously when we realize that just as God created different personality types, He also created different spirituality types (and there is probably a high correlation between the two). There is no room for spiritual arrogance.

So What?

Since the Spirit continues to speak as revealer and interpreter, we find implications here for the form of church service we have practiced in most of our churches—where one person, almost always a man, does most of the speaking. Should there not be collective exhortation and teaching of one another by many exercising gifts of prophecy, teaching, message of wisdom, discernment, and so on?[58] Given all of our translations, interpretative helps, institutions, and collective spiritual maturity, are there not more people capable of expressing truth under the guidance of the Spirit? Again, community is a matter we will discuss in a subsequent chapter.

Similarly, our reading of Scripture should take on a new vitality as we realize the potential for hearing God's voice anew, of discovering the deeper or essential meaning. We wait expectantly for Him to reveal truth and understanding, and to confirm the message of the Spirit to our spirits. The Old Testament opens up as never before.

In our institutions we embark on a bold adventure—contemplative exegesis. While we continue to do grammatical-historical exegesis, we do more. We directly involve listening to the Spirit in our method; we practice community interpretation; we embrace the role of obedience to truth as a prerequisite to further learning.[59] We couple doing exegesis with learning how to be disciples in process of spiritual formation. We encourage the nurturing of spiritual gifts, particularly that of prophecy.

But how do we open the door to this more contemplative approach? Have we not been taught that spirituality is primarily cognitive maturity, learning more and more truth? How can my heart—my mind, my emotions and my will—also be enlarged to think, love, and do as God does? Clearly, we must change our concept of spirituality. That's what our next chapter is all about.

Learning by Living

Paul's letter had hit home. There was repentance, confession, and forgiveness. Still Paul had singled out two women to settle their disputes.

"Euodia, we have been deacons in this church for three years and it seems that we have been at odds most of this time. Perhaps we could talk about it and figure out why."

"Yes, I have been bothered by this too. Syntyche, it seems that the thing we usually argue about is how to know reality in our Christian experience. I mean, I give myself to careful study of Scripture, using the rules of Jewish rabbis and the apostles, and you just pray, meditate, and seek the Spirit's interpretation. I think I am seeking the Spirit's guidance also by my approach."

"I don't want to downplay the importance of these skills, but I wonder if sometimes the quiet voice of the Spirit isn't heard through overconcentration on all this work. Remember the example of Mary and Martha?"

"But I was one of the first women to be instructed this way," Euodia replied defensively. "Paul and Timothy went to great lengths to teach me Hebrew and I read all the doctrine I can. Am I to throw this all out? Besides, what really bothers me is all your hair-brained ideas that come, you claim, by special revelation—'words taught by the Holy Spirit,' you say. Well, I just can't buy it. If you're claiming special revelation, who can argue with you? Can't you see what it does? It makes you look so spiritual and the rest of us so...so natural and unspiritual. I'm glad that Paul has put you and your kind in your place by limiting prophesying and tongues in our worship. We will still have plenty enough of this ebullience, this enthusiasm of the Spirit and all the attending ferment and confusion!"

"Well, now! What spirit is leading you to talk like this?" Syntyche asked in some amusement.

"Oh, I'm just expressing my frustration. I know that in the end we are all after the same thing."

"What are you referring to?"

"Demonstrating that the power of God can transform anyone, making him a citizen of heaven," Euodia offered, "advancing the Kingdom by experiencing its coming in our own lives and by bringing others into relationship with Christ."

"Yes!" Syntyche affirmed. "Remember how the gospel did this for our first convert, the jailer and all his house?"

"Uh huh, what a wonderful event that was! To be saved and become united with Christ—I believe that's how Paul puts it—is life changing."

"But that's just the beginning, Euodia. I am concerned that sometimes our brothers think of salvation as static, as though it were only a past event. Our union with Christ is the basis for our continuing to grow in oneness with God. As we become one with God we become like Him in His character.

"Paul told us to follow his example," she continued, "and the goal of all his life is to know Christ—to know a person, not doctrine. Doctrine is important, but it only provides the structure. The relationship is the real thing. This is what delights Him and us, since He created us so that we are happiest when we truly know Him. Please, dear friend, remember that all your learning is a means to an end and not an end in itself."

"Yes, I know this," Euodia responded. "We learn more deeply what Scripture is all about by living it. This process of sanctification in each of us is a smaller picture of the cosmic war of God's Kingdom overcoming the evil one. And I'm sure that we understand Scripture better the more we know the One who wrote it. But I still think that the skills I have learned play an important part."

"I'm sure they do too, Euodia, and that's something you can help me with. But I think it's just as important to practice the other spiritual disciplines that Jesus did. There are many ways that we can participate in God's work in our lives through practicing love and truth."

"Yes, I think that this is a life-long growing process. Even just now we have experienced some of God's Kingdom coming in our relationship. So maybe this struggle we have had understanding each other will help us in some measure to understand God better and His Word."

If we want to understand Scripture, we need to grow in knowing the Author. And as we experience the coming of the Kingdom in our own lives, we will understand better what Scripture is all about. To this end we outline a model of spirituality based upon the paradigm of reality, which weds the objective truths of our faith with our subjective experience of them.

Chapter Seven

Spirituality

How Do We Get to
Know the Author?

"That I may know Christ"

(Philippians 3:10).

In at least one way, this is the most important chapter of our book. For to be able to interpret Scripture, we must be spiritual interpreters. If we would be good exegetes, we must be good. We need to know the Author of Scripture and be able to hear His voice. He must be more than a passing acquaintance.

A strictly grammatical-historical approach to reading Scripture champions getting to know all we can about the human author—his background, situation in life, cultural context, ideas, and attitudes. God is the primary Author of Scripture. He is more knowable than any human author. He has revealed Himself in Scripture, creation, and history, but the way we really come to know God is by integrating the knowledge from these sources into our personal relationship with Him. Only then can we learn His heart, character, attitudes, purposes. So to understand Scripture, we need to know intimately God the Author.

Our purpose here is to present a model of spirituality, based on the Kingdom center and the paradigm, which will help us to overcome sin and grow to know God and become like Him.

TRUTH IS A PERSON

Sometimes we act as if truth is something to be mastered, as though we can write down bits of truth on flash cards and memorize them when we have nothing better to do—like when we are sitting in a traffic jam. And this is true in part. Truth is propositional. It can be expressed in statements for others to hear or to read and understand. Scripture verses and biblical doctrines are statements of truth.

We know instinctively, though, that truth is more than this. Our faith rests not merely in a collection of beliefs. There must be something more solid, more permanent behind these statements of truth. (We are talking about truths rather than facts. By *truths*, we mean the meaningful things of life. *Facts* have to do with things such as how many days are left until Christmas—a certain number may be true or false, but this is not a truth by our definition.) Truth is not just what we know, but it determines what we do. There must be truth behind these truths. Truth has something to do with what is good and bad, right and wrong. Truth is moral as well as propositional, serving as the basis for our ethical decisions.

But what makes truth true? What makes certain things right or wrong? Is the moral realm governed by some absolute law that exists in and of itself? No, a Person stands behind this truth. Truth is ultimately *Personal* because God Himself embodies His truth.[1] Our faith rests in a Person. If, at rock bottom reality, truth is a Person, then we must get to know this Person in order to really understand truth. We are missing something if we are merely memorizing Bible verses or theological doctrines. We can't master truth until truth masters *us*.

This begins to explain why we have put a model of spirituality in a book on hermeneutics. There are three reasons.

First, if we are searching for the divine Author's meaning in Scripture, it helps greatly to get to know Him who is truth. We attempted to demonstrate in the last chapter that the Spirit's teaching ministry is ongoing. He speaks not only through Scripture, but immediately, Spirit to spirit. This means that we need to build a relationship with Him so that we can know Him and become more like Him. We need to think, feel, and will as He does in order to understand things from His perspective. This is what it means for truth to master us. So, if we are going to interpret the Bible in partnership with the Exegete, we are necessarily talking about spiritual formation, about growing in holiness and in Christ's likeness. Understanding this process will help us to incorporate our spiritual life and its exercises into the life-long process of understanding Scripture. Interpretation is primarily the task of disciples, not academics.

Second, growing in Christ is part of the actualization of God's Kingdom. Every day the Spirit battles within us against sin, a microcosm of the raging war between the Kingdom of God and the dark powers of the universe. Victory within is slowly won as we grow in relationship with our God. As the Kingdom is actualized *in* us, God is able to work *through* us, in our relationships with others, to bring others into His Kingdom and help them grow in relationship with Him, and in this way, to actualize His Kingdom rule on earth. When we pray, "Your Kingdom come; Your will be done," we must first mean, "Your Kingdom come in me; please help me to do Your will." Then, through personal experience, we understand better this Kingdom mission that Scripture is all about.

Third, every method of interpretation assumes a model of spirituality and flows from it. We believe we have put together a model that works better than those which Protestant Christians have historically used[2] and contributes to our hermeneutical approach. Because of how our model naturally flows from the paradigm, it ties together the biblical truth for our spiritual life and our experience of that truth, capturing both the head and the heart of our faith. It picks up the twin themes of love and truth and explains why the spiritual disciplines actually work in help-ing us to know God, become more like Him, and serve His Kingdom mission. It does this by describing more carefully what exactly is our spiritual problem and what is the goal of spiritual growth, and by showing how the spiritual disci-plines logically relate to the problem and the goal. The hope is that if we understand all this better, we will be encouraged enough to believe that it can actually work so that we will be inspired to pursue God with all of our hearts.

THE PROBLEM: OUR SIN

Certainly we all recognize the presence of evil. Any model of spirituality must deal with the sin which hinders our knowledge of God and His truth, and which corrupted our original sinlessness.

Union

God created humankind, man and woman, as His image on the earth. It is God's preeminent purpose to actualize all that He is and all that He says is true in His creation. So we were created, our glory being to reflect the glory of God. God delights in His glory. His glory is most visibly manifest when we (and every aspect of creation) conforms to and reflects who He is, thus radiating His glory by representing His nature as His image. Ultimately this is how God is glo-rified in all things.

As man and woman in the Garden, we were one with God. Our entire being, our thoughts, emotions, and will, were wholly aligned with Him. We glorified Him as we manifested His nature, being in union with Him. We were to join His purpose of bringing an end to the sin which had infected the universe...until we sinned.

While God is glorified also in the judgment of sin, we are able to glorify God willingly only by being in union with Him. Now because we have sinned we are no longer in union with God. We do not think His thoughts, feel His emotions, will His will. To the extent that we do not, we do not reflect His nature, and we do not glorify Him. And deep inside our hearts we long to be one with God again, though we may not know it, because it is this for which we were created. Now we are faced with the problem of how to regain this union with God. To do this we need to understand the nature of sin within us that destroys it.

Pride

The essence of sin is pride. The essence of pride is what we are going to call *self-definition*.[3] This urge to self-definition involves an affective (emotional) element of self-love. It is a disposition of spirit which says, "I love myself and I will define for myself who I am." It is an attitude that causes us to refuse to accept whatever is true, especially about ourselves. In this way pride violates both love and truth. We create in our minds an image of who we are or who we wish to be, and then we set out to convince ourselves and everyone else that we truly are what we claim to be.

Now, this pride is wrong in violating love and truth, but not as love and truth *per se*. Since God Himself is love and truth, pride at its core offends the character of God and usurps His place. Satan tempted Eve to eat the fruit, forbidden by God, with the promise, "You will be like God, knowing good and evil." Eve desired to be like God and ate the forbidden fruit to actualize her *self-image*.[4] Satan, too, in the epitome of pride, had defined himself as equal to God and set out to usurp His place: "I will be like the Most High" (Isaiah 14:14). Humanity is deserving of God's wrath because we suppress the truth in unrighteousness (Romans 1:18). We define ourselves as wise. This causes us to refuse to acknowledge God for who He is, to seek independence from God, and to pursue what we think is the good life. This is manifest in every sort of sin, including blatant idolatry (1:19-32). Sin is idolatry, and the idol is self-image, who we have defined ourselves to be. We then redefine God, truth, sin, and righteousness to serve our self-image. Created by God in His image to worship Him, in pride "man creates God in his own image. It is his own self that he falls down and worships."[5]

Interestingly, this pride can be manifest in two ways: arrogance and insecurity.[6] When we are arrogant, we are seeking glory for whoever we have defined ourselves to be. If we have defined ourselves as capable, we make known our abilities and accomplishments to receive affirmation of our self-image. If we have defined ourselves as giving and kind, we look for opportunities to be praised for it. Now, we may very well be these things in truth. Behind arrogance, though, is the belief that our being these things is due to our own effort. We take the glory to ourselves.

Often, though, we act arrogantly to guard our self-image when there is some threat to unmask that we may not be who we have decided we are. Deep down inside, arrogant people are insecure. They are afraid to find out they are not who they think they are, or that someone else is better than they are in whatever way they value. This is often manifest in jealousy or a critical spirit. They are guarding the image of themselves which they have erected and in which they have placed their identity, their basis for self-valuation.[7]

Many people, though, do not display arrogance, but insecurity, the second way that pride is manifest. They openly display the fear that they may not be who they think they are. They act weak and self-debasing in order to receive what they are really seeking—affirmation of their self-image. They may enter relationships in which they are quite dependent in order to gain from the other person the affirmation they desire. It may very well be that behind co-dependency (and even suicide attempts) is pride.[8] We will use anything that works for the purposes of pride, including insecurity.

Humility

If sin is what keeps us from God, then holiness is what we want to pursue in order to grow closer to God. The essence of sin is pride. The opposite of pride is humility. Humility, defined in a particular way, is the core of holiness.

The essence of humility is embracing truth. Humility is a disposition of spirit which loves and accepts truth. "Put in simple terms, humility means to live as close to the truth as possible: the truth about ourselves, the truth about others, the truth about the world in which we live."[9] When some truth comes along which threatens self-image, humility embraces it, and that part of self-image is destroyed. This is important: it is not *self* that is destroyed, but *self-image*. As self-image is torn down, *identity* is established. This identity is based on truth. As we embrace truth, we receive our true self. Our false self and love of it are put to death. In any particular where self and truth conflict and we choose truth, love of self is replaced by love of truth. "He is truly meek [humble] who truly knows and is conscious of himself as he actually is."[10]

This process is what the Bible calls repentance. Its effects are most easily pictured in the basic issue of sin and salvation. When we embrace the truths of our sin and of God and His salvation in response to the gospel, our old person dies and we become new creatures in Jesus Christ. This is the beginning of our self-image being destroyed (in the death of the old person) and our identity being established (in the creation of the new person). This means that *our fundamental identity is who we are in Christ*. This identity is a legitimate source of strength and confidence and appreciation because it is based on truth. As we continue to embrace truth, we grow in our identity in Christ.

Notice that this definition is not what is commonly understood as humility. Humility is usually thought of as some sort of self-deprecation, often manifest in polite modesty. After all, are we not, in humility of mind, to "consider others better than [ourselves]" (Philippians 2:3)? Perhaps this exhortation is better rendered "let each of you regard one another as more important than himself" (NASB). This fits better with what immediately follows: "Do not merely look out for your own personal interests, but also for the interests of others" (2:4). This attending to others, giving ourselves in service, was perfectly exemplified in the humility of Christ (2:5-11). He did not believe others to be better than Himself as a person, for that would have been a lie. But He did consider others better, or more important, than Himself in that He, who was very God, took on our nature and gave Himself in ultimate service to die for us. It is only the one who knows his identity who has strength to attend to the reality of others and truly serve them. "Jesus knew that the Father had put all things under his power, and that he had come from God and was returning to God, so he got up from the meal, took off his outer clothing, and wrapped a towel around his waist" and proceeded to wash the disciples' feet (John 13:3-4). The one who is proud is continually defending herself, hiding in relationships, claiming her rights, seeking honor for herself to serve her self-image. To the extent that we know the whole truth about ourselves, we are free to love and serve others, even to death, as did Jesus.

We need to tell the whole truth about ourselves. Paul states elsewhere, "I say to every one of you: Do not think of yourself more highly than you ought, but rather think of yourself with sober judgment" (Romans 12:3). Self-deprecation that is contrary to truth is not required, and indeed can be sinful.[11] This helps us understand the answer to a question that most of us ask at one time or another. Have you ever wondered why God can hate pride so vehemently and demand our humility, and at the same time command us to worship and praise Him? On the surface He seems proud and egotistical.

But since humility embraces truth, God Himself is the ultimate example of humility. He is everything He claims to be. He is everything true and beautiful and good and holy. For Him to proclaim otherwise would be to lie. For God to engage in polite modesty would be an abomination. When we forsake our pride and its accompanying resentment that we are who we are, and instead we come to see God for who He truly is, we joyfully, gladly praise Him and delight in who He is. We have finally begun worshipping the One who is truly praiseworthy. For God to create us in any other image would have been to make us less than we are. For God to call us to love and worship and delight in anyone other than Him would be to cause us gravest harm. God embraces the truth of who He is. It just so happens that He is everything praiseworthy! Thus God's humility, especially manifest in Jesus Christ, is our model. God's call, indeed His demand, for our humility is the call to be like God Himself.

Humility requires us to tell the truth about ourselves. This includes unpleasant as well as pleasant truths. We are sinners. But we are also glorious because God in His grace has made us so. He created us in His image and is recreating us in the image of His Son, and there is no image higher, more excellent, more glorious. And He has given us gifts, abilities, and talents so that we may have the joy of serving Him. To acknowledge these is not pride, but freedom to use them for Him. We honor God when we embrace all the truth about ourselves. And as we do, our pride and self-image are destroyed while humility and our identity are established.

Truth

To embrace the truth, we need to know what it is and where to find it. God embodies truth. He is Truth. We cannot love and pursue truth without loving and pursuing God. Otherwise, the truth we pursue is not truth, but what we have decided is truth. Nor can we ostensibly pursue God in order to get truth. We will not get it, for we are not loving God; instead, we are using God to actualize our image of ourselves as one who pursues and conforms to truth. How noble pride can appear! We must love God in order to pursue truth. It is as we pursue knowledge and love of God that we come to understand truth. We see God for who He is, and in reflection, who then we truly are. And it is as we get our self-images out of the way that we are able to see God more clearly.

This means that the truth of self and the truth of God facilitate each other. Self-knowledge and knowledge of God are interdependent. Beholding God is the key to the destruction of sin. "We, who with unveiled faces all reflect the Lord's glory, are being transformed into his likeness with ever-increasing glory" (2 Corinthians 3:18). This is sometimes a difficult and painful process. But we remain under

His knowing, yet loving gaze because we trust Him that He works for our highest good. Too often we venture only to peek at the mirror through our fingers.

Love

This pursuit of God and His truth is not merely an intellectual enterprise. Humility is embracing the truth, a disposition of spirit that loves and accepts truth. Conversely, pride is not an apathetic self-definition caused by ignorance, but involves self-love. To be true humility, seeking the truth must involve the affections of the heart.

It is possible to apprehend some measure of truth and not be humble. The question is one of the disposition of the heart. Does the heart desire to obey the truth the mind sees? To be apathetic or hostile toward the truth the mind has received is to have mere "speculative knowledge," as Jonathan Edwards calls it. Spiritual understanding, on the other hand, sees the beauty of the truth the mind has comprehended and has an inclination toward it or will for it. "A clear distinction [cannot] be made between the two faculties of understanding and will as acting distinctly and separately."[12] There is no neutral stance toward truth. Upon receiving truth, we accept it; or if we do not accept it, we have rejected it. Ultimately, our mind and affections and will cannot be separated. Our whole being is oriented either toward or away from the truth. Thus true humility involves the affections of the heart.

The source of this bent toward truth in humility is love for God. "Love the Lord your God with all your heart and with all your soul and with all your strength. These commandments that I give you today are to be upon your hearts" (Deuteronomy 6:5-6). Thus in Torah, immediately following the declaration of who is their God, comes this command to love Him in response. To fear the Lord is to love Him, and to love Him is to fear Him. This fear is not the hopeless terror of the demons who know about Him but do not love Him. This fear is the loving awe and reverence for the Almighty God who, amazingly enough, loves us first—and for our good! There are many commands to fear

God, all entailing the concept of obedience. Even more numerous are the commands to love God, with that love almost being defined as obedience to His commands (11:1, 13, 22, 30:6, 16, 20). To fear God is to love Him. And this love is love in action—obedience.

All three concepts of love, fear, and obedience are contained in one verse: "What does the Lord your God ask of you, but to fear the Lord your God, to walk in all his ways, to love him, to serve the Lord your God with all your heart and with all your soul, and to observe the Lord's commands and decrees that I am giving you today for your own good?" (Deuteronomy 10:12-13). And Jesus said, "If you love me, you will obey what I command" (John 14:15). "The one who says, 'I know him,' but does not do what he commands is a liar, and the truth is not in him; but if anyone obeys his word, God's love is truly made complete in him" (1 John 2:4-5). The one who loves God embraces His truth and obeys it.

The two essential characteristics that mark out the Christian are love and humility. "No graces are more counterfeited than love and humility. For these are the virtues where the beauty of a true Christian is seen most clearly."[13] "If you want to be like [Christ], then have meekness and charity."[14] The two are necessarily related. We cannot love the truth we cannot see, and so we must have humility before we can have love. "According to the measure of your meekness or humility shall you have charitable love."[15] Yet, unless for love of God we are inclined toward the truth we see, we do not have humility. Each is required for the other; each facilitates the other. Both are perfectly manifest in Jesus Christ, who is our model both for humility (John 13; Philippians 2) and love (1 John 3:16).

God Is Love and Truth

We must never forget that love and truth are first and foremost Personal, not only ethical and propositional. "God is love" (1 John 4:11). Jesus said, "I am the truth" (John 14:6). The verity of ethics and truth statements is derivative, not absolute. They are only true because they come from God, flow forth from and reflect His nature. It is impossible to have real understanding of love and truth in the ultimate sense apart from an intimate knowledge of God. Many try, by a variety of philosophies and revolutionary movements for sociological and personal development, to live in love and truth apart from God. This is pride.

Christians are especially susceptible to the sin of pursuing love and truth for the sake of pride. The more we grow in the knowledge of God and His truth, the more likely we are to define ourselves as humble, truthful, and loving—everything He wants us to be. But there is only one baby step between pursuing love and truth in every Christian way and attempting to use God to fulfill our self-images for the sake of our pride. We end up pursuing sanctification for the purpose of pride rather than pursuing God for love of Him. What is designed to be a living, transforming relationship is reduced to some legalistic ethical code.

In summary, for us to be good interpreters of Scripture we need to deal with our problem of sin. The basis of all sin is pride. The essence of pride is self-definition. This self-definition erects an image of self in opposition to truth. It hates and fears truth, for it destroys self-image, the product of self-definition. In our sin we put ourselves in the place of God, defining for ourselves who we are, and redefining God and everything else to suit our purposes. Because of our sin, we are no longer in union with God. We think our thoughts, not His, love our self-image, not Him and His truth, desire our will, not the will of God. Thus, created to glorify God by manifesting His nature, we instead glorify ourselves. We worship whom we serve. We worship ourselves as we do every evil and seemingly good thing to serve our self-image. Sin is this: we worship an image, the idol of self, and to this self-image we willingly sacrifice anything on the altar of pride.

THE PREMISE: UNION WITH CHRIST

If sin is the destroyer of union with God, then the Destroyer of sin must be the restorer of that union. God's victory secures a new union. Our model of spirituality is bankrupt if Jesus Christ is not at its center. It is our union with the incarnate Christ that provides, among other things, the basis for our hearing him.

Death Do Us Part

Sin separates us from God in two ways. Objectively, sin separates us from being in relationship with God at all. Though we exist, we are dead. Separation from God is death. Because God is holy, He cannot be united with anything that is sinful. Though we unwittingly follow His sovereign rule, we are outcasts of His blessed Kingdom. Subjectively, it makes us so that we are not like God in His holiness. Because we are not in relationship with Him, we cannot image Him on the earth to bring Him glory. We are rebels, proud enemies of His Kingdom, seeking glory for ourselves. In our sin we are utterly lost and helpless to make up for our sin and reconcile ourselves to God. We are resentful and jealous of God, unable to love Him or to desire to know Him. In His love God had mercy on us, and He Himself provided a solution to our separation from Him.

He gave His Son as a sacrifice to pay the penalty of death for our sin. We sinned. He died. God incarnate died in our place. This is the one thing that we must grasp by faith in order to receive life from Him. "For what I received I passed on to you as of first importance: that Christ died for our sins according to the Scriptures, that he was buried, that he was raised on the third day according to the Scriptures" (1 Corinthians 15:3-4).

United with Christ

If we wish to be united with God, we must embrace the truth. The most fundamental truth we must embrace is who we are in relation to God. God is God and we are not. In our sin we define ourselves as God. This is high treason, and we are sentenced to die.[16] But in His most amazing grace, God desires relationship with us and offers the gift of life. When we finally submit to all of this as true and "believe in him who justifies the ungodly" (Romans 4:5), He makes us one with Christ. In this act of faith (which is itself God's gift to us), we have taken the first step in destroying self-image and building identity in Christ.

Everything that God gives us, He gives us *in Christ*, a phrase so often repeated in the New Testament. It is in Christ that we have our entire salvation, from election through glorification, from beginning to completion. When God makes us one with Christ, He makes His history to be our history. To understand this better, let's take a quick look at each important part of the mystery of being one with Christ.

1. Our entire salvation, including growth in our spiritual life, originates in the eternal *election* of God. He chose us for salvation, apart from anything we would do, by His own free will. "Praise be to the God and Father of our Lord Jesus Christ, who has blessed us in the heavenly realms with every spiritual blessing in Christ; for he chose us in him before the creation of the world to be holy and blameless in his sight" (Ephesians 1:3-4). Though He chose us, He chose us *in Christ*. He never thought of us for our salvation apart from our union with Christ. And the purpose for which He chose us is that we should be holy and blameless before Him. Then we image Him and advance His Kingdom.

2. God united us with Christ in His death, burial, and resurrection (Romans 6:3-4), and in doing this, gave us *justification* and *sanctification*.[17] Jesus' death for sin becomes our death, so we no longer have to die for our own sin. Jesus' sinless life becomes our life, His righteousness our righteousness (5:12-21). God now sees us in Christ, and our criminal record is wiped clean (Colossians 2:14). In this union with Christ in His death, we are justified before God—declared "not guilty." We no longer carry the guilt of our sin and its penalty of death (6:23). Because He has imputed to us Christ's righteousness, we are sanctified—declared holy and set apart for Him. "But you were washed, you were sanctified, you were justified in the name of the Lord Jesus Christ and by the Spirit of our God" (1 Corinthians 6:11; see also 1:2).

3. God "has rescued us from the dominion of darkness and brought us into the kingdom of the Son he loves"

(Colossians 1:13). In doing so, He granted us *adoption* as His children. He has brought us into His Kingdom, into relationship with Him. God reconciled us to Himself. We who were enemies are now His friends. We now have a new family identity. We were once in Adam and now we are in Christ. God has given us the right to be called children of God.

4. God has united us with Christ, not only in His death, but also in His resurrection. He has given us life and made us into new persons in *regeneration*. "If anyone is in Christ, he is a new creation" (2 Corinthians 5:17). "Do not lie to each other, since you have taken off your old self with its practices, and have put on the new self, which is being renewed in knowledge in the image of its Creator" (Colossians 3:9-10). Our old self (who we were in Adam) is entirely done away with. We have put on the new self (who we are in Christ). From conversion on we have a single, new nature.[18] Our adoption as children and our transfer from Adam to Christ is not some sort of legal fiction, written down in a record book but never made real. He has made it real by coming to dwell in us through the Spirit. Not only are we in Christ, but He is in us. We have received "the Spirit of adoption as sons" (Romans 8:15; cf. Galatians 4:5), and by Him we are also born again (John 3:5-8), making us children by birth as well as by adoption.

5. Finally, our entire salvation, clear through *glorification*, is guaranteed, for it is already effectively accomplished in Christ (8:29-30). We will be glorified with Christ: "When Christ, who is your life, appears, then you also will appear with him in glory" (Colossians 3:4; notice that this promised glorification, along with our death and new life in Him, v. 3, is the basis for growing in holiness, v. 5: "Put to death, therefore...."). Creation longs for and eagerly awaits the revealing of the children of God in glory (Romans 8:18-19). In receiving a spirit of adoption as children of God, we are heirs with Christ, and as such will be glorified with Him (vv. 15-17). Because of His love for us, even now God has seated us with Christ in the heavenly places (Ephesians 2:4-6).

The Nature of This Union

We know that God has made us one with Christ. We know that means that His history is ours, including His life, death, and resurrection. But in what sense exactly are we one? What is the nature of our union with Christ?

First, it is *spiritual*. Primarily this means that the bond of our union with Christ is the Holy Spirit. So close is the identity of the Holy Spirit with Christ that He is called the Spirit of Christ (Romans 8:9-11).[19] The Holy Spirit mediates the presence of Christ in us. This union is also spiritual in that it is characterized by spirit. Our union with Christ is a real union. God has not just declared us one and left it at that; He has made us really one. It is not merely a feeling of oneness that comes from shared goals and affection. It is certainly not a physical union. It is a union of Christ's Spirit and the spirit of His people, such that He dwells in us and we in Him, a union effected by the Holy Spirit.

Second, it is *mystical*. Our union with Christ is mystical in that it is a mystery (Ephesians 5:32). It is something that was once a secret, hidden in the mind of God, and has now been revealed in His Word. Paul writes of "the glorious riches of this mystery among the Gentiles, which is Christ in you, the hope of glory," a mystery once hidden but now made known to his saints (Colossians 1:26, 27). It is also mystical in the usual sense of the mystical life of faith. "The life of faith is one of living union and communion with the exalted and ever-present Redeemer....The life of faith is the life of love, and the life of love is the life of fellowship, or mystic communion with him who ever lives to make intercession for his people and who can be touched with the feeling of our infirmities."[20] It is a life of reciprocal love. "Though you have not seen him, you love him, and even though you do not see him now, you believe in him and are filled with an inexpressible and glorious joy" (1 Peter 1:8).

And last, it is *corporate*. We are not united with Christ just as individuals, but as a community. We were chosen in Him before the foundation of the world (Ephesians 1:4). Just as we were not thought of as individuals apart from Christ for salvation, neither were we thought of apart from each other. Though we are all saved at differing times in history, we were all elect in eternity. When our election is actualized in our personal history as union with Christ, we are made one with each other: "We were all baptized by one Spirit into one body," and corporately we are Christ's Body (1 Corinthians 12:13, 27), the whole Church (Colossians 1:18; 2:19; 3:11-15). Jesus prayed for us to be one as He and the Father were one, and that He and the Father and we might all be mutually indwelling (John 17:19-23; note that this is all related to our sanctification in the truth). Does it not make sense that if we each are one with Christ that we are also one with each other?[21] He desires for Himself a people, and one day He and His people will celebrate their union with Him as His bride in the marriage supper of the Lamb (Revelation 19:7-9).

This In-between Time

Our entire salvation has been accomplished in Christ from the foundation of the world, but for now we seem far from glorified! How does all this relate to our lives now? Do we keep on living in the same way as always, until someday we die and are made perfect in heaven? "By no means! We died to sin; how can we live in it any longer?" (Romans 6:1-2) Since we have died with Christ, we have died to sin. "The death he died, he died to sin once for all" (6:10), and so we too are dead to sin. "Our old self was crucified with him so that the body of sin might be rendered powerless, that we should no longer be slaves to sin" (Romans 6:6).

We also have been resurrected with Christ so that "we too may live a new life" (Romans 6:4). Christ died to sin, but He lives again, and "the life he lives, he lives to God. In the same way, count yourselves dead to sin, but alive to God in Christ Jesus" (6:10-11). The life we live outwardly is to be consistent with the new life within us. By nature we now love what God loves and think His thoughts after Him so that we do as He wills. We walk in a manner worthy of our calling (Ephesians 4:1).

How then is sin accounted for? If it is according to our nature now to do right, why do we do wrong? This new

172 • BEYOND THE OBVIOUS

nature is still affected by sin. "The new self described in the New Testament...is genuinely new, though not yet totally new."[22] We no longer have a sin nature, but we do have a sinful nature. This sinful new nature is in the process of becoming like Christ; as Paul indicates, we "have put on the new self, which is being renewed in knowledge in the image of its Creator" (Colossians 3:10). If the new nature were totally new, why would Paul have to speak of it being renewed?

But we can take heart in this because God has provided everything we need for life and godliness (2 Peter 1:3). Since He has given us a new nature, we are not only free from the penalty of sin, but also the power of sin. "He who has died [with Christ] is freed from sin" (Romans 6:7). We are justified through our union in His death, but we are saved by our union in His life: "For if while we were enemies, we were reconciled to God through the death of his Son, much more, having been reconciled, we shall be saved by his life" (5:10). The Spirit of life within us empowers us to live in holiness (cf. 8:2).

THE PROMISE: HIS HOLY SPIRIT

The whole promise of God for growing spiritually may be summed up in this: God has given us His Holy Spirit. "In him, you also, after listening to the message of truth, the gospel of your salvation having also believed, you were sealed in him with the Holy Spirit of promise" (Ephesians 1:13). Crucial to our model of spirituality is the Holy Spirit. After all, this is a model of *spirituality*. Dare we neglect Him when we try to interpret Scripture—the very documents He inspired? We sense the need to give renewed prominence to Him.

The Spirit is our Helper. He empowers us in several crucial things, and apart from Him the spiritual life is impossible.

Mutual Indwelling

It is an astounding truth, incomprehensible in its implications for our lives: God dwells in us and we in Him. This mutual indwelling is not just a mind game. Whatever is true for us is meant to be experienced by us.

Jesus very clearly taught us about this. On the night before His crucifixion, at the Last Supper, Jesus taught His disciples for the last time (called the Last Discourse, found in John 14-17). Near the beginning, Jesus promised, "On that day you will realize that I am in my Father, and you are in me, and that I am in you" (John 14:20). This idea of vibrant, intimate, mutual indwelling is woven throughout His whole discourse. He ended with His well-known High Priestly Prayer, praying "that all of them may be one, Father, just as you are in me and I am in you...I in them and you in me" (17:21, 23). If anybody's prayer is going to be answered, it's Jesus'.

Jesus said that "in that day" His disciples would know that they were in Him and He in them. To what day is He referring? The day that the Helper was to come: "I will ask the Father, and he will give you another Counselor, the Spirit of truth, to be with you forever....you know him, for he lives with you and will be in you" (14:16-17). This is the Holy Spirit (v. 16), whose coming is another crucial element woven throughout the discourse. The Spirit's coming to be in us is the indwelling of Christ in us. And it is through the Spirit that we dwell in Christ (1 Corinthians 12:13, 27).

The Holy Spirit indwells every believer: "If anyone does not have the Spirit of Christ, he does not belong to him" (Romans 8:9). What, then, is the meaning of Christ's command, "Abide in me" (John 15:4)? The answer is found in our understanding of God's purpose. What He says is "true in heaven" for us (essential reality), He wants us to make true in our lives on earth (existential reality).[23] Jesus said that He abides in us (again, through the Spirit) and we in Him, so He commands, "Abide in me." We do dwell in Him, therefore we are to make this true in our experience and abide in Him. We will often experience this as warm intimacy, love, peace, and joy (15:9-10; 16:20-22). These things delight God as much as they delight us. He wants love and worship from our hearts.

Knowing God

Our older brother Moses is an example for us of one who had closest intimacy with God. "The Lord would speak to Moses face to face, as a man speaks to his friend" (Exodus 33:11). This reminds us of Jesus' words: "I no longer call you servants because a servant does not know his master's business. Instead, I have called you friends, for everything that I learned from my Father I have made known to you" (John 15:15). And "the Counselor, the Holy Spirit, whom the Father will send in my name, will teach you all things and will remind you of everything I have said to you" (14:26). These words are not for Jesus' apostles only. Moses prophesied this coming of the Spirit. God had taken of the Spirit who was upon Moses and placed Him upon the seventy men who were to help him, and when they prophesied one time, Joshua was jealous for Moses. Moses responded, "I wish that all the Lord's people were prophets, and that the Lord would put his Spirit on them!" (Numbers 11:29). This is exactly what God promised in the coming of the Spirit in the New Covenant (Joel 2:28-29; Jeremiah 31:31-34; Ezekiel 36:26-27, 37:14), the age in which we now live. So the intimacy which Moses had with God, speaking with Him face to face, is ours through the Spirit.[24] The Holy Spirit is the One through whom we can know God directly, "The Spirit himself testifies with our spirit that we are God's children" (Romans 8:16).

Obeying God

As we have already seen, love and fear of God are necessarily manifest in obedience. It is the Spirit who enables this obedience. God has promised that by His Spirit we may keep from sinning. Paul is very clear on this, "Live by the Spirit, and you will not gratify the desires of your sinful nature" (Galatians 5:16). It is by the Spirit that we put to death the deeds of the body (Romans 8:13). God will not allow us to be tempted beyond what we are able, but will provide the way of escape (1 Corinthians 10:13).

This means that whenever we are presented with a conscious choice to sin, by His Spirit we can choose to obey.

We as believers, by the Spirit, can and should choose never to sin. Then, as we are transformed by the Spirit within to be more like Christ, our unconscious, spontaneous responses to trials and temptations are holy and pleasing to God. When we disobey, we grieve the Spirit, and He is not able to work. We do not have to do anything to get Him to work in us; it is His desire to do so. We may actively participate in His work, and we must certainly do nothing to hinder it. He will not force us to become more holy in any particular in which we are refusing to be made so. If by the Spirit we choose to obey, we abide in Christ, and the Spirit is free to work within us to make us more holy.

It is important to note that as important as obedience is to glorifying God, obedience is not God's purpose per se. God's purpose is our conformity to the image of His Son, and thus to God himself (Romans 8:29). Obedience is both the means and the result of this increasing holiness.

Serving

The mutual indwelling of God and us in love is to be manifest in service to others. Again, to abide in God is to abide in love (John 15:9-10), for God is love (1 John 4:8). We do not know God if we do not obey Him (2:3), nor if we do not love (4:8), for His commandment is that we love one another (3:23). If we cannot love our brother, we cannot love God (4:20). This love is not an objective attitude or an emotion only, but is manifest in practical choices. Love serves and provides for needs and dies for another, as did Jesus (3:16-17). The fruit of love in service is the proof that we are abiding in Christ (John 15:5, 8).

It is the Spirit who empowers us to love and to serve. Love is the fruit of the Spirit (Galatians 5:22), and to live a life of love necessitates living by the Spirit (v. 25). The Spirit has given us all sorts of gifts as members of the Body of Christ, the Church, so that we can serve one another in love. First Corinthians 12:1-11 states eleven times that the Spirit gives these gifts and empowers us to use them. Whether they are speaking gifts or serving gifts (Romans 12:6-8), they are manifestations of the Spirit for the common good (1 Corinthians 12:7). We are to teach and admonish one another in all wisdom in songs and hymns and various sorts of prophecy so that the Word of Christ might dwell in us richly (Colossians 3:16; 1 Corinthians 12:8-10).

In short, we are to speak the truth to each other in love and serve with all our gifts for the building up of the Body in love, so that we might all attain to maturity and the fullness of all that is ours in Christ (Ephesians 4:7-16).

Returning to Jesus' discourse in John, the Spirit is given to us not for our benefit only, but so that the world might know that we are His, and that God sent Him (17:18, 21, 23). Ultimately, His purpose in coming to us is to convict the world and to glorify Jesus by making Him known (16:7-15). It is the Spirit who empowers us to witness of Jesus Christ (Acts 1:8, 4:29-31; 1 Corinthians 12:3).

The key to God's mission, then, is the mutual indwelling of God and His people. As Moses prayed, what is it that distinguishes us from all the other people who are on the face of the earth, if it is not the very presence of God? Paul has made clear that this indwelling of God is not merely an individual reality, but a corporate reality as well. We are the Body of Christ, made one by the Holy Spirit and indwelt by Him. We, the Church, are the presence of Christ upon the earth. His Spirit empowers us to live and speak in love and truth. All people will know that we are His disciples by our love for one another (John 13:35). And when a person from the world is convicted by the truth we speak, he will fall on his face and worship God, declaring, "God is certainly among you" (1 Corinthians 14:25).

In summary, God has promised that we can know Him directly and obey Him by His Spirit which He has placed within us. His power is effected in us as we abide in Christ. As we abide in Him, we are filled with His Spirit, and He is able to do His work of making us like Christ. If we embrace the truth of His promises and by faith pursue them, they will be actualized in us. The more we seek to be identified with Christ, the more He reveals Himself to us. He keeps on teaching us. We are thus increasingly accountable for the truth given us, but with the truth He gives us the power to obey it. In this way the Spirit makes our objective union with Christ increasingly subjectively real. We then more perfectly glorify God in manifesting His nature. From the overflow of this union with Him, we give our lives in serving others out of love. By this demonstration of truth and love in our lives, the world comes to know that God is among us, and His mission is accomplished.

THE PROCESS: IMITATING CHRIST

"The longing to behold is inseparable from the longing to be."[25] We become like whatever we worship. God wishes us to be one with Him as Christ was one with Him. This is to say that He wants our entire being, thoughts, emotions, and will, to be wholly aligned with Him. In this way we are then like Christ in His humanity. God's goal for us is conformity to the image of His Son. It is to this end that we are predestined (Romans 8:29). We become like Christ in His perfect human nature as we seek to "know him, and the power of his resurrection and the fellowship of sharing in his sufferings, becoming like him in his death" (Philippians 3:10). But how do we seek to know Him? What do we do to become increasingly identified with Him?

We are to put sin to death and imitate Christ. Unlike Christ who was sinless, it is necessary for us to mortify pride. When we discover some truth that conflicts with our self-image (the reality we have created) we need to act upon that truth deliberately, and thus put pride to death in that particular area. If we will pursue God, pride must die in us. "Either God or sin must die in my life."[26]

We need also to imitate Christ. The Thessalonians became "imitators of the Lord" (1 Thessalonians 1:6). Paul exhorted his readers, "Be imitators of me, as I am of Christ" (1 Corinthians 11:1). We are to have the "mind of Christ" (2:16). We are to imitate Him in His self-sacrificing life: "This is how we know what love is: Jesus Christ laid down his life for us. And we ought to lay down our lives for our brothers" (1 John 3:16; cf. Matthew 11:28-30).

Spiritual Disciplines

Again the question arises, How do we do these things? What actions do we take to mortify sin and imitate Christ? The answer is that we do what He did in the lifestyle He lived. What He did may be discovered by reading the Gospels. He practiced what we call spiritual disciplines. They are tailor-made for our human nature to train us for godliness (1 Timothy 4:7). Using them, we learn obedience. The fact that they have been used throughout the ages universally in all religions, including Christianity, may speak to the fact that they fit who we are. It is only our twentieth century antinomian society that finds the disciplines strange.

What are these spiritual disciplines? The lists differ, but here is one well-known suggested list: the inward disciplines of meditation, prayer, fasting, and study; the outward disciplines of simplicity, solitude, submission, and service; and the corporate disciplines of confession, worship, guidance, and celebration.[27] We see the majority of these exercised in the life of Christ. Each of our lists may be a bit different according to our particular needs. To this list we may add suffering in the providence of God.[28] We have been called to suffer as Christ did, following his example (1 Peter 2:21). We are to seek to identify with Christ in the fellowship of His sufferings (Philippians 3:10; Colossians 1:24).

A most pressing question about the disciplines is, Why do they work? We should note first what is *not* the reason they work. They do not gain us points with God, as though we can earn His favor. They have no value in themselves. They are means we can use to pursue God for love of God. "Self-denial is never a virtue in itself. It has value precisely in proportion to the superiority of the reality embraced above the one denied."[29]

They work because they help us embrace this reality by doing two things. First, they strip away love of self and other things. Through means such as fasting, simplicity, and solitude, we deliberately deny the fulfillment of sensuous desires which may replace God. As we use the disciplines to put pride to death, we crucify the love of self that is pride's energy. All this is for the purpose that we might love God.

The disciplines also help us to receive truth. As we have seen, truth is essential for sanctification. Our new nature "is being renewed in knowledge in the image of its Creator" (Colossians 3:10). We have been granted "everything we need for life and godliness through our knowledge of him who called us" (2 Peter 1:3). Manifestations of our new nature prove that we are not unfruitful "in the true knowledge of our Lord Jesus Christ" (1:5-8). Jesus prayed that God would sanctify us in His truth (John 17:17).

In study, we find truth in His revelation, especially Scripture; "Your word is truth" (John 17:17). In meditation upon Christ, we find truth; "I am the way, the truth, and the life" (14:6). In prayer we are united with the God who is truth; our purpose is "complete and entire and absolute identification with the Lord Jesus Christ, and there is nothing in which this identification is realized more than in prayer."[30] In solitude and silence, we are better able to hear the Spirit who speaks the truth. In community we confess truth, the truth of God and of ourselves, we worship the God of truth, and we celebrate Him, as is pictured in the ordinances.

Grace

The question should arise, If we are doing so much work in the practice of the disciplines, how is sanctification by grace? These disciplines are means of grace. We ourselves do not effect our sanctification by the working of these works.[31] If we could, then the unbeliever in another religion may effect the same holiness of God through them. By them we may train ourselves to think and behave differently, for God has given us extraordinary power to work. But we are more than just the sum of our thoughts, attitudes, and habits.

First, God by His grace works in us to will and to work according to His good pleasure (Philippians 2:13). This verse is immediately preceded by the command "work out your salvation with fear and trembling" (2:12). We can work because God works in us to do so. By His grace we desire to work, and by His grace we do the work. The Holy Spirit is the power behind our putting to death the deeds of the body (Romans 8:13). "If we live by the Spirit, let us also walk by the Spirit" (Galatians 5:25).

As we walk by the Spirit in the disciplines, we are in a position to receive grace to be changed. By ourselves we can make great headway in self-discipline. We can change our habits. What we cannot change is who we are essentially. There is a part of ourselves about which we can do nothing. We as believers, by the Spirit, seek to train the mind, will, and affections to reflect God's. As we do this, we place ourselves in a position to be changed by the Spirit in His essence so that the mind, will, and affections are, in fact, in union with God. Thus the whole work of sanctification, as salvation itself, is by His grace and through His initiative and accomplishment. It is by His grace that we are permitted to participate in His work. Ultimately, our sanctification is all of God, and all the glory is His.

Jesus Our Example

It may be difficult to understand how Jesus can be our example in the disciplines since He had no sin. Yet He is our example because the crucial issue is the embracing of truth. This He did. For us, mortifying pride and embracing truth are both involved and are really the same thing. To embrace some revealed truth requires us to renounce the corresponding lie of self-definition we created. Every situation in life presents us with this choice anew. Christ was presented every moment in life with the choice to sin or not to sin. As He embraced truth every time, He learned and grew in godliness in His humanity (Hebrews 5:8). Because He had no sin in His nature, He always chose truth and His embracing truth mortified no pride. Though He learned obedience in His humanity, no change in His essential being was effected, since He was wholly pure. So we can participate in the disciplines as He did and grow in truth, but in us this also necessarily mortifies pride.

We can see how the disciplines enable us to mortify pride and receive truth in a specific example of solitude or silence. Much of our speech is filled with lies and justifications, all designed to serve our self-image. Refraining from them in silence counteracts this and enables us to hear God. If we lie, we confess it to the one to whom we lied and tell the truth. In this we put pride to death and embrace truth. In this same way, all the disciplines help us to grow in love and truth, replacing our pride with humility and making us more like Christ.

Finally, it may seem as if, through the practice of the disciplines in faith (our part) and the gracious activity of God in changing us (part of His part), we should be able to eradicate sin from our lives. But truth is essential to sanctification. This is why we cannot attain to sinless perfection this side of glorification. While we need not and should not commit willful sin, we are lacking in truth to know the entirety of God and His holiness and to conform to it. "Now we see but a poor reflection; then we shall see face to face. Now I know in part; then I shall know fully, even as I am fully known" (1 Corinthians 13:12).

We will know fully when we see Christ. In one sense we can never know God fully because He is infinite and we are finite. Knowing Him will be eternal discovery. But this verse asserts that we will know fully in some sense. It appears that this full knowledge finally removes the root of sin because we become like Him (in His purity) when we see Him as He is (1 John 2:29-3:3). Until then, truth will continue to disclose our sin to us—and not primarily sin we commit in ignorance of some unknown law, but ways, previously hidden from us, in which our pride, selfishness, and faithlessness are manifest in violation of the character of God which we already know. Not until we see Him will we be completely like Him, the exact image of God.

THE PROSPECT: ONE WITH GOD

"Love is properly a complete union of the lover and the beloved."[32] This is our hope and our destiny. We will be like Christ. At the very least, this means that we will be pure as

He is pure (1 John 3:3), without sin as He is (vv. 5-6), righteous as He is righteous (v. 7). What is truly ours now in our union with Christ, and that for which we are purifying ourselves in hope (v. 3), will be fully ours when we see Him. According to our paradigm, our essential reality will be perfectly actualized in our existential reality. Not only the penalty of sin and the power of sin, but also the presence of sin, will be abolished. At last we will be fully united with God. Christ is the perfect image of God and the exact radiance of His glory; we will be like Him. We will know God fully and love Him and His truth with our entire being. Thus we will fulfill our created design as the image of God, perfectly reflecting His nature.

SO WHAT?

There are, of course, many practical implications of any model of spirituality, but for the purpose of this book, we are interested in the impact of our model on interpretation.

1. The definition of pride as self-definition rather than merely self-love points out that sin violates not just love, but also truth. This essence of sin pervades our entire being. We are unitary persons; while the common divisions of mind, emotions, and will are convenient for analyzing and describing ourselves, these are all integrated with each other within us in such a way that one affects all. This means that we cannot say that sin affects only our willingness to accept the truth as though sin only distorts our will. It also affects our mind so that we cannot even understand the truth beyond a superficial level.

2. The spiritual disciplines help us to discover truth and to love and embrace it. We need to be intentional in our participation with the Spirit's work in changing us and eradicating the sin within us that keeps us from understanding the truth. We are then better fitted to hear the Spirit in and through the Word and in addition to it. This means that spiritual formation is an essential part of understanding Scripture, and its practices should be incorporated into our method of interpretation.

3. We should listen to the Spirit as He leads us in understanding Scripture and finding deeper meaning in it. This includes both meaning unknown (perhaps) to the human authors and its meaning for our own lives and the world around us. Skill in listening for the Spirit and discerning His voice should especially be made part of the practice of interpretation.

4. Personal experience brings a measure of understanding that mere study cannot. Personal experience of God and the coming of His Kingdom in our own lives will help us understand Scripture to a depth that we could not otherwise.[33] This means that understanding Scripture is a lifelong process and not merely the result of doing a few exegetical exercises and following a few hermeneutical rules.

5. We understand the Bible in order to relate to God, not relate to God in order to understand the Bible.[34] If God's highest priority was for us to have a perfect, finished theology, He would have given us a textbook on it instead of the Bible. Instead, He wrote the Bible in such a way as to lead us to relationship with Him—it is sufficiently clear that we can know Him, but not so clear that we don't need Him. Understanding the Bible helps us relate to God which helps us to understand the Bible, in a circular fashion. But always the real goal is to know God, become like Him, and accomplish His Kingdom purpose on earth. There is no escaping His call to discipleship if we would be good interpreters of His Word.

How One Church
Changed the World

The spiritual awakening at Antioch had been going on for over a year. Just when and how it began was unclear. Most traced it back to Simeon (also known as Niger), who had come from his home at Cyrene, a port of North Africa. More than fifteen years earlier he had been worshipping at the Cyrenian synagogue in Jerusalem when his whole life was transformed. For it was he whom the Romans forced to carry the cross for Jesus when He no longer could.

Upon hearing the news of the resurrection, he was deeply moved. When later the Spirit baptized the disciples with fire on the day of Pentecost, he was among the first to believe. Along with his first convert, Lucius, Simeon had carried the gospel to the Gentiles at Antioch when passing through selling dates and wool. As they taught the gospel and prophesied, God brought to faith many from various ethnic groups and races to join the converted Jews who had already believed.

So great was the spiritual movement that Barnabas was sent from Jerusalem to assist Simeon and his friends, Lucius and Manaen (part of the royal Herodian family of Judea). As even more responded to his preaching, Barnabas sought Saul from Tarsus to help them. Together these five taught great numbers of people. They were the first in the Roman world to be called Christians. And yet God had even greater plans for these five.

As the numbers grew and even more joined the ranks of teachers and prophets, Simeon became burdened for other Gentiles. He sought out Barnabas and Saul and the rest of the leaders to share his idea. "I think that the Spirit is telling us that we should use Antioch as a base to reach the great peoples of the East, including the Parthians, Medes, and Elamites. The trade routes will bring us to vast numbers of Gentiles."

This sparked an even bolder idea for Saul. "Yet think of the advantage we already have in being able to speak Greek throughout the Roman Empire. Why, we can go all the way to Rome and beyond. Think of being able to claim the entire empire for our Lord! I think that the Spirit would have us go west." Manaen and Lucius suggested an outreach to the south.

All of the suggestions had merit. Which was to be pursued? Simeon suggested that the matter be laid before the entire body of Christians for their discernment.

For three weeks the believers prayed, fasted, and worshipped. They debated the merits of the various proposals. Simeon and Lucius had the advantage of personal finances. Manean had his connections with the royal family. Both Barnabas and Saul had the experience of several years of ministry, and Barnabas had the total support of the church at Jerusalem. If ever a controversy arose over Gentile salvation, it would be important to have the support of James and Peter and the rest of the apostles and elders. Saul had several things in his favor: his special revelations of Christ, his calling as the apostle to the Gentiles, and his training in Scripture. By his interpretation he powerfully persuaded Jews to find Jesus throughout Isaiah and the Psalms of David.

Finally, on the fourth Sunday, the Holy Spirit spoke clearly in a prophecy through Simeon. "Set apart for me Barnabas and Saul for the work to which I have called them." With additional fasting and praying, all the church discerned this to be God's voice. On the fifth Sunday the other prophets and teachers placed their hands on them to send them off.

Saul said, "We are convinced that the Holy Spirit is the actual sender today. We will take John Mark along as our helper and recorder. We will go first to the Jews in the synagogues before turning to the Gentiles. We fulfill Isaiah's prophecy of a light for the Gentiles. Continue to pray for us. We will give reports about all that God does so that you may participate with us."

Little did the Christians know how much began on that day.

Composed of believers—past, present, and future—the Body of Christ is God's presence on earth. This community of faith, committed to love and truth, advances the Kingdom by exercising spiritual gifts to build up the Body and bringing others into relationship with God. It is in this community that truth is discovered from Scripture as we wrestle with present day questions from living and interacting with the world, empowering us to be the prophetic voice for our world today.

Chapter Eight

Community

Fellow Pilgrims
on a Trek for Truth

"Let the word of Christ dwell in you richly
as you teach and admonish one another"
(Colossians 3:16).

It is absolutely breathtaking to think of what God has made us to be! Like so many Bible truths, we know it but we don't *really* know it, or our spirits would well up with purpose and we would gasp in speechless wonder at the mystery of how the living God fills such mundane things as our own lives. We are the Church, the Kingdom of God upon the earth. We are the object of His constant attention, and it is through us that He is working out His purpose in the universe.

Attendant with this hermeneutic we are proposing is a renewed theology of the Church.[1] This is one of the reasons that we are including such a chapter in a book on hermeneutics. For quite a few years now, our theology of the Church has focused on peripheral details such as the right form of church government and the role of women in ministry. We need to regain an understanding of the *essence* of the Church and a sense of our purpose.

We also need a chapter on community because we are designed to grow spiritually in community. Community plays a crucial part in helping us to grow in love and truth, which is necessary for understanding Scripture. Further, truth is discovered in community, and the community provides a check for individual interpretation. The Spirit is at work in this process, slowly revealing more of God and His truth and maturing the Church as she struggles with challenges in engaging the world for His Kingdom.

THE PRESENCE OF GOD

The People of God

To get an idea of what the Church really is, let's go back to our definition of the Kingdom of God. In the broader sense, the Kingdom of God is His royal rule over all creation, including those who are in rebellion against Him. In the narrower sense, the Kingdom of God is favored relationship with God and the enjoyment of Him and all His blessings. Those who do not choose to come into relationship with God are excluded from the Kingdom (in this narrower sense). He empowers those who are in relationship with Him to love Him and obey Him willingly from their hearts. In this way the rule of God is accomplished through relationship with His creatures.

So the Kingdom of God is comprised of those who are the people of God, those in whose hearts God reigns. In the Old Testament, this was (for the most part) the nation of Israel, over which Yahweh was King. Today this is the Church, made up of Jews and Gentiles. Words spoken to Israel are now true of the Church: "You are a chosen people, a royal priesthood, a holy nation, a people belonging to God....Once you were not a people, but now you are the people of God" (1 Peter 2:9-10; cf. Deuteronomy 10:15, Isaiah 62:12, Hosea 1:9, 10). Israel was a political Kingdom under Yahweh; the Church is a spiritual Kingdom under Jesus Christ, Yahweh in the flesh.[2]

God in Human Flesh

The incarnation of God in Jesus Christ is the key to understanding who we are and what is our purpose. He was God walking on the earth: "Emmanuel, God with us" (Isaiah 7:14). In His person the Kingdom of God has come near. We who believe have been made one with Christ and with each other. His Spirit dwells within each one of us and within all of us corporately. We are His Body and He is our Head. As the Body of Christ, *we together mediate the presence of the living God upon the earth!*

The Kingdom is *here*, in us, because Christ died and was raised and inaugurated the end of the age when the Kingdom of God is upon the earth. The Kingdom is *near*, in us, because we are the presence of Christ on the earth and we still await the full realization of His reign. It has always been true that God dwelled among His people and they mediated His presence on the earth. But now God's people mediating His presence on the earth have been raised to new and glorious heights, since we have been united with Christ who has ascended to the throne and has sent His Spirit to dwell within each of us and all of us together. We incarnate God upon the earth.

Advancing the Kingdom

We are the Kingdom, and yet we wait for Him to come again and actualize His Kingdom in all the earth. What are we to do in this in-between time? We are to build the Kingdom! This is exactly God's purpose for us. We must not forget that every single moment until He accomplishes His will, God is working to actualize His Kingdom on the earth. He does this with or without our intentional participation, but because more is usually accomplished through the one who deliberately participates, we may as well jump in and help!

So just what do we do to help? We advance the Kingdom in three ways.

First, we work to actualize the Kingdom of God in our own lives by growing evermore to love and obey Him from our hearts and become like Him. This is what spiritual formation is all about.

Second, we build the Kingdom by building each other up in Christ, helping each other and the whole community to grow to maturity by exercising the gifts the Spirit has given us to serve others for their good. As we do these first two things, those who do not yet believe will see the evidence of God's presence in love and truth in each one of us and in our community.

Third, we build the Kingdom as we bring others into relationship with Him by witnessing to them of God's person and work with our lips and our lives.

Now let's take a look at two parallel passages of Scripture, one from John and one from Paul, which explain these three things and how they all work together.

John 13-17. Jesus promised that the Holy Spirit would come and would live within us (14:16-17). He is the Spirit of truth, come in the name of Jesus, who teaches us all things (v. 26) and guides us into all truth (15:13). Because of the coming of the Spirit we know that Jesus is in the Father, we are in Jesus, and He is in us (14:20). The whole Triune God dwells within us and we in Him! It is through the Spirit that we come to know Jesus (cf. v. 21). If we love Him, we will obey Him (v. 23).

Because Jesus actually lives in us and we in Him, we are to abide in Him and He will abide in us (15:4). We are to live out what has been made true for us. It is as we do this that we are able to bear good fruit, for apart from him we can do nothing (vv. 4-5). As we bear good fruit, we glorify God and prove to be Jesus' disciples (v. 8). He chose us for this purpose (v. 16).

All of this is so that the world might believe in Jesus. It is for this purpose that He has sent us into the world (17:18) They will know that we are His disciples by our love for each other (13:35) and by our good fruit. The Spirit not only makes us one with God, but one with each other as a testimony to the world. Jesus prayed,

I pray...that all of them may be one, Father, just as you are in me and I am in you. May they also be in us so that the world may believe that you have sent me. I have given them the glory that you gave me, that they may be one as we are one: I in them and you in me. May they be brought to complete unity to let the world know that you sent me (17:21-23).

Also, the Spirit testifies about Jesus, as we are to do (15:26-27), and He convicts the world of guilt, righteousness, and judgment (16:8).

The Holy Spirit is the key to everything. It is through Him that we are one with God and with each other. It is through the Spirit that Jesus discloses Himself to us. As we abide in Christ through the Spirit, we are able to obey Him, love Him, love each other, and produce good fruit. We are also sanctified by the truth (17:3), and the Spirit is the Spirit of truth. As we produce good fruit in love and holiness in the truth by the Spirit, others come to believe in Jesus when we testify of Him in conjunction with the Spirit. So the Kingdom of God is actualized in us and in the world as we know Christ, become more like Him, and witness of Him by the Spirit through our lips and our lives.

1 Corinthians 12-14. For Paul, too, the Spirit is the key. It is as we practice the gifts of the Spirit by the Spirit (1 Corinthians 12:4-11; cf. Romans 8:9-16; 12:6-8) in demonstration of love and truth that people recognize the presence of God is among us and thus encounter the Kingdom of God. "We were all baptized by one Spirit into one body [the Body of Christ]...and we were all given the one Spirit to drink" (12:13).

All of us have been given various sorts of gifts, all from the same Spirit, to each one of us according to His will (vv. 4, 11). All of these gifts manifest love or truth or both, but whatever their primary ministry, we are to practice them in love or they accomplish nothing (chapter 13). We are to excel especially in the gifts that build up and strengthen the Church (14:12, 26). We know from the context of this passage and from others of Paul's writings that this pouring out of ourselves in serving or speaking in love and truth is a witness to the world. In this passage, especially when the gift of prophecy is exercised, the unbeliever is convicted, "so he will fall down and worship God, exclaiming, 'God is certainly among you!'" (vv. 24-25).

About Spiritual Gifts

We have mentioned spiritual gifts several times in this book, especially in this chapter, and have tipped our hand as to what we believe regarding whether any have ceased. Let's take a moment to address this directly.

We believe that all the gifts of the Spirit are still operative today. In our opinion, the biblical support for the cessation of the more spectacular gifts is weak.[3] Such a reading of Scripture seems to be informed unduly by our Western, scientific world view and the fact that we don't see incredible but undeniable miracles of healing occurring through a person's ministry today.

But what about the witness of history? We don't see such miracles today, so if God continues to reveal Himself throughout time, should that not inform us how to read Scripture?

We do take very seriously the witness of history, as we explain in the next chapter. This is, in part, why we believe that the gifts have not ceased. There have been, and continue to be, reports of such miracles in various parts of the Church throughout time. While it is possible that every such report since the close of the Canon is indeed false and merely legendary, unless we are going to adopt such an extreme position, we have to account not only for the fact that we see few miracles (at least in our culture), but also for the fact that some still do occur somewhere. What reading of the biblical text accounts for all this?

First, there is the chance that God does not perform such miracles in our midst because we do not believe in them (rather than our not believing in them because He no longer performs them). This could be analogous to what happened for Jesus and His disciples. In some cities they performed fewer miracles than in others. "He did not do many miracles there because of their lack of faith" (Matthew 13:58). Yet when friends brought a paralytic to be healed by Jesus, "he saw their faith" and healed him (Matthew 9:2; many similar cases could be cited). While we condemn the practice of blaming ill people for not having enough faith, there must be something to this statement in the Word of God. We can't just ignore it.

There is another explanation that we think better accounts for all of this. The Church is not merely the local congregation. It is one Body. It is transtemporal, including all who belong to it, past, present, and future. And it includes every congregation in every part of the world at a given time. This is how God views the Church.

Therefore, those who believe that God will provide all the gifts to every individual congregation are misled by their myopia. The Spirit dispenses the gifts as He wills. This means not only to individuals within a local congregation, but also to congregations within the Church. He may bestow certain miraculous gifts in some cultures and not in others, and in some times and not in others, according to the need. (This is the implicit view of those who believe that the Spirit still gives these gifts, but that He gives them more often in places such as frontier missions in order to confirm His Word.) This way of looking at the Church in relation to spiritual gifts makes better sense of Scripture and our corporate experience.

COMMUNITY OF TRUTH

We know that the Church is a community of both love and truth. Both are essential (though if Scripture emphasizes one over the other, it is love). But for the purposes of a book on hermeneutics, we need to focus on truth.

The community contributes to our understanding of truth in several ways. First, community is the place where spiritual growth occurs; sin is destroyed and Christlikeness is formed as we come to know God in community. Second, the community holds the deposit of truth and passes it on to each of us. Third, the community provides a check for what we perceive to be the leading of the Spirit into truth in Scripture and all of life. And fourth, community is the place where truth is hashed out as we bring questions from our own lives, engage our world, and interact with Scripture and the truth handed down to us. The product of this is the development of theology, which is the ongoing distillation of God's truth in history.

Growing in the Truth

The stereotypical image of someone who pursues union with God is a secluded monk with his head in the clouds. Though a number of the disciplines require withdrawal from others for at least a short period of time, the pursuit of holiness is not designed by God to be an individualistic, impractical, otherworldly endeavor. In fact, we practice the majority of the disciplines, not in isolation apart from the rest of the world and its challenges, but rather in the context of relationship and in the midst of the vicissitudes of life.

Together we learn God's truth and the truth about each other and ourselves, truth that both affirms and humiliates us. When we do this together in community, we practice and receive love and grace. This can be very scary, but it can hardly be matched in its overwhelming power for rebirth and growth in holiness and freedom from fear. "Every new step of community is a threat to the false self. [In the context of community] the false self will die and the true self will come into its fullness and completion."[4] This is the principle "As iron sharpens iron, so one man sharpens another" (Proverbs 27:17). We come face to face with the image of God in each other and scrape ourselves on each other's rough edges. If we really live with each other in true *community* (and not just exist individually in a collective),[5] we are impelled to embrace God and His truth, thereby putting to death our false self and growing in identity in Christ.

In fact, God has *designed* us to pursue godliness in the context of community. He indicated this in His *creation* of man and woman together as His image to mirror the communal nature of God in the Trinity, and in His *re-creation* of believers in Christ, which, among other things, means with others in the Body of Christ. If we try to pursue God by ourselves, we will fall short. First, we will fail to mature as much as we would have in community. God has designed us to grow in relationship, and some of the greatest challenges to sin and sanctity occur in interaction with other people and institutions. If we don't try to grow in the way that God has designed, it simply won't work. And second, we will fail to manifest the communal nature of God. Then we will fail to manifest two aspects of God's nature: holiness and community. Since God is glorified as all of creation is conformed to His nature to reflect Him, His glory is accomplished less by one who withdraws from this world He seeks to redeem.

Remember, we understand Scripture better as we get rid of blinding sin and experience the coming of the Kingdom in our own lives, individually and corporately. Community plays a crucial role in this.

Handing Down the Truth

Very few of us, if any, learn everything we know about our faith from Scripture directly. It may be true to say that the majority of what we learn is actually passed down to us from the faith community in which we grow up spiritually. One of the chief functions of community is to hand down the truth to its spiritual children.

What we are usually taught by the community is a *deposit of theology*, a condensation of the most important truths in Scripture, such as we find in a catechism or a creedal statement. Granted, it is closely tied to Scripture, and Bible-centered churches teach this theology from the biblical text. But it still remains that this doctrine, this *tradition*—though it is derived from Scripture—acts also as a grid through which we read the Bible. This is why we generally understand the Bible the way that our community does and not the way a significantly different community does. A Lutheran understands the Bible quite differently at some points than a Pentecostal does. It is not possible to teach "pure" *Scripture* because what we are teaching is always something of our *interpretation* of Scripture.

Realizing this may be uncomfortable for some. All of us want to be secure that what we believe is indeed the truth. However, we needn't worry because our interpretation of Scripture is normally close enough to what the Bible actually means that we can be confident that we know the essentials of the truth. This is shown by the fact that we all agree on the meaning of the central things of Scripture required for salvation and feel free to disagree on the less clear, minor points. But it is our tradition, the deposit of truth (2 Timothy 1:13-14; perhaps also Colossians 2:6) handed down to us by the community, which helps us to understand these major and minor issues in Scripture.

Now, this tradition is always subject to revision by Scripture (which we explore more thoroughly in the next chapter), but we nevertheless do and *should* use it to understand Scripture. Why should we go over the same ground again (as though God's Spirit has not worked in others before us) and start from scratch to formulate such things as the doctrine of the Trinity or the relationship of the deity and humanity of Christ? We shouldn't. The community passes on to us all that has been distilled so that we can go on from there to discover truth in interaction with Scripture and life in our own day.

Safeguarding the Truth

Hand-in-hand with the trust of passing down the truth goes the responsibility of safeguarding the truth. The community defines who belongs to the community and who does not. A major definer of who belongs and who does not is whether they affirm certain core truths the community upholds (for examples, 1 John 2:18-23, the confession of Jesus as the Christ; 4:1-6, the confession of Jesus as having come in flesh; 2 John 9-11 warns of those who depart from the teaching about Christ). Any person or idea that deviates from this essential truth called *orthodoxy*, is considered heretical and outside the community. The community defends itself and the truth by fighting against these ideas.

Once in awhile, the Church gets it wrong and ends up fighting against the truth, usually by mistaking a minor point for an essential, as we did when we persecuted Galileo for saying that the earth revolved around the sun rather than vice versa. We look stupid for awhile and eventually come around. Though we are occasionally misguided and overzealous, one of the responsibilities of community is to contend for the truth.

What happens on this larger scale between the Church and the world also occurs on a smaller scale within the Church. Let's look again at the gift of prophecy. One of the criteria for evaluating prophecy (or any claim of speaking from the Spirit) is whether it is in accord with previous truth (Deuteronomy 13:1-5; 1 John 2:27). When anyone brings a prophecy, all in the community (and especially the others who have the particular gift of prophecy) are to evaluate its truthfulness (1 Corinthians 14:29-32). The community evaluates new theological ideas, interpretations of Scripture, and any instructions or revelations from the Spirit in the same manner.

We are a Spirit-filled community (Ephesians 5:18), empowered by Him to perform the very important function of safeguarding the truth in discerning the spirits as a check on individual interpretation of Scripture and the leading of the Spirit. Perhaps one of the reasons we fear the free exercise of the Spirit in these matters is that we don't practice true community so that we can feel confident in His work in us corporately to keep true to the faith in the exercise of such freedom (cf. 2 Corinthians 3:17).

Whatever frustration we may experience concerning the slowness of the Church to change, we need to recognize that guarding the truth is a God-given function of the community. We ought to be thankful for it. He has designed community so that it reinforces the accepted norm in order to give society structure and cohesion. Just because our faith community reinforces the accepted norm doesn't mean that all the individuals are closed to exploring challenging questions.[6] We can discuss things one-on-one and in small groups that we can't in the larger community until the whole community is brought up to speed. When we recognize God's design for community to safeguard the truth, we can be thankful and work within it.

Discovering the Truth

As we can see in the exercise of prophecy, the community is not only to safeguard the truth, but also to discover the truth. Community is the place where theology is hashed out. Here we bring the questions and concerns we encounter in our personal lives and in our world. Personal and corporate experience plays a role in discovering truth and understanding Scripture because theology always relates to real life—if it doesn't, it isn't "good theology." Here we explore together possible revelations from the Spirit, interpretations of Scripture, and new theological ideas. Together we process all these things in light of what we already know, not only to safeguard the truth we have received, but also to progress corporately in our understanding of the truth.

This discovering truth in community happens (or should happen) not only for each individual, but also for the community itself. The smaller community shares a common theological tradition and corporate history that should be tested in the larger Church community. Each community seems to act as though it has some corner on the truth. But let's be realistic. When we consider the plethora of Protestant denominations, let alone Roman Catholicism and Eastern Orthodoxy (both of which contain many, many genuinely saved believers), how likely is it that the small group of Baptists, for example, somehow contains the purest distillation of God's truth? Maybe it does, but whatever church we are a part of should not *assume* it does (as every church seems to) and put up straw men from these other traditions and set fire to them. We should read broadly and interact genuinely with people from these other traditions to check our understanding of Scripture and the truth.

We can learn not only from the Church in other traditions, but also in other cultures. Even a single tradition takes on different "flavors" in different cultures because our broader social culture influences how we understand Scripture and truth. Most of us haven't the good fortune to be part of a multi-cultural church. We need to interact, at least in reading but preferably in person, with Christians from other cultures. They help us to see beyond our cultural biases which color the way we understand truth.[7] For example, Christians from the more group-oriented cultures of Africa and Asia bring correctives to the overly individualistic slant of the Western Church's idea of salvation and of our theology in general.

The histories of various parts of the Church contribute to the theology of the whole. For instance, the Church, in what was once the Soviet Union, did not have the advantage of all the books and tools that the Western Church has, but unknown to us, it developed a rich theology of suffering forged in the crucible of oppression. In our efforts to develop a true, full theology, we must listen to all parts of the Church and incorporate into one theology the particular aspects God has taught each through their cultural values and corporate experiences.

One implication of this is that it is perhaps time that we learn to interpret Scripture and do theology in groups. We need others to check our traditional and cultural biases. The explosion of knowledge in all scholarly fields makes it impossible in this day for one person to master everything, and it is difficult to find a discipline that does not have implications for interpretation of Scripture and doing theology. It will take some time for this to catch on in our individualistic culture, but it will eventually become a necessity.

The reason that we are to *discover* truth and not just safeguard it is that God continues to unfold His truth in history (see chapter 9), and we must reformulate it and progress in our understanding of it in order to be relevant to the world. Few churches do this very well.

Balancing Love and Truth

How do we balance the responsibility to safeguard the truth with the responsibility to discover the truth? Are we required to believe whatever the community decides? And how do we handle it if—after all prayer, study, and discussion—we still disagree? When do we submit, and when do we break from the community?

These are difficult issues. Positive change and discovery of the truth comes through challenging the accepted norm of the community, so these struggles are reality for a great number of people as God works to mature His Church.

The answer is found in balancing love and truth. There is definitely some measure of truth required for fellowship together as the Church. These are the core truths of our faith. So, while we can build friendship with a Mormon in order to win him to the Kingdom, we can't fellowship in a Mormon church as part of the Body of Christ. We do not submit to the doctrines of such a church and should not attend it (unless, perhaps, we are going there in order to build relational bridges and to learn more about their beliefs to be used later for apologetic purposes). The same may go for mainline Protestant churches which have abandoned the gospel (although in some of these it may be possible to be an evangelist). The key is that we do not fellowship with them in our hearts as a community of truth.

Yet we are free to disagree with a true community of the faith on issues that are less than central, and if we have been part of a community for a reasonable amount of time, we are free to attempt to influence it according to our conviction. This takes much love and wisdom. Love recognizes that growth in truth is a process, and it proceeds patiently and attempts to avoid dissension.

Stress and even conflict are virtually unavoidable in the process of change, and are not bad in themselves. But there comes a point at which the stress being caused to the community is not warranted by the importance of the issue being contended, and so love drops the issue for the sake of the community.[8] The greater the importance of the truth being contended, the more disturbance is warranted and can be expected.

Wisdom is able to discern when to contend for change, what means to use and how quickly to do it, and at what point to submit or leave. Certain common-sense principles apply also. It is fruitless to go to a Pentecostal church expressly for the purpose of convincing them that the miraculous gifts of the Spirit have ceased.

Love submits to the community in all minor things not worth contending for. We will never find a church with whose doctrine we agree exactly. If an issue arises that is worth pressing, love seeks the best way to do this and quits if change doesn't happen and the stress is not warranted by the importance of the issue. If the issue is central to the faith, truth may require leaving the community if it abandons an essential of the faith.

There is some gray area here. Some issues may be important to us but not central to the faith. If the community affirms its position and the issue is important enough to us, we have the luxury in most areas in North America to worship with another community. When this is not available, we need to submit to the community. Its healthy growth and function in the mission is more important than accuracy on a less-than-essential issue. If our view is right, God may well show this to the community in time, but our pressing too hard, too soon certainly will not help His work.

We can't forget that God's ultimate goal is for us to grow in intimacy with Him and to bring others into the same relationship, not to develop a perfect theology. But since His purpose is for us to grow in the truth, this is not an excuse for sloppy theology. We should recognize, though, that the decision of the community regarding an issue may be God's leading for that community for that time, even if it is short of what we come later to understand as fuller truth. We also need to have the humility to realize that we may be the ones who are wrong—and even if we are right, we still don't have all the truth. We arrive at all theological answers knowing that they will be superseded.

Maturing in the Truth

God is slowly maturing the Church in the truth throughout the ages as He continues to work in her and in history. The Body is growing not only in numbers but in maturity; Jesus said that He would build His Church and Paul spoke of its growing maturity (Matthew 16:18; Ephesians 2:19-22; 4:11-16). To think that we have the final formulation of truth is to believe that there is no more left to be revealed, and that we have overcome the boundaries of our own time and culture to come up with a perfectly full and accurate formulation of truth that will transfer to all other times and cultures and last forever. This is obviously not true.

But what we do *contributes* to the maturity of the Church. How we engage the world and interact with God and His truth over our questions in community today is an organic part of His preparation of the Church tomorrow. They pick up where we left off (although there are plenty of repeat mistakes throughout the history of the Church). Just as what He has done in the past is for our benefit (cf. 1 Corinthians 10:6-11), so also what He is doing in us is for the benefit of those who follow us (as well as for us).

In some mysterious way, what happens with us is also for the benefit of those who preceded us. "These were all commended for their faith, yet none of them received what had been promised. God had planned something better for us so that only together with us would they be made perfect" (Hebrews 11:39-40). The Church is all those who are the redeemed people of God, from every people and tradition, whether alive or physically dead or yet unborn. Death does not exit us from the Body. What God does in history in any one moment is for the maturing of the whole Church. Somehow, what we do helps to mature Paul, Augustine, Calvin and Luther, and others in the faith.

John saw what we will be in the end. "Then you made them a Kingdom, Priests for our God, Priest-kings to rule over the earth" (Revelation 5:10, *The Message*).[9] The end is here now and is progressively being realized. What we will be is what we are. Jesus Christ is Prophet, Priest, and King.[10]

The Church, as the Body of Christ, is also prophet, priest, and king.[11] Look at that verse again. "Then you made them a Kingdom, Priests for our God, Priest-kings to rule over the earth." We have already seen that we are prophets to the world, speaking to them the gospel of God and warning them of impending judgment. We see also that we are priests to God and that we will reign with Him.

It is God who will accomplish this! He is able to keep those who are His. We can rest in this confidence as we endeavor to hold fast to the Head and engage the world for His Kingdom.

So What?

We need each other. We are, in fact, one in the Body, whether we recognize it or not. In the only abiding reality, we are brothers and sisters in Christ, regardless of how we relate to each other according to the flesh. Together we are the Body of Christ. Nothing helps us to grow spiritually more than to see love and truth actualized in each other's lives—God "fleshed out," made incarnate again. And nothing draws the world to Christ more than our mediating His presence, together as one, imaging His character as we actualize His Kingdom on earth (so John 13:34-35).[12]

What God has made us to be should give us insight on how we should do interpretation and ministry. Our hermeneutic and our ministry must be, in a sense, ecclesiocentric.[13] Few people are converted directly by a book. There is a sense in which the faith community and Scripture interpret each other. The Church fleshes out the truth of Scripture, making it tangible, interpreting God's Kingdom to the world of its day. Likewise, Scripture ultimately calls forth the community in which it can be understood rightly and gives the community its self-understanding and its mission in relation to God and the world. We need to recapture a sense of the value of ourselves as the Church to each other and to the world in God's Kingdom mission, so that the Word becomes once again a living, walking, loving, healing, proclaiming, reconciling, dying Person.

We cannot fulfill God's purpose for us as His people unless we do the hard work of loving and exploring and dying to discover true community, and with it, a dynamic life foreign to many of us now. Mostly, we coexist socially as a collective of individuals. We fall far short of all that we can be as one in Christ, an organic whole that is greater than its parts and is held together by something more than an institutional structure.[14]

When we have experienced this true community life, we understand Scripture better and are no longer so afraid of the potential abuses of freedom in the Spirit. We will not adopt a fortress mentality and focus primarily on keeping the truth we have safe and passing it on to those who are already insiders. We will embrace also our responsibility to engage the world, in order to continue to discover the truth God is unfolding and to proclaim Him to the world in which God has placed us, and not just to each other in the world of yesteryear.

Heresy, though a real evil, will never kill the Church— but dead orthodoxy just might. It is leprous, eating away at our spirit, dulling our sense of God and what He has made us to be and do. The Spirit-filled community life He has called us to is what keeps us vibrant and healthy, resistant to both diseases of heresy and dead orthodoxy. And it is what empowers us to fulfill God's purpose for us in accomplishing His Kingdom mission.

Vignette Nine

History Is Holy
Because God Is in It

"*Say, Philologus, did you read Saturday's* Alexandrian Times? *There's a story in there about how diggers have uncovered what they believe to be the remains of Sodom and Gomorrah underneath the southern end of the waters of the Sea of Salt," Julia announced.*

"*Yeah, I saw it. It led me to think about the meaning of history."*

"*I've been thinking too," she replied. "This shows that our Scripture is reliable. The destruction of Sodom and Gomorrah described in our book of Beginnings was an actual event, and not just some myth or allegory as some say."*

"*Well, that's true, but we Christians should see some other meaning in their destruction and its confirmation. It's what Jesus pointed to. Remember, He said that as wicked as Sodom and Gomorrah were, it will go better for them in the judgment day than for the cities of Chorazin, Capernaum, and Bethsaida."*

"*Oh, I see what you're driving at. You take them as examples of degrees of punishment according to the principle, the greater the light, the greater the judgment. Because our cities of Judea have rejected the light of the gospel in unbelief, their judgment is more severe than that of Sodom and Gomorrah who didn't receive this light."*

"*That's true, too, Julia, but you're still missing my point. We have been conditioned to think that God's miraculous interventions in our history together form a special sort of holy history. You know what I am talking about, the Passover, the Exodus, the conquest of the land under Joshua, the reign of our great King David, the fall of Jerusalem to Nebuchadnezzar—things like these. All of these events, and especially the incarnation and death of Jesus, are supposed to be a holy history. It parallels ordinary history but stands above it, as though God just pops into ordinary history to perform a miracle once in awhile and keeps out of everything the rest of the time. I don't think this is true."*

"*You don't? I don't understand."*

"*Well, I think that when Jesus referred to Sodom and Gomorrah He was validating the fact that all of history is revelatory. These still speak today. It is not just through their destruction at God's miraculous intervention but also through their subsequent history that God still speaks. The former event is recorded in our Scripture but the latter is recorded in our newspaper—sort of a new revelation for our contemporary society. Both events communicate truth—truth about God, about the fallen state of man, about moral laws that reflect His nature even if never written down. The former revelation gives us insight to enable us to interpret their recent discovery.*

"Let me give you some other examples. Our historians have praised the Roman conquest of the last strongholds of the Greek empire—Carthage and Corinth—about two hundred years ago. But as it turns out, the Romans were conquered by Greek customs and ways, often immoral ones, so much so that some think that Rome herself is crumbling from within because of this Greek influence. Didn't such an event prepare for Christ by showing us that no matter how mighty a kingdom might be it does not stand by might alone? Or, remember the edict of our Emperor Claudius just last year by which he forced all of the Jews out of Rome, and us Christians with them? Didn't that reveal that God wanted us and others to plant the gospel of the Kingdom in regions beyond as we settled elsewhere? God works in all of history, revealing Himself, not just in the events recorded in our Scripture."

"Okay, I see what you mean. But I'm still impressed more by the big events. You know, where God speaks audibly to someone, as to Moses, or does some miracle. That's real revelation."

"I know how you feel, Julia, but when you think about it, it is just as beautiful and powerful that He works in quiet ways. One day Christ will come in power and glory, on a white horse and with eyes aflame. But when Jesus came the first time, He came not as royalty would to a palace, but as a baby, born to an obscure couple on an obscure day at an obscure place attended by obscure shepherds. Jesus' presence in all of our obscure moments makes our entire history sacred."

God is the Author of both Scripture and history, and all of history is revelatory. Thus, revelation continues as history unfolds. What God does in history helps us to understand what He says in Scripture, from which we interpret history.

Chapter Nine

Kingdom History

History Is His Story

"Your Kingdom come, your will be done on earth
as it is in heaven"
(Matthew 6:10).

GOD WORKS IN ALL HISTORY

We know that Scripture is God's revelation to us, but we do not often stop to consider that God also reveals Himself to us in *history*. This should not surprise us, though, because Scripture is about what God is doing in history. When we think through the implications of the Kingdom center and the paradigm of reality, our appreciation of history changes. What God is doing at the individual level in the spiritual life and in the community, He is also doing at the cosmic level as He works in all of history. This, in turn, affects how we understand God's truth, ourselves, and our purpose in life.

History Is Revelatory

God reveals Himself in *all* of history. God doesn't just pop into history once in awhile and otherwise follow a policy of "hands off." He holds all things together, and were He to sit back and just watch for even a nanosecond, the very atoms would fly apart! He actively works in history in and through natural[1] means, immanently, in cause-and-effect relationships, physical laws, philosophical development, and social and political relationships. He is no less active in these ways than He is when He supersedes the laws He set up.

It takes no special power for Him to break natural laws. We seem to think that a miracle is some great and mighty act that is more powerful than the so-called natural laws, as though it takes more of His power to perform a work that supersedes these usual principles than to set them up in the first place and work within and through them. No, a miracle is rather a gift of grace for our encouragement. It only seems mighty or especially caring because we are faithless and think that He is not working or paying attention to us when He is working quietly within the natural laws He created.

We can see in Scripture that God works in both ways. He clearly performed miracles for Israel in bringing the plagues on Egypt and in parting the Red Sea. But He preserved David from Saul and brought him to the throne over several years through creative thinking and political moves. The clearest example of God working in both ways is in the death and resurrection of Jesus. God and God alone raised Jesus from the dead in opposition to all natural laws. Yet Jesus, "delivered up by the predetermined plan and foreknowledge of God, [was] nailed to a cross by the hands of godless men and put to death" (Acts 2:23).

God's action in history is a macrocosmic view of the way He works in every moment in each of our lives. The Spirit moves in peoples and cultures no less than He leads in an individual life. Our collective thoughts and experiences are the furnace in which theology is forged. Just as personal experience plays a role in understanding Scripture, so does our corporate history, cultural movements, and contemporary life questions develop our understanding of Scripture. Not only does He mature a person throughout her life, but He is teaching the Church throughout the ages.

Revelation Marches On

In a sense, God's revelation is continuing. While every theological formulation, as a non-canonical, man-made construction, is still subject to revision by examination of Scripture, it is nevertheless a product of the Spirit's work in the Church in history. We do not reformulate each doctrine every generation. Church councils' decisions are considered orthodoxy, so much so that anyone who does not hold to the doctrine of the Trinity or to the proper view of the two natures of Christ is considered a heretic.

This is how theology works.[2] While a new theological idea may not claim to be a result of direct revelation from the Spirit, it is the product of the Spirit's work in history as He slowly unfolds truth. A person (or a small group) develops a theological idea or an interpretation of Scripture, in interaction with the culture and questions of his day, and in some way puts the idea before the Church.[3] Immediately we set to work on it, checking it out, especially with Scripture. If it doesn't measure up, it is discarded; and if it violates one of the core doctrines of revelation, it is labeled as heresy. If it passes muster as a helpful idea, it is allowed to stand until we have a better understanding of Scripture, and then the idea is modified or superseded by another that works better. In this way, church tradition is always subject to Scripture (contrary to Roman Catholicism).

Progress of Revelation

The fact that a theological idea is modified over time should not trouble us. It does not prove that it was not inspired by the Spirit. God gives as much truth as we need or can handle at a given time. He also works within the historical circumstances of the time. Thus the Spirit may well lead in the interpretation of some part of Scripture or in the formulation of some theological idea and allow it to be imperfect, knowing that it serves its purpose for the time and will eventually be corrected. For example, not all of the doctrines formulated in the Reformation were correct or have been universally adopted, but what Protestant Christian will deny that the Spirit led in the recovery of "justification by faith"? Even minor points of this doctrine are under continual discussion. Not everything in the Reformation was correct, let alone final.

This is similar to the "progress of revelation" in Scripture. God did not dump all His truth on humankind at once. He slowly revealed it over time, adding dimension to theological truths and specific details to prophecies. (This is evidenced also in the way biblical writers found deeper meaning in previously written Scripture.) The Torah, the first five books of the Old Testament, were written by Moses after God made a covenant with the nation of Israel. These books of the Law served as the core revelation for Israel. The books of the prophets and Israel's history and wisdom literature all came afterward. We would be hard-pressed to find much of anything in these later works that is not an elaboration of an idea (perhaps in incipient form) already in the Torah. Specific details of prophecies were slowly unfolded as well. For example, looking back we can see that the coming of Christ was prophesied in Genesis 3:15-16, but certainly the first hearers of this prophecy did not know all that we now know.

In this unfolding of revelation, God worked within the historical circumstances of the given time. For instance, the patriarchs were polygamists. Over time, monogamy became the norm. Jacob married Leah and Rachel, who were sisters. The Law later forbade marrying a wife's sister while the wife was alive. It's quite likely that Jacob's experience had something to do with this development. Another time, five sisters approached Moses and asked if they could inherit their father's land since they had no brothers. Moses asked the Lord, who said that women could inherit land if their father had no living sons. The circumstance gave rise to the revelation. Presumably, if they had not asked, God would not have volunteered the information.

Such ideas may make some people feel uncomfortable. The "Sunday school" picture of the writing of Scripture is God hitting someone with a *heavy revvy* (a sudden flash of revelation) while the author frantically writes down the words as they come into his head. The fact is, though, that much "revision" went on before divine revelation ever got inscripturated. The beautiful chiasms and parallelisms in poetry didn't just flow out of the quill. There were plenty of "wadded up" parchments and scratched out words.

Not everything God told the prophets made it onto paper. There are two versions of the book of Jeremiah, one from Israel where he spent his life, and one from Egypt where he was taken by people who were left behind in the Babylonian captivity. We know for certain that some of Paul's letters didn't make it into the Canon. Countless nameless scribes helped put the Canon together (who wrote about Moses' death at the end of the books that Moses wrote?) and faithfully translated the meaning of the text as the Hebrew language changed over hundreds of years. (In some places a *the* makes all the difference in meaning. Who put all the *the's* in the text when Hebrew later developed this word?)[4] Yes, sometimes the Word of the Lord came in a way as striking as a smack in the head; but He also worked almost unnoticed through the normal processes of life.

We can be confident that the Spirit is working in the development of theology even if there are minor corrections later. This does not mean that there were errors in Scriptural revelation. Nor does it mean that our theological ideas are revelation in the same way that Scripture is. Perhaps we can think of it as *Revelation* and *revelation*. Revelation with a capital R is what is contained in Scripture. The Canon is closed since the climax of history and revelation has occurred in the life, death, and resurrection of Jesus Christ. Revelation with a lower case r is still ongoing in history. The Revelation in Scripture serves as an interpretive norm for revelation in the rest of history.

Help from Our Fathers

We can take theological development as revelation-in-progress. We should pay particular attention to those areas of broad agreement in the Church, universal doctrines tested by the Community against Scripture over centuries. As we said, the core ideas in these doctrines are just a step away from being normative revelation for us.[5] As such, they in turn affect how we interpret Scripture. Just as personal experience plays a role in understanding Scripture, so also does corporate experience in the form of tradition play a role.

We should make use of universal doctrine (particularly from the Patristic period) in doing theology.[6] We must acknowledge the legitimate role of tradition. Granted, the tradition we advocate consists only of the core doctrines universally adopted as orthodoxy because they have passed the test of Scripture over time, but that only demonstrates our point. Scripture is first, but it is not alone.

These universal doctrines should help determine with whom we will fellowship and work as brothers and sisters in Christ. Lesser doctrines, as important as they may be for us individually or for our community, should not divide us and threaten the peace and unity of the Spirit and the Kingdom mission.

This does not mean that we should all belong to one church. We often decry the plethora of denominations as a sad commentary on our disunity, longing for the one mind and perfect understanding we imagine will be true when the Kingdom is realized on earth. There is no question that we have been guilty of petty quarreling to the shame of God's name. But there is another way to look at it. Yes, it is less than the best, but maybe we are running ahead of the Spirit and this is God's design for the in-between times. (Israel demanding a human king rather than God as King was also less than the best, but it was actually a crucial part of God's divine plan for Himself to reign physically as King on the earth.) We can and should work toward the unity that we will have in full someday, realizing at the same time that denominations provide a God-given freedom to disagree and to learn in this time of imperfect knowledge.

Different denominations with their distinct theological traditions are a means whereby God leads us corporately to wrestle through understanding truth. Our differences are things that haven't been settled yet. We can joyfully engage

in irenic and lively discussion of such issues, agreeing to disagree for the time being, trusting that God will eventually
bring the truth to light if and when we really need it. Even
the apostle Paul, the recipient of normative revelation, graciously tolerated differences on less significant issues until
God should bring light to the situation (1 Corinthians 7-
10). Dissension, not difference, dishonors God
(1 Corinthians 14). We are free to set these small things
down and clasp hands in fellowship and mission, a powerful
witness to the world. When we do this, we are of one mind
in the Spirit, as the Bible commends.

Learning from the Enemy

Evangelicalism harbors a strong streak of anti-
intellectualism. We believe that we have the truth. The
world wars against the Kingdom of God, so we are a little
leery of its philosophies. For these reasons, historically, we
have stayed away from the universities. Until recently, sta-
tistics have revealed that evangelicals were significantly
behind the norm in their educational levels. Typically, we
have reacted strongly against new ideas and philosophies
and scientific advances, only to incorporate later their good
parts when we have come to terms with them.

Because God reigns over the whole world and works in
all of history, we should not be afraid, but listen for His
voice in the world's philosophies that threaten Christianity.
They mean to war against God and His Kingdom, but
unknown to them, God is using them for His Kingdom. Yes,
they are far from the truth, but that does not mean that
there isn't some truth there. God uses them to instruct and
even to rebuke us. So often we think we have the truth and
are satisfied. We become sluggish and institutionalized,
interested in holding our ground. We adopt a fortress mentality, trying to defend ourselves from the evils of the world,
when we should be on the offensive, engaging the world
and learning all we can in order to bring others into relationship with God and advance His Kingdom.

Until He comes, our job is never done. We never
"arrive," and it is presumptuous of us to sit around in

complacent satisfaction. Just as God used the more evil Babylonia to discipline Judah, so He chastises us into action, using the enemies of the truth to teach us things that we should be teaching the world! For example, Liberation theologies have redefined salvation in terms of self-actualization and freedom from class, racial, and economic oppression. This is a rebuke to the complacent, materialistic Western Church. Though it has lost the essence of the truth, Liberation theology takes more seriously the plight of the poor and the disenfranchised and calls us into account for the ways we participate in the economic oppression of two-thirds of the world. Though we may feel helpless to do anything about it, we are nevertheless accountable through corporate solidarity, being part of a system that uses and abuses others for its own gain.

Another example is New Age theologies with their creation spirituality. They take seriously the interconnectedness of all creation[7] and our responsibility as stewards of it. The evangelical Church has caught on and is doing some very good work in this area now, but we are a Johnny-come-lately in the work. Now, New Agers have gone overboard and worship nature, but stewardship is a *biblical* teaching. We should have been *leading* the effort to save the environment.

Also at the core of New Age theologies is an appreciation for mystical experience. They promise various sorts of union with God or a god. This is attractive to people not because they are sinful, but because God has created us with this desire for union with Him. We may pervert that desire and pursue it in some way that makes us the god, but the desire itself is God-given.

We need to take this seriously in evangelical spirituality. The fulfillment of this desire is an inherent part of the gospel (see chapter 7). We've gone too far in the historical pendulum swing toward the cognitive side of our faith. It's time now to hold onto the good, solid Bible truth that we have and reach out for a deeper experience of it in the more mystical aspects of our faith. We need to recapture the whole gospel or lose the lost to New Age spiritualities that falsely promise to fulfill one of humanity's deepest desires.

Liberation and New Age theologies have denied the truth in pursuit of their own passions, but they have brought to our attention truths that strike at the heart of American culture's core values. Materialism (the pursuit of material gain), utilitarianism (the exploitation of human and natural resources for gain and valuing them for their function rather than their being), and individualism (with its denial of corporate solidarity and community responsibility) are all core values of our culture. The Bible teaches against them in their extreme forms, but much of the evangelical Church is so enculturated by the world around it that it has missed these biblical truths and their implications. The Lord of the universe rules all of history, and if we listen in humility, we can learn what He would teach us through those who oppose us, even though they know less than we do about the truth.

KINGDOM HISTORY IS HIS STORY

God's World View

Because God reveals Himself in all of history, we can think of Him as its Author, just as He is the Author of Scripture. His authorship of Scripture and of history are inextricably related in two ways. First, the meaning of historical events is not inherent in the event itself. This is demonstrated in that different people give different interpretations of the same event. So, in order to understand God's revelation in history, we need to have the interpretation of His actions to tell us what they mean, and this is found in Scripture. Second, Scripture is largely about history. God acts in history. Scripture recounts the highlights of God's historical acts and what they mean. God cannot be the Author of Scripture without being the Author of the history it talks about. Scripture and history tell the same story.

The fact that people interpret events differently raises a question that postmodernism asks: Is there such a thing as history? Remember, language is just the highest expression of each person's response to the common experience of life, something that all people experience and know about (see Appendix A). This common experience of life has no objective reality in the sense that there is only one right way to experience it. This means that language refers to nothing objective, so that behind words is not truth but only more words (someone else's expression of their experience to which we respond). Any attempt at writing history, then, is only that person's interpretation of things. There is no way to evaluate it as right or wrong because there is no History (correct interpretation of an objective reality) to test it against.

While we take very seriously postmodernism's emphasis on the subjectivity of interpretation and the role of language in expressing it, we do not agree that there is no objective reality to interpret and talk about.

Now, there is some question as to what a historian is supposed to do. Is she supposed to recount, as accurately as possible, the events that occurred and explain why they occurred, by tracing the currents of thoughts and feelings in the parties involved (which is one kind of interpretation)? Or is she also supposed to interpret what those events mean (in themselves) and what they mean for her people in her own day?[8] The first task is more easily done since the results can be checked by normal methods of historical research. But many historians don't stop there. The task of interpreting meaning is extraordinarily difficult and the results nearly impossible to evaluate since the interpretation is determined by the person's world view. But who can say who has the right world view?

Maybe there is an answer. It is simplistic, but it just might work. God is the Author of history; in it He is telling His story. To understand history, we need to look for the Author's intended meaning. We need to try to understand the Author's horizon (which is essential reality), to look at things from God's world view. In order for us to understand what He means by what He does, we need Him to explain

Himself to us. He did this when He revealed, through divine inspiration, the correct interpretation of His actions to the writers of the Bible. Therefore, Scripture contains the correct interpretation of history. To be certain, it does not recount and interpret every event; but it does explain the crucial elements that reveal the plot. The interpretation of history contained in Scripture is thus the standard of accuracy against which to measure all other interpretations.

Salvation History

This brings us again to criticism of the idea of salvation history. The first criticism is that salvation is not the goal of God's action in history; glorifying Himself by establishing His Kingdom is. We discussed this in chapter 4.

The second criticism is that salvation history, as it is formulated by Oscar Cullmann (its latest major proponent), does not include all of history, but only certain events selected out by God and connected with each other by divine choice rather than by all other historical events. So there are historical gaps between the actual events in salvation history, making it a special strand of history unfolding within universal history.

The problem with this is that it is not true to the way Scripture indicates that God works in history. God is the God of the whole world, working His purpose and revealing Himself in all of history (cf. Acts 17:24-31). The high points of God's action are connected by immanent historical processes in which He worked. If there are giant gaps between events connected only by some divine bridge, the salvation history in which we are placing our faith is open to the charge of being *suprahistorical*. This needlessly calls into question the historical basis of our faith, which the apostles quite vociferously defended. If our faith lacks historical basis, it has no basis.

Kingdom History

An ahistorical faith is invalid because historicity is exactly what the actualization of the Kingdom demands. God is actualizing His Kingdom on earth, essential reality in existential reality. We'd like to suggest that instead of salvation history as the biblical (and historical) center, we should think of Kingdom history.[9] Kingdom, rather than salvation, is the central idea. This Kingdom history is not a special history *per se*. Instead, all of history is a story properly told from God's perspective.

The biblical account contains the high points of this story, the most crucial elements for understanding the whole plot. Nevertheless, all the smaller details and seemingly less significant events are necessary for the development of the story. The crucial events cannot happen in a vacuum. All of history, not included in Scripture, is still part of one and the same story as the high points recounted in Scripture, providing the setting and the causally-related historical contingencies in which the events in Scripture occurred.[10]

Interpreting History

As we implied, this Kingdom history found in Scripture is the interpretive key to all of history. We should use it to understand history, past and present, and maybe even to attempt to prognosticate the future. This means that the historian must be a theologian, if he wishes to interpret history for meaning as well as for reconstruction.

So What?

The fact that God works in all of history to bring about His Kingdom has several practical implications, both for the way we should think about ourselves and our lives, and for the way we should read Scripture and do theology.

First, all of us are participating in the progress of God's revelation. It is in the seemingly mundane daily activities of our lives that theology is tested: working for daily sustenance, giving birth, changing diapers, cleaning house, living in community with spouse and children, relating to friends, parents, neighbors, bosses, and civic authorities, fixing things that break and fighting weeds in the yard, going to school and learning that we don't really know anything, getting hurt, embracing tragedy and triumph, battling sickness and wrinkles and fat, being surprised by joy, growing old and dying, and wondering, Why?

It is in the little day-to-day things that we wrestle with the big questions, whether consciously or unconsciously. In interaction with people closest to us and the larger culture around us, we answer those questions, whether we know it or not. And all the while we are developing a theology by which we run our lives. We bring all this with us as we take our part in the Church. Corporately we struggle to deal with the problems and questions of our time, attempting to answer them from God's perspective to offer hope and stability to ourselves and the world. As we come to understand God in our history, God slowly reveals more of His truth in history. We each play a part in this, no matter how small. *Nothing* in our lives is in vain.

Second, we need to study the Bible, to get to know the Author intimately, and identify ourselves increasingly with Him in order to understand all things from God's world view.

Third, we can and should learn from history. We are not very big on the value of history in our culture, and this is to our detriment. We are missing a vital avenue of learning about God.

Fourth, we can and should use history (and especially the universally adopted teachings from the time of the Church Fathers) to help us understand Scripture better and to do theology. Two thousand years of history since the Resurrection may be able to convince us that any attempt to make the Kingdom of God visible on the earth (through a political state or a utopian society) is doomed to failure for this in-between time. This is something that Augustine and others of his time didn't understand.[11] Therefore, we will read certain passages of Scripture differently (more true to what God intended) than they did.

And fifth, we can and should—though cautiously and in great humility—interpret historical events of our day from the Author's perspective. In our history He is telling His story. The main story line is found in Scripture, which serves as the interpretive norm for our understanding of history. Jesus Himself expects us to understand His Scripture enough to be able to discern the times (cf. Matthew 24, where Jesus' instruction implicitly encourages us to examine history; cf. also 16:1-4).

Processing the truth found in Scripture, history, and the community, and applying it to our present time empowers the Church to be the prophetic voice to our world.

A Letter to Paul

The church of God of the twentieth century in the West, to Paul, the Apostle. Grace to you and peace in God our Father and in our Lord Jesus Christ, which you have in full measure!

We are writing to you to ask you a few questions about some problems we are having. In your letters you often quoted Scripture to prove the truth of what you were teaching, but you did not spell out how we ourselves are supposed to read Scripture. We have been working on this question of hermeneutics now for the last two millennia, and the debate has only intensified.

From our present perspective, the way you quoted Scripture is puzzling. When you biblical writers read Scripture, you seemed to find meaning there that the human authors could not have intended.

Now, some say that you did not do this. You read Scripture according to a strict grammatical-historical hermeneutic, and that any other hermeneutic undermines the authority of the Bible. Others say that you did find deeper meaning in Scripture, but since you were inspired by the Spirit, we can't do the same. Still others are beginning to believe that we can read Scripture the way you did. Some of them are even suggesting a mild version of new hermeneutical theory in postmodernism.

We're wondering, who's right? Did you or didn't you practice the grammatical-historical hermeneutic? Did you discover God-inspired meaning in Scripture beyond what the human authors intended? If you did, how did you do it? And can we do the same? If so, how do we validate the meaning found?

Related to this whole issue is the question of the role of the Holy Spirit in interpretation. Does a person have to have faith in order to be able to understand Scripture? And if so, does this undermine the rational and historical nature of the Christian faith? What meaning can an unbeliever understand, and what meaning can he not?

And the questions get tougher. Does the Spirit still speak to us directly today or only through Scripture? And if He does still speak, how authoritative is it? And is what He reveals in any way new truth? If so, how does this relate to the authority of the

Bible and how we formulate theology? Some claim every whim as revelation from the Spirit and abuse the authority that they can gain with it. Others brush off all such experiences as illegitimate. So many people are smug and suspicious. We can't seem to understand each other and come to agreement on the truth.

From the time of the Church's infancy, we have been basing our hermeneutic on the current world view, at least in part. Some have used such methods as allegory and radical historical criticism. Did you biblical writers also just use your contemporary methods in some modified form? It seems there have always been some faithful followers in every age who used whatever methods they were taught, but still understood the truth.

But what about you? Did you use a particular hermeneutic, whether you were conscious of it or not? Is there some biblical, transtemporal world view on which our hermeneutic should be based? What criteria should we use to distinguish the timeless truth of Scripture from its historical contextualizations?

We have many more questions, but we will quit for now. In our struggling to know the answers, factions have arisen. Feelings have run high. We can't even hear each other's earnest desire for the truth in our fearful defense of what we believe it to be. A few answers sure would be nice. These questions have everything to do with our ability to understand truth and to be the prophetic voice for God and His Kingdom to the world today. Under the guidance of the Spirit, we will just have to continue to work through these troubling issues until that day when we know in full.

Greet all who are with you on our behalf. We will see you before we know it.

Since we are rather doubtful that Paul will return our letter, we close our book by giving our suggested answers to some of the questions above. Then we survey where this hermeneutic might take us, and invite any fellow explorers to come along.

Chapter Ten

The Big Question

Where Does This Hermeneutic Take Us?

"Now we know in part"

(1 Corinthians 13:12).

We come to the end of our proposal. We are suggesting that the biblical authors practiced something more than the grammatical-historical hermeneutic, and that we can do the same. A biblical passage contains one basic sense (which we have called *essential meaning*), of which there can be many historical particularizations (which we have called *existential meaning/reality*). Sometimes the original human authors were not conscious of this broader sense and intended only the historical particularization about which they wrote. In these cases the Holy Spirit intended in the text deeper meaning of which the human author was unaware.

Using the paradigm of reality, we can distinguish in the text between essential reality, existential reality, and actualization. These are to be a reflection of the biblical world view of God actualizing His Kingdom on earth. The biblical authors read Scripture from this perspective and under the guidance of the Spirit, often discovered meaning there that is inextricably related to, but also beyond, the original author's intention. We can do the same.

Any so-called deeper meanings must be related to the Kingdom center. The validity of any theological formulation and any personal instruction from the Spirit can also be checked by this. We have also the help of the Holy Spirit, spiritual transformation in personal relationship with God, the community of faith, and history to aid us in the interpretation of Scripture and the discovery of truth. Our hope is that this hermeneutic we are suggesting will better empower us as the Church to mediate the presence of God upon the earth and be the prophetic voice to our world today.

By way of further summary, we will recapitulate the answers to several key questions. Then after we take a quick look at where we should go next, we'll wrap up.

LET'S ANSWER A FEW QUESTIONS

About a half-dozen questions about this paradigm are often asked. We have answered most of them in bits and pieces throughout the book, but now we want to give succinct, and in some cases, more thorough answers.

Are you saying that this paradigm is the hermeneutic of the biblical writers?

As we said in chapter 5, we are not saying that the biblical writers consciously thought through this paradigm to find deeper meaning as they read their Bible. It is unlikely that they followed any single exegetical procedure. For example, according to Hays, Paul offers "helter-skelter intuitive readings, unpredictable, ungeneralizable." Modern scholars who adhere to a "conception of exegesis as a rule-governed science have frequently sought to retroject such a conception onto Paul by ascertaining the methods that he employed." However, such classification, while useful, suffers from "ex post facto artificiality." The modern concern for "methodological control in interpretation is foreign to him."[1] Hays' comments apply to the other biblical authors as well. Part of the reason that they didn't go off the deep end in finding deeper meaning is because they believed in the historicity of the faith.

What we are saying is that the biblical writers were so immersed in Scripture's world view that they interpreted what they read from this perspective, finding deeper meaning in the original sense. As Hays says of Paul, his hermeneutic "reads Scripture primarily as a *narrative* of divine election and promise" [italics his], except we believe it to be a narrative about the Kingdom. It is God's act in Christ that illuminates a previously uncomprehended narrative unity in Scripture.[2] For Paul,

> original intention is not a primary hermeneutical concern. He is not constrained by a historical scrupulousness about the original meaning of the text. Eschatological meaning subsumes original sense.... True interpretation depends neither on historical inquiry nor on erudite literary analysis but on attentiveness to the promptings of the Spirit, who reveals the gospel through Scripture in surprising ways."[3]

The paradigm codifies what happens unconsciously by the leading of the Spirit, so in this sense the paradigm could be called the hermeneutic of the biblical authors.

Can we practice their heremeneutic?

Our position, that we can reproduce the hermeneutic of the biblical writers, is anchored in the conviction that such a hermeneutic is discoverable and transferable. That is, it is a hermeneutic which involves submission to the Scriptures for what they might instruct us regarding this topic. It is based in the presupposition that the Bible speaks transtemporally and transculturally with regard to theology, ethics, and hermeneutics. It certainly is no technical, outlined source book on hermeneutics, but neither is it such for theology and ethics.

Our fears regarding subjectivity and heresy should not deter us; subjectivity and heresy always have existed well apart from reproducing the hermeneutic of the Bible.

Many in the Church already do practice the biblical

writer's hermeneutic, just as they did, unconsciously and by the leading of the Spirit. But we recognize this is subject to abuse. Without some objective criterion, it would be difficult to discern what is an authentic reading and what is a misreading of the text. This is one major reason that some people may object to practicing the hermeneutic outlined in this book. The controls provided by the Kingdom center are still not scientific enough for some.

How does your paradigm address the concerns of those who object to deeper meaning?

The paradigm ties the deeper meaning of Scripture to the literal meaning. The Kingdom center provides an objective criterion for evaluating whether we have discovered a legitimate deeper meaning, or applied Scripture in a way contrary to its intent. It embraces the role of the community in discerning the validity of a suggested deeper meaning.

The process is no different for this than it is now for exegesis and theological development. Interpretations and doctrines are posited at a point in history. From there they are tested by the Church as its members wrestle with truth in their historical circumstances. Gradually, truth is affirmed—some of which becomes orthodox, nearly as authoritative as Scripture itself. Other, more uncertain interpretations are held in tension. In the end, all interpretations, including deeper meanings and doctrinal formulations, are subject to Scripture.

Why should we practice this hermeneutic and find deeper meaning?

Some might object, "Following the grammatical-historical hermeneutic gets us everything we need, so why should we look for more?" A better question is, "If deeper meaning is there, why shouldn't we look for it? What are we missing that we are unaware of?" Justification is surely deep enough to get us saved, but it doesn't encompass all that a deep and full life with Christ promises. Further, this hermeneutic better empowers us to find meaning for our lives in Scripture and to contextualize its message for those who need to hear it.

The most important reason, though, is that the biblical writers find deeper meaning. They must have had a reason for doing so. If the Bible is our source for theology and ethics, why is it not also the source of our hermeneutic? We usually object to finding deeper meaning because of fear or contemporary philosophical concerns. Either we attempt to prove that the biblical authors used the grammatical-historical hermeneutic, or we give a theological reason why we can't practice their hermeneutic—they were inspired and we are not. We have addressed these concerns. Fear should not hold us back. The love and freedom God has given us in Christ has liberated us from fear. We can practice this freedom in reading Scripture with confidence.

Do you have any suggestions of deeper meanings in Scripture?

We have been working with this hermeneutic only for a short time. Interpretations and theological ideas are supposed to be tested over time. Any ideas we have are untested, and speaking in historical time, are off the top of our heads. Yet here are some examples, most of which are commonly known and not original with us.

1. Ezekiel and Isaiah prophesy about Satan as well as the historical kings. There is debate about whether these prophecies refer also to Satan. Even if we think they refer to Satan, the language is so extreme that the original writers themselves may well have known that what they were writing described more than just the human king to whom they referred. Yet no later Scripture passage interprets these passages as referring to Satan.

2. Genesis 3:15-16 is commonly considered the *proto-evangelium*, the first promise of the coming of Christ, though no later Scripture passage interprets it as such. It can be argued that the fact that this passage refers to Christ is only an existential unfolding of the essential meaning readily apparent in the passage—the triumph of man. This would mean that finding Christ here is not a deeper meaning since the essential meaning was known to the human author. While we accept this objection as viable, it may not

convince others who see this as another example of deeper meaning in which prophecies are applied to Christ that were not so intended by the original human author.

3. The Old Testament Joseph may be interpreted as a type of Christ, though no later Scripture passage does this.[4]

4. We may be able to extend some analogies and types that the biblical writers began in order to see what we might learn from them. For example:

a. Interpreting the bread and wine in the story of Melchizedek in Genesis along the lines that it is used in Hebrews.

b. Extending Paul's analogy in Galatians between Hagar, who stands for Mt. Sinai and the old covenant, and Sarah, who may stand for Mt. Zion and the new covenant (which are not explicitly mentioned in the text), and making connections between this and comments on Mt. Zion in Hebrews (which is strongly influenced by Pauline theology).

c. Extending Paul's analogy, in Galatians, of the law as a tutor to that of guardian and trustee, with its various ramifications.

d. Extending the implications of covenant according to English custom of testament as the author of Hebrews extends it according to Roman custom.[5]

5. We could look in the tradition that for centuries has been finding deeper meanings and evaluate some—the Contemplative tradition. Many allegorical meanings may have been valid ones.

As we noted in chapter 5, the distinction between finding divinely intended deeper meaning in a passage and finding meaning for one's own day can be fuzzy, even in the writings of the biblical authors. Let's take the book of Hebrews as an example. The author of Hebrews was addressing particular problems of a particular audience. This is readily recognized by all and guesses are made as to who the audience is, based upon the problems the author appears to be addressing. To address these problems, he uses Scripture to prove his arguments, but he interprets these Scriptures from the perspective of the Christ-event, finding meaning that goes beyond the literal meaning and using it to support the theology he is developing in answer to the problems of his audience.

We usually treat the book of Hebrews as though it is presenting a rather flat, abstract theology, deposited once and for all in its final form. Yet our very attempt to discern who the audience is by the problems he addresses, implicitly recognizes this possible truth: the author of Hebrews was developing theology from the perspective of the audience in response to their needs and experiences.

I recently listened to someone's paper on the hermeneutic of the author of Hebrews. He was asked what problems the author was addressing, and what relevance the book has for readers today who are not faced with the same needs and experiences. His answer was that today's audience may have some trouble relating directly to it, and that the relevance would have to be shown to them.

Perhaps this is making an incorrect assumption; maybe the theology of Hebrews, as it is presented in the book, is not supposed to have direct relevance, as though its meaning is our starting place for finding meaning for ourselves. It may be that the author of Hebrews (and other authors) is an example for us of how to practice a postmodern evangelical hermeneutic. Our starting place for finding meaning is our own horizon, our own world, experiences, needs, and questions, just as those of his audience were the starting place for the author of Hebrews. We then answer these questions by developing theology based on reading Scripture (one anchor and horizon) from the perspective of the Kingdom center (another anchor and horizon), of which the Christ-event is the crux, just as the author of Hebrews did.

Notice one very important thing: while our questions are the starting point for the formulation of the theology, the actual conceptual content is provided by the meaning found in some way in Scripture. Our assumption of the proper answer from our own horizon cannot be grounds for dismissing the text.[6] Today we are more likely to try to find a passage in Scripture that can be abstracted and applied to our question, or to answer it from the perspective of a whole system, rather than to use Scripture the way the author of Hebrews did. But there is no reason that we cannot do what he did.

This is not very different from what we profess we are doing in systematic theology, where we develop theology from the perspective of our questions based upon biblical theology, which is theology developed from the perspective of the questions asked within the Bible. The problem is that we don't seem really to be doing systematic theology. We appear to be reading the Bible through centuries-old dogmatic categories and organizing it accordingly, rather than developing an authentic systematic theology for our own day. Perhaps part of the reason we seem frozen in Reformation categories is that our Reformation hermeneutic (the grammatical-historical hermeneutic) may not permit us enough freedom. This hermeneutic that we are proposing permits us the freedom to do what the author of Hebrews did.

What this implies is that there is more than one meaning in the text. This is true, in a qualified sense.[7] We wrote in chapter 5 of the essential meaning of a passage as though there is only one, for the sake of simple presentation of an already complicated concept. Yet that is a bit simplistic. It works well for explaining how a biblical author found a deeper meaning in a passage because he presented only one deeper meaning. But careful thinking will reveal that that is not all that is possible, for this reason (and perhaps others): the meaning of a passage depends upon how much of the passage is selected. The meaning of a word is different from the meaning of the sentence in which it appears, and the meaning of the sentence is different from that of the passage and the story and so on. Therefore, the essential meaning of a word may be different from the essential meaning of its sentence and its passage and its whole story. This is why the biblical writers could take a verse and give it meaning that was (an application of the essential meaning) in the range of its literal meaning, but not the same meaning it had in its original context. So the essential meanings found may vary, at least according to how much of a passage is selected.

Another reason that there may be more than one meaning in a text is that different questions can bring out different meanings that are objectively in the text, but are not the main point of the author. They are not the meanings that appear to be the single intention of the author, which the grammatical-historical hermeneutic claims is the only meaning of the text. One example of this is provided by Erickson.[8] In Matthew 10 Jesus' main point was to teach people not to fear in being His disciples because God takes care of them. To show them this, He pointed to how God takes care of the birds. His intended meaning was, *God takes care of you, so don't worry—confess Me.* But is not a valid meaning of the text also that God takes care of the rest of creation?

Diogenes Allen provides an excellent example of theological development from meaning that is objectively there in the text, yet not the primary meaning. He uses the parable of the Good Samaritan to develop a New Testament view of justice and personhood that strikes at the heart of Western democratic theory.[9] He took the questions that our theory implicitly asks and used meaning in the text (found by asking our questions), to challenge the answers our theory presupposes. All of that meaning is there, but Jesus' purpose was simply to answer the question, "Who is my neighbor?"

These sorts of meanings, like those suggested by Erickson and Allen, do not seem to be quite like many of the meanings found by the biblical writers in their interpretations of the meaning of particular passages. The sorts of meanings above seem more like *other* meanings rather than deeper meanings. (These other meanings were not divinely intended meanings unknown to the human author, but they may provide deeper meaning—as in meaningfulness—for the reader.) These sorts of meanings may be the most important found, but the line between the two may often be fuzzy.

What is the relationship of your paradigm to the grammatical-historical hermeneutic, and other things that we already do?

The paradigm incorporates the practice of the grammatical-historical hermeneutic and goes beyond it. The essential (or deeper) meaning of a passage is related to the literal meaning, and the literal meaning is found using the grammatical-historical hermeneutic.

This last statement needs to be qualified. The literal meaning is found using the grammatical-historical method, but it is not the automatic result of that method. This is because the literal meaning of a book is a biblical theology, a central conception of what the book is all about. The grammatical-historical hermeneutic provides the basic data with which to work, the bits and pieces of meaning that are to be put together in one coherent whole, that is, biblical theology. This is why understanding meaning in the Bible cannot be reduced to historical or literary science, but will always be part art. This is also why we say that the existential meaning[10] of a text is *roughly* equivalent to what is found through the grammatical-historical method. It is yet again one of the reasons that we say the existential meaning is *roughly* the meaning that an unbeliever can understand. (Other reasons include the fact that through the Spirit's work, experience, and growing maturity we understand the same basic meanings at ever more profound levels and make connections not seen before.)

Using the paradigm as a hermeneutic is very much like other methods we use. One of the ways we figure out how to apply Scripture to our lives is through principalizing or discerning timeless truths. This is very much like looking for the essential meaning of a text. The paradigm helps us to find timeless truths and principles more precisely by giving us criteria for distinguishing them from changeable elements of the text and by relating them more directly to the central theme of the Bible. This will keep us from falling short of the timeless truth or principle by mistaking some stage or application in the progress of revelation as the end. It will also keep us from reading in contemporary philosophy as the essential meaning, as many allegorists and theologians such as Bultmann did.

Using the paradigm is also similar to the canonical method. Every text is interpreted in light of the entire canonical context, which we also advocate. The canonical method simply falls a step short in a couple of ways. It does not espouse a specific theological center, which some consider to be a positive attribute of the method. But since it does not do this, the only deeper meanings that can be said to be in texts are those that have already been explicitly uncovered by later writers.[11] The paradigm helps us to discover deeper meaning for ourselves.

Typological and analogical methods also are incorporated within the paradigm. The paradigm simply gives understanding of how the types and analogies were found in the first place and how we might do the same. This also goes for the allegorical method at its best, and every other method that espoused literal meaning and deeper meaning tied to the literal meaning. The paradigm explains the connection between the meanings so that we might discover the deeper meaning with more assurance and a sense of objective control that the grammatical-historical hermeneutic provides in finding the literal meaning.

Application and contextualization of Scripture can also be done with more certainty with the paradigm. Such purposes were often the occasion for the biblical writers themselves to find deeper meaning in their Scripture. Not only does the paradigm help us to find deeper meaning in the Bible for our own lives, but it helps us to distinguish between this meaning for us and the deeper meaning of a passage.[12] This way we keep from absolutizing a Spirit-led application to our own situation as being true for everyone for all time.

It is also similar, in many ways, to the views of reader-response approach, which is being advocated in restricted form by some evangelicals. However, the paradigm provides better control in that the range of meanings that can be found is governed by its intrinsic Kingdom center.

The paradigm is similar to many good things we have always done; we think it just works a little better. It should be quite similar to what we have already been doing since God has been at work all along, bringing increasing clarity to how we are to do it. Anything radically different would, in effect, say that He has not been revealing to us all along how we are to understand His Word.

Because it is so similar to many things we have always done, we can be accused of setting up a straw man (who espouses the grammatical-historical hermeneutic) and tearing him down. But if there are people who hold to the common definition of the grammatical-historical meaning as the single intention of the human author and the view that no other meaning exists, then we have not set up a straw man. Now, this definition has been so qualified of late (as to include types and meanings the human author is not aware of and fulfillments unknown and unforeseen by him)[13] that it is no longer the same definition. Further, reading to find these meanings violates this basic principle of the grammatical-historical hermeneutic: the text is to be read in its "plain" sense unless there are clues within the text itself that it is to be read otherwise.

Now, if a person wants to expand the definition of the grammatical-historical meaning to include all these things, then we are in basic agreement with her and cannot stop her. However, we must admit that it is no longer the same definition, and we need to investigate how this revises our exegetical methodology. We should be honest in admitting that we are, in fact, practicing the grammatical-historical hermeneutic and something more than that. After all, if the world of which the Bible speaks (essential reality or the Kingdom of God) is not precisely the same as the world of the text (the existential reality or historical circumstances in which the text was written), how can we practice only the grammatical-historical hermeneutic and yet exhaust its meaning? God and His Kingdom are not reducible to grammar and history.[14]

We will be hesitant to admit that we are using something more than the grammatical-historical hermeneutic until we have a new construct in which to think—one that better fits our understanding and experience—to replace the old one (rather than just stretching it until it is hardly recognizable). We believe our paradigm may provide a good way to find deeper meanings and other meanings within the range of the grammatical-historical meaning of the text. Our Kingdom hermeneutic affirms meaning as primarily the assertions of the human author, which serve as the vehicle and the boundary for all meaning found.

Often our praxis is better than our theology or our idea of proper methodology. Reading the Bible with the paradigm as a hermeneutic yields results similar to what we already do when we read Scripture devotionally.[15] It allows us to be more intentional in the process and to practice it with more security. We can discern between the Spirit's leading and our own ideas, and affirm with more assurance and less apology the meaning that the Spirit reveals.

WHERE DO WE GO FROM HERE?

Our approach to hermeneutics affects in significant ways how we do biblical and systematic theology and contextualization. Space permits only some initial observations.

To have a viable biblical theology, according to G. Osborne, we must meet certain criteria.[16] It must (1) correspond with all aspects of Scripture, (2) show the historical and dogmatic coherence in the relationship of the Testaments,[17] (3) unite the various strands of theology in the Bible, (4) reflect canonical history as it links the biblical message of salvation and the Church's attestation of faith, and (5) be based on exegesis and hermeneutics. Our paradigm of reality united to a Kingdom center provides a basis for doing biblical theology in such a way that these criteria can be met.

The paradigm of reality also provides a plausible model for constructing systematic theology. It fulfills Osborne's five components of theological construction.[18] Following him, it embraces the ultimate authority of Scripture, the place of tradition, the community, personal experience, and the role of philosophy, though it is neither derived from philosophy nor dependent on it. It arises within Scripture itself. Our paradigm meets the additional criteria of verification or validation, which are coherence, comprehensiveness, adequacy, consistency, continuation, and cross-fertilization.[19]

Osborne, among others, calls for a new model of systematic theology which departs from neo-Platonic and Aristotelian patterns of thinking.[20] This is a timely invitation to us all, for we face a postmodern world and the Church has never been so diverse as now. The bulk of the Church today has never known the Renaissance and the Reformation with their cultural, rational, and spiritual legacies. As Dyrness asserts, it is appropriate that African, Latin, and Eastern legacies participate in the interpretation of Scripture and the formulation of doctrine.[21] Osborne describes this new approach to theology as showing an interdependence of doctrines and more balance between competing systems. It will present this in a narrative approach or *story theology* form, putting an emphasis on praxis rather than abstract meaning.[22] The paradigm of reality with its Kingdom center may hold potential for being at the core of such a new model.

The paradigm of reality may serve well to bring about a more united Church. It helps to distinguish the non-essentials from the essentials and to enable true bonding to occur around the latter. It appears to be compatible with amillennialism as well as premillennialism. It may provide progressive dispensationalism with a new approach to hermeneutics not far from early dispensationalism's broader understanding of meaning.[23]

What about contextualization and application? Contextualization involves such matters as the form and content of the assertions of Scripture, two[24] or three[25] horizons, deculturalization, principle-making, abstractions, and validation of application based on the degree of continuity between audiences of the ancient past and the present (that is, the degree of transfer).[26] The paradigm of reality anchored to the Kingdom center provides much more specific guidance in formulating contextualization, and compels us to apply Scripture along lines the original author/Author intended.

Contextualization also involves the discernment of universal moral absolutes. The way we view the relationship of the Testaments is fundamental to discerning which Old Testament laws are moral absolutes and which are not.[27] While absolutes must be consistent with the progress of God's redemptive program, this is too limited as a criterion. The Kingdom center, with its joint concerns for truth and love, for transcendence and immanence, is a better criterion than redemption.[28] God in redemption does not merely restore the status of creation, as this view claims; He uses redemption to bring us to a level of nobility and relationship unachievable apart from the Incarnation.

In addition, rather than doing contextualization only after doing exegesis, biblical theology, and systematic theology in a linear process, the paradigm of reality calls for discovering the truths of essential reality as part of exegesis because of the dual authorship of Scripture. This results in a much more holistic and integrative exegetical-theological-applicational process, which is also in line with the multi-dimensionality of meaning.

Finally, concerns for developing a biblical world view that is consistent with reality, internally coherent, and open[29] are well met by the paradigm of reality. Throughout our discussion we have been emphasizing that the paradigm of reality is a total world view. It makes sense that God's world view should be the biblical center, and the paradigm of reality with its actualization of the Kingdom center provides this. It seems to fare better than other centers in answering world view kind of questions. To be relevant and viable, it must tell us of ultimate reality and account for reality as we find it. It must tell us who God is and what He is doing, explain why life is the way it is, reveal who we are, how we relate to God and others, and what our purpose is. It must do all this in a coherent, consistent manner. The paradigm appears to do this well.

So where do we go from here? This depends in part upon any feedback we get. If someone points out a fatal flaw, we start from scratch. Otherwise, we will continue developing the entire system to demonstrate whether or not it makes sense of Scripture and answers the needs of the Church. How does it help us understand ordinary and extraordinary passages and solve sticky theological and practical problems? We will also need to show how it does meet all the criteria mentioned above. The underlying philosophical system will need to be developed comprehensively, and findings from linguistics, psychology, and such, will need to be taken into consideration. Explicit hermeneutical/ exegetical methodology will have to be outlined. We will need to explore what the Scriptural criteria are for validation of meaning in the Bible. In short, we need to show how it works and what difference it makes. If it doesn't help the Church to accomplish its God-given mission to mediate the presence of Christ and to proclaim His truth in love to a deteriorating world, then it's useless.

WE'RE IN THIS TOGETHER

We are all part of the Body of Christ and, in various ways, engaged in doing theology for our generation. Truth is tested in community. After having tried it out awhile on a few people, we are now putting this idea before those of us who are interested to think it through and evaluate it together. If you don't think it works, we welcome your ideas on why it doesn't. If you think it has possibilities, perhaps you will join us in testing how it works for exegesis and contextualization.

One colleague, a former missionary who now teaches theology in the States, said after reading one of our papers, "Get this thing out there and let a few of us give it a try." In obedience to everything we have written in this book, we do this gladly and with eagerness to learn together. If you decide to give it a try, we'd love to hear your results.

We, as brothers and sisters for all eternity in Christ, work together for the coming of the Kingdom of God on earth. The Spirit Himself is our *esprit de corps*. We affirm this with joy and delight and thankfulness to God. While we do not prepare the world so that Christ can come in the flesh, we seek His coming every time we beseech Him and endeavor for His Kingdom to be realized in healing and forgiveness, in grace and peace. We seek Him in relationships and broken lives, in triumph over exploitation and injustice, in the transformation of God's enemies into His children through relationship with Him, and in their empowerment in purity and service to others in love and truth for the glory of Christ and His Kingdom.

No matter what our eschatology, we can work and pray for His coming in our own day, until that day when "the kingdom of the world has become the kingdom of our Lord and of his Christ; and he will reign for ever and ever" (Revelation 11:15). Maranatha!

Appendix A

Postmodernism and the Paradigm of Reality

A shift in the whole way we think seems to be taking place before our eyes. While it is still too early (historically speaking) to tell how permanent it will be, it is already highly influential in every realm of human knowledge and will continue to be for some time. Like every philosophy or human idea, postmodernism is a mixture of good and bad. To be responsible Christians, we need to understand it in order to learn from it and to address our world effectively with God and His truth.

SUMMARY OF THREE PHILOSOPHICAL PERIODS

To this end we will give a brief summary of premodern, modern, and postmodern thought.[1] Then we will attempt to evaluate the hermeneutic we are proposing in light of postmodern concerns to see whether our hermeneutic makes use of the positive discoveries of postmodernism, or merely reverts to premodern views and approaches.

Premodernism

The premodern age is characterized by a dogmatic approach to Scripture, authorized by the Church and exemplified by allegory. Private interpretation is not allowed; reading and understanding the Bible must be done within the framework of the life and doctrine of the Church. The Scriptures function as conventional signs, so interpreters use ordinary linguistic and literary resources to perform their task. Yet biblical interpretation has to cohere with the philosophical and theological system of thought inherited from Plato, whereby the visible world is an imperfect imitation of the unseen realities behind it. Therefore, language is essentially "the outward expression of inner ideas or thoughts."[2]

While this era acknowledged the historical content and context of Scripture, it relativized them (often by figure and allegory) to fit the world view which viewed meaning as the outward expressions of an inner reality (metonymic meaning).[3] So the views of self, world, text, language, and meaning were shaped by a Bible read in light of the current world view. The best representative figure of this era is the priest.

Modernism

During the modern period, epistemology (how do we know truth) has come to predominate over concerns about metaphysics (what is reality) and the orderliness of the universe. Epistemological foundationalism has prevailed, meaning that knowledge can be justified only by "finding indubitable 'foundational' beliefs upon which it is constructed."[4] The idea is that there should be unchangeable beliefs as the foundation of knowledge. For Descartes, the foundations of knowledge were intuitions; for Hume and others, sense experience became the foundation upon which all scientific knowledge was to be built. Many challenged these positions, however, so that skepticism has been an ongoing aspect of foundationalism.

In regard to a theory of language, the modern period has embraced the view that language represents the objects or facts to which it refers, or that it expresses the attitudes or emotions of the speaker. Hence, language is representational and expressive. McKnight calls this the descriptive idea of language—it describes an objective, natural order. It is framed on the model of truth by correspondence; that is, something is true if it corresponds to what it refers. So the "criterion of truth is related to the external source of the description rather than to the inner consistency of the argument."[5] Yet language itself has been elevated from a tool of human intercourse to a master, "determining the way cultural phenomena and even humankind itself are perceived."[6] In recent times, language has become more important than humanity, text, and all cultural expressions.[7]

Reflecting the impact of the Renaissance and Reformation, the modern world view has replaced authority with critical human reason as the ultimate criterion for truth. With this, the idea of progress and the principle of evolution have gone hand in hand, along with the concepts of probability in making judgments and analogy based in human experience.

In regard to metaphysics, the modern period has embraced the attempt to understand reality by reducing it to its smallest part, called atomism or reductionism. In ethics and political philosophy, the individual is given priority over the group or community.[8]

In this age, as in each of the others, people are trying to find consistency between their world and the text. That is, they are trying to take their world view and see how the text relates to it. For the modern era, the old dogmatic approach of the ancient and medieval church has been superseded by the historical-critical method of the Enlightenment. This approach has permitted a variety of approaches, including the existential hermeneutics of Bultmann (and others) and canonical and sociological exegesis. It is the source and foundation of the grammatical-historical method. Even nonhistorical approaches emphasizing the text and/or readers, rather than the author, derive from this approach.

With regard to the Bible, the historical-critical method has triumphed.[9] By using all the tools of language study and historical and literary criticism, the interpreter achieves the goal of objective, scientific understanding of the text. The Bible makes sense intellectually and religiously. Scholars have produced a historically accurate understanding of the ancient times when the texts were made. Yet as exegesis has become more and more refined and technical, it has moved further and further from the common Christian.[10]

In summary, the modern era is characterized by the supremacy of reason, the autonomous self, optimism, the right of freedom (academic, moral, political, religious), globalism and tribalism at the same time, propositional truth, inductive Bible study, and neglect of the role of the Holy Spirit in interpretation. The person who best epitomizes the modern period is the scientist (such as Carl Sagan).[11]

It is helpful to compare the premodern and modern approaches, as explained by Millard Erickson.[12] They agree on the objectivity of reality, the referential understanding of language (it refers to something beyond itself; it has an object), and the correspondence theory of truth (ideas are true because they correspond to the state of existence as it is). The differences are as follows: the premodern period fixed this truth or objective meaning in some external (Platonic forms or ideas) or transcendent (the mind of God) realm; while the modern era, more nearly Aristotelian, located objective meaning in experience in several ways. Rationalism found universal truth in a pattern of reason or thought since the order of the human mind corresponds to reality; empiricism found reality in the patterns of experience in the world; and humanism found objective meaning in the self or the individual (as in existential theology).

Erickson (noted above) finds that the premodern era found meaning within the text in a literal or straightforward manner (he is obviously excluding the allegorical and other senses which departed from the literal), the meaning intended by the author. Hermeneutics and exegesis were basically the same. In the modern era, historical criticism sought to determine the history and meaning of the text, which may not be the surface or obvious meaning. In either case, however, the meaning resides in the text, not in the reader.

Postmodernism

Postmodernism in its most radical form turns everything of the preceding eras on its head. For example, in science, Einstein's theory of relativity, Heisenberg's quantum physics, and other scientific advances have all encouraged the idea of relativity. In philosophy, foundationalism is crumbling: there is no truth. In linguistics, interpretations are merely interpretations of other interpretations. The reader rules as the supreme determiner of meaning (although some, such as McKnight, affirm that the text and author are interactive, so that not just anything goes). Just as words find their meanings from sentences and sentences from words, and sentences from larger narratives and narratives from sentences, so also texts find their meanings from life and life from texts. Various life contexts bring out different meanings in texts. In this way, many meanings are found.

Because anything goes in hermeneutics, various forms of criticism are employed to find meaning according to a predetermined criterion, such as feminist or liberationist criticism. In ethics, because social problems are not going away and because there is no absolute truth, we struggle for a basis for ethical decision-making.

Postmodernism considers that the totality of knowledge is a man-made fabric or network subject to experience. Meaning is determined not by its reference, but by its multiple uses in discourse; and *language makes possible both ideas and experience*, rather than the opposite (where ideas and experience determine language).[13] Finally, postmodernism embraces an organic "view of community in ethics and political philosophy—a corporate metaphysics."[14] Indeed, language and the search for knowledge are communal achievements.

The text as language is the focal point, the medium, for changing the reader. Interpretation becomes a "hermeneutical paradigm of understanding by participative dialogue" with the text so that

> reader and text are mutually transformed. The reader is transformed not by capitulation but by conversion, the text is transformed not by dissection but through multiple interpretations to which it gives rise by its surplus of meaning.[15]

Scientific criticism is necessary, but inadequate. "Revelation is not primarily...a matter of more or better knowledge, but of deeper and richer encounter."[16]

Because the cultural rule of science has ended, the postmodern era is characterized by epistemological relativism so that the Bible is just one of many tongues and Christianity is just one of many options. In this sense, "Christianity is intellectually relevant"[17] as one voice among many. Christians can remain faithful to their native language, "to preserve the integrity of the biblical tongue."[18]

In summary, the era is characterized by a denial of objective truth and a unifying center, pessimism, process (instead of solution), spirituality, aloneness, sense of shame (rather than sin and guilt), physical and sexual abuse, irreverence, cynicism, sensuality, and lack of ideology. The representative figure of this era is the rock musician.

We have been describing postmodernism in its extreme form, what is known as *deconstructive postmodernism*.[19] It rules out an objective approach to the facts of experience, and objective referents for words. In literary criticism and in theology, the aim is to "deconstruct the traditional objects of thought and traditional methods of the discipline."[20] The criteria of internal consistency and coherence are considered inapplicable.

A less extreme form of postmodernism is liberationist. It focuses on social and political forms and seeks to change them. It may be third world, black, or feminist. It does not go quite so far in its denial of logical consistency and objective truth.

Constructive postmodernism seeks to revise or rebuild the modern worldview. This approach often takes the form of process metaphysics.

Finally, conservative or restorationist postmodernism, as constructive postmodernism above, seeks to retain much of modern theology, but retains it on the basis of its value in premodernism. It recognizes that the modern world view embraces appropriate and irreversible changes in the way we think of reality. It doesn't "throw out the baby with the bath water" in its evaluation of previous eras.

IS OUR HERMENEUTIC POSTMODERN?

At this point we should make a disclaimer. We never intended to create a postmodern hermeneutic. This hermeneutic was developed intuitively, by reading the Bible from what seemed to be the world view of the Bible. When we began intentional exploration of the method as a hermeneutic, we used it first for interpreting the New Testament, in order to make sense of the tensions within it between who we are in Christ and the injunctions regarding social institutions. Then it occurred to us that we might be able to use this hermeneutic to explain how the New Testament authors found meaning in the Old Testament beyond that of the grammatical-historical hermeneutic. Quite honestly, at this point we knew very little of postmodernism. In fact, we had written most of this book before we began discovering its relevance to postmodernism. But as we began researching postmodernism, we were delighted to discover that our hermeneutic reflects, at least on the surface, some postmodern concerns.

This leads us to observe two things. First, we are by no means experts on postmodernism or philosophy in general. We are not the best qualified analysts to evaluate our own hermeneutic, but we are the best qualified people we could persuade to do it on such short notice! Our grasp of the issues is basic so our observations will be as well. Second, if our proposal proves to be of any value and is in some respects genuinely postmodern, we will have done it entirely by accident. This is not all bad. It is simply evidence again of how God works quietly every day in His ordinary people so that through our collaborative efforts we discover what He has next for us. Given our limitations and our need for each other, we welcome any help from others in this evaluation, and especially from those to whom God has given particular training in these things.

Parts of postmodernism we must categorically reject. The pure subjectivism and denial of an absolute, objective truth characteristic of deconstructive postmodernism is incompatible with evangelical belief. While some good can be gained from liberationist perspectives, we must draw the line at organizing reality from those presuppositions in such a way that the Bible is discredited and even discarded.

Still, there are many good things that we can gain from postmodern discoveries. In order to evaluate our hermeneutic in light of such things, we will first compare notes with ideas from Edgar McKnight's *Postmodern Use of the Bible*.[21] Then we will see how our hermeneutic measures up to the guidelines for a postmodern evangelical hermeneutic in Millard Erickson's *Evangelical Interpretation*.

Gleanings from Postmodernism

Space permits only a few observations and cursory ones at that. Though we cannot agree with many of McKnight's conclusions, we nevertheless appreciate his denial that "anything goes" (61), his desire to remain in some sense faithful to the text (85), and his validation that "the horizons of previous dogmatic and historical approaches...provide control and constitute limitations for the new approaches" (67).

> The new approaches have developed from the conviction that the meaning and significance of the text are not limited to those meanings that conventional historical criticism is designed to recover. Meaning is not reduced to the nexus of historical relationships. Text is not simply a historical source. There is no contradiction between historical study and the more comprehensive model, for the text is *intended* to produce an

effect on the reader, in part perhaps by the quasi-literary activity of the reader's imaginative reconstruction of events that explain the formation of the text (85, italics his).

While we do agree that meaning is more than what can be reduced to history, and that the text is intended to produce an effect on the reader, we need to be careful of the last part. It is true that requiring the reader to reconstruct imaginatively the history behind the text may produce an effect on her, but in saying this we do not want to collapse the "causes" that gave rise to the text into the "effects" that the text produces on the reader, as McKnight seems eager to do.

> Even when the reader appears to be analyzing the text scientifically and discussing the objective structures and causes for such structures, the result of the activity is in part a creative construction of the reader, a construction of *cause*, which is a result of the *effect* of the text in the first place. The meanings behind the text and in front of the text coalesce. The various "causes" that criticism has attempted to discern behind the text need not be ignored. They can be reconceptualized in a radical reader-oriented approach as "effects"—the results of the constructive or imaginative work of readers in front of the text, which not only helps them make sense of the text but also coincidentally makes sense of the world and of themselves. "Causes" will not be denied but will be relativized (175-176, italics ours).

We recognize that reconstructing bits of data/meaning gained by historical methodologies into a comprehensive meaning of the whole text is a creative enterprise carried on from the perspective of our horizon. Nevertheless, we maintain that texts have objective meanings apart from anyone's interpretation, and that it is possible to come to understand that meaning. The text and the reader are on opposite sides of a hermeneutical spiral. The reader does make meaning from the data in and behind the text from her own perspective. Nevertheless, this meaning is continually subjected to scrutiny in light of such data so that the meaning that the reader constructs is ever closer to the meaning of the text as it actually is. While we may never arrive at that meaning perfectly, nevertheless, we can understand it sufficiently to obtain truth.

In emphasizing this possibility, we want to stress again that the meaning cannot be reduced to these causes, though they are a crucial means of our finding meaning. A reader-oriented approach

> refuses to accept the enabling conditions of biblical texts as the cause and the explanation of those texts. These "causes" may then be seen as past and present devices for reader-meaning rather than as a reduction to historical meaning. There is no need for denial of the fact that certain states of affairs or developments operated in some sense as sources for biblical writings and that biblical writings now reflect those enabling conditions. But attention is to be paid to the realities behind the text (as far as they can be ascertained or imaged) in order to understand the text as a pattern of meaning that continues to have an effect on readers (175).

We can affirm this in cautious measure. We would suggest that the causes behind the texts are transtemporal realities of the human condition, reflecting enduring human tendencies, questions, needs, and the transcendent realities of the spiritual realm. Since these more basic causes/realities continue for us, the text is able to have meaning for us and affect us today. We are able to relate to the worlds in the Bible because the most basic realities in them are much like our own. In the process, "the text often challenges the conceptions and ideologies with which the reader begins, and the reader's world is modified or recreated ideologically" (176). Having said this, we affirm that "since the contemporary relevance is mediated and not direct, the reader cannot ignore the ancient circumstances of the text's origin. The reader should not attempt to visualize the writers as intending (in a narrow sense) to communicate with contemporary readers in their particular situations" (220-221).

So the text does determine the boundary of meaning. But this cannot be equated with the author's intended meaning as it has usually been defined.

The intention of the author has been used in literature to guard against undue subjectivity in interpretation. Biblical scholars who are interested in a hermeneutic approach to the Bible as literature and history-oriented scholars sometimes equate intentionality with narrow pragmatic purposes and uses. Literary scholars, however, do not speak of the author's intention in terms of the limited meaning of which an author is conscious or the meaning that is explicitly expressed in the text. [And then he goes on to quote Hirsch to support this view] (248).

This and other observations open up the possibility of multiplicity of meanings. McKnight describes the creative process of the reader interacting with the text within the bounds of language structures in order to make meaning. Then he writes:

The result of the process is a synthesis made by the reader. It is an actualization of the discursive structures of the text. It must be remembered, however, that this actualization cannot be equated with the text. Other actualizations are possible (235).

This is explained by the observation that

readers who wish to make sense of biblical texts may not give uncritical allegiance to some radical deconstructive views, but they can benefit from contemporary emphasis on the fact that no particular context, no particular theme or topic, allows saturation of all the data of a text. The meaning of a text is inexhaustible because no context can provide all the keys to all of its possibilities (241).

In the final analysis, we differ from McKnight here in that we believe there is one theme or context that allows saturation of all of Scripture's data and provides the key to all of its possibilities. This is the Kingdom center, or the world view of our omniscient God. Now, because of our limitations and the finitude of our historical perspective, we understand only part of this. So we can affirm that no single *human* context can provide all the keys to unlock all of Scripture's meaning.

All of this creates the impression that interpretation truly is a matter of one's own opinion. It cannot be, however, since the general meaning of the whole text provides the boundaries for other meanings found in it. The main meaning can usually be ascertained by common sense methods and agreed upon by most people. This meaning is often not in dispute, but the question of whether there are any other meanings besides this one is. We affirm a freedom for a multiplicity of meanings (usually subsidiary) within this boundary and the limits of the words and sentences of the text. McKnight seems to go a little further than this, though.

> Truth is discovered and expressed in terms that make sense within a particular universe of meaning. It is not some final objective trans-historical and trans-human expression of truth, for truth in such a form does not touch us. But meanings that are consistent with the various systems that cohere in a particular universe of meaning are true—or truthful....

> Instead of giving up any attempt to find meaning, we may observe that human beings continue to make sense and to build upon that common sense observation. Even if the sense is not some final synthesis of meaning, a meaning is discovered or created, which is satisfying for the present location of the reader. This meaning is a result of the nexus of signifying systems, which include the reader or the readership. Since these systems are dynamic, meaning is dynamic, and *final meaning* continues to recede (59-60, italics his).

We affirm that, in some sense, meaning continues to unfold because of God's action in history to reveal His truth. We participate in this unfolding by interacting with Scripture (and all that is meant by this) from the perspective of our times. Consequently, no formulation is final and theology is continually being discovered and refined.

Nevertheless, we hold out for a final meaning in the end and affirm that we have the essence of that final meaning now, and in a real sense, always have had. (McKnight implicitly affirms this in his quote from Alan Richardson, 185.) Basic truth regarding the nature of God and humanity, the relationship between the two, and the human condition remain unchanged. His observations here will prove helpful, though, in informing how we approach demonstrating the truth of the Bible in a postmodern culture.

There is ultimate, objective truth, and yet there is room for a multiplicity of meanings within the boundary of this final meaning. Our paradigm permits the discovery of such meanings while providing a control in the form of the Kingdom center of Scripture and the sense of the grammatical-historical meanings of passages of various sizes.

Guidelines for a Postmodern Evangelical Hermeneutic

The handiest means of evaluation we have available to us is the set of guidelines Millard Erickson developed specifically for a postmodern evangelical hermeneutic. We will briefly summarize each of the eleven guidelines, and following each summary, make observations regarding our proposal. The comments regarding our own hermeneutic are better understood after reading our whole book, and in some cases, may be confusing or even troubling if not interpreted from the perspective of the whole. Also, for those without sufficient preparation, the sentence summaries of Ericksons's guidelines may be meaningless. We encourage you to read the few pages where he develops each in several paragraphs.[22]

1. An evangelical approach must take seriously the rejection of foundationalism and may need to be more like presuppositionalism, and show how its system of assumptions is more consistent and coherent and better fits the broad sweep of experience than other systems do.

Here Erickson is thinking more broadly than our modest

attempt in this book. We wrote only with an evangelical audience in view, addressing evangelical questions delimited by certain shared assumptions. We have not attempted to make an apology for our hermeneutic to the rest of the world. Further, in this book we have not developed the entire system.

Nevertheless, our proposal seems to fulfill at least partially this guideline. Our approach is definitely presuppositionalist and not foundationalist. Our appeal is that it better fits the data and individual and collective experience, but we are comparing only with the prevailing evangelical hermeneutic, and in a lesser way, with the historical and contemporary methods that Christians have espoused for explaining the phenomena of deeper meaning. We are not comparing it with approaches that are fundamentally incompatible with evangelical presuppositions. We do develop other areas related to our hermeneutic to demonstrate, in some measure, its consistency and coherence and better accounting for experience. We have developed far more than what is contained in this book. It is sufficient for now to say that we are taking the general approach outlined by Erickson.

2. An evangelical hermeneutic will re-evaluate what language signs signify, and Erickson suggests that the referent of a word is the concept, not the actual thing, much like ancient Platonism.

It is here that we immediately resonated with Erickson's proposed guidelines. Our idea of the essential reality/essential meaning of a text seems to fit precisely what Erickson is talking about. At the very least, this allows there to be a fuller meaning beyond what may have been intended by the human author (who may have only intended the "thing" and not consciously the broader concept to be interpreted later beyond his intent), but still within the range governed by the grammatical-historical meaning. This permits us to develop theologies and find meanings that are in some sense within the text, but not consciously and singly intended by the human author. This essential meaning takes us a long way toward finding the meaning for our day and for contextualizing the message to different audiences. We affirm verbal inspiration, but maintain that the real locus of revelation is in the essential meaning of a passage. We trust that our paradigm is not a reversion to premodernism in its similarity to Platonism, but we are not able to say definitively that it is not.[23]

3. A postmodern hermeneutic will have to consider the fact that meaningfulness rather than meaning is the main issue for many people today.

A major goal of our hermeneutic is to facilitate meaningfulness of the Bible. In fact, the line between meaningfulness and meaning is fuzzy. We will be criticized by some because it will not always be easy to tell whether meaning found using our hermeneutic is meaningfulness for today or divinely intended meaning (as the biblical writers seemed to find) for all time. This distinction is difficult to make even in the use of Scripture by the biblical writers since they were using Scripture to address the people and conditions in their day. In any case, our hermeneutic is strong in the area of addressing the desire for meaningfulness.

4. The meaning of individual biblical propositions may be better demonstrated through showing the meaning and meaningfulness of the system as a whole, and then the individual parts to that system.

This is precisely the approach we take in our entire system, the majority of which is not in this book. Specific verses and whole passages may not be made to apply directly to contemporary issues, and even if they are, they will not be accepted on that basis. The Bible holds no authority in our broader culture, so quoting passages will accomplish nothing. And even among Christians, the broader system that interprets a particular passage must be demonstrated, since we are commonly aware that passages can be understood in different ways depending upon from what system they are interpreted. Again, simply quoting a passage will not do. We continue to work on the development of our system to demonstrate the meaning of all the parts.

5. Related to the previous guideline, the meaningfulness of biblical passages will be demonstrated by showing how they address core human needs.

The system we are developing does this. Where individual passages do not address these needs directly, their meaningfulness can be shown by how they fit into the system which addresses these needs. The presuppositional system which proves persuasive will be the one that not only fits human experience, but meets the deepest human needs. This is not developed directly in this book, but it is often addressed peripherally, and one of the goals of our hermeneutic is to facilitate this meaningfulness of biblical passages. The biblical world view of the Kingdom, upon which the paradigm is based, directly addresses many of these core human needs.

6. A postmodern evangelical hermeneutic will make use of phenomenology to identify human needs and elements of human experience to which the Bible can be related.

This guideline is a little confusing. Phenomenology is to be used to identify elements of the experience of secular humanity which transcend the limits of its own categories. So phenomenology appears to be more of a hermeneutic for evaluating secular hermeneutics for finding meaning in life, rather than for understanding meaning in the Bible. The results of this analysis through the use of phenomenology are the human needs or experiences to which the Bible can be related. In this sense, phenomenology seems to be a hermeneutic for Scripture since these needs and experiences are then the perspective from which Scripture is read for the purpose of finding meaning (including meaningfulness). It is in the use of phenomenology that an evangelical hermeneutic will be postmodern and not just premodern, according to Erickson. We are guessing that it will be postmodern rather than premodern because meaning in Scripture will be found from the perspective of experience, not just from the perspective of predetermined dogmatic categories superimposed upon the Bible.

If we have correctly understood this guideline, we appear

to be in basic agreement with it. We do not discuss phenomenology specifically. We do advocate the discovery of "new" truth in part from the basis of personal and collective experience, and even call this truth "revelation." At the very least, we encourage the formulation of doctrine from the perspective of questions being asked or needs that should be addressed as a major part of contextualizing the truth.

7. A postmodern evangelical hermeneutic will not limit itself to natural, historical explanations for the content and the production of the text since postmodernism has discovered that the universe is not a law-bound, self-sustaining system, and that supernatural explanations cannot be ruled out as an assumption.

We take seriously God's work in ordinary human processes to accomplish His will through immanent historical means, as well as through acts that violate so-called natural laws. In this sense, we have not reverted to premodernism. However, we also directly assert that God has supernaturally caused everything, including the production of the Bible. We take very seriously His co-authorship and assert that He intended meaning unknown to the human author. According to this guideline of Erickson's, we are indeed postmodern.

8. In the postmodern world, hermeneutics will be carried on in groups, and not just as individuals.

We strongly affirm the role of community in discerning and discovering meaning. It is an integral part of our hermeneutic. A more postmodern idea is that of the community determining what is a legitimate reading of a text. We embrace this in recognizing the role of community in safeguarding and handing down the truth. Yet, as postmodernism has observed, the community is not ultimately determinative since individuals are able to find meanings that disagree with those of the community. We affirm this as a legitimate possibility in recognizing that God uses individuals to change the community as they posit ideas for meaning before the community for consideration. We probably emphasize a stronger role for community than postmodernism does in determining the legitimacy of a reading,[24] but we balance this with the reminder that community is the whole community of faith from all traditions and cultures and times.

This book itself was written by two people and its ideas discussed with many others. As a whole, evangelicalism (even more so than our culture, which is changing in this regard faster than we are) hasn't caught on to working in groups yet. Quite frankly, we have found it difficult to find some forum for vigorously exploring this book's ideas and related topics. Until we place a higher premium on community and working together—or until we are forced to do so by the explosion of knowledge and the sheer impossibility of doing significant work alone—hermeneutics will continue to be primarily an individual effort submitted to the community for review and interaction. It may well be that with the shift of the Church's balance from the West to the Third World, we will learn community better. It is endemic to that region, which will pass by the West if we don't learn it.

9. A postmodern evangelical hermeneutic must have a genuinely philosophical basis and be part of a larger, carefully thought through philosophical system.

Here we fall miserably short. Our hermeneutic has a philosophical basis, just as every idea does, but we probably don't know what it is. From the very beginning our primary concern regarding the viability of our hermeneutic has been the soundness of its philosophical basis. Apart from becoming linguists or philosophers (and the case could be made that that is what we should have done), we can only submit our ideas to those so trained for evaluation. And it seems that the best (and in some cases the only) way to do that is to put it into print for someone to find and criticize.

Our lack of qualifications in these two areas obviously does not mean that we are barred from coming up with anything helpful. It does mean that what we have done needs to be tested by those better qualified in these areas. Even that is not definitive since in time, one paradigm replaces another and ideas are tested through history. In light of this, we decided to submit our ideas to the community now since our own system assumes that no matter how carefully it is prepared and completed, no formulation is final.

10. More work needs to be done in *metahermeneutics*, or hermeneutical theory rather than practice.

Our book is definitely more about hermeneutical theory than practice. This theory is being submitted for review, and if it is found helpful, practice will develop further from it.

11. A postmodern evangelical hermeneutic will take into account global and multi-cultural issues.

Our proposal directly addresses this in the role of community and makes plenty of room for meaning to be found from various perspectives. We warn ourselves that much of the concern of postmodernism derives from the West and we may well be myopic as far as the global Church is concerned. From the beginning, we have been concerned that the perspective of the whole Body universal must be appreciated. This is one reason why we have tried to cultivate our hermeneutic from the Bible alone so as to let its world view, that is, its view of reality, and its practice of interpretation, inform ours. We agree that it is time for that part of the Church existing in the West to listen to that part of the Body found in the rest of the world.

CONCLUSION

As best as we can tell, our proposal is a genuinely postmodern evangelical hermeneutic. It takes into consideration such postmodern concerns as multiplicity of meaning, the role of the reader in making meaning, community, the possibility for the supernatural, meaningfulness, meaning being demonstrated in a nexus of systems, and more. At the same time, it does not abandon the good things from modernism, such as understanding historical causes and conditioning of the text and the developmental nature of its contents. It does not merely revert to premodernism. Above all, we believe that it is a biblical hermeneutic.

Appendix B

Reproducing the Hermeneutic of the Bible

We have shown that the world view of Scripture focuses on two perspectives of reality, with the Kingdom as its central theme; that this world view should include how the biblical writers do interpretation; and that their interpretation finds additional, divine meaning that often goes beyond the meaning intended by the human author. We proposed that this world view with its special practice of interpretation should be imitated by us. We believe that we can and should follow the hermeneutic of Scripture, even when it finds additional meaning—yet we cannot claim canonical normativity for our interpretation (this is the third alternative adopted in chapter 1).

The major objections against our reproducing the biblical hermeneutic are fear of where it will lead, and ambiguity regarding the accuracy of the results. Let us address both of these concerns.

OBJECTIONS ADDRESSED

Regarding the fear, it is important to remember that the Holy Spirit is guarding His Church. We provide particular corollaries that give parameters to hermeneutical freedom, namely the work of the Holy Spirit, the community of faith, a revised model of spirituality, and interpretation of history as well as Scripture from the Kingdom center. Besides, one cannot dismiss a truth because of its problems.[1] Refusing to pursue essential meaning is just as likely to keep us from *truth* as it is to keep us from *error*.

Second, how are we to know if we have arrived at correct meaning? The process is no different for this than it is now for exegesis and theological development.[2] Interpretations and doctrines are posited at a point in history. From there they are tested by the Church as it wrestles with truth in its historical circumstances. Gradually truth is affirmed, some of which becomes orthodox, nearly as authoritative as Scripture itself (e.g. the conclusion of the Council of Nicea regarding the deity of Christ, as explained above). Other more uncertain interpretations are held in tension. In the end, all interpretations and doctrinal formulations are subject to Scripture.

Only time will tell. Until Christ comes, we may never know for sure if an interpretation is truth (1 Corinthians 13:9-12; 2 Peter 3:17; 1 John. 2:26-27). Little more ambiguity is admitted by searching for a deeper sense because although Scripture is the final rule, our hermeneutic determines somewhat the results of our exegesis—and sixteen hundred years after the close of the Canon, we cannot even agree on our hermeneutic!

ADVOCATES CITED

There is a growing impetus from many quarters for us to practice the hermeneutic of the Scriptures. The suggestion of canonical criticism that the Bible as Canon is "a veritable textbook of hermeneutics on how to adopt and adapt wisdom from any part of God's creation";[3] extremes such as reader-response criticism which take us further and further from the literal meaning, from authorial intention; the plethora of attempts to find an acceptable hermeneutic; the cautions of modern studies in the meaning of meaning; the increasing diversity and universality of the Church; the passing of the modern age and its patterns of thinking and knowing; and the existence of an approach at hand in Scripture all compel us to let Scripture finally speak for itself in this vital area.

Voices here and there throughout the Church, both in the past and now, have affirmed that we should follow the practice of the biblical writers themselves in their finding additional meaning in their use of previous Scripture. We trace here a few of these contemporary voices. Obviously our presentation builds upon the study of the previous chapters which sought to expose the existence of a deeper, essential meaning (as in chapter 3).

D. Moo takes exception to the literal one-meaning view of Kaiser and others. He believes that this approach may commit the "intentional fallacy," does not allow adequately for the divine intention, and does not allow for the "added" meaning that a text may take on as a result of the ongoing writing of Scripture (the growth of the Canon).[4] Moo can embrace a *sensus plenior* explanation for the additional meaning the New Testament discovers in the Old, but prefers a canonical approach and its witness to salvation history. He believes that we can reproduce with caution the exegesis of the New Testament, applying similar criteria to our own interpretation, but we do not have the same revelatory authority to make the specific identifications which the New Testament makes.[5] This deeper or extended or fuller meaning is always based on the meaning intended by the human author.

R. Longenecker believes differently. We may duplicate the literal use of the Old Testament by the New, but not its method when it involves *pesher*, *midrash* or allegory. These require a special revelatory stance.[6] Yet what if these three methods are part of their "literal" or usual way of interpretation? Is it proper, or even possible, for us to distinguish these when they did not? Are we not imposing an artificial distinction on first century writers which they would not recognize? The approach of Longenecker, which is typical of evangelicals, grants, in the words of Hays, "hermeneutical veto power to a modern critical method of which Paul himself was entirely innocent. From the perspective of faith it is not clear why this should be so."[7]

M. Silva, in departing from his co-author, W. Kaiser, believes that there is more to the biblical message than is apparent on the surface. Because of the primary origin of the Bible in the mind of God there is "considerable meaning in the biblical text that the human authors were not fully aware of." He bases this on both literary and theological grounds. Meaning need not be identified completely with the author's intention. However, authorial meaning is indispensable or primary.[8] Elsewhere he argues that Scripture must be the source of our methods of interpretation; otherwise we are "in practice denying the authoritative character of their scriptural interpretation...and to do so is to strike at the very heart of the Christian faith."[9]

R. Hays writes in a similar vein. He believes that we can interpret Scripture with the same freedom that Paul did. Paul's interpretations of his Scripture are normative and his interpretive methods are examples for us to follow. To try to separate the theology from the method which presents it is to practice "intellectual schizophrenia." It is not possible to accept Paul's message "while simultaneously rejecting the legitimacy of the scriptural interpretation that sustains it." We end up formally identical to the rabbis when we view Scripture as belonging to a "holy past in which we no longer can presume to participate." We cut "the lifeline between Paul's time and ours." If Paul's hermeneutic is wrong, then it can only lead us astray.[10]

S. L. Johnson believes that the very issue of inerrancy itself is at stake in the matter of how the New Testament uses the Old. In contrast to Kaiser and Radmacher, cited in Appendix F, he sees inerrancy bolstered by reproducing the hermeneutic of the biblical writers. Basing his view on the dual nature of Scripture, Johnson notes that "the biblical interpreter is interested not only in what the inspired author meant but also in what God meant." To the question whether we can reproduce the exegesis of the New Testament, Johnson answers:

> Unhesitatingly the reply is yes, although we are not allowed to claim for our results the infallibility of the Lord and His apostles. They are reliable teachers of biblical doctrine and they are reliable teachers of hermeneutics and exegesis. We not only can reproduce their exegetical methodology, we must if we are to be taught their understanding of Holy Scripture.[11]

K. Snodgrass acknowledges the tendency of the New Testament writers to use the Old in ways "different from their original intention." Whether we should interpret the Old Testament the same way the New Testament writers did is uncertain, he seems to say. Yet he is convinced that we have not "completed the interpretive task until we have determined how a text does or does not correspond with Jesus' ministry or the ministry of the church."[12]

G. K. Beale, in his approach to typology, shows that Christ as the center of history is the key to interpreting earlier portions of the Old Testament and that there is dual authorship. He believes that we can and must reproduce the exegetical method of New Testament writers in order to feel "corporately" at one with them, although we may not be able to claim that our interpretation is normative.[13]

Klein and his co-authors support the idea that readers create meaning in their interaction with the text. Under certain controls, including the author's intended meaning, we may read texts with fresh meaning, not limited to the original sense.[14]

McCartney and Clayton affirm that we can discover a fuller, divinely intended meaning in addition to the grammatical-historical one. They give several controls for doing so.[15]

D. Bock advocates a complementary hermeneutic. By this we read the Bible and find meaning at two different levels: the historical-exegetical and the theological-canonical. In the latter we discover that a text may have a force beyond what the original author could have grasped.[16]

B. Chilton identifies Jesus' hermeneutic as that of "fulfilled interpretation" and believes that we can reproduce it.[17] In contrast to *midrash*, *pesher*, and *targum*, with their concern to contemporize the text, Jesus goes further by introducing His own insight. So we cannot stop with the question of what a text means—we must see how the text freshly speaks of the activity of God. Jesus makes "God's present activity, not the text, his point of departure." He does not use present circumstances to explain Scripture, but uses Scripture to assert God's meaning and action for the present. "God's activity is the 'text,' and scripture is only the vehicle of expressing the present reality of God." So the text becomes a reflection of Jesus' experience of God. Jesus fulfills what is lacking in the text itself.

Finally, we could add here all those interpreters and authors of texts on hermeneutics (Ramm, Mickelsen, etc.) who believe that we can find additional types in Scripture beyond those identified in Scripture. Typology lies outside grammatical-historical interpretation so our practice of typology engages us in discovering a form of additional or deeper meaning.

CONCLUDING THOUGHTS

While writers approach and pursue differently the question of reproducing the hermeneutic of Scripture, they do hold in common the belief that it can and should be reproduced in some respects. They call the result of such things the deeper meaning, divine meaning, additional meaning, or new meaning. We favor essential meaning for the other terms fail to characterize the nature of this meaning, and some raise other problems concerning revelation and dichotomy of meaning. Most importantly, essential meaning readily reflects the biblical world view of Kingdom reality.

And so there are many voices[18] calling for reproducing the hermeneutic of the biblical writers, and we join ours with them.

The Kingdom Center as Rule and Relationship

The Kingdom center, with its dual nature of rule and relationship, permeates the Bible from cover to cover. We briefly demonstrate this here.

THE WITNESS OF THE OLD TESTAMENT

This center begins with the very reason why God created man and woman: they are to exercise rule over the world on behalf of God (Genesis 1:26-28; Psalm 8) in offensive action against the realm of darkness. Yet they are made in His image and He walked with them in Eden (ch. 2). God's presence among Israel distinguished them from all other peoples. He, as the eternal King, delivered Israel at the Red Sea, and in His unfailing love, the angel of His presence led and guided them (Exodus 15:18, 13; 23:20-24). Israel was to be a "kingdom of priests" (Exodus 19:6—a role now given also to Christians, cf. 1 Peter 2:9); and He delivered them from Egypt on eagle's wings and brought them to Himself as His treasured possession (vv. 4-5).

God was King over Israel (Deuteronomy 33:5), both in a transcendent sense (from the heavens, v. 26) and in an immanent sense (He was their refuge with everlasting arms under them, v. 27). So when Israel sought a human king, God interpreted it as a rejection of Him as their true King (1 Samuel 8:7). Yet He promised that David and his sons would be as His sons and He would be as their Father (2 Samuel 7:14). This promise is ultimately fulfilled only in the new heavens and new earth, when God will dwell with the saints and they will be His people and will see His face (Revelation 21:3, 7; 22:4). The Abrahamic covenant was cast in the form of ancient Near Eastern royal land-grant treaties, and the Sinaitic covenant—with all of Deuteronomy and Joshua 24—had the form of Near Eastern suzerainty-vassal treaties. So even the form of the covenant itself reminds us of Kingdom rule and relationship.

Perhaps the psalms of David and others best demonstrate this Kingdom center and its dual nature. Just citing the instances where both rule and relationship exist back to back would include, we estimate, about a third or more of the psalms, beginning with Psalm 2 and ending with Psalm 149. Particular examples include Psalms 2, 5, 7-11, 16-19, 22 (especially), 24, 29, 33, 44-47, 53, 55, 57, 59-61, 65-68, 72-74, 76, 78, 80, 84, 86, 89, 90-100 (most of which are labeled *Royal Psalms*), 102-111, 113, 115-119, 123, 132, 134-136, 138-139, 144-150. So great is the emphasis on relationship with God, that if we were to include such concepts of God as "almighty," "sovereign," and the like, to capture His transcendence, then virtually every psalm presents this double emphasis. The ideas of love and faithfulness are frequent reminders of God's immanence throughout the psalms.

An instance from each of the Major Prophets will illustrate their rich portrayal of this Kingdom center. The coming Ruler on David's throne will be called the everlasting Father and the Prince of Peace (Isaiah 9:6). In future days God will restore Israel to the land (Jeremiah 30:3), will raise up David their king for them (v. 9), and will be with them (v. 11). Israel's Ruler will arise from among them

(v. 21) and they will be His people (v. 22; 31:1, 33) and all will know Him (v. 34). The future prince, David, will reign forever and will alone eat in the presence of the LORD (Ezekiel 34:21-24; 37:24-28; 44:3). The very last words of this prophet emphasize God's immanence. The name of the city will be, "The LORD Is There" (48:35; cf. Revelation 21:22-22:5).

The so-called Minor Prophets continue this emphasis. Joshua the priest (immanence) is crowned as king (transcendence) to rule, to show that there is harmony between the two offices (Zechariah 6:13). By its date, Malachi is the very last book of the Old Testament. And here God is again presented as a great King whose name is to be feared among the nations (1:14). Yet His immanence is emphasized also: He loves Israel (1:2), is their Father (1:6; 2:10), and promises that He will make those who fear Him His treasured possession and object of compassion—as a father his son (3:17). We could go on and on.

Some of the motifs used to relate the Testaments (as discussed in chapter 3) reinforce the Kingdom center. For example, the promise of God, promise and fulfillment, Christology and others usually can be identified with the Kingdom. While covenant is a key concept, it, like the greater concept of redemption, is part of the yet greater Kingdom center. Indeed, covenant and redemption serve to secure the rule and relationship of God. They find the basis of their existence in the Kingdom. The emphasis on relationship by covenant, especially the New Covenant, is strong in the Prophets. In Ezekiel alone we are told that it includes the Spirit, peace, and people becoming the people of God (11:19-20; 16:60; 18:31; 20:37; 34:25-31; 36:26-28; 37:14, 23-28; 39:22-28).

THE WITNESS OF THE NEW TESTAMENT

In the New Testament, the pattern of the Old, where God was revealed as King over all the earth and as Yahweh in covenant love with Israel, is enhanced. Jesus intimately brings the Kingdom of God to all who believe in Him. The new birth accomplishes this (John 3:3, 5). In Him the

Kingdom is present (Luke 17:21).

The New Testament begins with the magi seeking the King of the Jews (Matthew 2:2). The angel announces Jesus as Emmanuel—God with us. The nearness of the Kingdom is the substance of both John's and Jesus' preaching (3:2; 4:17). It is the center of the Sermon on the Mount (5:20), and its coming is the focus of the Lord's prayer (6:10). The Kingdom is forcefully advancing (11:12), and its nature is explained by the parables (ch. 13). A scribe of the law must also be instructed in the Kingdom of heaven to discover old and new things. The Transfiguration is a foreview of the Son of Man coming in His Kingdom (16:28-17:12). The triumphal entry heralded Christ as King (21:4) and when the gospel of the Kingdom has been preached in all the world, the end will come (24:13). At His return He will sit on His throne as King and judge the nations (25:31), yet His disciples will reign with Him. Finally, Jesus is tried and crucified as King of the Jews (27:11-44). After the resurrection, He commissions His disciples with all power in heaven and earth and yet, He is with them always (28:18-20).

Similarly, Acts witnesses that the Kingdom was the substance of what Jesus taught His disciples before His ascension (1:3) and what they are to await (1:6-8). Peter preached that Jesus was to sit on David's throne (2:30), yet to be believed as both Lord and Christ (2:36). In Paul's preaching, the gospel of grace is thought of as equal to the Kingdom as he summarizes his three years at Ephesus (19:8; 20:24-25; also Colossians 1:13; 4:11), and as Luke summarizes his two years at Rome (28:23, 31). Indeed, Paul sought, at the end of his life, to be brought safely to the heavenly Kingdom (2 Timothy 4:18), with the Lord standing beside him until then (4:17).

While the Epistles do not frequently use the word "Kingdom" per se, they nevertheless continue this emphasis on rule and relationship. For example, Jesus reigns over all rulers and powers, yet is head of His body the Church in which all are brought near and in which God dwells (Ephesians 1:20-2:22). For believers, the Kingdom is not a matter of external things but of righteousness, peace and joy of the Spirit (Romans 14:17). Even when it is not referred to directly, the Kingdom perspective is the world view from which the Epistles were written, providing the basis for all the instructions within them. Reading them from this perspective helps to unlock their meaning.

In Hebrews, Jesus is both King (1:8-9) and Priest (2:17), Creator (1:10-12) and Brother (2:11-12, 17). He is the divine Son on His throne (1:8-9) and yet He died for us (2:9). Because He died He is the Son of Man already crowned with glory and honor (2:5-9), our Melchizedekan Priest-King (ch. 7), and the Author and Perfecter of our faith (12:1-2). He is the Son over God's house which we are (3:6). While God is a consuming fire (12:29), we are to draw near to Him (10:22). Significantly, we have already arrived at Mount Zion, at the heavenly Jerusalem, and come to angels, to the Church of the firstborn, to the spirits of the righteous, to God the Judge of all, and to Jesus the mediator of the New Covenant (12:22-24). Most significantly, we are receiving in the present a Kingdom which cannot be shaken (12:29). In our essential reality we have arrived!

Finally, Revelation shows that believers are a kingdom of priests (1:6, 9; 5:10). While Jesus is King of kings and Lord of lords (19:16), the overcomers will rule with Him over the nations (2:26-27; 3:21; 20:4, 6; 22:5). God will dwell with His people (21:3-7), and they will see His face (22:4). The ultimate purpose of rule and relationship is the glory of God in our union with Him, and it is achieved in this, the eternal state—fulfilling Jesus' prayer in John 17.

Appendix D

Kingdom Light on Difficult Issues

I n the following pages we show applications of the paradigm of reality involving existential reality, essential
reality, and actualization to specific cultural patterns and
social institutions. To save space and time we will present
this in a concise format, much like an outline. While some
clarity is lost, we think that showing how the paradigm
works in many cases and situations is of greater benefit.

PARADIGM APPLIED TO VARIOUS CHRISTIAN DILEMMAS

A. *The Worship of God (John 4:19-24)*. Jesus spoke about
the worship of God to the Samaritan woman. *Existential
reality:* Jews have no dealings with Samaritans; "salvation is
from the Jews" (v. 22); Messiah is present (v. 26). *Essential
reality:* "God is spirit, and those who worship him must worship in spirit and truth" (v. 24); in Christ Jesus "there is neither Jew nor Greek" (Galatians 3:28; note also Romans
10:12; 1 Corinthians 1:24; 12:13; Colossians 3:11). *Process:*
an hour is coming when the Father is worshiped "neither in

this mountain nor in Jerusalem" (v. 21); "an hour is coming, and now is, when true worshipers shall worship the Father in spirit and truth" (as opposed to the physical, v. 23). With the arrival of Messiah and His Kingdom, the nature and means of worshiping God have changed. There is a necessity to change (v. 24), to actualize the Kingdom now. The presence of God among His people in the new heavens and new earth (Revelation 21-22) is in process of realization now. We are His temple (2 Corinthians 6:16-18). We are to be a spiritual people of God whose whole lives are worship carried out in our bodies wherever we are. There is no earthly center of worship wherein God particularly dwells; every place is sacred where the believer is because God dwells in the believer.

B. *Neutral Things: Food Sacrificed to Idols (1 Corinthians 8; 10).* The early Church struggled over the potential compromise with paganism if believers ate food which had first been sacrificed to idols. *Existential reality:* the strong eat and the weak do not eat food sacrificed to idols (1 Corinthians 8:7, 9-10); there are different levels of knowledge or maturity (8:7). *Essential reality:* idols are nothing; there is no God but one (8:4-6); food does not commend us to God (8:8, i.e., it does not effect spirituality); all things are lawful (10:23); everything is the Lord's (10:26); there is freedom to eat (8:9; 10:25-27); God's glory is paramount (10:31). *Process:* abstain from freedom to eat if offense is made, causing another to stumble (8:9-13; 10:28-29), and so sin against Christ (8:12); partake with thankfulness (10:30); do all (eating or abstaining) to the glory of God (10:31); give no offense to Jews, Greeks, or the Church of God (10:32); please all men, seek their profit, that they may be saved (10:33); follow Paul's example and Christ's (11:1). The essential reality of total freedom can be pursued unless circumstances (i.e., love, to avoid offense to the gospel) dictate otherwise. The old restraints of the Law regarding clean and unclean animals, etc., have already disappeared (cf. Acts 15:29; for other neutral things, see Romans 14:1-23).

C. *The Rights of an Apostle and Ministers (1 Corinthians 9:1-23).* *Existential reality:* Paul and Barnabas (and all ministers) need sustenance while they preach the gospel but their motives may be misunderstood if they live on offerings and do not support themselves (v. 6), while others do not; they endure all things (v. 12); they use no income from the gospel (v. 15). *Essential reality:* Paul is free and an apostle (v. 1-2), with attendant rights; he is free, a slave to none (v. 19). *Process:* Although Paul has a right to food and drink (v. 3), a right to a wife (v. 5), a right to support from the gospel (v. 12-14), he foregoes his rights (v. 12, 15, 18); he becomes all things to all men, including a slave, a Jew, under law, without law, and weak (v. 19-22); in order to win as many as possible (v. 19); for the sake of the gospel (v. 12, 18, 23). Freedom and rights exist to be exercised, but for this apostle it is a personal choice not to exercise them in order to avoid any occasion for misunderstanding and to secure a greater response to the gospel.

D. *Lawsuits between Christians (1 Corinthians 6:1-8).* *Existential reality:* Christians are having disagreements and taking each other to court before unbelievers (v. 1, 6), thus wronging and defrauding brothers (v. 8). *Essential reality:* saints will judge the world (v. 2) and angels (v. 3); they are brothers in Christ (v. 5). *Process:* Christians are competent to judge trivial cases and matters of this life (v. 2-3) between brothers (v. 5). They should be judged before competent saints (v. 5) but not before unbelievers. If this is not possible, they should allow themselves to be defrauded and wronged (v. 7-8). Here the believers are already suffering defeat (v. 7) if they have lawsuits with one another. In love they should let the implications of essential reality control their affairs. If necessary, they should allow themselves to be defrauded and wronged, presumably to avoid bringing offense to the gospel.

E. *The rule of Mankind (Hebrews 2:5-18).* *Existential reality:* at the present time we do not see humanity, though crowned with glory and honor (2:7), exercising the rule over the entire creation that God ordained for them (Genesis 1:26-27) and which David reiterated (Psalm 8). They do not yet rule "the world to come" (2:5). *Essential reality:* we see Jesus, the representative man, crowned and ruling with glory and honor because He suffered death for all. He is bringing many sons to glory. Both Jesus, who sanctifies, and we who are sanctified, are of the same family, so Jesus is not ashamed to call us brothers (2:10-11). *Process:* we are to see Jesus as crowned with glory and honor; His death destroyed the devil with his power of death and freed us from the slavery caused by the fear of death. He helps us, not angels. He has been made like us in every way in order to be a merciful and faithful high priest, to make atonement for our sins, and to help us when being tempted (2:9-18). We are to consider this exmple of Jesus (3:1), hold fast our confidence and our hope (v. 6), take care not to fall away from the living God through unbelief (v. 12), encourage each other (v. 13), fear and be diligent in obedience to the faith (4:1, 11), hold fast our confession (v. 14), and draw near to Jesus, our high priest, for help when we are weak (v. 16). We are to do all of this so that we will receive in full what we now have in being made partakers of Christ, who has already been crowned with glory and honor. This is how we begin to actualize His rule as ours.

THE PARADIGM APPLIED TO VARIOUS INSTITUTIONS

A. *Slavery (1 Corinthians 7:20-23; Colossians 3:22-25; Ephesians 6:5-9; 1 Timothy 6:1-2; Titus 2:9-10). Existential reality:* there are enslaved believers and free believers (1 Corinthians 7:21). *Essential reality:* there is neither slave nor free man in Christ Jesus (Galatians 3:28; Colossians 3:11); there is no partiality with God (Colossians 3:25); a slave is the Lord's freedman, a free man is Christ's slave (7:22); a slave is bought with a price (Colossians 3:23); a slave is a slave of the Lord Christ (Colossians 3:24; Ephesians 6:6); slaves and free are baptized by one Spirit into one Body (1 Corinthians 12:13). Masters have a Master in heaven (Colossians 4:1; Ephesians 6:9); believing masters and slaves are brothers (1 Timothy 6:2). *Process:* one should remain in the condition in which one is called (7:24); yet it is better, if one is able, to gain freedom (7:21), appropriating essential reality; one should not become a slave of men (v. 23). Slaves are to honor their masters and to serve well, and not take advantage of believing masters, but to serve them even better, since they are beloved brothers (1 Timothy 6:1-2); masters are to grant justice and fairness to slaves (Colossians 4:1). Slaves should serve fearing the Lord (Colossians 3:22; Ephesians 6:6-7), working heartily for the Lord, receiving reward from the Lord without partiality (Colossians 3:23-25; Ephesians 6:8); and they should show "all good faith that they may adorn the doctrine of God our Savior in every respect" (Titus 2:10), and prevent the name of God and doctrine from being spoken against (1 Timothy 6:1).

In the institution of slavery there is the significant encouragement by Paul for slaves to reach for essential reality, that is, freedom, presumably depending upon the circumstances. Yet, if this is not possible, by giving Christian masters better service (cf. Galatians 6:10), slaves are viewing life from the perspective of the Kingdom of God. Though they are not actualizing their equality in Christ, they are living out the principle of His people loving and serving one another. The slave who serves a believing master serves his brother, one he loves, and so benefits the Kingdom of God. Essential reality clearly makes a difference! If the social institution can be changed without greater evil, that is, civil unrest, anarchy, and the like, ensuing: and causing harm to the gospel, it should be changed.[1] In Philemon 8-21, Paul virtually requests freedom for Onesimus, slave of Philemon. The gospel teaches that there is no real difference between slave and free in the Church of Christ. Both are gifted without distinction (1 Corinthians 12:13). Historically, slaves were admitted to baptism, Christian worship, the clergy, and martyrdom. The slave Callistus became bishop of Rome (A.D. 222).[2]

B. *Government (1 Peter 2:13-17; Romans 13:1-7).* *Existential reality:* governments are instituted by God for the entire course of this age (2:13-17; Romans 13:1-2; Genesis 9-11); they are God's servants (13:4, 6). *Essential reality:* believers are "free people" having "freedom" (2:16); they belong to the Kingdom of Christ (Colossians 1:13); their citizenship is in heaven (Philippians 3:20); and they are of God's household (Ephesians 2:19). *Process:* believers submit themselves to "every institution," including government for the Lord's sake (v. 13); it is the will of God to silence the talk of ignorant people (v. 15); they should honor the king (v. 17); they should not use their freedom as an excuse to do evil, but use it as God's servants for His purposes (v. 16), which requires submission to government for the sake of the gospel; they submit because of punishment and conscience (13:5).

The essential reality of being free from every human institution of human government is moderated by concerns for justice, order, rule, and peace in society (1 Timothy 2:1-2: "pray that we may live a quiet and tranquil life in all godliness and dignity"), to serve the progress of the gospel (vv. 3-4). To the extent that government supports the law of Christ, to the extent that they are coexistent, believers obey the government (incidentally) in the course of living according to the law of the Kingdom, which is the law of love. To the extent that government is mandating neutral affairs, believers obey, even though they are free, as true missionaries adopting the cultural norms in which they are living in order to further the cause of the gospel. Yet believers in Christ ultimately are citizens of God's realm and this allegiance surpasses all others. So when government mandates oppose God's law, the Christian obeys God rather than men (Acts 5:29).

C. *The Home (Colossians 3:18-21; Ephesians 5:21ff; 1 Peter 3:1-7). Existential reality:* the home is instituted by God for the entire course of this age and through the Messianic Kingdom. Children are inexperienced and immature, needing teaching and guidance. Patriarchy is the prevailing cultural pattern.[3] The husband is head of the wife (5:23).[4] Yet the man has his birth through the woman (1 Corinthians 11:12). *Essential reality:* there is neither male nor female in Christ Jesus (Galatians 3:28), whether adults or children; husbands, wives, and children are fellow heirs of the grace of life (1 Peter 3:7). *Process:* the wife submits to her husband as to the Lord (Colossians 3:18; Ephesians 5:22, 33); she submits in everything as the Church submits to Christ (5:24). The husband loves his wife as Christ loved the Church (5:25), as he loves himself (5:33), and should not be embittered toward her (Colossians 3:19). He nurtures and cherishes her. Children should obey their parents (both of them) (Colossians 3:20); and fathers should not exasperate their children to cause them to lose heart (3:21).[5] Yet since male and female are one in Christ (Galatians 3:28), mutual submission and love should prevail in the community of faith (Ephesians 5:21; cf. 1 Corinthians 7:3-4; Colossians 3:12-17; 1 Peter 3:8; 5:5), at worship and in the home. Submission and love are mutual: to love is to submit and to submit is to love.[6]

Essential reality should be actualized in the home as a microcosm of the Church. Just as essential reality impacted the institution of slavery, so it should impact the home. Children need to submit because they are children and need guidance. The goal of believing parents, though, is not to treat them as children until they leave home, imposing their will simply because they are the parents. Rather, their goal is to raise up their children in the faith and to empower them deliberately as brothers and sisters in Christ, and to engage in mutual submission in the faith with them as they are able and mature enough to do so. So also the only enduring relationship between believing husband and wife is that of brother and sister in Christ; there will be no marriage in heaven. This one essential relationship is to inform how they are to interact in their marriage. So the biblical injunctions regarding marriage have this end in view, slowly but surely working toward the actualization of who they are in Christ, within the bounds of the prevailing cultural patterns for the sake of the gospel. Contrary to Roman and Jewish custom, in Christ the husband is now to love his wife, while the wife is now to submit herself willingly.[7]

In summary, a Christian is free from every institution because she belongs to a new order within the eschatological dominion of Christ. Yet she is to use this freedom, not to rebel, but to submit to all social institutions as the roles are then presently defined to further the gospel, disobeying only when those roles require immoral conduct. Further, she is to submit to the discipline of the institution when she must disobey that institution in order to obey God. This suffering for her faith is both judgment and grace for the purging from sin and progress in sanctification, and for the privilege of following in the steps of Christ, eventually to share also in His glory.

PARADIGM APPLIED TO THE ROLE OF WOMEN IN THE CHURCH

A. *Propriety (Customs) in Worship (1 Corinthians 11)*. *Existential reality:* men and women are praying and prophesying in church (v. 4-5) without proper regard for traditions (v. 2), customs (v. 4-6), "nature" (v. 13-15) and "practices" (v. 16). Additionally, (1) "Christ is the head of every man; the man is the head of a woman, and God is the head of Christ" (v. 3). (2) Man is "the image and glory of God; woman is the glory of man" (v. 7). (3) "Man does not originate from woman, but the woman from man" (v. 8). Yet the man has his birth through the woman (v. 12). (4) Man was not "created for the woman's sake, but woman for the man's sake" (v. 9).[8] *Essential reality:* (1) male and female each fully reflect the divine image (Genesis 1:26-27); (2) there is neither male nor female in Christ Jesus (Galatians 3:28). (3) Men and women are gifted without distinction based upon gender (i.e., sex) (cf. Romans 12:4-8; 1 Corinthians 12; v. 13 says that we were all baptized in one body); (4) There is interdependency in the Lord ("in the Lord neither is woman independent of man, nor is man independent of woman") (v. 11). (5) There is common dependence upon God ("all things originate from God") (v. 12). *Process:* believers should follow the propriety of custom (man should not cover his head; woman should cover her head, vv. 5-10); woman should have a symbol of authority on her head "because of the angels" (v. 10);[9] proper decorum (peace) should prevail (v. 16) while men and women equally exercise gifts.

This and the other matters of existential reality are used to guide the exercise of spiritual gifts in the community at worship. They are cited to enforce "traditions" from the apostle (v. 2).[10] The references to the three "heads" then support the past "traditions" of v. 2 as well as those Paul subsequently introduces: customs (v. 4-6),[11] "nature" (13-15),[12] and "practices" of the churches (v. 16). Yet it is implicit in the context that the process must go further, to actualize essential reality in existential reality. When the sole reference is made to the believers' identity in Christ (v. 11), interdependency upon one another (v. 11) and common dependency upon God (v. 12) are the principles. These principles correspond to the idea of mutual submission in Ephesians 5:21. Indeed, verses 11-12 are set in contrast to the rest of the passage with its emphasis on custom in worship. The "however" (v. 11) breaks off the discussion and emphasizes what is important.[13] The truth as it is in Christ (vv. 11-12) means there is no distinction, no priority, no inviolable rule. What Paul has written before must be modified by this verse and the closing words of verse 12: "all things are of [originate from] God." In effect he corrects the tradition, or guards against its misuse, by adding that man is dependent upon the woman and has his birth through the woman. The "oneness" of man and woman and "their consequent interdependence are rooted in their common dependence upon God and faith in Christ."[14] The future conditions of the Kingdom are beginning to be realized by the mutual exercise of these gifts (cf. Joel 2; Acts 2), without distinction based upon gender (1 Corinthians 12:13).

B. *Order in Worship (1 Corinthians 14)*. *Existential reality:* there are multiple numbers of people speaking at the same time: in tongues (v. 27); with prophecies (vv. 29-33); and women are speaking (vv. 34-35). *Essential reality:* (1) there is neither male nor female in Christ Jesus (Galatians 3:28). (2) All are gifted (v. 26). (3) God is a God of peace, not confusion (v. 33). *Process:* all should desire spiritual gifts (v. 1) including tongues and prophecy (which is better than tongues) (v. 5; cf. 12:31). Yet believers should follow certain rules for order. (1) Tongues: no more than three speak and one at a time with an interpreter (vv. 27-28). (2) Prophecy: only three at most, each in turn (v. 29-33). (3) Women: avoid disruptive speech in the church (vv. 34-35).

The reasons for the rules are: (1) to edify the Church (v. 12, 26); (2) to maintain peace (v. 33); (3) to keep order (v. 40); (4) to allow for careful weighing (v. 29); and (5) to allow for the instruction and encouragement of everyone (v. 31).

Essential reality calls for men and women to participate fully, an advance over the institutions of the Old Testament. Yet the chief concern is that order and peace and unity should prevail in the community of faith. Prophets and speakers in tongues (men and women), with the aside addressed to women speaking inappropriately, are regulated. The prohibition regarding women cannot mean that they are not to participate at all in light of the points of essential reality and context (including 1 Corinthians 11; 12).[15] Again, these gifts anticipate the Messianic Kingdom when they will be fully realized; men and women will prophesy (Acts 2:17-18).

C. *Ministry in the Church (1 Timothy 2)*. *Existential reality*: during worship, discord and lack of unity occur in the church at Ephesus. Also Adam was created first (v. 13); Eve was deceived, not Adam (v. 14). *Essential reality*: there is neither male nor female in Christ Jesus (Galatians 3:28); all are brothers and sisters in Christ (cf. 1 Timothy 5:1-2). *Process*: during worship, men should pray in every place (v.8) and women should dress modestly and be adorned by good deeds (vv. 9-10); a woman should quietly and submissively receive instruction (vv. 11-12). Paul does not permit a woman to teach a man nor to exercise authority over a man (v. 12); elders are men (only? see 3:1); deacons are men (and probably also women) (3:8-11); women shall be saved (or preserved) through childbearing (2:15). One should exhort an older man as a father, younger men as brothers, older women as mothers, younger women as sisters (5:1-2).

We discover that Paul wants men to pray as characterized by lifting holy hands and by peace. He wants women to dress modestly, avoiding braided hair, jewelry, and expensive clothing. Instead, he wants them clothed with good works that befit godliness. Also, they are to learn quietly with entire submissiveness. Paul does not permit a woman to teach or exercise authority over a man, but to remain quiet. The rest of the passage gives the explanation or cause for Paul's exhortation ("for," v. 13), and the consequence (v. 15) if conditions are met. We note that the thrust of all of Paul's exhortations are occasioned by a concern for decorum or quietness and godliness—concerns that pervade the epistle.

At this point, we would normally engage in application. But here we run into a major difficulty. Is the meaning for us the same as the grammatical-historical meaning? That is, are Paul's exhortations to mean the same for a contemporary local church, and the same for the universal Body also?

When we do interpretation by means of the paradigm of reality, we first make determination of the existential reality, or grammatical-historical meaning of the text, as just shown. Then we search for the essential reality. It is the second step of interpretation itself, a step of integrating the text with Kingdom reality, before we do application. Here we seek to ascertain what the presence of the Kingdom brings to the meaning of the text.[16]

What eternal truths realized in the Kingdom should we bring to bear on this text dealing with roles of men and women in the local expression of the Body of Christ? The pertinent truths would include the essential oneness and equality of all in Christ (Galatians 3:28), leading us to affirm that a Christian's essential identity in Christ is unaffected by what one wears or what roles one fulfills; but in turn essential reality should affect what one wears or does. We also realize that gifting by the Spirit is without gender qualification (also 1 Corinthians 11; 12; 14; Ephesians 4; Colossians 3; Romans 12; and others).

Thus we come to the third step of the paradigm—actualization of essential reality in light of truth and love. This step initially leads us to affirm that all may dress any way they wish and may fulfill any given role—as gifted by the Holy Spirit—to edify the local church in a context of decorum and godliness (traits also of the Kingdom). Thus Paul's explicit exhortations are limited in nature and not universals for all time. By way of application, the results are obvious. However, this is not the end of the matter.

Even a solely literal interpretation must conclude that Paul is not setting particular standards, but general ones. His concern, for example, is not to set forth standards of dress, for he ends up exhorting his readers to be clothed with good works. He isn't so much banning jewelry or certain clothing or hair styles because these are relative to various cultures. The kind of clothing and appearance is relative, incidental, clearly existential and not universal. If this is true of verses 8-10, it seems helpful to extend this conclusion to the rest of the exhortations about women learning and teaching (which are relative to various cultures). They are limited, being occasioned by concerns for decorum and quietness. Then Paul, in verses 13-15, explains by way of illustration what he means.

The appeal to creation and the Fall does not itself make the exhortations universal any more than the appeal to creation makes universal the fourth commandment to keep the seventh day holy (Exodus 20:8-11). It seems that there are three reasons why this commandment is limited: obedience was never universally enforced nor expected of Gentiles in the Old Testament; it was never repeated in the New Testament, and, in fact, Jesus seemed to overturn it; and it is virtually unobserved in the practice of the Church throughout time. Essential reality would have us treat all days the same (cf. Colossians 2:8, 16-23), as days of Christ's triumph. As the Sabbath was to be servant of man, so every day is to be for the believer. However, believers are to meet regularly together to celebrate, to instruct, and be instructed. So out of necessity, some day must become the common day of gathering. Theoretically, this could be any day of the week. Traditionally, the Church has decided on Sunday to commemorate Christ's resurrection.

Why, then, on the matter of Saturday worship do we excuse or release Gentiles throughout Old Testament history and all believers of the present, yet not make room for all Christians on the matter of women's role in ministry, which seems to be not as weighty? Why should we not expect that these exhortations enjoining women's silence be observed by all Christians in all public meetings and in all institutions if the appeal to creation and the Fall has this significance? Do we not expect modest clothing and good works in all walks of life and not just in the assembly? It seems we may be making an unwarranted division in the text between verses 8-10 and 11-12.

The appeal to creation and the Fall seems not to establish universals because in the final analysis, even the order of creation and depth of Eve's culpability are existential or accidental (in the philosophical sense), not essential to the identity of man or woman or the reality of sin (it is actually traced to Adam; Romans 5). This is why Paul can say to the Corinthians that both men and women should learn from the example of how the serpent beguiled Eve (2 Corinthians 11:3).

So the end result is that cultural patterns are to be taken into consideration for the sake of the gospel. Yet for all cultures, it is appropriate that order and godliness should prevail, especially in the behavior of women for whom the liberating gospel has provided unprecedented freedom in all cultures. This again is the expressed concern of the very last words of v. 15: women shall be preserved through the bearing of children "if they continue in faith and love and sanctity with self-restraint."

Certain other observations are in order.[17] Paul cannot be setting the standard of absolute silence for women, in light of the fact that Corinthians, allowing women to speak in the church, is written from Ephesus while 1 Timothy is written to Ephesus. Also, the Epistle to the Ephesians itself encourages the community to participate in the gifts without gender limitation. The only exception to this would be the case that 1 Timothy is meant as a corrective to a local, temporary problem which has arisen and thus does not represent the teaching for all the churches, as 1 Corinthians and Ephesians as cyclical or circular epistles seem to do. In addition, the overriding concern of 1 Timothy is the securing of peace and unity (note 2:11-12 for "quietness"), as in 1 Corinthians. Finally, the provisions of the new covenant seem to indicate a change in the institutions of government, home, and the Church (believers become the temple of God; we all become priests, kings, and prophets), and this means a change in the roles of men and women within them. In light of this and much more, it seems that the full participation of women in ministry is not to be denied.

Throughout Scripture we are enjoined to heed the dual concerns of truth and love in the actualization of essential reality. Although the truth leads to freedom in dress and roles, love leads to restraint and selflessness. We forego rights out of love for one another and for God and His gospel, that it not be slandered. This is a chief concern by which the New Testament restricts the freedom of actualizing essential reality (e.g., Ephesians 4:15: "speaking the truth in love"). So, finally, we say that dress is important, that modesty and godliness and decorum and refraining from speech must all take place if to do otherwise in a particular culture brings slander to the gospel and stands as a barrier to people coming to Christ. Truth and love are also essential reality; it is these which finally guide the believer's conduct and not the creation order or the Fall. So we seek to actualize essential reality as far as possible within the twin constraints of love and truth.

The issue of the role of women in ministry is too complicated and deals with too many passages to treat it thoroughly here. We have briefly reviewed the passages above from a more egalitarian perspective to challenge our traditional readings and to stimulate thinking. Reading these Scriptures and thinking through the issue from the perspective of the Kingdom/paradigm helps us to refocus the discussion. As important as exegesis is to this issue, "microexegesis" will never solve it. We weigh evidence differently based upon the larger picture from which we interpret it.

The paradigm of reality raises questions to help us think through the larger picture behind this issue. What is the essence of man and woman? Is there any essential difference between man and woman? Even if there isn't, there are obvious, significant, God-designed existential differences. How determinative of roles are these differences to be? Is the general pattern that many see in (pre-Fall) Genesis to be normative, a moral absolute that it is a sin to break, or descriptive of general trends, to which there will be many God-created exceptions? What is the relationship of essential reality and existential reality in this time before glorification? If the existential differences between the sexes are to be determinative during the present time, why do we not apply them across all institutions including government and work? What makes communities of faith different? Are the prohibitions just temporary submission to the cultural situation for the sake of the Gospel? Or are they moral absolutes?

These sorts of questions explore our views of basic realities and allow us more easily to see if we are applying them systematically so that our theology/worldview is internally consistent and coherent. No matter what position on this issue we each begin with, these sorts of questions can help to think through our positions more thoroughly and either alter our view or provide us with a stronger foundation for the view with which we began.

FINAL OBSERVATIONS

The various demonstrations of our paradigm as a hermeneutic or interpretive grid serve to show the essential meaning of various texts. We discover that essential reality emphasizes such matters as the glory of God, freedom, identity in Christ, truth, love, equality, oneness, and the Kingdom.

The paradigm does not have to be explicitly evident in every biblical topic. Rather, it helps to establish a pattern of thinking, a divine world view, from which the authors write because it reflects God's purposes in history. These are Kingdom purposes. We believe this world view informs all the writers of Scripture. We find ourselves compelled to re-examine repeatedly our interpretation in light of Kingdom reality.

Revelation Determines Our Hermeneutic

The hermeneutic we have proposed to allow us to interpret Scripture as the biblical authors did implies a particular view of revelation. The goal of hermeneutics is to "get meaning." Now, the means for getting meaning need to match the kind of revelation it is. To illustrate what we mean, we will describe some past ideas of what revelation is and how this shaped the hermeneutic for how to get meaning out of the Bible. Then we will explain our own proposal for how to define revelation. If the concept of revelation is wrong, then the hermeneutic almost certainly is too. So we need to take a look at the idea of revelation inherent in the hermeneutic we have described.

A SELECTIVE HISTORY OF REVELATION

Nineteenth-Century Liberal Theology

Liberal Theology was radically antisupernaturalistic. It believed the descriptions of miracles to be merely the authors' attempts to describe what Jesus meant to them. It began with the assumption that miracles do not occur, so it attempted to reconstruct "the historical Jesus" who inspired the biblical writers to create the "Christ of faith." The method used to strip away the supernatural elements of Scripture in an attempt to describe Jesus in purely historical terms was called *historical criticism*. This method matched Liberal Theology's idea of revelation. *The purely human Jesus Christ was the unique revelation of God*, not as a divine-human savior, but basically as the model Christian. Such a purely human revelation of God fit well with the prevailing idea that humankind is in harmony with God. The radical historicism (rejecting everything supernatural) of Liberal Theology eventually came to be rejected. Among other criticisms came the question of how a purely *human* Jesus could be considered the unique revelation of God.

Twentieth-Century Dialectical Theology

Karl Barth's break with Liberalism resulted in Dialectical Theology which dominated the twentieth century.[1] He challenged the idea that humankind was in basic harmony with God, believing instead that there is a radical disconti-nuity between the two so that God is not to be found any-where in history. The endeavors of Liberal Theology had been a waste of time, preoccupied as it was with historical data and ignoring the message of Scripture. Barth, a pastor, was concerned to interpret its message for his twentieth-century congregation.

Dialectical Theology criticized Liberal Theology for pro-ducing nothing more than bits and pieces of historical data without meaning. In an attempt to make the Bible relevant to twentieth-century modern man, Dialectical Theology engaged in *theological exegesis* to interpret the meaning of the Bible for its day. In contrast to the idea that humankind is in harmony with God, it considered God to be "wholly other," so much so that He could not even be found in his-tory. This is exactly opposite of Liberal Theology, which searched for revelation of God *only* in a historical Jesus. Dialectical Theology, then, gave little place to historical study in the goal of understanding Scripture. Instead, in order to understand the text, the reader of Scripture already must have had a faith encounter with Christ.

In the introduction to his commentary on Romans, Barth stated that the Bible needs to be understood in light of its "subject matter" (what the text is ultimately about). He considered the subject matter to be the Spirit of Christ. Since the Spirit of Christ is outside history, this is how the historically-bound Scripture, written in another time and culture, can speak to any person at any time in history. *The Spirit of Christ is revelation*, and understanding comes in encounter with Him. Scripture is not revelation (or the Word of God), but the Word can be found *among* the words of the text, witnessing to the Spirit of Christ.

Notice the implication of the idea that the Bible is to be interpreted *in light* of its subject matter. Since the subject matter of Scripture is the suprahistorical ("outside of history") Spirit of Christ, and God cannot be found in history, then understanding of Scripture can be gained only by divine enablement. A person has to have a faith encounter with the Spirit of Christ before he can ever understand Scripture since he has to interpret it in light of this Spirit of Christ. But the Spirit of Christ is so "wholly other" that He cannot be found in history. The result is that the historical basis of the Christian faith is undermined. Further, an unbeliever cannot understand Scripture at all, so he cannot use Scripture to get somehow to the Spirit of Christ. This means that a human has no way of initiating contact with God. Revelation is found only in encounter with the Spirit of Christ in faith, and that only by God's initiative.

This is why Barth disparaged historical study in favor of *theological exegesis*. Why do much historical study if God is not found in history? So he went on to describe the meaning for today, which is supposed to be the product of reading Scripture in light of the Spirit of Christ encountered by the exegete (reader of Scripture). The interesting thing is that Barth actually did engage in some historical study. He gave it only a preliminary place, however, and passed quickly from it to theological exegesis. Eventually it was pointed out to him that his idea of revelation contradicted the method he used to get meaning. If revelation is only in the Spirit of Christ and not in history, why do any historical study at all? The fact that he did some historical study indicated that there must be some positive relationship between history and revelation. For these reasons, Barth was criticized for being ahistorical and Kantian in his view of revelation. Once these things were pointed out to him, he changed his mind to express a positive relationship between revelation and history. But he still insisted that the reader of Scripture had to have a prior faith encounter with the Spirit of Christ in order to understand the Bible.

Oscar Cullmann

Oscar Cullmann is a twentieth-century New Testament scholar famous for his concept of salvation history. He was a contemporary of Barth and Bultmann (and as of this writing, he is still alive and in his 90s). In his early years, he agreed with Barth that the subject matter of Scripture is the Spirit of Christ and that the reader had to have a prior encounter with Him in order to understand it. He differed with Barth, however, in that he gave a greater place to historical study. Instead of having only a preliminary role before theological exegesis, Cullmann maintained that theological exegesis is to be resubjected to the historical meaning of the text. He saw these two as being in perpetual interaction with historical study providing a control for theological exegesis, which in turn clarified some elements of the biblical text.

A few years later, however, he changed his mind. In the interchange, which revelation—from the Spirit of Christ or from Scripture—had priority? He decided that requiring personal faith for understanding undermined the historical nature of the Christian faith, and that the determinate meaning of the faith is found in the events on which it is based. If the Christian faith is truly based on historical events, then a description of that faith should be understandable to everyone, regardless of whether they believe.

This means that an unbeliever can read Scripture and understand its basic message.[2]

This conclusion follows his concept of revelation. In his mature theology, he described revelation as *God's saving acts in history* ("event" for short) and *the divinely inspired interpretations of those events*.[3] Together these events and their interpretations, all linked in a chain, equal what he calls salvation history (*Heilsgeschichte*). Revelation is now found in history, not only outside of history. This salvation history, not the Spirit of Christ, is the subject matter of Scripture, which is the Spirit-inspired written record of these events and their interpretations. And what is the proper method of interpretation for a historical revelation that is written down? What we call the *grammatical-historical hermeneutic*. Even an unbeliever can do this, which is exactly Cullmann's point. Any sort of understanding that a believer gains from his personal faith experience, and any theological ideas he gleans from the text of Scripture, must be resubjected to the understanding of the text gained by grammatical-historical methods. According to Cullmann, this hermeneutic provides a control for the message and meaning of the Christian faith since it arrives at the meaning of the text on its own terms.

The interesting thing is that Cullmann knows the biblical writers did not follow a strict grammatical-historical hermeneutic in interpreting previously-written biblical texts. He even accounts for this fuller meaning with his concept of salvation history. When a new event (special act of God in history) comes, "corrections of the interpretation of past saving events are undertaken in the light of new events. This, of course, never happens in such a way that an earlier account is disputed. Rather, aspects formerly unnoticed are by virtue of the new revelation now placed in the foreground."[4]

So there seems to be an inherent contradiction in Cullmann's thought. He himself attempted to practice "purely scientific exegesis," following the grammatical-historical hermeneutic. He wanted to hear the message on its own terms only and did not seek to go beyond it to find any deeper meaning. The implicit view of revelation is that it is found only in salvation history which is expressed in the grammatical-historical meaning of the text. Yet he is perfectly aware that the biblical writers did not practice this hermeneutic. It follows that revelation for them must have been different from what Cullmann believes it to be for us now. He actually describes this differing revelation in his explanation of the unfolding of salvation history:[5] (1) the prophet (or apostle, whoever is receiving the revelation) has faith in the previously recorded events and interpretation as salvation history; (2) he witnesses a new event in his own day and receives a divine revelation about that event; (3) he reinterprets the previous record of events and interpretations (meaning Scripture) in light of this new event and its revelation, only in such a way that it does not contradict the previous meaning, but makes it fuller.[6] This sounds quite similar to the hermeneutic we are proposing. The concept of revelation that is implicit in it is similar to the one we will propose shortly.

Evangelical Scholarship

Compared with the radically antisupernatural theologies of those from the Liberal school and Rudolf Bultmann (who is famous for "demythologizing" Scripture of all its miracles), and even the more moderate Karl Barth, Oscar Cullmann was the European theologian-of-choice for evangelical scholars. He has a very high view of Scripture as inspired and authoritative (though not inerrant), he strongly emphasizes the historical nature of the Christian faith, and he embraces a revelation that can be found in the text by the grammatical-historical hermeneutic. Because of all this, his work has had a significant effect on evangelical theology.

The criticism we made of Cullmann we also make of most evangelicalism. Most trained evangelicals practice the grammatical-historical hermeneutic (at least in theory), and churches from Bible-centered traditions basically teach lay people how to read Scripture the same way. Many of the more conservative Protestant evangelicals, as good heirs of the Reformation, believe that the Holy Spirit speaks to the believer today only through Scripture and not directly. They have confined the role of the Holy Spirit to interpretation of Scripture which helps the reader to accept that it is true (the work of illumination), rather than helping her to understand meaning (the work of some sort of revelation). Revelation (special revelation, at any rate) is found only in Scripture, so the process of interpretation is essentially a cognitive one. This is why most seminary courses on interpreting Scripture say they affirm the role of the Holy Spirit, but do not spell out what it is or translate it into a methodology that accommodates His role.

Summary

Before we present our proposal for a concept of revelation, we should briefly summarize. Liberal Theology considered a human Jesus to be the model Christian; he was the unique revelation of God. Using methods reflecting strict historicism, it sought to strip Scripture of its supernatural elements to find the "historical Jesus" behind the "Christ of faith" described by the miraculous language. Dialectical Theology went entirely in the opposite direction and regarded revelation as the totally suprahistorical Spirit of Christ. Faith was required for understanding Scripture, and there was little place for historical study in doing theological exegesis.

Cullmann regarded revelation to be God's saving acts and the interpretations of them in salvation history as recorded in Scripture. The meaning of the Christian faith is found in and must be governed by the grammatical-historical meaning of the Bible. Any personal faith experiences must be made subject to this meaning. Evangelical scholarship in general agrees with Cullmann. It rarely speaks of events as revelation, and Jesus as revelation, a little more often. This is not because it does not consider them to be revelation, but because we know of the events and Jesus only through the written record of them. For all practical purposes, the Spirit-inspired Scripture is revelation. Therefore, the means of accessing the meaning of this revelation is the grammatical-historical hermeneutic.

OUR PROPOSED IDEA OF REVELATION

For reasons we have hinted at above, we differ with Cullmann and the prevailing view in evangelical scholarship. Along with our proposed hermeneutic goes a slightly different view of revelation. After we explain more thoroughly our criticisms of Cullmann, we will present our proposed view of revelation and its inherent controls for meaning in the Bible.

Criticisms of Cullmann

The hermeneutic of Cullmann (as well as its common evangelical counterpart) is not the hermeneutic of the biblical authors, and therefore does not function on the same view of revelation. Cullmann explains how the biblical authors arrived at fuller meaning but does not adequately deal with why we can or cannot do the same. And he certainly does not practice the biblical hermeneutic. In his own words, "I know no other 'method' than the proven philological-historical one."[7]

We believe Cullmann lands where he does because he has misidentified the subject matter of Scripture. He thinks the subject matter is salvation history. For him, the object of faith is a chain of salvation historical events. A person hears that these events have occurred and what they mean. He places his faith in these events and thereby aligns himself with that salvation history. In doing so he becomes incorporated into that history and it becomes his own history more truly than his earthly history.

To evangelical ears this sounds a little off. We don't place our faith in a history but in God. God Himself is the object of faith. Paul said that his all-consuming goal was to know Christ (Philippians 3:10), not some chain of events. Jesus Himself defines eternal life for us: "And this is eternal life: that they may know you, the only true God, and Jesus Christ whom you have sent" (John 17:3). Eternal life is gained by not aligning ourselves with a history of events. It comes by "believing in him who justifies the ungodly" (Romans 4:5), and then this salvation history is made our own history as a gift.

Having said all this, it is important to point out that a primary way of knowing God and putting faith in Him is through hearing and believing what He has done. But what He has done flows out of who He is. His acts in history are designed to point to who He is in Himself. It is He whom we are to believe and know and with whom we are to align ourselves. The ultimate subject matter of Scripture is God. But isn't this exactly the error that Barth made, having the subject matter be something outside of history? No, because in Scripture God reveals Himself and His characteristics, but He does so first and foremost through historical events that He has then interpreted to explain Himself in our lan- · guage. For this reason He is able to prove that He is what He says He is by pointing to what He does in history.

There are, then, really two subject matters of Scripture. God is the ultimate subject matter but He is a God who has revealed Himself in history. So the penultimate subject matter is God's action in history to bring about His Kingdom on earth. (Here we differ with Cullmann about the center of Scripture; we believe that it is God's Kingdom rather than salvation history. See chapter 9.) This way, making the subject matter of Scripture to be ultimately God, a suprahistorical reality, does not mean that we sacrifice intellect or that faith is required for a basic cognitive understanding of Scripture. Instead, He has revealed Himself in our concrete reality which can be understood cognitively so that we will come to believe in Him. So yes, the subject matter of Scripture is God's acts in history and we must align ourselves with this history. This is penultimate, though. The true goal is to put our faith in God Himself and to align ourselves with Him. But we usually know Him first, perhaps primarily, and certainly most explicitly through His acts and their interpretations, which are contained in Scripture.[8]

We should deal with one last thing regarding Cullmann. One of the evidences he gives for "event" being central rather than God, is that "imperatives" (commands to obedience or ethical action) in Scripture are based on events rather than on God's character. For instance, we are commanded to stop sinning because Christ died for us, rose again, and made us into new creatures when we were made one with Him through faith (Romans 6-8; see chapter 7). This pattern is called indicative-imperative, and it is especially prominent in Paul's epistles.

The problem with this is that it is misleading. The Bible does, in fact, make ethical appeal based upon the character of God. "Be holy for I am holy" (Leviticus 11:44-45; 1 Peter 1:15-16). "Be perfect as your heavenly Father is perfect" (Matthew 5:48). "Walk in a manner worthy of him" (Ephesians 4:1; Colossians 1:10; 1 Thessalonians 2:12). The reason we *are* to be holy and to do right is that this is the way God is. The reason we are *able* to be holy and to do right is that He has done all things necessary for us in Christ. The events provide the basis for our ability. God's character provides the reason He makes the claim and our motivation for obeying it.

Revelation as Spirit and Letter

Corresponding to the idea that God and the story of His Kingdom action in history are the dual subject matter of Scripture is a redefined locus of revelation. The revelation is not only in the text, as the grammatical-historical hermeneutic implies, nor is it only in the Spirit of Christ, with Scripture being only a witness to that revelation, as Barth seems to say. Instead, revelation is in the Word, which is the self-revealing of God. This Word is expressed both in the person of Jesus Christ and in Scripture, both of which are explicitly called the Word.[9]

This would seem to open up the Pandora's box that Cullmann has tried to shut and lock: if both of these are revelation, then Scripture, with its historical orientation, cannot serve as a control for the revelation given in the personally encountered Spirit of Christ. This, of course, is not necessarily true. We must not forget that the Spirit of Christ, whom we personally encounter, is the same Spirit who inspired Scripture. God is the same yesterday, today, and forever. He will not contradict Himself. Direct revelation from the Spirit is just as authoritative as Scripture, at the very least for the individual receiving it. But it will be consistent with the revelation in the written Word. It is in this sense that Scripture provides the control.

This seems to fit better the biblical data. We made the case above for unmediated communication with the Spirit and His ongoing ministry in revealing the truth (see chapters 6 and 7). In Scripture God gives two criteria for discerning whether a prophecy really comes from the Spirit. First, if it is prophesying some event, then the event must come true (Deuteronomy 18:22). God does what He says He will do and no one can stop Him. Second, it must be consistent with what the Spirit has taught in the past, regardless of what miracles the prophet performs or events he foretells (Deuteronomy 13:1-5; 1 John 2:27). God does not change. What He has taught in the past is contained in Scripture. So the meaning of Scripture provides the control for revelation from the Spirit.

At this point it is extremely important to understand what we mean by "Scripture provides the control for revelation from the Spirit." Scripture does not *control* the Spirit, but only provides the knowledge of the truth in order to discern what is the *true* Spirit. The Spirit is just as authoritative as the Scripture He inspired. Unmediated revelation from Him to an individual believer is just as authoritative and just as true. But consistency with Scripture is how we tell what sort of spirit a revelation is from (1 John 4:1-3). If something claiming to be a revelation does not violate the clear teaching of Scripture, it is allowed to stand until such a time as it may be proven wrong as we come to understand Scripture better.[10] See also 2 Peter 1:16-19.

This idea of revelation being both the Spirit (in direct encounter with the Spirit of Christ) and Scripture, opens up the possibility of practicing the hermeneutic of the biblical authors. Let's review for a moment Cullmann's description of how the biblical writers found deeper meaning. First, they understood and believed what Scripture said, basically according to the human author's original intention. Then they witnessed a new event in their own day and received a revelation from the Spirit regarding its interpretation. In light of this new event and interpretation, they reinterpreted the previous Scripture, finding deeper meaning than the human author intended.

We are advocating that we can do something similar. Since the Holy Spirit is a source of revelation, under His guidance we may find deeper meaning written in Scripture.

There is, of course, one big problem with this. We have said that the way we tell if something is from the Spirit is if it is consistent with what He has already taught in Scripture—understood in its plain sense. But if we are trying, by the Spirit, to find deeper meaning in Scripture, then how can the plain sense be our test for the authenticity of that meaning?

It can in two ways. First, the suggested deeper meaning must not contradict or violate the plain sense. In fact, it must be related to it (in that it must be within the range of the sense of the grammatical-historical meaning). Second, the fuller sense must be governed by the central theme of Scripture—the actualization of the Kingdom of God. (In other words, it is the essential reality as expressed in the existential reality of the text. See chapter 5.) The reason that it must be related to the central theme is that the search for the deeper meaning is actually a search for the divine Author's intended meaning. The meaning He intends to convey must be related to the central theme of His revelation or it doesn't fit. (This is also true for "other" meanings objectively in the text but which are not the main points of the human author. See chapter 10.) And how did we discover this central theme? By using the grammatical-historical hermeneutic in the plain sense of Scripture. Our theological formulation of Kingdom history as the center of Scripture is checked, like all other biblical theology, by the grammatical-historical meaning of the text.[11]

In this idea of revelation, what meaning can and cannot an unbeliever understand? It was Cullmann's contention that making the subject matter to be the Spirit of Christ and requiring the reader to have faith in order to understand, ultimately undermined the historical nature of revelation.

Our answer to what an unbeliever can and cannot understand involves a recognition that the Bible speaks of two worlds. In so far as the text speaks of our world, our language is sufficient; there is a one-to-one correspondence of what is written about and some concrete element of our world. But the Bible also speaks of another world, of God and His Kingdom and the entire spiritual realm, for which our language is not quite as adequate and of which understanding is more limited. Since the world about which the Bible speaks is an extension of our world (or rather, our world is an extension of this world), which was created by God in such a way that it reflects the spiritual world, some measure of understanding can be gained of this world from the perspective of our world.[12]

But it follows, does it not, that the more experience a person has of this other world of which the Bible speaks, the more she cognitively (and not just experientially or affectively) understands it? The one who believes participates more and more fully in this other world of God and His Kingdom. Participation in the Kingdom brings increased cognitive understanding of the Bible (and of our world, incidentally, since it derives its meaning from this other world). There is meaning that the unbeliever cannot know.

The unbeliever can understand the Bible in some measure because it speaks of events that have occurred in our world. This understanding is enough for him to come to faith and to be held accountable for rejecting this truth if he does not (in keeping with Cullmann's concern regarding the implication of Romans 10:4). But the Bible seems to indicate that it takes the empowerment of the Spirit for any person to understand sufficiently to come to faith. Both Calvinists and Arminians have affirmed this. (The latter simply believe that this is a common, prevenient grace of the Spirit available to everyone who will have it, and not specially given only to those preordained by God to belief.)

How does this undermine the historical nature of the faith? Cullmann himself asserts that the events had to be interpreted through divinely given revelation about the event. How is it that this does not undermine its historical nature? More importantly, though, if we could not understand event apart from divine enablement, how are we better equiped to understand the interpretation of the event apart from the Spirit's aid? The reader's will is involved in choosing constructs to make sense of the text, so that volition affects cognitive understanding.[13] The unbeliever needs help to understand and not just to receive the truth.

So what does all this look like in practice? First, the reader of Scripture should (ideally) understand it according to the human author's intended meaning so that she herself knows the bounds of deeper meaning. Then, through prayer and meditation on Scripture, history, present life events, and personal relationship with the Spirit of Christ, she makes herself open to new insights through the leading of the Spirit. (This can be done individually or in a group.) This must be done for the purpose of knowing and glorifying God.

Following this, she (or the group) needs to submit the insight to the larger Christian community in some way so that they can test its validity over time. (This is the way that interpretations of Scripture and theological ideas have been tested throughout the history of the Church, and the same process can work for testing interpretations of deeper meaning in Scripture.) As it continues to stand the test of time (and place), it will become part of theological tradition, and it can be thought of as true. But it will never be normative in the sense that it should be made part of Scripture because the Canon is closed. Further, scriptural insight gained later may disprove it in some way, so tradition is always subject to Scripture. Once in a long while a doctrine is so universally approved for so long that it becomes orthodoxy, and those who do not believe it are considered heretics or unbelievers.

Summary

If this idea of revelation is true, we have the best of both worlds. Revelation is found in direct encounter with the Spirit of Christ for us, just as it was for the biblical authors. He can guide us in finding deeper meaning in Scripture. But Scripture (and the events of which it speaks) is also revelation, just as it was for the biblical authors. The Spirit we encounter directly is the same one who inspired the Bible. The deeper meaning must not violate the plain sense of Scripture, and it must be governed by its central theme. Thus the human author's meaning is the divine Author's meaning also. But the divine Author's meaning may go beyond the human author's, unknown to him. And while revelation in the Spirit and in Scripture are equally authoritative, the meaning of Scripture, as found by the grammatical-historical hermeneutic, serves as the criterion for discerning the truth of a deeper meaning or some theological construction possibly discovered by the Spirit.

In contrast to the common practice in evangelical scholarship, this definition of revelation would permit us to practice the biblical hermeneutic in finding deeper meaning without going off the deep end. It gives a more specific role to the Holy Spirit in interpretation so that the method used should not be merely an academic exercise. Perhaps the process of interpretation would include some of the practices of the Christian spiritual life (see chapter 7).

Appendix F

Deeper Meaning and the ICBI Statement on Hermeneutics

MEANING AND AUTHORITY

Earlier we reviewed the concerns of Glenny, Erickson, and others who struggle with the problem of meaning and significance. In this same vein is E. Johnson, who distinguishes sense from meaning. Meaning for him appears to be a combination of sense and reference. He holds that there is but one defining sense, shared by both the human author and the divine Author. Yet there may be several referents which are not shared. Thus the divine reference "will be fuller than the human reference in the shared meaning. The human author truly refers to the reality but not fully."[1]

So Johnson would redefine *sensus plenior* as follows. "What we are therefore proposing is that the *author's intention* expresses a *single, defining textual sense of the whole*. The single sense is capable of implying a fullness of reference.

This is not *sensus plenior* but *sensus singular* as expressed in the affirmations of the text. But it also recognizes the characteristic of *references plenior* [italics his]."[2] So Johnson seems to allow for only a single sense but multiple references. He appears to limit authorial intention to the sense since he writes about an authorial ignorance of the subject matter and ignorance of his own meaning, that is, "all the implications of all possible reference."[3] At first blush, Johnson's view appears to be quite similar to W. Kaiser's[4] (but not close enough, according to Kaiser, as we will soon explain).

How does Johnson's view differ from ours? We affirm that there is one sense of the text, and that this sense is the essential meaning. This essential meaning is usually garbed in some historical particularization, which we call the existential meaning of the text. There can be many other historical particularizations of that one sense, which are commonly called referents. Everyone affirms that God intended more referents than the human author was aware of. In contradiction to Johnson (and to Kaiser), however, we also affirm that the human author may not have been aware of the general sense.

He may only have understood, intended, and affirmed the historical particularization of which he wrote—the existential meaning of the text. In the inspiration of the recording of that historical particularization, then, God intended the sense (essential meaning) of which the human author was unaware. When this occurs, this sense is so-called deeper meaning in the text. We affirm, along with the ICBI statement, that this does not compromise the authority of Scripture.

Johnson presented his position in the volume on hermeneutics that represents the findings of the International Council on Biblical Inerrancy, Summit II, held in 1982. His study, as with all the others, had two respondents: E. Radmacher and W. Kaiser. In their responses they make clear their belief that Elliott has separated human and divine intentions. This brings about different senses and raises questions of authority. They defend single meaning and condemn both multiple meanings and the impossibility of knowing an author's meaning.

Radmacher is especially concerned about authority. As the original author's meaning is *evaporated*, so goes his authority. He believes that such an approach brings "hermeneutical nihilism and subjectivism."[5] Radmacher also raises concerns about separating the authors and subjugating the human author's ignorance to divine omniscience, thus making the Bible less than a truly human document. He believes that 1 Corinthians 2:10-13 shows that human authors knew the things of the Spirit and were taught the deep things of God by Him. He also questions the claim that "the human author did not share fully in the divine author's meanings" as he understands Johnson's identification of authorial intention with the "sense of the whole."[6]

Kaiser also addresses what authority consequent senses of Scripture would have. He rebuts Johnson on the ground that the divine Author's intention could not be separate and different from that of the human author without the fuller sense becoming a different or double sense. Kaiser will allow only different applications, clarifications, implications, illustrations, principles, propositions, and others of the same sense. Their authority depends on how closely they reproduce the original sense of the text. If *sensus plenior* goes beyond the consciousness of the human author, then it has no force, authority, or normative status. Kaiser clearly rejects both the canonical and sensus plenior approaches. If these approaches bring additional meaning, then the battle for an inerrant Bible has been lost.[7] It is "to give away with the left hand all that was won with the right hand in the contest for an inerrant Bible."[8]

Note here the expressed concern for an inerrant Bible. Kaiser seems to equate any approach other than the literal (the single meaning intended by the human author) with a denial of inerrancy. We believe this is unfortunate. For if a single instance exists where later Scripture finds meaning beyond the literal (e.g., Paul's allegorizing of Galatians 4), then later biblical writers did not treat prior Scripture as inerrant, according to him. And others do not consider inerrancy and authority to be put in jeopardy by a deeper sense.[9]

THE CHICAGO STATEMENT AND DEEPER MEANING

To many evangelicals, the International Council on Biblical Inerrancy represents the standard on biblical authority and interpretation. While the responses of Kaiser and Radmacher argue against essential or deeper meaning, this is not the position of the Council itself as found in its published document, "The Chicago Statement on Biblical Hermeneutics." How does the paradigm as a hermeneutic fare in light of the findings or affirmations of the Chicago Statement? Is essential meaning consistent with the affirmations of the Council? We believe it is.

When dealing with interpretation in general, the Council adopted affirmations upholding single meaning. Article VII affirms that "the meaning expressed in each biblical text is single, definite and fixed." Article IX affirms that the horizons of the writer and interpreter could not "fuse" in such a way that what the text communicates to the interpreter is not ultimately controlled by the expressed meaning of Scripture. And Article XV affirms the need to interpret the Bible according to its literal, or normal (grammatical-historical) sense, "the meaning which the writer expressed." The article denies the legitimacy of any approach which attributes to it meaning that the literal sense does not support.[10] We believe that the discovery of essential meaning, at least, does not violate this denial for it is consistent with the so-called literal meaning of the author, although it is not limited to it.

Yet the preceding articles deal with biblical interpretation in general. More pertinent to our study is the article specifically dealing with Scripture's use of Scripture. Article XVIII reads in full as follows:

WE AFFIRM that the Bible's own interpretation of itself is always correct, never deviating from, but rather elucidating, the single meaning of the inspired text. The single meaning of a prophet's words includes, but is not restricted to, the understanding of those words by the prophet and necessarily involves the intention of God evidenced in the fulfillment of those words.

WE DENY that the writers of Scripture always understood the full implications of their own words.

When Geisler, commenting on Article XVII, says that the "interpretation of a biblical text by another biblical writer is always within the confines of the meaning of the first text,"[11] he seems to go too far in light of his comments on Article XVIII. In the latter he deliberately discusses the problem of whether God intended more by a passage of Scripture than the human author did. He acknowledges that evangelical scholars are divided on the issue, some holding that the single meaning may be fuller than the purview of the human author. The prophet may not have been conscious of the full implications of the single meaning shared by God and the prophet. This meaning may not always be fully "evidenced" until the prophecy is fulfilled. He writes: "It is important to preserve single meaning without denying that God had more in mind than the prophet did." God was conscious of something more than what He and the prophet actually expressed in the text. He notes that the denial "makes this point clear by noting that biblical authors were not always fully aware of the implications of their own affirmations."[12]

Geisler is a bit confusing with his use of *meaning* and *implications*. This *more* that God had in mind seems to be meaning, not just implication. The discovery of essential meaning is in keeping with these concerns, we believe. It stays within the confines of "single meaning" as expressed in the article above.

When we turn to the section of the Council's study of the Use of the Old Testament in the New, R. Youngblood in his response quotes favorably J. Wenham as saying that the Holy Spirit, in guiding the writers, "intended a deeper meaning than they understood."[13] In a similar vein, he quotes S. L. Johnson that "the intention of the secondary author must be subordinated to the intention of the primary author, God Himself."[14] Finally, Youngblood quotes G. von Rad as saying: "Christ is given to us only through the double witness of the choir of those who await and those who remember."[15] These statements strongly support the idea of a divine meaning beyond the author's intention.

One of the most significant statements regarding the discovery of additional meaning beyond the literal is located in S. L. Johnson's response to the study by R. Nicole on the use of the Old Testament in the New. Johnson writes that exegesis must be grammatical, historical, and theological to allow (under the last term) for dual authorship. In calling for a new approach to the study of prophecy and the problems thereof, Johnson notes that the old is not infrequently better than the new. He quotes Steinmetz in his article as saying:

> The medieval theory of levels of meaning in the biblical text, with all its undoubted defects, flourished because it is true, while the modern theory of a single meaning, with all its demonstrable virtues, is false. Until the historical-critical method becomes critical of its own theoretical foundations and develops a hermeneutical theory adequate to the nature of the text which it is interpreting, it will remain restricted— as it deserves to be—to the guild and the academy, where the question of truth can endlessly be deferred.[16]

While we may disagree with Steinmetz's evaluation of medieval theory, we accept his conclusion and call for modern re-evaluation. We believe that the application of the paradigm of reality as a hermeneutic begins to meet the need for a hermeneutical approach adequate to (because it reflects) the nature of the text.

For the Curious
and the Careful

NOTES - CHAPTER 1

1   These last terms can prove troublesome, as we explain in chapter 3.

2   We discuss this whole matter in greater depth in chapter 3.

3   See, for one sampling of additional passages, M. Erickson, *Evangelical Interpretation* (Grand Rapids: Baker, 1993), 14-15. Also D. Hagner, "The Old Testament in the New Testament," in *Interpreting the Word of God*, ed. S. Schultz and M. Inch (Chicago: Moody, 1976), 92-103, shows that the literal sense is inadequate in almost two dozen instances including some of those we discuss.

4   The Greek here (and similarly in Hebrews 1) may be rendered by *of*, *about*, or *to*.

5 Regarding Psalm 45, there are some who believe the subject is some king of Israel other than Solomon. Human beings are addressed as God elsewhere: Psalm 82:6-7; Exodus 7:1; 21:6; 1 Samuel 28:13. In any case, most interpreters see these two passages (2 Samuel 7:14; Psalm 45:6-7) as speaking about some merely human king first, and then, by another layer of meaning, about Christ (see commentaries by Kidner, Leupold, Perowne, Calvin, etc.).

6 The words, *a little lower*, refer to position in Psalm 8:5, but probably to time (*for a little* [while] *lower*) in Hebrews 2:9. This is a change from the literal sense that even Calvin recognized in his commentary on Hebrews.

7 See discussion of the difficulty of this example in E. Johnson, "Author's Intention and Biblical Interpretation," in *Hermeneutics, Inerrancy and the Bible* (Grand Rapids: Zondervan, 1984), 416ff.

8 The examples of 1 Corinthians 10 and Galatians 4 are especially important to include in our discussion. They are not prophecy *per se*, but show that the Old Testament—even in its historical-narrative sections—has a deeper meaning beyond grammar and history.

9 For a more technical form of this study, see our work elsewhere: J. De Young and S. Hurty, "Reproducing the Hermeneutic of Jesus: Kingdom Reality as a Biblical Hermeneutic," a paper presented to the Evangelical Theological Society, Washington, D.C., Nov. 18, 1993. We cite various studies of this problem passage. See also J. De Young, "The Function of Malachi 3.1 in Matthew 11.10: Kingdom Reality as the Hermeneutic of Jesus," in *The Gospels and the Scriptures of Israel*, ed. C. Evans and W. Stegner (Sheffield: Academic Press, 1994), 66-91.

10 "The coming one" is a messianic title used in such places as Psalm 118:26; Daniel 7:13; Malachi 3:1-2;

Matthew 3:11; Mark 11:9; Luke 13:35; 19:38; John 1:15, 27; 6:14; Acts 19:4; Hebrews 10:37; Revelation 1:4, 8.

11 Jesus in His answer to John (11:5-6) alludes to several Old Testament passages regarding the work of Messiah (Isaiah 35:5-6; 42:18; 61:1). Though these uses of the Old Testament are instructive in their own right concerning Jesus' self-awareness, they are not as crucial as what Jesus says from the Old Testament about John.

12 This paradox of verse 11 suggests that with the arrival of the Kingdom, values and standards by which we judge greatness have been radically altered. It suggests also that the Kingdom is growing and will continue to grow to include all sorts of people. Indeed, Jesus says that the Kingdom is "forcefully advancing" (it cannot be held back) and forceful men are laying hold of it (v. 12).

The exact force of the verb *biazetai* and the noun *biastai* ("forceful men") is debated. It may be passive (*is stormed* positively by the people or *advanced forcefully* by John and Jesus); or it may be middle (positively, *forcefully advances* (NIV), or negatively, *suffers violence* (NRSV) by the people). It seems best to take it as middle, as per the NIV. While these words are difficult to interpret, it seems that they at least speak to the eagerness, resolve, and commitment people exert to enter the Kingdom at the preaching of John and Jesus. And somehow the least person in the Kingdom would experience greater benefits or privileges or power than John. Just what this means we will later discuss.

13 Some assert that this is a point which Matthew, reporting Jesus, wants to emphasize—that John is in the era of fulfillment, not in the time of prophecy. That is why he uses a preposition for "until" (*heos*) differing from the one (*mechri*) that Luke uses. See R. Gundry, *Matthew: A Commentary on His Literary and Theological Art* (Grand Rapids: Eerdmans, 1982), 210. Others see it the

opposite way. See D.A. Carson, "Do the Prophets and the Law Quit Prophesying before John? A Note on Matthew 11.13," in *The Gospels and the Scriptures of Israel*, ed. C. Evans and W. Stegner (Sheffield: Academic Press, 1994), 179-194. We see John as the bridge, the hinge, between two eras.

14 Since elsewhere in His preaching Jesus has said that the Kingdom has already come (Matthew 4:17), then here He must be thinking of the Kingdom in its narrower sense of the realization of the physical reign of Messiah. Or, Jesus may have intended no doubt at all about the coming of the Kingdom. His words simply show how difficult it is to grasp the arrival of the Kingdom, especially prior to the cross. See D.A. Carson, "Matthew," in *The Expositor's Bible Commentary*, F. Gaebelein, ed. (Grand Rapids: Zondervan, 1984), 8:268. By either view, the Kingdom is present.

15 One more important point needs to be made. The *formula* used in introducing quotes or uses of the Old Testament often helps to explain the particular importance or kind of use of the quote (direct fulfillment, indirect fulfillment, analogy, etc.). There is a special introductory formula here which seems to emphasize direct fulfillment. The words, *this is the one concerning whom it is written*, occur only here and in the recounting of the same story in Luke 7:27. (There are similar words, *it is written concerning*, in Matthew 26:24). This stresses the significance of the statement in the mind of Jesus. More particularly it stresses the important place of John in prophecy.

16 We notice that Malachi 3:1 demonstrates the use of the Old Testament in the Old Testament, for the words of 3:1 are already familiar. The first words (*I will send my messenger*) recall Exodus 23:20-24 where Yahweh (the LORD in most English translations) promises to send His angel before Israel to bring her through the wilderness to the place He has prepared. The angel has the name

of Yahweh in him and has the authority of Yahweh to bring judgment on the evil inhabitants of the land of Israel. The point of Malachi 3:1 is that now a messenger of judgment will come to Israel herself before Yahweh comes to set up His Kingdom.

The second phrase of Malachi 3:1 reflects another earlier promise from the prophets, Isaiah 40:3: "A voice of one calling: 'In the desert prepare the way for the LORD; make straight in the wilderness a highway for our God.'" The person whose voice Isaiah heard calling to prepare the way of Yahweh in the desert, that the glory of Yahweh might be revealed to all flesh (v. 5), is here in Malachi identified as *mal'ak*, "messenger," whom Yahweh will send before Him (i.e., before His coming). See C.F. Keil, *The Twelve Minor Prophets* (Grand Rapids: Eerdmans, n.d.), 2:457.

The following verses after Isaiah 40:3 again place emphasis on the Kingdom, the Sovereign rule of God over the nations and over Israel (40:10-24; 41:21; 43:15; 44:6). Yet He is also Israel's Redeemer, Sustainer, and Lover (40:28-31; 41:8-20; 43:1-4).

So Malachi takes up earlier promises of God's presence and deliverance for Israel in a future day. From Exodus he draws the promise of a messenger, an angel, who has God's name and authority. By his use of Exodus, Malachi would have us realize that God will supernaturally deliver His people safely through another great wilderness experience. From Isaiah, he draws the idea of a messenger preparing the way for God Himself to come as Redeemer and King. Malachi adds the newer elements that the LORD, heralded by the messenger, will come suddenly to His temple; that the messenger is distinguished as *Messenger of the covenant*; and that he is linked to or is Elijah the prophet.

17 This is another instance where the Old Testament gives hint to the idea that when God comes, He comes as both Priest and King (as well as Prophet) (see also

Psalm 110:1, 4; Zechariah 6:11-13; Deuteronomy 18:15).

18 We compare the various texts of our passage in the original languages to discover what differences may exist among the Hebrew Old Testament (known generally as the Massoretic text or MT), the Greek translation of the Old Testament known as the Septuagint (symbolized by LXX, representing the tradition that seventy Jews completed this translation in Egypt about 250 B.C.), and the Greek New Testament. The English translation of all of these would be inadequate at this point. This step is necessary in order to discover what points of interpretation may rest on a change, however minor, in the wording of these texts in the original languages.

In summary, we can say that the quote in Matthew 11:10 is closer to the Hebrew MT of Malachi 3:1 than to the Greek LXX. When we compare the LXX and the New Testament, there are three differences of little significance. See G. Archer and G. Chirichigno, *Old Testament Quotations in the New Testament* (Chicago: Moody, 1983), 164-165. When we compare the MT with the LXX and the New Testament, we find that the remaining differences show that the LXX and MT are in agreement in wording against the New Testament (that is, the two former texts are closer to each other than they are to the New Testament), and these again are without grammatical significance.

However, some minor changes that Jesus makes in His use of Malachi do suggest major significance for interpretation and theology. These concern, in addition to those discussed in our study, His use of *who* in Matthew 11:10.

The LXX of Exodus 23:20 (except for its initial Greek *kai*, "and") is exactly the same as the first clause of Matthew 11:10. This leads Gundry to conclude that Jesus is citing Exodus 23:20, and using *hos*, "who," in place of *kai*, "and," as a literary device to connect the quotes from both Exodus 23 and Malachi 3:1. See R. Gundry, *The Use of the Old Testament in St. Matthew's Gospel* (Leiden: E. J. Brill, 1967), 11-12. Gundry's view is supported by rabbinic exegesis; the homiletic literature on Exodus 23:20 shows that the sermon was given on Malachi 3:1-8, 23-24, according to K. Stendahl, *The School of St. Matthew and Its Use of the Old Testament* (Philadelphia: Fortress, 1968), 50. Stendahl notes that this fusion of texts may point to an Aramaic version used in the synagogues.

This would mean that Jesus may deliberately want to point to Himself as the angel sent before Israel in the desert. This would be an amazing yet subtle indicator to those open to seeing it (remember Jesus' words in Matthew 11:15: "He who has ears, let him hear"). Yet whether Jesus is citing Exodus is, in the end, not necessary to resolve, for it seems that Malachi at least alludes to Exodus. So Jesus alludes to Exodus through Malachi. In a sense, this means that the first and second *messengers* of Malachi 3:1 (that is, the first *messenger* may be derived from the angel of Exodus and has God's name, and the second is called, *Messenger of the covenant*) have much in common.

19 This is so if the quote is based on Malachi alone and not also on Exodus.

20 Thus the Synoptic Gospels (Matthew, Mark, Luke) and John seem to be in contradiction. We will resolve this later when we discuss our hermeneutic.

21 Another significant question concerns whether there is any Jewish basis at all in the first century for the belief that Elijah's coming is connected with the coming of the Messiah. In our more technical study cited above, we marshall the strong evidence for such belief and leave it for the curious reader to pursue it there and elsewhere. The most obvious support are the words of Malachi 3:1 and 4:5.

22 Part of the resolution depends on how many persons are to be identified in Malachi 3:1 (see our more technical study for fuller discussion of this problem). We believe that there are two persons in addition to Yahweh the speaker ("I" translated above as LORD): the messenger, and the Lord expanded (by means of the *waw*, a Hebrew connective) by a second title as the Messenger of the covenant, rather than three persons—the messenger, the Lord, and the messenger of the covenant. Hence, the Lord and the Messenger of the covenant are titles for one divine Person. He is also related to Yahweh in some way. The use of LORD and Lord seems to be similar to the use of LORD and Lord in Psalm 110:1 which Jesus used first (Matthew 22:44-45), and then other writers of the New Testament (Hebrews 1:13), apparently both to distinguish Himself from Yahweh and also to argue for His oneness in deity.

23 R. Hays, *Echoes of Scripture in the Letters of Paul* (New Haven: Yale, 1989), 180, has a similar list in the form of questions to get to the same point of concern regarding the reproduction of Paul's hermeneutic. They are: "(1) Are Paul's specific *interpretations* of Scripture materially normative? (2) Are Paul's interpretive *methods* formally exemplary? (3) What are the appropriate *constraints* on interpretive freedom?" He answers the first two questions yes and gives three constraints to answer the third question: God is faithful to His promises; Scripture must witness to the gospel of Christ; and interpretation must mold readers into a community of love (190-192).

24 C. H. Dodd, *According to the Scriptures* (London: Nisbet, 1952), 127. Our remarks in this paragraph reflect the concerns of Hays, *Echoes*, 182.

25 Hays, *Echoes*, 189, thinks it is deceptive for three reasons: a clear, authoritative text of unchangeable meaning is untenable, for the reader contributes to the act of interpretation; to separate Paul's hermeneutical freedom from ours cuts off the word at its roots; and it

provides a "smokescreen for self-deception for those who will in fact continue to generate their own transformative readings of Scripture while pretending not to do so" (189).

26 Yet even on the subject of the Canon, there is a pluralistic view within the Church, as one compares the Roman Catholic and Eastern traditions with the Protestant. See C. Evans, "The Function of the Old Testament in the New," in *Introducing New Testament Interpretation*, ed. S. McKnight (Grand Rapids: Baker, 1989), 164-165; and R.T. Beckwith, *The Old Testament Canon of the New Testament Church and Its Background in Early Judaism* (Grand Rapids: Eerdmans, 1985), 478-505.

27 This translation takes the verb as an indicative or statement. The form can also be read as an imperative or command: "*Search....*" The point being made is not materially affected.

28 Gundry, *Use*, 213ff., traces every one of Matthew's hermeneutical principles to Jesus, including the case of Malachi 3:1 in Matthew 11:5,10,28 and 29 where Jesus assumes the role of Yahweh.

29 As Gundry, Ibid., points out, a messianic interpretation heightens the meaning of any passage of Scripture. In note 2 Gundry adds that underlying "Jesus' interpretation is the idea that Scripture may contain a divinely intended significance higher (or deeper) than the human author intended." Terms in Psalm 110:1, 4 are proof of this.

30 See the appendix on reproducing the biblical hermeneutic for an elaboration of these concerns.

NOTES - CHAPTER 2

1 If you have not yet read the introduction, please go back and read the last four paragraphs.

2   We refer you for additional information on this history to several general studies on biblical hermeneutics. See G. Osborne, *The Hermeneutical Spiral* (Downers Grove: InterVarsity, 1991); W. Klein, C. Blomberg, and R. Hubbard, *Introduction to Biblical Interpretation* (Dallas: Word, 1993); D. McCartney and C. Clayton, *Let the Reader Understand* (Wheaton: Victor, 1994); R. Stein, *Playing by the Rules* (Grand Rapids: Baker, 1994); and W. Kaiser and M. Silva, *An Introduction to Biblical Hermeneutics: The Search for Meaning* (Grand Rapids: Zondervan, 1994).

   We are aware that every history is an interpretation and that history in a real sense is what we make it to be. This is our attempt to understand it.

3   Kaiser and Silva, *Hermeneutics*, 212. See also R. Longenecker, *Biblical Exegesis in the Apostolic Period* (Grand Rapids: Eerdmans, 1975), 20-48.

4   See these rules in Kaiser and Silva, *Hermeneutics*, 213-214; and Longenecker, *Exegesis*, 34-35.

5   See examples in Klein, et. al., *Interpretation*, 23-28.

6   Longenecker, *Exegesis*, chapters 2-7.

7   See Chapter 3 for an elaboration of this approach.

8   Kaiser and Silva, *Hermeneutics*, 221. While Kaiser argues that this school still held to a single sense or meaning, and believes his generic prophecy approach is close to the Antiochian school, it appears that he fails to give as full a place to the spiritual as does this school.

9   See D. Moo, "The Problem of *Sensus Plenior*," in *Hermeneutics, Authority, and Canon*, eds. D. A. Carson and J. Woodbridge (Grand Rapids: Zondervan, 1986), 182.

10 The four are the historical, aetiological (the origin of things), analogical, and allegorical.

11 According to D. Steinmetz, "The Superiority of Pre-critical Exegesis," *Theology Today* 37 (April, 1980): 31.

12 This information comes from Steinmetz, "Pre-critical Exegesis," 31. This comes close to our proposal for a hermeneutic.

13 Yet Luther allowed for an allegorical interpretation when theological sense cannot be derived from a text in any other way. And most Protestant interpreters allowed for a *sensus mysticus* or *spiritualis* alongside the *sensus literalis*; they simply insisted that this was part of the one sense intended by the Holy Spirit. See also Moo, "Problem," 183. See also F. Farrar, *History of Interpretation* (Grand Rapids: Baker, rep. 1961), 335. Even Calvin saw some uses of the Old Testament in the New as *pious deflections* (347).

14 McCartney and Clayton, *Reader*, 93-94.

15 Klein and et. al., *Biblical Interpretation*, 41. The Spirit's role is to confirm, not to illumine, the truth, Calvin believed.

16 This view was revived in more recent times by the Dutch theologians Bavinck, Kuyper, and Berkouwer, according to J. Rogers, "A Third Alternative: Scripture, Tradition, and Interpretation in the Theology of G.C. Berkouwer" in *Scripture, Tradition, and Interpretation*, ed. W. Gasque and W. Lasor (Grand Rapids: Eerdmans, 1978), 74-75.

17 McCartney and Clayton, *Reader*, 98.

18 According to Steinmetz, "Pre-critical Exegesis," 29, Tyndale distinguished between the "storybook" or nar-rative level of the Bible and the "deeper theological meaning or spiritual significance implicit within it."

19 K. Bockmuehl, *Listening to the God Who Speaks* (Colorado Springs: Helmers & Howard, 1990), 126. Many of our ideas at this point in the text are a summa-ry of 121-126. For a similar view of Luther and Calvin

on this matter, see D. Lake, "The Reformation Contribution to the Interpretation of the Bible," in *Interpreting the Word of God*, ed. S. Schultz and M. Inch (Chicago: Moody, 1976), 186-195.

20 Ibid., 130. Significantly, in contrast to the position of our discussion, in which we argue for the democratization of the gift of prophecy, in Reformed thinking the gift of prophecy has virtually disappeared or been monopolized.

21 This may be changing, however. With the significant rise of home Bible studies in contemporary America, there is again an expressed concern how theology—our very view of God—is changing. Such groups promote community and revitalize faith, yet may do little to increase biblical knowledge, and often replace explicit creeds with implicit norms of the group. They are part of the quiet revolution transforming society, adding fuel to the fires of cultural change. Such are some of the observations delineated in two significant articles in the Feb. 7, 1994, issue of *Christianity Today*.

22 See J. Miller, "The Emerging Postmodern World," in *Postmodern Theology*, ed. F. Burnham (San Francisco: Harper, 1989), 3.

23 See the fuller discussion of these influences and results in E. McKnight, *Postmodern Use of the Bible* (Nashville: Abingdon, 1988), 44-53.

24 Kaiser and Silva, *Biblical Hermeneutics*, 226; McCartney and Clayton, *Reader*, 20-21.

25 Kaiser and Silva, *Biblical Hermeneutics*, 227.

26 McCartney and Clayton, *Reader*, 100. Schleiermacher's grammatical interpretation was complemented by his "technical" interpretation whereby he sought to discover an empathetic or subjective appreciation for the author by both analytically comparing him with other authors and by intuitively transforming himself into the

author. This attempt to combine the objective and subjective allowed Schleiermacher to use reason as a criterion for truth.

27 Ibid., 102.

28 McKnight, *Postmodern Use*, 46. He identifies the historical-critical method as consisting of three principles: correlation, the influencing of one event upon another in a chain of events by a cause and effect relationship; criticism, the questioning of past judgments so that they are not viewed as true or false but as more or less probable; and analogy, meaning that such judgments of probability assume that present experience is similar to the experience of past peoples (47). McKnight does well in showing how world view has influenced the interpretation of Scripture in all eras, whether the premodern dogmatic approach, the modern historical-critical method, or the future postmodern one. For a critique of the historical-critical method, see G. Maier, *The End of the Historical-Critical Method* (St. Louis: Concordia, 1977); and E. Linnemann, *Historical Criticism of the Bible* (Grand Rapids: Baker, 1990).

29 McCartney and Clayton, *Reader*, 109. So the New Testament world view must be demythologized, i.e., the existential truth within the myth must be restated in a way acceptable to modern people. There can be no objective world view, for such is counter to faith and insecurity. Nor can God be spoken of objectively lest He cease to be God.

There is much for which to fault Bultmann. His major error was failure to see that he used his own subjective world view to pronounce judgement upon the Bible's own words concerning its world view. Also Bultmann could not allow the spiritual and physical worlds to coexist (111).

30 Klein, et. al., *Biblical Interpretation*, 47-48. Three basic assumptions of neo-orthodoxy are: (1) God is a subject,

not an object; hence one can only know Him in a personal encounter; (2) a great gulf separates the transcendent God from fallen humanity so only myths, not history, can reveal Him; (3) truth is ultimately paradoxical in nature (48). See the standard works on interpretation cited above for further help and clarification of this and other matters such as existentialism.

Also see Appendix A for other ramifications for interpretation and history.

31   This is the heart of our own approach: discovery of the biblical center (world view), and tying to it the biblical hermeneutic.

32   While synchrony is by far the more important in interpretation (since the contemporary users of a language determine its meaning), we must also consider diachrony when we come to the New Testament. This is so because the New Testament restates terminology and a world view derived not from the Greek usage of the day but from the Old Testament hundreds and thousands of years before it.

33   McCartney and Clayton, *Reader*, 116. The sense concerns "the general functional meaning of a word, phrase, sentence, etc., within the language as a whole," the "what" of a discourse, the mental linguistic response. The reference is "the extra-linguistic reality to which it refers in a particular context," the "about what" of a discourse. Since the "meaning" of most words in a sentence is their sense and not their reference, the place of context is strategic for interpreting the biblical text and getting to the original intention of the author.

34   G. Osborne, *The Hermeneutical Spiral* (Downers Grove: InterVarsity, 1991), 368. We follow Osborne's discussion for the development of these various critical approaches (368-386). See also N. Gulley, "Reader-Response Theories in Postmodern Hermeneutics: A

Challenge to Evangelical Theology," ch. 12 in *The Challenge of Postmodernism: An Evangelical Engagement,* ed. D. Dockery (Wheaton: Victor, 1995), for his critique.

35 Regarding structuralism, A. Blancy, "Supplemental Theses," in *Structuralism and Biblical Hermeneutics,* ed. and trans. A.M. Johnson, Jr., (Pittsburgh: Pickwick, 1979), 180, writes: "The meaning is always plural....The meaning grows richer by never becoming fixed. The structural method never ends. It is aesthetic, not ethical."

36 Osborne, *Spiral,* Ibid., 375. It is especially timely that our proposal for a new hermeneutic is part of a paradigm of reality (a world view), for it brings us to the only authoritative source, the Bible, for a Christian world view.

37 Ibid., 377.

38 Ibid., 380; 383.

39 Some words to ponder come from Steinmetz, "Pre-critical Exegesis," 36. He quotes C.S. Lewis as saying: "An author doesn't necessarily understand the meaning of his own story better than anyone else." Steinmetz adds: "The act of creation confers no special privileges on authors when it comes to the distinctly different, if lesser task of interpretation....Authors obviously have something in mind when they write, but a work of historical or theological or aesthetic imagination has a life of its own."

Later he observes that medieval exegesis stands between two extremes: the single, original meaning intended by the author and accessible by grammatical-historical interpretation; and the literary relativism of the present era which excludes the author. Rather, the Bible contains both letter and spirit; the original meaning limits a field of possible meanings which are possible in the encounter between the author and reader (37).

40 J. Sanders, *Canon and Community* (Philadelphia: Fortress, 1984), 61ff., shows that canonical criticism discovers how the biblical community re-presented and resignified earlier tradition, that the canonical process is never ending, and studying both the text and the social context make up hermeneutics (77ff.).

See criticism of the new criticism in J.D. Brown, "Barton, Brooks, and Childs: A Comparison of the New Criticism and Canonical Criticism" *JETS* 36/4 (Dec. 1993): 481-489. He finds disharmony between secular and biblical approaches because of different presuppositions, the questions asked, and the application of authority.

41 Erickson, *Interpretation*, 99. Regarding the rise of deconstructive postmodernism, he timely observes: "Differing times and differing contexts call for differing approaches to hermeneutics." Indeed, the changes today are so great that a major paradigm shift away from the foundations of modernism is occurring. This means that the framework within which thought occurs is changing, not just a change in thinking. The very future of Western culture may be at stake. Erickson cites Diogenes Allen, who writes: "What is crumbling are the pillars of western society, which were erected during the Enlightenment" (108).

From another standpoint, J. Rogers, *Scripture, Tradition, and Interpretation*, 83, writes that evangelical theology is in need of "a new theory, model, or paradigm by which to understand Scripture." He believes that there is need for a third alternative to the rationalism of the grammatical-historical approach and subjectivism. It would be, he believes, the approach of Augustine, Calvin, and Luther. The model should be "a functional, not a philosophical one" (84). As we will show, we think that our model addresses these concerns.

42 By *the Bible's world view* we do not mean that there is no variation in a biblical world view from Genesis to

Revelation, nor do we deny that the Bible contains many world views within its pages. We mean that there is a general world view running from beginning to end which distinguishes the Bible's from all other world views.

43 Erickson, *Interpretation*, 101. Interestingly, Erickson characterizes the premodern and modern periods as the transcendental and experienced periods.

NOTES - CHAPTER 3

1 Two questions are always before us. First, how does Scripture interpret itself? That is, what method do biblical writers use to interpret earlier writers? Second, how should we interpret Scripture? Most feel that the biblical method should impact our method, and we also believe this. So throughout, we assume that the Bible's method of interpreting itself is also the model for Christians.

2 V. Poythress, *Understanding Dispensationalists* (Phillipsburg: Presbyterian and Reformed, second ed. 1994), 82-86, says that using terms such as plain, normal sense is inadequate. It puts the focus on words, yet sentences are the key. Also it treats the text as written directly to the modern reader, whereas grammatical-historical interpretation treats rightly the text "as if it were written in the time and culture of the original author" (85). Although it historically stands for the grammatical-historical meaning, the idea of the term *literal* is faulty also, for it can mean the first-thought meaning or the flat meaning, overlooking figurative language, etc. (82-86ff.). Grammatical-historical means to interpret according to the context, allowing for figurative and symbolical language. While we will continue to use *literal interpretation*, we are aware that often it is thought incorrectly as opposite to figurative sense.

3   E.D. Hirsch, *Validity in Interpretation* (New Haven: Yale, 1957), 8. See W. Kaiser, *The Uses of the Old Testament in the New* (Chicago: Moody, 1985), 218-220, for application of this distinction to the use of the Old Testament in the New.

4   Also Kaiser, *Uses*, 63ff. More broadly, W. Klein, C. Blomberg, R. Hubbard, *Introduction to Biblical Interpretation* (Dallas: Word, 1993), 97-98, write that the goal of hermeneutics is to enable interpreters to arrive "at the meaning the biblical writers 'meant' to communicate at the time of the communication, at least to the extent that those intentions are recoverable in the texts they produced" (see also 133-138).

5   W. Kaiser and M. Silva, *An Introduction to Biblical Hermeneutics* (Grand Rapids: Zondervan, 1994), 41. This fine text goes far to explain the different concepts involved in meaning, including referent, sense, intention, and significance. Unfortunately, Kaiser does not allow the divine intention to exceed the human one, and refuses to acknowledge the possibility of a difference between divine and human intentions by claiming that passages cited as such do not pertain to the writing of Scripture (40). However, he then cites the passage of 1 Corinthians 2:6-16 as his support for a totally equal divine and human intention, which has nothing to do with writing Scripture either (as we will show in a later chapter)!

Also R. Stein, *Playing By the Rules* (Grand Rapids: Baker, 1994), 38-46, maintains the usual distinction that meaning is determined by the author, significance by the reader. Yet he places implications within the concept of meaning, and an author may not know all the implications of what he writes.

6   M. Erickson, *Evangelical Interpretation* (Grand Rapids: Baker, 1993), 16. See also, V. Poythress, "Divine Meaning of Scripture," *Westminster Theological Journal* 48 (1986): 245-248.

7 Yet if the Holy Spirit is distinguished in Scripture's authorship, should He not be in its interpretation?

8 See the appendix for discussion about these matters as discussed in "The Chicago Statement on Biblical Hermeneutics" drafted in 1982 by the International Council on Biblical Inerrancy, and by others.

9 A literal hermeneutic may discover that a deeper sense also may belong to Malachi. Malachi means *my messenger* and so there is a play on words implicit to 3:1. Malachi himself is God's sent messenger. Yet, Malachi says also that God will *send* Elijah, and both sendings are followed by references to the coming of the awesome *day of the Lord* (3:2; 4:5). Kaiser (*Uses*, 82-84) argues that an actual Elijah was not in Malachi's mind. In this sense, at least, Jesus and Malachi are not far apart.

So in its narrowest form the literal method limits the meaning or significance of the prophecy of Malachi 3:1 and 4:5 to a single actual Elijah to come in the Day of Yahweh. On the other hand, if a broader literal meaning is pursued so that meaning includes significance, then more than a single person may be in view, and even a metaphorical Elijah. Yet this approach cannot account for two comings and two or more people fulfilling this, especially since the characteristics attending the promise in Malachi will not be fulfilled as envisioned until the second coming. In addition, a literal hermeneutic fails to give certainty or sufficient guidelines for discovering the deeper significance. Should a literal method work here, there remain other places where it does not.

10 W.J. Beecher, *The Prophets and the Promise* (Grand Rapids: Baker, 1963 [1905]).

11 K. Barker, "The Scope and Center of Old and New Testament Theology and Hope," in *Dispensationalism, Israel and the Church*, ed. C. Blaising and D. Bock

(Grand Rapids: Zondervan, 1992), 323-328, calls it the progressive fulfillment of prophecy.

Barker's idea of progressive fulfillment seems to suffer the same faults as does Kaiser's view. (1) It says nothing of dual authorship with the Holy Spirit as co-author (324), treating the Old Testament as secular literature when the New clearly did not. (2) It focuses on progressive stages or climaxes, while it seems better to think of progressive development, a progressive actualization more and more throughout any and all stages, as our approach will suggest, just as progressive revelation suggests. (3) The *both-and* idea still suggests a dual mindset (294, 328). Yet it should be more; it is *here, but not yet* in ongoing actualization. (4) It does not represent a total world view so as to provide an approach for hermeneutics, as well as theology, which finds biblical authority. (5) Our approach will allow for community contributions to progressive revelation even beyond the Canon. Hebrews 11:39-40 is still applicable during the whole present age.

12 Kaiser, *Uses*, 204.

13 More precisely, Kaiser (*Uses*, 230) defines generic prophecy as that which "envisages an event as occurring in a series of parts, often separated by intervals of times, yet, expressed in such a way that the language of the Old Testament may legitimately apply either to the nearest, remoter or climactic event. Thus, the same word, with the same sense or meaning of the Old Testament authors, may apply at once to the whole complex of events or to any one of its parts in any particular era without destroying what the author had in mind when he first gave that word."

14 Yet Hebrews reflects a preference for putting the divine Author over the human author so that it never attributes Scripture directly to a human author. Perhaps this explains its own anonymity: it wants its message received as divine. Finally, God is also the co-Author of

New Testament Scripture.

We are not saying that Kaiser rejects dual authorship; he doesn't. Rather, he rejects it as an explanation for deeper meaning.

15 This and other reasons lead P. Payne to assert that it is fallacious to equate meaning with the human author's intention. See P. Payne, "The Fallacy of Equating Meaning with the Human Author's Intention," *JETS* 13 (1970): 243-252.

Furthermore, it does not seem that generic promise is an all-encompassing hermeneutic applicable to all forms of literature. In addition, even with Erickson's (*Interpretation*, 19-31) concessions, there is no guiding central theme and no pattern whereby we can reproduce this hermeneutic.

The fact that biblical authors use later Scripture to interpret earlier Scripture contradicts another standard of strict grammatical-historical interpretation. Hebrews alone does this repeatedly. For example, Hebrews 2:5-10 uses Psalm 8 to interpret Genesis 1-2; and 3:7-4:11 uses Psalm 95:7-11 to interpret the rest of Genesis 1, Joshua, and 1 Kings. Paul in Galatians 4:21-26 uses Isaiah 54:1 as the basis of his figurative interpretation of Genesis and Exodus.

16 Kaiser and Silva, *Hermeneutics*, 34-45.

17 Ibid., 42.

18 Erickson, *Interpretation*, 31-32. We give here in greater detail his contributions. Erickson writes in defense of single authorial intention and at the same time criticizes the view of Hirsch and Kaiser who champion it (14ff.). (1) He departs from separating meaning and significance because they tend to represent *then* and *now*. So he would use meaning to include both signification and significance, to allow future situations to be included in signification. (2) The understanding of intention

is too narrow, so he proposes the use of *affirms* or *asserts* to focus on the product of the intention rather than the process, and so "avoid any appearance of conscious intention as a requisite for meaning" (23). Affirmed meaning includes both future persons and situations as well as those originally addressed. (3) Writers such as Hirsch and Kaiser limit the type of meaning to the referential and disregard expressive and conative ideas, that is, the affective and volitional. These last two concepts refer to the attitudes of the speaker and what action or changes in attitude he wills. Communication involves affective, volitional, and cognitive dimensions. (4) They don't deal adequately with the use of the Old Testament in the New and with prophecy in general. Did the prophet have multiple meanings in mind? What of prophecies yet unfulfilled (such as the Apocalypse)? Doesn't God have more knowledge about their fulfillment than the human author? (5) They don't deal adequately with the complexity of communication (there may not be just one big idea or central meaning of a passage). (6) In order to prevent subjectivism they fail to set apart sacred Scripture from other literature, treating the Bible as a secular book. Yet doesn't dual authorship exist?

So in addition to what we have already indicated as the changes Erickson would make to literal interpretation, he would also expand authorship to include the Holy Spirit as co-Author; and he would allow the principle of Scripture interpreting Scripture. This apparently supports a canonical approach, although he may still be thinking, as Kaiser does, of antecedent theology informing a given text.

19 W. E. Glenny, "The Divine Meaning of Scripture: Explanations and Limitations," paper presented to the Evangelical Theological Society, Washington, D.C., Nov. 19, 1993, 24-25. Glenny adopts the suggestions of Erickson (see endnote above) and goes further. He

endorses a divine meaning from the standpoint of the idea of meaning because for him, meaning is multi-dimensional with three aspects: the original significa-tion (literary content) of the text; the *sensus plenior* or canonical level of meaning; and the significance of the text to the hearer as he makes application of a text. So meaning and significance are only different dimensions or aspects of meaning. He adds that the divine, fuller meaning must be an extension of the concept found in the original verbal meaning. The divine meaning can-not violate or annul the original affirmation of the text, but must be within the field or range of the original meaning. Glenny denies that the divine meaning is a different or a new meaning of a text. It is simply anoth-er dimension or aspect of one meaning, of the concept in the original context (28). Similarly, Poythress ("Divine Meaning") argues that since God could fore-see all applications of Scripture, these enter into His meaning at the outset of dual-authored Scripture (278-279). We substantially agree with these suggestions (see Paul, Galatians 3:8).

20 Kaiser and Silva, *Hermeneutics*, 41.

21 Ibid., 246. On the basis of divine authorship, he "can hardly doubt that there is considerable meaning in the biblical text that the human authors were not fully aware of." On both literary and theological grounds, he holds that "the meaning of a biblical passage need not be identified *completely* with the author's intention" (italics his).

22 Even Hirsch, *The Aim of Interpretation* (Chicago: University of Chicago, 1976), 79-80, has modified his position on meaning and significance, allowing authori-al will to be disregarded in certain constructions, a change Kaiser, *Uses*, 204, laments. This change could have been foreseen because of certain remarks made by Hirsch in *Validity*, 24-25, 122-123, according to Kaiser, *Uses*, 204, n. 6. See also Glenny, "Divine Meaning,"

8-11. Hirsch, "Meaning and Significance Reinterpreted," *Critical Inquiry* 11 (Dec., 1984), 202-225, also believes that meanings with a future directed intention may have many different future fulfillments as long as these can be subsumed by the original intention-concept, are exemplifications "of a broad and still valid concept" (217). So meaning can tolerate a small revision in mental content but not a big revision, as long as "the adjustment is in the spirit of the historical speech intention" (222-223).

23 So for different reasons, people are finding literal interpretation inadequate. Note, for example, F.F. Bruce, "Interpretation," in *Baker's Dictionary of Theology*, ed. E.F. Harrison (Grand Rapids: Baker, 1960), 293. He asserts that "grammatico-historical exegesis is not sufficient for the interpretation of the biblical documents....Theological exegesis is also necessary, although it cannot override grammatico-historical findings." He appeals to the part that the Holy Spirit fulfills in opening the Scripture for us as the risen Christ did for the apostles. More recently, Bruce writes of an "increment of meaning" in the Scriptures derived from the experience of Christians through the ages. F.F. Bruce, "Interpretation of the Bible," *Evangelical Dictionary of Theology*, ed. W. Elwell (Grand Rapids: Baker, 1984), 565-568. This *increment of meaning* gives to Scripture a fuller meaning. It is supplied by the *whole of Christian history*; what the Bible "has come to mean in the experience of Christian readers, generation by generation, has added something to its meaning for Christian readers today" (567).

E.E. Ellis, *Paul's Use of the Old Testament* (Edinburgh: Oliver & Boyd, 1957), 147-148, defines Paul's exegesis or interpretation as *grammatical-historical plus*. For him exegesis provides the possibilities for what a text says; the meaning of the text arises from an added factor—in the meaning of an event for its later fulfillment. The same could be said for Jesus' interpretation.

W. LaSor, "*Sensus Plenior* and Biblical Interpretation," in *Scripture, Tradition, and Interpretation*, ed. W. Gasque and W. LaSor (Grand Rapids: Eerdmans, 1978), 272, finds that there are passages where something deeper or fuller than the literal and spiritual meanings exists. He calls this the fuller or *sensus plenior* meaning. He relates the failure of the grammatical-historical method to the current dominance of the scientific world view where anything beyond scientific process is ruled out. The literal meaning is the basic meaning, "but if it is the only meaning, then God is not speaking to us; he spoke to men of old—or so they believed—and that was that" (265). We observe that there are historical matters on the horizontal plane and theological matters on the vertical plane, and these are intertwined.

R. Longenecker writes that biblical exegesis has a revelatory stance, a claim to special inspiration, which took the authors beyond the literal method. The additional methods include allegory, midrash, and pesher, to be discussed below.

C.F.H. Henry, *God, Revelation and Authority* (Waco: Word, 1979), 4:281, writes of additional *nuances* which may occur when the New Testament applies the Old. He goes on to say that the Spirit as inspirer of the prophets and apostles, "thus stretches the evident meaning to embrace what is not contrary to the writer's intention but need not have been consciously intended by him." He cites 1 Peter 1:10-12 in support and says that the analogy of Scripture must be taken into account when seeking to understand authorial intention.

D. Hagner, "The Old Testament in the New Testament," in *Interpreting the Word of God*, ed. S. Schultz and M. Inch (Chicago: Moody, 1976), 92-103, shows how the literal sense is inadequate in almost two dozen cases.

V. Poythress, "Divine Meaning," 253-258, argues that on the basis of dual authorship, human meaning and a narrow grammatical-historical approach are inadequate. Because Scripture has a divine Author, he opposes *sensus plenior* and instead favors reading later revelation into earlier passages. Communication involves getting to know the author, including expressive and volitional aspects of the divine Author, as revealed throughout Scripture. Since God intends that Scripture be applied today, the applications we make are part of God's intention—His meaning. A strict grammatical-historical approach is inadequate and does not characterize New Testament usage (225, 275-279).

Even Erickson, *Interpretation*, 29, acknowledges that in the matter of the use of Scripture by later writers, the human author's intention may not be identical with the divine intention, and that the human author was not fully conscious of his own meaning.

E.R. Clendenen, "Postholes, Postmodernism, and the Prophets: Toward a Textlinguistic Paradigm," ch.8 in *The Challenge of Postmodernism: An Evangelical Engagement*, ed. D. Dockery (Wheaton: Victor, 1995), writes that it is often possible to extend an authorial intention and world beyond the human author by means of the canonical context and textlinguistics.

D. Bock argues for a complementary hermeneutic functioning as a result of the progress of revelation within a historical-grammatical-literary reading of the text. It is to read a passage on two levels in light of the event itself and/or in light of following events. Because of the latter, God may mean more than He originally did, but never less. So subsequent revelation can always expand on earlier revelation. See "The Son of David and the Saints' Task: The Hermeneutics of Initial Fulfillment," *BibSac* 150 (Oct.-Dec.1993): 445-447. Elsewhere he identifies this as the *historical-exegetical* reading and the *theological-canonical* reading; the latter may develop the force of a passage beyond what the original author could grasp. See "Use of the Old Testament in the New," in *Foundations for Biblical Interpretation*, ed. D. Dockery, K. Mathews, R. Sloan (Nashville: Broadman & Holman, 1994), 107-109.

In addition, commentators on Hebrews affirm that the latter finds a "different sense from that it bore in the consciousness of the original writer" (Delitzsch, 112); that the original meaning is "the germ and the vehicle of the later and fuller meaning" (Westcott, 69); and that texts of the Old Testament are interpreted "not according to the understanding of their human author, but in the way in which the Christian revelation elucidates them" (P. Hughes, 84; see 395).

Even Calvin, in his commentary on Hebrews (58-60, 95, 208-209, 226-229), several times acknowledges that the author, when citing the Old Testament, turns from the literal sense and embellishes the meaning. See also his commentary on Galatians (134-137).

See also C. Evans, "The Function of the Old Testament in the New," in *Introducing New Testament Interpretation*, ed. S. McKnight (Grand Rapids: Baker, 1989), 164-165, 192-193. He affirms that modern principles are inadequate to describe the biblical method that finds new meanings in earlier texts.

M. Terry, *Biblical Hermeneutics* (Grand Rapids: Zondervan, rep. 1974), acknowledges that not all of the meaning of Old Testament typology was understood by the authors, and that there are more types to be discovered (344-346). *Deeper meaning* is acknowledged (140, n. 1). Unfortunately, he never discusses such key passages as Psalms 8, 110, 125, etc., or the places in the New Testament where they are cited.

Indeed, virtually all texts on hermeneutics (Ramm, Mickelsen, etc.) acknowledge that the grammatical-historical approach is inadequate, for they acknowledge that typology, which is clearly present in Scripture, is outside this approach. They even support our discovering additional typology.

Additional interpreters are cited in this chapter, and in Appendix B dealing with reproducing the hermeneutic of the New Testament.

While Kaiser recognizes the place of theological interpretation (*Uses*, 204-212), he refuses to allow subsequent, progressive revelation to influence earlier Scripture, and confuses normativity, authority, and truth—distinctions which we will later make. Yet biblical writers use later Scripture to interpret earlier Scripture (e.g., Hebrews 7 uses Psalm 110:4 to interpret Genesis 14 regarding Melchizedek).

24 Erickson, *Interpretation*, 18, and Kaiser, *Uses*, 20-23, 189, 209, 216), attempt to explain these passages differently. Kaiser repeatedly misrepresents 1 Peter 1:10-12 as saying that the Old Testament prophets spoke not "only for themselves but also for us." Yet Peter does not say this; rather to the prophets "it was revealed that they were not serving themselves but you"—the believers of the present era. Peter makes no mention that they were serving themselves in their prophesying but affirms just the opposite. In a note (p. 216, n. 49), Kaiser acknowledges this but affirms that it is the figure of speech known as ellipsis by which the word "only" has been left out for the sake of emphasis. While this may be possible it is not certain. Peter at least suggests that they did not understand everything.

25 This is the verb *anapleroun*.

26 For example, see Hebrews 1:5, 6, 7, 8, 10, 13; 2:12; 3:7; 4:3, 4, 7, 8; etc.

27 As LaSor, "*Sensus Plenior*," 266, points out, there is spiritual meaning(s) because God is a spiritual being and his purpose is redemptive (we would say Kingdom-actualizing).

28 According to Hays, Paul's "original intention is not a primary hermeneutical concern." He is not constrained "by a historical scrupulousness about the original meaning of the text. Eschatological meaning subsumes original sense." See R. Hays, *Echoes of Scripture in the Letters of Paul* (New Haven: Yale, 1989), 156. He further writes that Paul does not follow any single exegetical procedure. He offers "helter-skelter intuitive readings, unpredictable, ungeneralizable." Modern scholars who adhere to a "conception of exegesis as a rule-governed science have frequently sought to retroject such a conception onto Paul by ascertaining the methods that he employed." However, such classification, while useful, suffers from "ex post facto artificiality." The modern concern "for methodological control in interpretation is foreign to him" (160). Hays comments: "Paul's readings characteristically treat Scripture as a living voice that speaks to the people of God. Scripture must speak to us and must speak of weighty spiritual matters" (165). For example, Deuteronomy 25:4 is used in 1 Corinthians 9:8-10 (165); note v. 11, and Romans 4:23-24; 15:4; 1 Corinthians 10:11; Romans 10:5-10 (165).

D. Steinmetz, "The Superiority of Pre-critical Exegesis," *Theology Today* 37 (April, 1980), writes: "The notion that Scripture has only one meaning is a fantastic idea and is certainly not advocated by the biblical writers themselves" (32).

So also Poythress, "Divine Meaning," 279, asserts that we should not require biblical writers to confine themselves "to a narrow grammatical-historical exegesis."

Even Calvin in his commentary on Hebrews affirms that the apostles were not scrupulous in quoting the Old Testament, and exercise great freedom (227-228).

29 As suggested by Bock, "Son of David," 447.

30 There is little uniformity in nomenclature here. The first six (including literal) are more or less structural

models recognized somewhat universally, and then we grouped all the remaining motifs or concepts under *theological methods*, loosely defined to include any concept serving as a theme or method. See J. Weir, "Analogous Fulfillment: The Use of the Old Testament in the New," in *Perspectives in Religious Studies* 9 (1982): 67-69; Longenecker, *Exegesis*, 28-50, who posits the literal, *pesher*, *midrash*, and allegorical methods; and other authors such as Kaiser, Baker, Verhoef, etc.

31 Longenecker, *Exegesis*, 41.

32 Ellis, *Paul's Use*, 139-147.

33 K. Stendahl, *The School of St. Matthew and its Use of the Old Testament* (Philadelphia: Fortress, 1968), 183-184.

34 Longenecker, *Exegesis*, 70ff.

35 C.H. Dodd, in his *According to the Scriptures*, shows this well.

36 Longenecker, *Exegesis*, 32.

37 Ibid., 37. See also Ellis, *Paul's Use*, 139-147.

38 Ibid., 37, 56-70, 126.

39 M. Silva, "New Testament Use of the Old Testament," in *Scripture and Truth*, ed. D.A. Carson and J. Woodbridge (Grand Rapids: Zondervan, 1983), 161. He believes that the differences between biblical and rabbinic interpretation are *quantitative* rather than *qualitative*. B. Chilton, *A Galilean Rabbi and His Bible* (Wilmington: Michael Glazier, 1984), shows that targumic material was also used by Jesus and believes it to be the key to His use of the Old Testament.

40 I.H. Marshall, "An Assessment of Recent Developments," in *It Is Written: Scripture Citing Scripture*, ed. D.A. Carson and H.G.M. Williamson (Cambridge: University Press, 1988), 13-14. See also R.H. Gundry, *The Use of the Old Testament in St. Matthew's Gospel* (Leiden: E.J. Brill, 1967), 208, 213;

K.J. Thomas, "Torah Citations in the Synoptics," *NTS* 24 (1977):96. So also LaSor, *"Sensus Plenior,"* 272, rejects Jewish methods as explanations for these uses of the Old Testament in the New.

41 G. von Rad, "Typological Interpretation of the Old Testament," *Essays on Old Testament Hermeneutics,* ed. C. Westermann, trans. J.L. Mays (Richmond: John Knox, 1963), 21.

42 In seeking to identify typology, we must avoid the extreme of going too far and forcing from the text those types and antitypes that have virtually no support in the text. The other extreme doesn't go far enough, for it makes a type nothing more than an example or pattern. See D. Baker, *Two Testaments: One Bible* (Downers Grove: InterVarsity, 1991 rev.), 199. He denies that it is exegesis, prophecy, allegory, symbolism or a method or system. Yet the New Testament uses it as a method of interpretation. While Baker recognizes the need that the type be historical and have correspondence to something that fulfills it, he seems to ignore as essential to typology (1) a predictive element; see S.L. Johnson, *The Old Testament in the New* (Grand Rapids: Zondervan, 1980), 55-56; (2) the impact of redemption history; see Kaiser, *Uses,* 106-110; and (3) heightening or climax; see L. Goppelt, *Typos* (Grand Rapids: Eerdmans, 1982), 18, 200-202.

43 Yet this very point that typology, like symbolism and prophecy, involves both the symbol and what it symbolizes (hence two dimensions), makes some like Poythress, *Understanding,* 113, move away from using literal and in its place grammatical-historical interpretation.

44 Baker, *Two Testaments,* 190. See also R. France, *Jesus and the Old Testament* (Downers Grove: Inter-Varsity, 1971), 41-42.

45 von Rad, "Typological," 36-39.

46 P. Verhoef, "The Relationships Between the Old and the New Testaments," in *New Perspectives on the Old Testament,* ed. J.B. Payne (Waco: Word, 1970), 280, warns against making typology more than one aspect of the *scheme of redemptive history.* Other ways to connect the Testaments are legitimate.

47 For an excellent defense of the idea of reproducing the New Testament practice of typology, see G.K. Beale, "Did Jesus and His Followers Preach the Right Doctrine from the Wrong Texts?" in *The Right Doctrine from the Wrong Texts?* ed. G.K. Beale (Grand Rapids: Baker, 1994), 399-404.

48 W. Pannenberg, "Redemptive Event and History," *Essays on Old Testament Hermeneutics,* ed. C. Westermann, trans. J. Mays (Richmond: John Knox, 1963), 327-329. Typology undermines the historical facts connecting the Testaments by being "a finally unhistorical, purely structural similarity." Yet this can be overstated, for typology embraces historicity.

49 Weir, "Analogous Fulfillment," 72, 75. Mickelsen, Wolff, von Rad, D.S. Russell, and De Vries all hint at analogous fulfillment, according to Weir. He finds that the analogous fulfillment model meets the four criteria necessary for the fulfillment of the Old Testament in the New Testament (66). Chilton, *Galilean Rabbi,* 184ff., prefers analogy over typology in his process called *fulfilled intepretation* (involving analogical, critical meditation, and experiential steps).

50 Longenecker, *Exegesis,* 93-95. The other three are corporate solidarity, correspondences in history, and eschatological fulfillment. Longenecker terms Christology *messianic presence.*

51 G. Hasel, *New Testament Theology: Basic Issues in the Current Debate* (Grand Rapids: Eerdmans, 1978), 155-164, thinks Christology is the center of the New Testament, but it should not become the structure upon

which to write a New Testament theology (164).

52 See Gundry, *Use of the OT*, 215-216. Hasel, *New Testament Theology*, 111-139, 148-153, shows that salvation history seems to be inadequate. In addition, Chilton, *Galilean Rabbi*, 154ff., argues that it is only an assumption that biblical history amounts to salvation.

53 It is possible to distinguish between a valid use of *Heilsgeschichte* and an invalid one. R. Allen has defended the moderate view which was, apparently, the position of the originator of the term, von Hofmann. See R. Allen, "Is There *Heil* for *Heilsgeschichte?*" A paper presented to the Evangelical Theological Society, Reformed Theological Seminary, Jackson, MI, Dec. 30, 1975. Allen goes on to suggest eight considerations or prerequisites necessary for a careful use of *Heilsgeschichte* (17-20).

54 Pannenberg, "Redemptive Event," 314-315. This is its error shared with existential theology in its reduction of history to historicity. Both *Heilsgeschichte* and existential theology are often employed as means to escape the feared destruction of faith caused by that kind of historical-critical investigation which seems to destroy the historical reliability of the Scripture. Pannenberg notes that "redemptive history is not a suprahistory, but because of its universal tendency essentially includes all events" (330). Yet in the end Cullman's approach to salvation history preserves canonical faith better than Pannenberg's, as T. Dorman argues. See T. Dorman, "Can We Speak of 'Canonical' Scripture? Oscar Cullman's Thesis in Light of Wolfart Pannenberg's Proposal." A paper read at the Evangelical Theological Society, Kansas City, MO., Nov. 21-23, 1991.

55 See Baker, *Two Testaments*, 203-233; Hasel, *OT Theology*, 181ff.; *NT Theology*, 127-132, where he cites Goppelt (*Theology of the NT*) as limiting salvation history to promise and fulfillment.

56 As Pannenberg, "Redemptive Event," 316-317, shows. He writes that reality is a linear history moving toward a goal, for God initiates new events in the course of His creation. This "history arises because God makes promises and fulfills these promises" (317). "History is event so suspended in tension between promise and fulfillment that through the promise it is irreversibly pointed toward the goal of future fulfillment" (317). "The goal here of Yahweh's action in history is that he be known—revelation....His action comes from his love, begins with his vow, and aims at the goal that Yahweh will be revealed in his aciton as he fulfills his vow" (317). We too see the significance of history relative to promise, and we devote a later chapter to it. W. Kaiser, "Biblical Theology of the Old Testament," in *Foundations for Biblical Interpretation*, ed. D. Dockery, K. Mathews, R. Sloan (Nashville: Broadman & Holman, 1994), 328-352, supports promise as the center.

57 Verhoef, "Relationships," 289-290, believes that the whole of the testaments is to be covered by each term, *promise* and *fulfillment*. Yet he acknowledges that this formula must be supplemented by such concepts as unity of perspective regarding the coming of the Kingdom of God and continuity/discontinuity (292).

58 R.E. Brown, "The History and Development of the Theory of a Sensus Plenior," CBQ 25 (1963): 262-285. Those evangelicals who seem to hold to some form of *sensus plenior* include S.L. Johnson, J.I. Packer, E.E. Johnson, W. Dunnett, P.B. Payne, W.S. LaSor, D.A. Hagner, and D. Moo.

LaSor, "*Sensus Plenior*," 274, takes this approach to be the fuller sense or fullness of meaning. It arises from God's redemptive purpose, so he labels it *purpose* (not prediction) *and fulfillment*. Fulfillment accomplishes God's purpose. It lies beyond the human author's intention. LaSor offers safeguards in finding the fuller meaning (275): it must always begin with the literal meaning (grammatical-historical exegesis); it must derive from the total context; and it must derive from Scripture, not some mystical or spiritual source (he seems to mean that it cannot contradict Scripture).

· 59 See D. Hagner, "The Old Testament in the New Testament," in *Interpreting the Word of God*, ed. S. Schultz and M. Inch (Chicago: Moody, 1976), 92-104, for a very fine defense of *sensus plenior* (which is actually combined with the canonical approach, *Heilsgeschichte*, promise-fulfillment, and typology). He discusses almost two dozen passages in this light.

60 Moo, citing Brown's defense of *sensus plenior*, shows that this meaning may have at times been dimly perceived by the human author as shown by the context (it need not be a meaning *reserved by God to Himself*—an objection raised by B. Vawter and endorsed by Kaiser, Uses, 209); that there is a relationship between the literal sense and the "fuller" sense; that it differs from typology since it concerns words rather than events; and that it differs from accommodation (God truly intends this meaning). D. Moo, "The Problem of *Sensus Plenior*," in *Hermeneutics, Authority, and Canon*, ed. D.A. Carson and J. Woodbridge (Grand Rapids: Zondervan, 1986), 201-202. See also Baker, *Two Testaments*, 193-194.

61 J.J. O'Rourke, "The Fulfillment Texts in Matthew," CBQ 24(1962):402-403, says that "we should not call a *sensus plenior* something which we cannot otherwise classify; that would be merely labeling a difficulty, not resolving it" (403). He believes that Matthew viewed his use of the Old Testament as legitimate and proper, but so varied from "our point of view that no completely satisfactory classifying of them has yet been produced" (403).

62 Moo, "*Sensus Plenior*," 205-206. He gives these advantages: (1) The meaning is built on the redemptive-historical framework of the Old Testament in the New;

(2) it is represented by the use of the Old Testament in the Old Testament; (3) it imparts a meaning not deliberately concealed from a human author but a meaning which unfolds as the Canon grows; (4) it is open to verification to some extent.

For other advantages, see Klein, Blomberg, and Hubbard, *Introduction to Biblical Interpretation* (Dallas: Word, 1993), 65-69. They give it cautious approval, but distance themselves from the canon criticism of J. Sanders who focuses on the Canon as a process rather than a product (68).

63 Thus Moo defines the canonical approach ("Sensus Plenior," 210). See the advantages of this approach for understanding the gospel of John in D. M. Smith, "John, the Synoptics, and the Canonical Approach to Exegesis" in *Tradition and Interpretation in the New Testament*, ed. G. Hawthorne with O. Betz (Grand Rapids: Eerdmans, 1987), 166-180.

64 J.I. Packer, "Infallible Scripture and the Role of Hermeneutics," in *Scripture and Truth*, ed. D. A. Carson and J. D. Woodbridge (Grand Rapids: Zondervan, 1983), 350.

65 J. I. Packer, "Exposition on Biblical Hermeneutics" in *Hermeneutics, Inerrancy, and the Bible* (Grand Rapids: Zondervan, 1984), 909-911. Packer discusses integration as his fourth point, following the literal sense, the grammatical-historical method, and the principle of learning. We will suggest a different second step in our approach.

66 B. Waltke, "A Canonical Process Approach to the Psalms," in *Tradition and Testament: Essays in Honor of Charles Lee Feinberg*, ed. John S. and Paul D. Feinberg (Chicago: Moody, 1981), 8. Waltke's four stages are the meaning of the original poet, the meaning in earlier collections of the Psalms at the time of the First Temple, the meaning in the final and complete Old

Testament Canon of the Second Temple, and the meaning in the full Canon including the New Testament (9). Waltke's approach rests on four convictions: the people of God are united by a common knowledge and faith; Scripture is inspired by God—He is the divine Author of the whole Bible; texts must be interpreted in light of the whole Bible; the Canon is closed (9-10). This allows Waltke to find additional meaning; we are in the heavenlies now and mystically participating in the future age (Galatians 4:26; Ephesians 1:3; 2:6, 19; Hebrews 12:22ff). Waltke has built on the work of Brevard Childs.

67 Yet Waltke's progressive meaning is not *sensus plenior*; the New Testament doesn't impose a new meaning on the Old but wins back the original and true significance, finding Jesus as the fulfiller of the ideal King of the Psalms ("Canonical Process," 16).

While our approach is very similar to Waltke's, we have some concerns regarding his approach. (1) Cannot the divine Author intend more than a human author? (2) Is his approach applicable to other portions of the Old Testament? (3) We believe that the conceptual center of the Kingdom is a better center than an ideal King concept. (4) Are there four actual stages and not five or six, since the New Testament Canon went through a four-hundred-year history? Also the New Testament does not seem to recogize such a development or progress in meaning. Rather, in regard to the use of Malachi 3:1, which alludes to Exodus 23 and Isaiah 40, the prophet seems to assume one continuous meaning from the Law onward and it is this which the New Testament similarly assumes. The same could be said of Hebrews' use of Psalm 110:4 which picks up Genesis 14; or of Hebrews' use of Psalm 40 used by Isaiah in the Servant passages.

68 B. Waltke, "A Response" in *Dispensationalism, Israel and*

the Church, ed. C. Blaising and D. Bock (Grand Rapids: Zondervan, 1992), 355. The "images of the old dispensation were resignified to represent the heavenly reality of which they always spoke" (358-359).

In an address at the Northwest Section, Evangelical Theological Society, Multnomah School of the Bible, Portland, Oregon, April 9, 1983, Waltke urged reconsideration of the fourfold sense which predominated during the middle ages. This approach greatly affects one's view of end time events, that is, eschatology.

V. Poythress has built on Waltke's approach by finding three contexts (original, intermediate canonical [prior to the text under consideration], and completed canonical). The later understanding is a fuller, divine meaning. See V. Poythress, "Divine Meaning," 241-279. See Glenny's excellent summary ("Divine Meaning," 16-17). Glenny also evaluates (17-19) the *multidimensional* approach of D.A. Oss and his "Canon as Context: The Function of Sensus Plenior in Evangelical Hermeneutics," GTJ 9.1 (1988):115-127. Yet Oss fails to distinguish the author's historical meaning from the later divine meaning, so that there is no discernible meaning for the original recipients.

69 We are aware of certain rabbinical guidelines, such as *pearl-stringing*, which are used to explain the linking of texts. But we are thinking more broadly here: What biblical center or theme gives an even broader grid?

70 By now many of our readers have begun to see the impact of these different approaches on the question of how prophecy about end time events (eschatology) will be fulfilled. We are basically divided between those who look for an actual reign of Christ on this earth and those who don't. The former champion literal interpretation that prophecy must be fulfilled for Israel in the forms in which it was given; the latter believe that prophecy will be spiritualized and fulfilled in the Church. These are standard generalizations. Each group

wants to be biblically sound and yet struggles over the issue of hermeneutics. For too long these approaches have gone unresolved. But the day for resolution may not be far off.

For example, in the camp of premillennialism, classic dispensationalists allowed for a spiritual interpretation of prophecy, particularly of the nature of typology. In the 1960s there came a tightening of this so that literal interpretation was designated one of the *sine qua non*, one of the essentials, of dispensationalism. More recently, progressive dispensationalists are more open again to a broader view of hermeneutics so that Israel and the Church do not have to be regarded as two separated peoples of God. Bock (cited above), whose work parallels some of our approach, is one such progressive dispensationalist.

71   Klein, et al, *Biblical Interpretation*, 138-145. See also N. Gulley, "Reader-Response Theories in Postmodern Hermeneutics: A Challenge to Evangelical Theology," ch. 12 in *The Challenge of Postmodernism: An Evangelical Engagement*, ed. D. Dockery (Wheaton: Victor, 1995), who finds the reader-response approach lacking.

NOTES - CHAPTER 4

1   For a similar description of this plan of the ages, see the fine summary of S. Ellisen, "Everyone's Question: What is God Trying to Do?" in *Perspectives on the World Christian Movement*, ed. R. Winter and G. Hawthorne (Pasadena: William Carey Library, 1981), 19-23.

2   The view of creation that is assumed in this account is based upon Bruce Waltke's *Creation and Chaos* (Portland, OR: Western Seminary, 1974), and others'. The theology of mission traced above remains essentially the same regardless of one's precise view of the creation account.

3   In the Hebrew, the verse means literally that God creat-
    ed man *as* His own image. This further emphasizes the
    sense of mission in God's creation of man.

4   See the helpful article suggesting a position very similar
    to ours by D. McCartney, "*Ecce homo*: The Coming of
    the Kingdom As the Restoration of Human
    Vicegerency," *Westminster Theological Journal* 56
    (1994):1-21.

5   The missionary purpose of Israel is set forth by W.
    Kaiser, Jr., in "Israel's Missionary Call," *Perspectives on
    the World Christian Movement*, ed. R. D. Winter and S.
    C. Hawthorne (Pasadena: William Carey Library,
    1981), 25-33.

6   Two interesting essays give additional food for thought
    concerning a visible Kingdom and its relationship to
    mission. The first is Ralph Winter's "The Kingdom
    Strikes Back: Ten Epochs of Redemptive History,"
    Perspectives on the World Christian Movement, 137-155.
    He discusses a possible historical pattern he discerns
    wherein a people is raised up and enabled to engage in
    God's mission for the whole world and is subsequently
    conquered when they become preoccupied with build-
    ing their own kingdom rather than engaging in mission.
    A prime example is the institutionalization of the
    Kingdom of God in the Roman Empire with
    Constantine.

    The second is Philip Yancey's "Ecclesiastes: The High
    Counterpoint of Boredom," *The Reformed Journal* (July-
    August, 1990):14-19. In it he wonders whether the
    decline of the Kingdom of God in Israel shouldn't teach
    us that the allure of the visible kingdom is empty. The
    spiritual Kingdom of God must be sought, beginning
    with the reign of God in the heart. This will naturally
    work itself out within institutions, fully manifest (with-
    in time) in the millennial Kingdom when earthly and
    spiritual authority are reunited. In the meantime, we

are to attend to God's mission by spreading the gospel of salvation through Jesus Christ.

7   So the Bible is both a record of God's perspective and part of God's record (in the sense that God's perspective is larger than the Bible).

8   See D. Griffin, *God and Religion in the Postmodern World* (Albany: CUNY, 1989), 14.

9   The more technical terms of a world view are known as *metaphysics* (what is real), *epistemology* (how do we know it), and ethics (what is good or moral). Does Scripture itself display concern for what we have called a world view? We do find the pattern of a world view presented within it. For example, John expresses concern for morals or ethics, reality, and truth (1 John 5:18-20). In each verse, one's relationship to God is the key for finding all three of these fufilled or defined.

10   For a good summary of various centers, see G. Hasel, *Old Testament Theology: Basic Issues in the Current Debate* (Grand Rapids: Eerdmans, 1991), 138-171. He reviews such concepts as covenant, the holiness of God, God as the Lord, the election of Israel, the rulership of God, the Kingdom of God, the dual concept of the rule of God and the communion between God and man, promise and fulfillment, Yahweh the God of Israel, Israel the people of Yahweh, and Yahweh Himself. He finds them all lacking. He argues against a single unifying concept because "the Old Testament message resists from within such systematization" (141). He rejects recent approaches because they are rooted in "philosophical premises going back to scholastic theology of medieval times" (154). Others agree that a single concept or theme is not "sufficiently comprehensive to include within it all variety of viewpoint" (153); that a single concept approach has "undeniable inadequacies" (153). Hasel advocates that one must search for an "internal key," from within the Bible itself, based on the inner biblical witnesses (159) to discover the theology

of the Bible. Hasel concludes that the unifying center of the Old Testament is God/Yahweh (168), and for the whole Bible adopts a "multiplex approach" to describe the relationship between the Testaments, citing seven concepts or schemes (191-193).

In spite of Hasel's reluctance to find such a center as ours, we think the Kingdom center is the internal key.

11 See W. Kaiser, *The Uses of the Old Testament in the New* (Chicago: Moody, 1985), 147; Hasel, *Old Testament Theology*, 139-141. See W. Kaiser and M. Silva, *An Introduction to Biblical Hermeneutics*, (Grand Rapids: Zondervan, 1994), 266, for the importance of covenant in covenant theology.

12 See endnote 10 for all that may be involved.

13 Others have talked about this dual nature of the Kingdom in other ways. For example, G. Ladd *A Theology of the New Testament* (Grand Rapids: Eerdmans, 1974; rev. 1993), 67, speaks of a twofold emphasis in the New Testament: "God's will is done in heaven; his Kingdom brings it to earth. In the Age to Come, heaven descends to earth and lifts historical existence to a new level of redeemed life" (Rev. 21:2-3). Citing Jesus' words regarding the fact that in the future realm people will not marry and cannot die (Luke 20:35-36) Ladd notes:

> "Here is a truly inconceivable order of existence. There are no human analogies to describe existence without the physiological and sociological bonds of sex and family. But this is the will of God: to conquer evil and to bring his people finally into the blessed immortality of the eternal life of the Age to Come."

14 R. France, "The Church and the Kingdom of God," in *Biblical Interpretation and the Church*, ed. D. Carson (Nashville: Thomas Nelson, 1984), 35-42, shows that the phrase *Kingdom of God* has a variety of areas of ref-

erence; cannot be identified with any specific situation, event or thing but rather denotes the overall conceptual framework of the saying; focuses primarily on men's relation with God; means, *God in control, God's initiative, God's purpose accomplished*; and its coming means "God in strength" (quoting B. Chilton)(43). See B. Chilton, *The Kingdom of God* (Philadelphia: Fortress, 1984), ch. 7: "God in Strength," 121-132. While we do not agree with everything said here, we concur with the suggestions regarding the breadth of the term and the emphasis on personal relationship with God. We believe these concepts fall within our perspective of the term, yet we place a greater emphasis on the "rule" dimension of it. See also Winter (endnote 6.

15 In the eternal state, God lives with us, we are His people and He is our God (Revelation 21:3, 7); as His servants we will see His face and reign forever (22:3-5).

16 O. Chambers, *My Utmost For His Highest* (Westwood: Barbour and Company, 1963), 248.

17 We do not mean only the simple fact that Christ is Yahweh, but all the implications of this statement as unfolded in the entire New Testament: Christ as Messiah, the coming of the Kingdom, the New Covenant, and the end of the age.

18 Chilton, *Kingdom*, writes in his own chapter, "God in Strength," that the words, *God in strength*, best represent the concept of the Kingdom in Jesus' teaching (124-127). Yet this seems to be a bit vague if we were to cover both transcendence and immanence.

19 The Kingdom may have different forms—in Israel, in Christ, in the Church, in the consummation. It may be past, present (cf. Colossians 1:13; 4:11), and future (1 Corinthians 6:9-10). "Thus it is always the same kingdom, which comes out of heaven and eternity, continues through the ages, and runs again into the eternity of

God." See E. Sauer, *The Triumph of the Crucified* (Grand Rapids: Eerdmans, 1966), 24-25.

The Kingdom center, though narrow enough, is yet broad enough as well. It reveals the inner hidden unity that can bind together the various theologies and themes, concepts and motifs in the Old Testament writings. This is the concern of Hasel, *Old Testament Theology*, 205-206.

20 For example, it meets Hasel's (*Old Testament Theology*, 139-170) concerns: it avoids a Canon within a canon; it arises within Scripture itself, not from external creeds, tradition or modern philosophy; it is broad enough to encompass all Scripture; it encompasses Christocentricity and *Heilsgeschichte*; and it avoids arbitrariness, subjectivity, and reductionism. It also promotes continuity over discontinuity.

The Kingdom center also seems able to meet Osborne's six criteria for a center. See G. Osborne, *The Hermeneutical Spiral* (Downers Grove: InterVarsity, 1991), 283. An adequate center must: (1) express the nature/character of the Godhead; (2) account for the people of God as they relate to God, their world and one another; (3) include the world of humankind as the object of God's redemptive love; (4) explain the dialectical relationship between the Testaments; (5) contain and sum up the individual emphases of diverse parts of Scripture; (6) account for other potential unifying themes and must truly unite them under a single rubric. And even those who suggest other centers explicitly recognize the importance of the Kingdom. For example, D. Wenham in his appendix to the revision of Ladd, *Theology*, 709-714.

21 Probably the Jewish standard of two or three witnesses is in mind here.

22 Ladd, *Theology*, 54; see also 56 and 58-67 for support for additional points we make. According to Ladd again

(412) we find that the unifying center in Paul is the "realization of the coming new age of redemption by the work of Christ....The unifying center is rather the redemptive work of Christ as the center of redemptive history." Now this seems to run counter to the idea of the Kingdom as the central theme for Paul. Yet Ladd goes on to say that Paul's message involving the two themes of justification and mysticism (the new life in Christ) is "one of both realized and futuristic eschatology." This, we believe, is simply another way of saying that the Kingdom, while belonging to the Age to Come, has in some form come to be experienced now in the person of Christ.

23 See France, "Church and Kingdom," 34. His chapter shows the breadth of meaning in the phrase, *Kingdom of God.*

24 R. Stein, *The Method and Message of Jesus' Teachings* (Philadelphia: Westminster, 1978), 60-79, says that the central theme of the teaching of Jesus is the coming of the Kingdom of God. In defining this Kingdom (75-79), he weighs several views: realized eschatology (the Kingdom is realized in the ministry of Jesus); consistent eschatology (the Kingdom is entirely future); and a harmony of both views. Stein prefers the last idea (as do we): the Kingdom is both here, as a present reality, but also not yet here, as a future reality. Similarly, D. Bock, "The Son of David and the Saints' Task: The Hermeneutics of Initial Fulfillment," *BibSac* 150 (Oct.-Dec. 1993): 449-57, writes that the Kingdom is present with Christ, in an initial form.

25 R. Saucy, *The Case for Progressive Dispensationalism* (Grand Rapids: Zondervan, 1993), 21. Scholars who see the Kingdom as such include dispensationalists and non-dispensationalists: Pentecost, McClain, Peters, Bright, Hoekema, Ladd, etc. Saucy faults both non-dispensationalists and dispensationalists for either missing this center entirely or wrongly defining it. And while

some in both camps embrace the Kingdom as such a goal, how it is to be achieved is the disputed issue. He suggests a mediating position whereby the distinctives of the second system above and the emphasis on one united people in the first system are retained. Israel will have a distinctive role in the future but there is no radical discontinuity between the present Church age and messianic Kingdom promises.

Saucy (20) does not see hermeneutics nor the purpose of God in history as the basic issue separating dispensationalists from non-dispensationalists. Rather it is the "way we understand the historical plan and the goal of that plan." While this may be overstated, we think that our approach tied to the Kingdom center satisfies the need for this understanding.

Recently, K. Barker, "The Scope and Center of Old and New Testament Theology and Hope," in *Dispensationalism, Israel and the Church* (Grand Rapids: Zondervan, 1992), 314-318, has gathered an impressive list of scholars who have written in support of the Kingdom as the central theme of Scripture. His list includes Bright, Glock, Peters, Ridderbos, Kohler, Eichrodt, Smith, Ladd, Lovelace, Davidson, Richardson, Sauer, Vriezen, McClain, Marshall, Saucy, and Goppelt. This list clearly shows a general consensus among liberal and conservative scholars, dispensationalists and covenantalists.

See also E. Sauer, *The Triumph of the Crucified* (Grand Rapids: Eerdmans, 1964), 144; Bock, "Son of David," cited above.

26 Saucy, *Case*, 27-29. A progressive dispensationalist, Saucy bases his view on several hermeneutical considerations: prophecy has eschatology within its scope and spiritual and material elements are not incompatible; typology does not mean that the shadow is absorbed in the reality; the finality of Christ and the progressive fulfillment of prophecies about Him; and the assumption

that Old Testament prophecies are still valid unless explicitly otherwise stated.

Both dispensationalists and non-dispensationalists see the Kingdom in some sense as this central theme of Scripture and history. Even the doctrine of the Church (ecclesiology) must be understood within the concept of the Kingdom. So S. Grenz, *Theology for the Community of God* (Nashville: Broadman & Holman, 1994), 620-624. The Church is a foretaste of the Kingdom. Grenz shows how the Kingdom is broader than the Church, produces the Church, and gives purpose to the Church. And all theology may be written from the Kingdom center.

27 Barker, "Scope and Center," 305-314.

28 We are indebted to Bock, "The Son of David," 447, for suggesting some of the significance of this verse.

29 The paradox is clear. The Scriptures say that we are receiving the Kingdom (Hebrews 12:29), that darkness and the world are passing away (1 John 2:8, 17), that it is the last hour and the last days (1 John 2:18; Hebrews 1:2). Yet it also says that the last days will be terrible times, (2 Timothy 3:1-5), that greater sin and the lawless one will come (2 Thessalonians 2:1-12), that unless the days of affliction are shortened even the elect would be deceived and destroyed (Matthew 24:22-24).

30 O. Chambers, *My Utmost for His Highest* (Westwood: Barbour and Company, 1963), 228, writes that the new birth gives a new power of vision (John 3:3) to discern God's rule. It is here all the time but is in the form that is true to His nature. Having His nature enables us to see His rule.

31 A reference to C.S. Lewis', *The Lion, the Witch, and the Wardrobe*. In his writings, Lewis sought to engage the two worlds of the real and fantasy, rather than keep them totally foreign. We see the (real) Kingdom engaging our fantasy (shadowy-existent) world.

32 See the fine article elaborating these matters as the mis-
    sion of the Church by G. Ladd, "The Gospel of the
    Kingdom," in *Perspectives on the World Christian
    Movement*, eds. R. Winter and G. Hawthorne
    (Pasadena: William Carey Library, 1981), 51-69.

33 The purpose of God is the key. According to some, we
    are to determine the nature of Scripture by the *purpose
    of God's revelation*, (see J. Rogers, "A Third Alternative:
    Scripture, Tradition, and Interpretation in the
    Theology of G.C. Berkouwer," in *Scripture, Tradition,
    and Interpretation*, ed. W. Gasque and W. LaSor (Grand
    Rapids: Eerdmans, 1978), 84ff.). If this is so (and there
    are concerns with this), then should we not determine
    its hermeneutic thereby? If its purpose is, in short,
    Kingdom history rather than salvation history, then
    should this not be the hermeneutical grid for all? See
    also Calvin in his commentary on Hebrews for its use of
    the Old Testament based in the author's purpose.

34 We acknowledge as our source of this phrase the fine
    work of M. Erickson, *Where Is Theology Going?* (Grand
    Rapids: Baker, 1994), 220.

35 While we could say that the Bible contains many world
    views, in the sense of multiple cultures and ways of con-
    ceiving reality, we affirm that the Bible itself propounds
    and assumes its own world view which often runs
    counter to that of the world around it and its authors.
    Its divine Author has revealed His own world view and
    it is this that we are to embrace.

    In an excellent writing on world view, P. Hiebert,
    "Epistemological Foundations for Science and
    Theology," rep. and ed. from *Theological Students'
    Fellowship Bulletin* 8 (March/April, and May/June,
    1985): 5-10 and 12-18, shows that every world view
    (idealist, pragmatic, determinist, etc.) except the
    critical realist has significant shortcomings for the
    Christian in light of Scripture. Evangelicals in particu-
    lar could greatly profit from his discussion. We find that

our world view of the Kingdom center satisfies the concerns of critical realism. Hiebert interestingly discusses the three aspects of theory, paradigm, and world view. In addition, Hiebert has analyzed personhood, society, and culture and suggests three different world views: the bounded set, the fuzzy set, and the relational set. The former are Greek, the last more in line with Scripture, he observes. We believe that our paradigm of reality is most in line with this last approach.

For an excellent discussion of world view, see C. Kraft, *Christianity in Culture* (Maryknoll, N.Y.: Orbis, 1979), 53-57. For the impact of world view on postmodernism, and vice-versa, see Griffin, *God and Religion*, 13-27.

NOTES - CHAPTER 5

1 Some things have come close. Oscar Cullmann's *Heilsgeschichte* has within it an explanation of how the biblical writers found deeper meaning in Scripture by viewing events of their own day from the perspective of this salvation history and receiving a divine revelation concerning a particular event as being part of salvation history and how it is related to prior salvation-historical events. The problem is that Cullmann embraces the grammatical-historical hermeneutic (including a conservative use of historical criticism) as the method we are to use today, which is different from the hermeneutic of the biblical writers. So, while his biblical center has within it a potential hermeneutic for interpretation, that is not the hermeneutic he uses.

Another example is Karl Barth and others who link the subject matter of Scripture to a hermeneutic. For Karl Barth, the subject matter of Scripture is the Spirit of Christ. Since the Spirit of Christ is outside of history, the method of interpretation he used was not the grammatical-historical hermeneutic, but what he called *theological exegesis*, so that that there was a correlation between the kind of subject matter and the hermeneutic used to understand it. However, a subject matter is not necessarily the same as a theological center, which is usually more specific. There is a much clearer connection between the hermeneutic we are suggesting and the biblical center it is based upon than we have yet encountered elsewhere. See Appendix E for a more thorough discussion of Cullmann and Barth.

2   The names of the parts of this paradigm were chosen for descriptive purposes only. They were the best words we could think of to describe what we meant. The words have been used before and in technical ways in philosophy or theology, and so they carry certain "baggage." You will find it helpful to dump the baggage (if you are aware of the ways these words have been used). Though the way we have used these terms may resemble ways they have been used in the past, we chose them apart from their technical uses in the past (and in fact, became aware of some of it only after devising the paradigm). In other words, don't read in anything technical you may already know or you may get confused.

3   The paradigm is not platonic dualism. It is not exalting a world of ideas over earthly entities. Both the existential and essential are realities. And it is the process of the paradigm that is unique; it actualizes the essential within the existential.

4   This thought, *that matter is affirmed and enduring*, was also the position of Erich Sauer. In *From Eternity to Eternity* (Grand Rapids: Eerdmans, 1966), he warns against overemphasizing the literality and historicity of the millennial Kingdom when "the true, essential core" is the eternal (169). Often the former are simply typical of the perfection of the new earth. The millennial Kingdom is not the real and final goal; eternity is. "In this deepest and noblest sense 'spiritualizing' is decidedly in place" (169). He suggests that in the millennial Kingdom the literal and spiritual will belong together;

that is, there will be "the literality of the outward and material and yet its essential purpose being for spiritual ends" (182); the clothing of eternal spiritual truths in material forms and yet the full reality of this literal material (182). In the Old Testament, the emphasis was on material things; in the New Testament, the emphasis is on the spiritual (though the material is real, as in baptism and the Lord's Supper: they go beyond the merely symbolic and the fact of remembrance and are associated with the reception of Divine blessings (see especially 1 Corinthians 10:16-21) (183). In the millennial Kingdom there will be both outward and spiritual aspects. The two will be "truly Christianized from within" and be "harmoniously united, the external and the internal, the visible appearance and the invisible spiritual life of the heart" (184).

5   In *The Triumph of the Crucified* (Grand Rapids: Eerdmans, 1966), Sauer points to the Incarnation for the precedent that "embodiment is the end of all the ways of God; the eternal is an actual, existing, spiritually embodied Reality" (181). For Sauer, this clearly set the Bible apart from Greek philosophy, especially Platonism with its ideal state containing no bodily element. Rather, the Bible knows nothing of *fleshless spiritualizing* (182). It emphasizes both realms harmoniously. The body is an important part of man's nature (2 Corinthians 5:3, 4). It is not redemption *from* the body but *of* the body (Romans 8:23).

6   The Apostolic Fathers reflect this same world view of Scripture. For example, Ignatius writes, "For this reason you consist of flesh and spirit, that you may deal tenderly with the things which appear visibly; but pray that the invisible things may be revealed to you, that you may lack nothing and abound in every gift" (Ignatius to Polycarp 2.2).

7   Actually, the deeper meaning for us is related to the

essential meaning of a passage which was usually understood by the human author. *The* deeper meaning is essential meaning unknown to the human author. This essential meaning (whether or not it was understood by the human author) is what we use to find meaning for our own lives. We explain this later in the chapter.

8   A different aspect of the idea of meaning is being emphasized here. In the case of looking for *the* deeper meaning in a passage (if there is one), we are looking for an objective meaning placed there by God. In the case of seeking deeper meaning in Scripture for our own lives, we are looking for a subjective sort of meaning, what Hirsch would call the significance or application for our lives that the meaning of a passage has. Someone may counter, Then why don't we call them *deeper meaning* and *significance* and avoid the confusion? We choose to call them both deeper meaning because (1) that is the term that everyday people would naturally use for both ideas; (2) Hirsh's distinction is problematic, and; (3) the word *meaning* encompasses both ideas. See Erickson's very helpful discussion related to this in *Evangelical Interpretation* (Grand Rapids: Baker, 1993), 19ff.

9   Much of this discussion applies also to using the paradigm in the New Testament, but we have a separate section for it to discuss some difficult questions particular to it.

10 The essential meaning of a text seems to be akin to what Millard Erickson has called "the signification behind the signification," a core meaning transferable for all time, very theological in nature. *Evangelical Interpretation*, 61.

11 See Appendix E for Cullmann's description of this.

12 The culture in which they were born and reared is now foreign because they have new core values and look at life very differently from their birth culture.

13 V. Poythress, "Divine Meaning of Scripture," *WTJ* 48 (1986), 246-247, makes the case that God intends in His writing of Scripture the applications that later believers are to make, so that application is part of meaning, which the original human authors could not have known. This is what we would call *deeper meaning* in the sense of "deeper meaning *for us*," referring to significance and application, in Hirsch's terms. In this sense we agree that there is deeper meaning in the New Testament unknown to its authors. But if deeper meaning is restricted to *essential* meaning unknown to the human authors, then we are inclined to say that, for the reasons given, there isn't any in the New Testament.

14 The letters themselves speak very clearly of churches in John's day. It is unclear whether John intended his messages to refer only to his contemporary church. Quite commonly, though, we have sought deeper meaning in his messages to them, going so far as to take them as God's description of the Church through various epochs.

15 Of old, God spoke through His prophets, but now has spoken through His Son (Hebrews 1:1-2). Revelation in Christ is final and authoritative, but it may not be exhaustive in the New Testament. There remains what we will know when we see Him as He is. Perhaps the Council of Nicea unfolded a bit of essential reality when it worked out the two natures of Christ using terms and concepts not found in the Canon of Scripture.

16 E. McKnight, *Postmodern Use of the Bible* (Nashville: Abingdon Press, 1989), 205. Yet we believe that the paradigm of reality as a hermeneutic is biblically derived and not imposed from without, as a modern philosophy is.

The entire history of interpretation can be told as a story of our perennially basing our hermeneutic on the contemporary world view. The odds are quite against us that we have avoided this error ourselves, especially since we do not have a thorough understanding of the philosophical basis of our suggested hermeneutic. Nevertheless, we are putting forth the idea that perhaps if there is a "biblical hermeneutic," it is based on the basic biblical world view, no matter how contaminated by our own world view is our attempt to find this.

NOTES - CHAPTER 6

1   G. Fee, *God's Empowering Presence* (Peabody: Hendrickson, 1994) 901, in his massive treatment of the Holy Spirit in the Pauline epistles, calls for a return to Paul's perspective that the Christian life is "essentially the life of the Spirit, dynamically experienced and eschatologically oriented—but *fully integrated into the life of the church*" (italics his).

He says this means that "our theologizing must stop paying mere lip service to the Spirit and recognize his crucial role in Pauline theology; and it means that the church must risk freeing the Spirit from being boxed into the creed and getting him back into the experienced life of the believer and the believing community" (902).

2   D. Wallace, "Who's Afraid of the Holy Spirit?" *Christianity Today* (Sept. 12, 1994), 35-38, writes from a cessationist viewpoint in his indictment of the evangelical neglect of the Holy Spirit. He presents seven theses to affirm the greater role of the Holy Spirit.

This neglect is also pointed out by C. Pinnock, "The Role of the Spirit in Interpretation," *JETS* 36/4 (Dec. 1993) 491. He cites illumination as the "gap in evangelical theology."

Most courses in Bible schools and seminaries teach exegesis as "the skillful application of sound hermeneutical principles to the biblical text with a view to understanding and declaring the author's intended meaning." This standard definition is inadequate and fails to establish the distinctive of biblical interpretation. In addition, the "hermeneutical principles" mentioned usually refer only to grammar and history, and make no special reference to the work of the Holy Spirit. Do we not then fail to distinguish the nature of Scripture from purely secular literature?

As an example of an approach which disavows any place to the Spirit, W. Stenger, *Introduction to New Testament Exegesis* (Grand Rapids: Eerdmans, 1993), simply omits all mention of the Holy Spirit in the process of interpretation and treats his method of interpreting the Bible as not "fundamentally different" from that used in a secular approach (1). While he admits that there is a "theological" question of what the text says today, he dismisses this concern as beyond his task as he sets forth the historical-critical method (5-6). There is no place for making the text relevant for today! He opposes allowing the Bible to speak "directly" and dismisses the idea of a "direct encounter between the biblical text and the reader as useless for any disciplined and responsible dealing with the text" (2). He uses the same principles for understanding Scripture as for other books. It is "the content of the Bible, not exegetical method itself, that makes exegesis a theological discipline" (1), he asserts. He omits any reference to such passages as 1 Corinthians 2; John 14-16; and 1 John 2.

On the other hand, we agree with the observations of F. Klooster, "The Role of the Holy Spirit in the Hermeneutic Process: The Relationship of the Spirit's Illumination to Biblical Interpretation," in *Hermeneutics, Inerrancy, and the Bible* (Grand Rapids: Zondervan, 1984), hereafter cited as *HIB*, who points out that understanding Scripture involves the entire being, the head and heart (462), and requires the gifts of the Spirit (468). He observes that scientific exegesis is a "specific kind of activity, but it is not of a higher order; it is not lord of correct interpretation"; it is not presuppositionless (469). He defines scientific exegesis as grammatical-literary-historical-theological-canonical (470). Why not add the word, *spiritual?*

Several centuries ago, John Owen argued that right interpretation is first by means of spiritual aids such as prayer and meditation, and secondly (and subservient to the first) by means of arts and sciences with all kind of learning. The Spirit alone is the "primary efficient cause" of our understanding Scripture. John Owen, *The Works of John Owen*, ed. by W. Goold (London: Banner of Truth Trust, 1967), 4:126, 124; see A. Lindsley, "A Response to the Role of the Holy Spirit in the Hermeneutic Process," *HIB*, 488, 492.

3 This is our perception of the practice of evangelical hermeneutics and exegesis. As the subsequent discussion and notes show, scholarly opinion is divided on whether illumination includes aid in understanding meaning or only aid in receiving the truth.

4 Based on the premise that apostles are no more, prophets are now in first place (cf. 1 Corinthians 12:27).

5 C. F. H. Henry, *God, Revelation and Authority* (Waco: Word, 1979), 4:278, notes this also.

6 Some may distinguish the Spirit's work of illuminating the text or speech (clarifying what is already there) from His teaching role (imparting new communication or revelation), but we treat them together. The two roles of illuminator and teacher mean that the Holy Spirit is an exegete. If Jesus is the one who exegetes (*explains, interprets*) the Father (also John 1:18), it is certainly appropriate to speak also of the Holy Spirit as He who exegetes both the Father and the Son, in Scripture and out.

7   Everyone who holds to the second option, that the Spirit helps us to understand Scripture, would also endorse the first option, that the Spirit helps us by enabling us to receive the Word.

8   There is considerable discussion about this question. It is interesting how widely assumed it is that illumination pertains to the aiding of the listener of the text so that he will receive or welcome the meaning of the text, that is, grasp its significance, rather than understand its meaning in the first place. For example, see W. Kaiser and M. Silva, *An Introduction to Biblical Hermeneutics* (Grand Rapids: Zondervan, 1994), 40-41, 167-169, 181-182. Yet on 23-24, Silva seems to deny this possibility; that is, the work of the Spirit is necessary to understand Scripture.

D. Fuller, "The Holy Spirit's Role in Biblical Interpretation," in *Scripture, Tradition, and Interpretation*, ed. W. Gasque and W. LaSor (Grand Rapids: Eerdmans, 1978), 189-198, also limits the Spirit's role to our response to the Word, not to aiding our understanding which even an unbeliever can do. He bases this on the meaning of *foolishness* in 1 Corinthians 2:14—that it points to the significance of truth, not its meaning, and the inadequacy of 1 Corinthians 2:13 to communicate anything if the intention can be known only to a believer.

Yet C. Ryrie, "Illumination," in *EDT*, ed. W. Elwell (Grand Rapids: Baker, 1984), 544-545, says it is the understanding of Christian truth; specifically, making clear the meaning of Scripture to the believer. He makes no mention of significance, only understanding. With Ryrie's view concurs Henry, *Revelation*, 4:272-295. Also, Klooster, "Role of the Holy Spirit," 461, affirms that the Holy Spirit works in the believing interpreter "to enable faithful understanding of the meaning of the passage under study."

M. Erickson, *Evangelical Interpretation* (Grand Rapids:

Baker, 1993), 33-54, does admirably well in refuting the view of Fuller and others. Fuller fails to appreciate adequately the doctrine of total depravity and its effect on the mind. He is faulty from a psychological standpoint, for he improperly divides the person into intellect, emotions, and will, failing to recognize a person's psychosomatic unity. He is problematic logically, for he has gone to an extreme in his desire to avoid a charismatic approach, giving no place to the Holy Spirit in interpretation. He is epistemologically faulty, for we come to understand not just by natural or mechanical processes of exegesis. And Fuller has a metaphysical problem in addressing how the natural and supernatural are related. It is on this last point that this position is most flawed.

Lindsley, "A Response to the Role of the Holy Spirit in the Hermeneutic Process," in HIB, 489, writes that an unbeliever is able to grasp an idea with the mind, but is unable to have a deep or full sense of "its truth, goodness or beauty." But it is not clear what the words, *its truth*, mean. Is not the truth in both general and special revelation ascertainable to some degree due to the image of God?

Geisler in HIB seems to agree with Fuller: the unbeliever may perceive the message of Scripture but does not welcome it to his heart (891-892). On the other hand, Packer divides Scripture into two levels: the unbeliever may understand the theoretical or notional level, but the Spirit is necessary to grasp the level of "the assent and commitment of faith to become experiential through personal acquaintance with the God to whom the theories and notions refer" (908-909). This also is not far from Fuller.

R. Stein, *Playing By the Rules* (Grand Rapids: Baker, 1994), 25, affirms that the unbeliever may understand the words of the sacred Author, but not the truth of the subject matter, not the experience. He later (65-71) clarifies this by saying that an unbeliever can understand a passage, but not accept its significance, values, implications, or truthfulness. So he follows Fuller's position.

It seems to us that there is historical content to be heard in the gospel or read in the text, and this content is cognitively accessible to the unbeliever by grammatical-historical interpretation. It provides the hearing upon which basis faith may come (Romans 10:14). Yet this falls short of the true hearing and understanding which manifests itself in believing and obeying (we expand on this at the end of our chapter and in Appendix E) and involves the entire person—mind, emotions, will.

The resurrection ministry of Jesus parallels that of the Spirit and testifies that interpretation involves both the heart and the head. On the road to Emmaus and later, it was necessary for Jesus to encourage the disciples both to believe in their hearts all that the prophets had spoken (Luke 24:25, 32) and to open their minds so that they could understand the Scriptures (v. 45). This speaks to both the subjective and objective aspects of interpreting.

9   As in Erickson, *Interpretation*, 52. For Erickson, the ministry of the Spirit is necessary; He takes what is in the biblical text and helps us to understand what is already there. Moreover, the passages do not refer to the process of canonization; that is, they are not to be limited to the original circle of disciples and their completing of the Canon, Erickson affirms (42). He believes that these passages tell of the ongoing ministry of the Spirit to illumine the text. Yet, we believe Erickson himself is flawed in limiting these passages to the biblical text.

10 Verse 13 could be limited to Paul, since Paul repeatedly uses the terms, *we speak* found in verse 13, of his own ministry of speaking a message (vv. 1, 4, 6-7). Yet verse 13 probably refers to all believers, or to all who speak to

the church as prophets, apostles, and other ministers of the Word. Calvin takes v. 13 as of Paul. For other views see C. Kling, "The First Epistle of Paul to the Corinthians," in *Commentary on the Holy Scriptures*, by J. Lange (Grand Rapids: Zondervan, rep. 1960), 59-64; and commentaries by Hodge, Ellicott, Robertson and Plummer, Mare, and Carson (on chapters 12-14).

Another major view is that the whole passage of 2:6-16 is limited to Paul and perhaps in a derivative sense to those fellow-teachers who worked with him. For example, this is the view of W. Kaiser, "A Neglected Text in Bibliology Discussions: 1 Corinthians 2:6-16," *Westminster Theological Journal* 43 (1980-81):301-19. He disallows the inclusion of other apostles and bases this on the use of the verb *speak* used here instead of *preach* and *proclaim* (vv. 1-3) and the use of *but* in v. 16 (to put himself in contrast to the perfect and the members of the church in general). So Kaiser finds vv. 10-12 to refer to revelation, v. 13 to inspiration, and vv. 14-16 to illumination.

We think that it is too narrow to limit the passage to Paul, as though v. 13 refers to those who write Scripture, as in 2 Timothy 3:16. Inspiration is usually seen as a trait of the written text, not of the writers of it. See S. Grenz, *Theology for the Community of God* (Nashville: Broadman, 1994), 497-498, for the idea that it covers both the activity of the Spirit on the writer and the deposit of the writings. It seems more consistent to see at least Paul and all his fellow workers—Sosthenes, Cephas, Apollos, Timothy, Silas, Aquila and Priscilla, and others, apostles and non-apostles—involved and this explains the we in 2:6-16 and 3:9 (cf. 1:1, 12, 23; 3:5-9; 4:1, 6-13; 2 Corinthians 1:1, 19; Acts 18:1-20:6). None but Paul and Cephas wrote Scripture, as far as we know. While *writing* occurs in 4:6, 14, Paul in 2:6-16 refers more broadly to the message he and others *speak* (2:6, 7, 13), not write. This would fit

Paul and Apollos and other preachers well. Also, he commends the Corinthians for not lacking any spiritual gift (1:7), and this would include revelation (2:10; 14:26). So we think that 2:13 refers to Paul and any other preachers of and to the church there through whom revelation comes. It is not about inspiration of the canon.

11 This is so even though a different Greek word is used for *understand* in the two verses. Calvin, *Institutes of the Christian Religion*, trans. H. Beveridge (Grand Rapids: Eerdmans, 1970), 1:240, seems to agree, for he comments that our minds have to be renewed by "the enlightening of the Holy Spirit." Regarding 1 Corinthians 2:14, he says that the natural man has "no understanding in the spiritual mysteries of God" and that "they are made known only by the revelation of the Spirit"; he goes on to cite Ephesians 1:9 and 1:18 for support. He uses *understand* several times (see 484 also).

Ephesians 1:17-18ff. is Paul's prayer for the believers that the Father might grant them the Spirit of wisdom and revelation so that they may fully know Him.

First Corinthians 2:13 is very similar to 1 Peter 4:10-11a: "Each one should use whatever spiritual gift he has received to serve others, faithfully administering God's grace in its various forms. If anyone speaks, he should do it as one speaking the very words of God." This tends to support the idea of additional revelation from any Christian so gifted. The goal is the praise of God through Jesus Christ (v. 11c).

12 The verb *expressing* ("interpreting," NIV margin) is difficult to translate. It may refer to *interpreting* in light of verses 12 and 14 which speak about *understanding*, rather than revealing. It is used on at least a half dozen occasions in the Septuagint for *interpreting* dreams (Genesis 40-41; Daniel 5). Yet to interpret is *to express*, and *to reveal* is also appropriate; when one speaks by the

Holy Spirit, He interprets the message into human speech as He reveals it. The other prevalent view takes it as *comparing, uniting* or *combining* used by Paul in 2 Corinthians 10:12 (which is its only other use in the New Testament). It really does not matter; for *comparing* or *uniting* or *combining* would mean that the spiritual substance or content is combined with the spiritual form or means. Revelation is probably the basic idea. Also, revelation cannot be limited to Paul and his co-workers, for he assumes it as possible for any believer in 1:7; 2:10 and 14:26. For support of *interpreting* or *explaining* see Kling, "Corinthians," 61-62, and other commentaries for this problem.

13 Fee, *Presence*, 105, quoting Holladay, 47. This seems to be the meaning of 1 Peter 4:10-11 as well, and also 2 Peter 1:20-21.

14 The words *adapts* and *accommodates* are from John Calvin, *Commentary on the Epistles of Paul the Apostle to the Corinthians*, trans. J. Pringle (Grand Rapids: Baker, rep. 1979), 20:114.

15 Some would point out that the Bible emphasizes here and elsewhere the continuity of the divine and human intention in that the Spirit teaches the person, rather than speaking through him things unknown to him. We agree. This is the emphasis of Scripture. However, this is not *all* that the Spirit does. This is evident from the phenomena of Scripture using Scripture and from certain passages that indicate this.

A personal example might help in understanding this. I was on the phone with a friend within minutes of needing to leave to catch a plane. I rehearsed all the things I had done to leave and what I had left to do, and then in closing the conversation, I said, "Well, I've gotta fly!" *After* the words came out of my mouth I realized the pun. I had not intended the pun at all. In fact, I *never* use the phrase, "I've gotta fly." I simply don't like it. My mind had unconsciously made connections between my being in a hurry and the fact that I was going to catch a plane soon, and, from among all the alternatives, chose an idiom that does not fit my personality to close the conversation. My words had a sort of deeper meaning that I had not intended at all. And we have all had other people point out a pun in our words that we had not intended and did not pick up ourselves until they mentioned it.

Now if this sort of thing can happen every day in the natural workings of the human mind, why can't it happen also by the aid of the Spirit in the writing and reading of Scripture? It seems to us to be quite conceivable that the biblical writers, while ruminating on all the Kingdom things they knew, wrote Scripture by the aid of the Spirit who intended more meaning in it than they knew.

16 These words of Paul are significant in providing a basis for our proposed approach of finding a deeper, divine meaning beyond the literal. The subject matter, the kind of revelation, determines the method of interpretation. The human intent lends itself to grammatical-historical interpretation, but the divine intent lends itself to another method of interpretation—which incorporates the role of the Holy Spirit. See Appendix E for elaboration of this.

17 It seems that Kaiser and Silva, *Biblical Hermeneutics*, repeatedly make this wrongly refer to the written Word (seven times in one paragraph) (40, 182). So also Erickson, *Interpretation*, 52, limits the Spirit's role of illumination to the biblical text. While Erickson argues against Fuller and supports the Spirit's role in interpretation, giving insight into meaning (he even allows for "deeper dimensions of understanding" that come from the illumination of the Spirit, but these are "not essential to salvation or to Christian fellowship") (54), in the end he makes an error similar to Fuller's. Erickson's own position does not arise from the text when he

limits the role of the Holy Spirit to giving "insight or understanding of the meaning that is in the biblical text." Yet there was no biblical text. While there was an Old Testament text, Paul cannot be limited to this. Erickson wants to avoid the subjectivity associated with giving the Holy Spirit the role of ongoing interpreter and revealer of the truth to His church. Yet this seems too narrow a limit on the role of the Spirit. And is there not subjectivity involved in determining the new insight or understanding?

Erickson writes similarly in *Christian Theology* (Grand Rapids: Baker, 1985), 250. This appears to be the view of Pinnock, "Role of Spirit," 497, although he says intended meaning can get *enriched, sharpened and enlarged* (495-496).

Henry, *Revelation*, also limits illumination to the biblical text. Following Hodge, 1 Corinthians 2:12 refers only to apostles (275-276); the Spirit illumines the meaning of the biblical text to believers (276ff.); special revelation comes only to the apostles (276); the Spirit also convinces believers of the Bible's truth (278, 282, 294); most scriptural propositions can be understood without the work of the Spirit (presumably he means that the natural man can understand much biblical truth) (278-279); that in some uses of the Old Testament in the New, the Holy Spirit "stretches the evident meaning to embrace what is not contrary to the writer's intention but need not have been consciously intended by him" (281); the whole Canon must be considered for a proper understanding of authorial intention (281); revelation can be derived only from the Bible and not also from the Spirit as "a second source alongside and independent of Scripture" (284—unless we share the office and gifts of apostles and prophets, he adds. But do we not share the gift of prophecy?). A major reason Henry shuns ongoing, direct revelation from the Spirit is that it may generate another "novel cult" (284).

While the doctrine of illumination is usually associated (especially for us) with the written Word, it need not be. Illumination is necessary for written or spoken revelation. Illumination is mediated communication; revelation is unmediated communication. 1 Corinthians 2:13 teaches unmediated oral revelation. In any case, the verse cannot be limited to illumination of the written text, for there was none. We must find support for this idea elsewhere.

Klooster, "Role of the Holy Spirit," 471, writes quite honestly when he says, "A precise definition of illumination does not seem possible." The doctrine cannot be "empirically demonstrated or rationally proven."

He cites Calvin's own inability to explain the inner witness of the Spirit: "I speak of nothing other than what each believer experiences with himself—though my words fall far beneath a just explanation of the matter." *Institutes of the Christian Religion*, ed. J.T. McNeill, trans. F.L. Battles (Philadelphia: Westminster, 1960), 1.7.5.

S. Grenz, *Theology*, 500-506, writes that the two processes of illumination and inspiration are intertwined, for the community was illumined to recognize the Canon of inspired writings. The compiling of Scripture took place within the community and its self-understanding. They were illumined to see God's addressing of them in these books. Grenz, however, also limits 1 Corinthians 2:13 to illumination.

Paul cannot be referring to the Old Testament, for he asserts that he speaks a message of wisdom—God's wisdom—hidden beforehand (1 Corinthians 2:7). Elsewhere he makes it clear that this came to him by special "revelation...which was not made known to men in other generations as it has now been revealed by the Spirit to God's holy apostles and prophets...this mystery" (Ephesians 3:3-9; cf. Colossians 1:25-26).

18 See the note above on the meaning of the verb *expressing or interpreting.*

19 Also Calvin, *Corinthians*, 113ff., sees it as the spoken word.

20 Also even the words, "We have the mind of Christ" (v. 16), are spoken probably of all believers and not just Paul and ministers of the message.

21 Verse 13 affirms a lot more. (1) The Spirit communicates revelation which is beyond or in addition to or not found in Scripture. (2) Paul (and in principle, others receiving this revelation) interprets, and in a sense, reveals this orally for the listeners with words which the Spirit teaches. (3) The verse includes both revelation from the Spirit and interpretation of this all by Paul. In this sense, Paul serves much in the manner of an Old Testament prophet. He gives two revelations, the spiritual things and the spiritual words. (4) Both the content of revelation and the mode of revelation come from the Spirit. (5) The words are both human and divine, not just divine, for Paul is taught them; he does not parrot them. (6) This verse, with verses 12 and 14, affirms that the Spirit both gives revelation directly and aids both our understanding and our reception of this oral revelation.

This verse apparently teaches that prophecy has two basic elements: the revelation (or content); and the interpretation (or meaning of it, and this may include the mode, such as words). When both are Spirit-sourced, there can be no error. When the interpretation is not given but left to man, error can occur. Hence Paul insists that others (perhaps other prophets, but probably the whole church) should discern a prophet's utterance and that the spirits of the prophets are subject to the prophets (1 Corinthians 14:29-32; cf. 1 John 4:1-3; 1 Thessalonians 5:21). The analogy to this is the gift of tongues, which needs to be accompanied by an interpretation. Perhaps this explains why the two gifts are dealt with together. In 1 Corinthians 2:13, Paul is dealing with both the prophetic Word and its interpretation as coming from the Spirit. This explanation of prophecy may be a better way to explain what W. Grudem and others mean when prophecy fails. It seems that D.A. Carson, *Showing the Spirit* (Grand Rapids: Baker, 1987), (162-165) basically agrees with us.

22 Ephesians 5:18 is to be interpreted somewhat akin to 1 Corinthians 2:13. To be filled with the Spirit is to let the Spirit within give expression to the spiritual truths in spiritual words to others. The exhortation is to "not get drunk on wine....Instead, be filled with the Spirit." The next verse regarding speaking to one another in various modes (psalms, hymns, songs) makes it clear that the parallel to v. 18 is Colossians 3:16: "Let the word of Christ dwell in you richly as you teach and admonish one another with all wisdom" in various modes (psalms, hymns, songs). This "word of Christ" can hardly be limited to the written text of Scripture. More likely it must include the ongoing revelation about Christ or from Him which comes to members of the Body in worship. Thus Ephesians 5:18 refers to the collective Body in worship and is to be interpreted as 1 Corinthians 2. This filling in community is the major emphasis (cf. Acts 2:4; 4:31), although there are instances of personal fillings (e.g., Acts 4:8; 6:3, 5; 6:10; 7:55; 9:17).

23 F. Farrar, *History of Interpretation* (Grand Rapids: Baker, rep. 1961), 340, records Luther as follows: "The multitude of Christians in believing that God spoke to holy men of old have altogether forgotten that he speaks to them still, though neither then nor now does he raise the finite to the capabilities of the infinite, so that neither they nor we were made either perfect or all wise, or on all subjects infallible, although moved by the Holy Ghost. There was a time when saints and martyrs had

no New Testament. As Zwingli said, 'He who is born of the Spirit is no longer dependent on a book.'"

24 R. Hays, *Echoes of Scripture in the Letters of Paul* (New Haven: Yale, 1989), writes that Paul's espousal of freedom in Christ (Galatians 5:1; 2 Corinthians 3:17) bears hermeneutical implications. We can read Scripture with freedom as we are illuminated by the Spirit (154). For Paul, God's Word "is alive and active in the present time, embodied in the community's Spirit-empowered life and proclamation" (171). The "true sense...is actualized in the community of Paul's readers only as a consequence of the hermeneutical transfiguration wrought intertextually in 2 Corinthians 3:7-18. True interpretation depends neither on historical inquiry nor on erudite literary analysis but on attentiveness to the promptings of the Spirit, who reveals the gospel through Scripture in surprising ways" (156).

25 W. Klein, C. Blomberg, and R. Hubbard, *Introduction to Biblical Interpretation* (Dallas: Word, 1993), take the view that the passages refer to "the inspiration of the Spirit in providing the New Testament canon of Scripture" (85, n. 8).

26 Points made by M. Erickson, *Christian Theology* (Grand Rapids: Baker, 1985), 251.

27 D. McCartney and C. Clayton, *Let the Reader Understand* (Wheaton: Victor, 1994), 76. They do not believe that an ongoing communication of the Spirit is taught in these passages.

28 See Erickson, *Theology*, 251-252, for a defense of the need to have both an objective word (written) and a subjective word (the inner witness of the Spirit) as the authority for the Christian.

29 Since there is a deposit of truth not revealed by the apostles—they did not inscripturate all that they knew (cf. John 20:30; 21:24-25; cf. Luke 1:1-4)—there is at least the suggestion that more may be revealed.

30 The truth is not in the text of v. 20, but is supplied from v. 21 (as also the NIV recognizes).

31 McCartney and Clayton, *Reader*, 77-78.

32 See S. Smalley, "1, 2, 3 John," vol. 51, *Word Biblical Commentary* (Waco: Word, 1984), 124. It seems that we can affirm more, that the words concern the teaching of new truth, that is, revelation, and not just interpretation.

33 See chapter 8 for fuller discussion of spiritual gifts.

34 Prophecy differs from teaching in various ways. The former refers both to foretelling future things by direct revelation, and to declaring or telling forth the mind of God, perhaps by the special, direct, and immediate revelation of the Holy Spirit. Teaching does not include foretelling, and seems to be not immediate revelation from God but the instruction resulting from deliberate attention to tradition or to the written Word of God. And these gifts are distinguished by Paul (1 Corinthians 13-14). See also J. Owen, *Works*, 4:469.

In addition, we suggest that prophecy itself may encompass all the speaking gifts, that all (apparently different) terms are merely different manifestations of broader understanding of the gift of prophecy. This enhances our argument that it is a universal gift.

35 Even the foretelling aspect was anchored to the past. The Old Testament prophet was validated by his "acumen for reading the past clearly and interpreting its meaning for their present time." Also C. H. Bullock, "Entre to the Pentateuch Through the Prophets: A Hermeneutics of History," in *Interpreting the Word of God*, ed. S. Schultz and M. Inch (Chicago: Moody, 1976), 76.

36 Fee, *Presence*, 908, notes that Paul's words, that "all may prophesy, one by one" (1 Corinthians 14:31),

reflect the promise of Joel 2. He goes on: "In Paul's view, to despise prophetic utterances is to quench the Spirit."

37 Both women and men exercise the gift (11:4-5); it appears to be limited to some (12:10, 28) but isn't; it will someday cease, when the perfect comes (13:2, 8-10); yet Paul wishes that all prophesy as the greatest gift (14:1-6-19, 24-33) and all should desire prophecy (14:37-39).

38 Owen, *Works*, 4:451ff., distinguishes prophecy as an extraordinary office and gift (1 Corinthians 12:28; Ephesians 4:11), as an extraordinary gift only (Acts 19:6; 21:9; 1 Corinthians 14:29-37), and as an ordinary office and gift (Romans 12:6). We are thinking primarily along the lines of his second and third categories, but do not wish to make prophecy to be nothing more than teaching or preaching the Word, as he does (452). Yet his distinction may help in the current debate over errant foretelling and the gift of prophecy.

39 See Chapter 8 for an elaboration of this.

40 While we are not to quench the Spirit, nor treat prophecies with contempt, we are to "test everything" (1 Thessalonians 5:19-21; cf. 1 John 4:1-3; 2 Peter 2; 3). This is just as it was in the Old Testament with the tests of fulfillment (Deuteronomy 18:17-22) and the truth (Deuteronomy 13). This implies that some prophesying may be wrong, and not from God in the first place, or that it has been wrongly interpreted.

41 These include limiting the number doing it; taking turns; yielding place to additional prophesying; and weighing one another's prophecy so that order and peace prevail. "The spirits of prophets are subject to the control of prophets" (v. 32)—they are not carried out by their own power but are subject to the prophets' "own judgment, choice, and understanding." Also J. Owen, *Works*, 470.

42 See Appendix A as it relates to postmodernism for further discussion on the additional meaning communicated in Scripture.

43 The verb *hearken* is from the same root as the word for "hear." So in this passage it is implicit that it is possible to hear and understand and yet neither hear nor understand fully. Israel was no different from the world in this regard. The biblical concept is that to hear and understand truly means to hearken, that is, to obey, to accept, to respond. Without this, full hearing and full understanding have not occurred. So the Spirit is necessary for both understanding and conviction of the truth so that belief follows. He, knowing who is to believe, assists their understanding of that which leads to their believing.

44 Note that we are writing here about meaning, not significance (following the distinctions of Chapter 3). That is, everyone, including those such as Fuller, Geisler, Stein, Kaiser, and Silva, and others, would agree that significance is not comprehended by an unbeliever (he will not submit to or believe the message as significant for him). But we are saying that he also will not fully understand the message. This is not just because hearing is biblically defined as also involving obedience, but also because Matthew 13 explicitly says that the heart or disposition affects, or at least is related to, hearing (and understanding) and seeing (and perceiving). All three go together; the whole person is involved. The modern equivalent of this is to say that meaning and understanding is cognitive (affecting the mind), affective (affecting the emotions), and volitional (affecting the will). On the basis of this unity, one cannot separate out the last two and assert that an unbeliever can do the first but not the last two. 2 Corinthians 3-4 agrees with this, as discussed above.

45 In this case (to make the equivalency for our purposes) these first three are not aided by the Spirit to enable

understanding. If, on the other hand, the two in the middle do understand it, this tends to support the idea that the natural man can understand the Word but doesn't bear fruit unless aided by the Holy Spirit. The former view is better, given the actual wording of the text.

46 M. Erickson, *Where Is Theology Going?* (Grand Rapids: Baker, 1994), 58, suggests that as postmodernism replaces our modern era, we may discover that human nature may not be as rational as previously thought.

47 Another argument in favor of our approach is this. Even for believers, there are levels of understanding. None of us fully comprehends what is spoken or written. We continue to mature in understanding. In Hebrews 5, the problem was failure to go beyond the elementary truths and become teachers of others. They remained babes needing milk. Applying again our paradigm of reality, we would say that this growth in understanding reflects the ongoing actualization of essential reality in the life of the Christian.

48 It is at this point that Erickson, *Hermeneutics*, 51-54, faults Fuller and others, and argues that the Holy Spirit is necessary to illumine—give insight or understanding or perception of the meaning that is in the biblical text. Hence he uses *illumination* in a different way than does Fuller. We simply disagree with Erickson that illumination is limited to the biblical text, for Paul was not referring to such when he wrote his words, there being virtually no text in existence.

49 This is our best understanding of this issue at this point. We are not linguists or psychologists, though we are continuing to read in the fields that inform this question. So we welcome insights from such fields that our readers may have on this question.

50 While all revelation about Christ must correspond to the message about Christ revealed in Scripture, all such

revelation has not been fully revealed. It may be final and adequate, but not exhaustive (cf. Deuteronomy 29:29). The *last days* in which God spoke by his Son (Hebrews 1:1-2) are still present. The very gift of prophecy suggests this, as do other spiritual gifts.

Someone may say that all that he knows of Christ is found in Scripture. This is manifestly not true. We do not know Him very well if it is limited to what we read of Him. We come to know far more of Christ in personal relationship.

In addition, it is the view of some that a few major contested portions of Scripture, debated as to their inspired (thus canonical) status—such as John 7:53-8:11 or Mark 16:9-20—are nevertheless valid historical and reliable teachings of Christ. Even Paul cites authentic but oral tradition (unrecorded before Paul—not found in the Gospels) from Jesus when he says that the Lord said that it is more blessed to give than to receive. It is conceivable that apocryphal and even pseudepigraphal documents from the era of the first few centuries contain authentic words of Jesus.

Clearly Deuteronomy 29:29 doesn't prohibit or discount the revealing of additional truth. When Moses spoke these words, there was yet to come the rest of the Old Testament and all of the New. Interestingly, it is verse 4 of this chapter that says that it is the LORD who "gives a mind that understands or eyes that see or ears that hear."

51 Interestingly, M. Silva, *Biblical Hermeneutics*, 267-268, suggests that the devotional use of the Bible—and even allegorical and reader-response interpretation—may have a place in interpretation. God works in spite of our ignorance of the grammatical-historical method, he says.

This matter of devotional reading is a little difficult to pin down. Two different kinds of things seem to happen in devotional reading that are akin to finding deeper meaning. In the first, the reader is so filled with Scripture and its world view that she unconsciously makes thematic or typological connections between texts so that she finds meaning akin to the sort that the New Testament authors found. (See Poythress' description of this in "The Divine Meaning of Scripture," *WTJ* 48 (1986): 274-275). This is primarily an *intertextual* sort of reading.

In the second, the reader is suddenly struck by a sentence or phrase as being God's guidance for him in a particular area of his life. The words are taken entirely out of context and read from the perspective of events in his life. An incident in Dietrich Bonhoeffer's life illustrates this. He was deciding to return to Germany instead of staying in the safety of America and writes this about 1 Timothy 4:21, "'Do your best to come before winter.' That follows me around all day. It is as if we were soldiers at home on leave, and going back into action.... 'Do your best to come before winter....' it is not a misuse of Scripture if I apply that to myself" (cited in R.B. Hays, *Echoes of Scripture in the Letters of Paul* (Yale University Press: New Haven, 1989), 178. The citation is originally from Dietrich Bonhoeffer, *Meditating on the Word*, ed. and trans. D. Gracie (Cambridge, MA: Cowley, 1986), 97-98.).

Many say that this sort of occurrence is simply a misguided use of the text. If these people also say that the Spirit cannot use anything else in such a manner to give a person specific directions or promises, then there is no inconsistency. But some of these people have no objection to the Spirit speaking to an individual in such a manner using something other than Scripture, as in the well-known incident in Augustine's life. While he was wrestling over the issue of sin and salvation, he heard in the voices of the children playing in the street, instructions from the Spirit, "Take, read." So he picked up the Bible lying on the bench, read in the book of Romans, and was saved. But if the Spirit can use such things as these, why is He not free to use His own Scripture in this way too? Again, in our desire to protect Scripture from abuse, we may find ourselves working against the Spirit.

The Kingdom center and the paradigm help us in different ways in these two types of devotional reading. The paradigm is a codification of what happens in the first kind of devotional reading. The second sort of devotional reading is totally without pattern. The Kingdom center can only help in acting as a check for weeding out impressions that cannot be the leading of the Spirit. (Obviously, it can act only as a check or control for a person who is sincerely seeking affirmation regarding an impression. The Kingdom center cannot act as a check for anyone who is so certain the Spirit is leading them that they will not listen to anyone. But such people would not be stopped by the stricter grammatical-historical hermeneutic either. These types of people are the reason that many would rather deny altogether that the Spirit speaks to anyone.)

52 Cited by A. Lindsley, "Response," 489. Paraphrasing Edwards, Lindsley writes that the Holy Spirit helps the believer "to understand more clearly the mutual relations of truths...a more lively sense of ideas."

J. Frame, "The Spirit and the Scriptures," in *Hermeneutics, Authority, and Canon*, ed. D.A. Carson and J. Woodbridge (Grand Rapids: Zondervan, 1986), 217-235, writes similarly. The Spirit does not give new words or revelation. In the process of knowing, the Spirit does not give new norms (reveal words), nor a new content (a new saving act in history); instead, He operates on the knower (our hearts and minds to illumine and persuade us) (229-230). The Spirit changes us so that we "acknowledge what is rationally warranted" (232). Although he acknowledges that Calvin is somewhat unclear on the Spirit's work, Frame is convinced that Calvin rejects new revelation, and Frame agrees with Calvin (233). Yet Frame fails to distinguish between revelation from the Spirit that is authoritative for an individual and what is normative for the whole church. He seems also to ignore totally the idea of the Spirit's aiding our interpretation or understanding of the revelation.

53 How the Book of Mormon fails this test of truth is illustrated by Joseph Smith's question regarding polygamy. He asks how such can now be allowed, given Jesus' teaching about a husband and wife forming one flesh. The angel responds by saying that it is new truth. Yet this is new "truth" that contradicts former truth.

54 In a sense we need not quibble here, for Jesus is the mine from which all treasures of wisdom and knowledge will be extracted (Colossians 2:3). There can be nothing new apart from Him. So all must be consistent with Him to be truth.

Other parallels might be made. The Law of Moses was new in the sense that it revealed new standards of relationship with God, or at least new ways by which the standards would be practiced. Yet it did not contradict or replace previous revelation, including the Abrahamic Covenant. This is Paul's point in Galatians 3:15-29. It is also Jesus' point when He said that He came not to destroy the Law, but to fulfill it. He certainly revealed new truth, but only such as gave the extension, continuity, and fullness of what was already there in seed form. Similarly, the use of the Old Testament in the New produces new truth, yet it is always in agreement with and not contradictory to earlier Scripture. See D. Bock, "Evangelicals and the Use of the Old Testament in the New, Part 2," *BibSac* 142 (October-December, 1985): 309.

55 See C. Evans, "The Function of the Old Testament in the New," in *Introducing New Testament Interpretation*,

ed. S. McKnight (Grand Rapids: Baker, 1989), 164-165 and sources cited there. This raises the issue of the Canon itself and the involvement of the Spirit in discerning it. Logically, it seems that since even the Canon is in dispute yet today between the Protestant church, the Catholic church, and the Orthodox church, we cannot be absolutely sure what is canonical. No verse of Scripture can help us here. And what of the first four hundred years when at least seven books of the New Testament canon were in general dispute, and some Christians even favored as canonical such books as the Didache or 1 Clement? If for almost four hundred years there was indecision regarding the Canon, was the Spirit limited to illuminating just twenty books until A.D. 400 or so? Did He not lead some in interpreting the truth of the disputed books, whether or not they became canonical? So truth exists both in and out of the Canon.

The author of 1 Clement 63.2, the earliest Christian non-canonical writer to address the Corinthians after Paul, considered himself to be writing by the Spirit. He wrote: "You will give us joy and gladness, if you are obedient to the things which we have written through the Holy Spirit."

56 Take the Council of Nicea (A.D. 325), for example. Emperor Constantine, having moved the capital of the Roman Empire from Rome to Constantinople in 323, brought substantial political unity to his empire. Yet religious controversy raged so strongly over the nature of Christ that public rioting often ensued. So he brought the churches of the East and West and Alexandria in the South together to come to some unity on the question. He felt that the Holy Spirit was leading him in this endeavor, and in the final creed of the Council, all but Arius (branded as a heretic) and two other bishops signed. Yet this final creed concluded with an amendment offered by Constantine himself

which utilized the crucial term, *homoousios*, "of the same substance," to make unmistakable the deity of Jesus Christ as one Person of the Godhead.

Was not the Holy Spirit active in the deliberations of this Council? Was not some degree of new truth discovered in the utilization of a nonbiblical, yet orthodox term, which spoke better to the heresy of the day than any term in Scripture? Would we not consider someone who denied the Nicean Creed to be less than orthodox, even less than biblical?

Perhaps there is a parallel in the current struggle over the word *inerrant*. While the term is nonbiblical, it may represent the best term orthodoxy can use today to distinguish those who view Scripture as authoritative in all its parts from those who don't. The International Council on Biblical Inerrancy sought to bring consensus on the issue.

Packer, *HIB*, 908, also points to the Spirit's leading the church to recognize the Canon. Yet he says that illumination "does not yield new truth, over and above what the Bible says; rather, it enables us to see what Scripture was showing us all along." We discover the Word yielding up to us its meaning, he affirms.

57 O. Chambers, *My Utmost for His Highest* (Grand Rapids: Discovery House, n.d.), 159.

58 This was apparently the way it was in those churches where the first English translation by Tyndale was first used and read.

59 Regarding obedience in this connection, Chambers, *Utmost*, says: "All God's revelations are sealed until they are opened to us by obedience....Obey God in the thing He shows you, and instantly the next thing is opened up... It is not study that does it, but obedience. The tiniest fragment of obedience, and heaven opens and the profoundest truths of God are yours straight away. God will never reveal more truth about Himself

until you have obeyed what you know already" (284). For October 12 he wrote: "Spiritual truth is learned by atmosphere, not by intellectual reasoning" (286).

NOTES - CHAPTER 7

1   See J. Dahms, "The Nature of Truth," *JETS* 28/4 (Dec. 1985): 455-465.

2   We will not be able to interact with these other models to explain in any detail how ours is an improvement over them. For a summary and evaluation of these other models and a more thorough presentation of our model, please see Sarah Hurty, "The Truth Shall Make You Free," Th.M. thesis, Western Seminary, Portland, OR, 1993. This thesis attempts to provide a theological basis for the Contemplative pursuit of mystical union with God and to explain why the spiritual disciplines work in sanctification by relating them logically to the essence of sin and the goal of sanctification.

3   By defining pride as self-definition we meet postmodernism's rejection of individualism and its concern for community.

4   This image of ourselves, which we create in violation of both love and truth, we will call *self-image*. Idolatry is an especially abominable sin in the Bible, and since image and idol are closely related terms, we could not resist using self-image to describe the product of pride. We use the word *identity* for all the good things that the word self-image often connotes in our common usage.

5   N. Snaith, "The Snare of Pride," *The Expository Times* 65 (August, 1954): 345-346.

6   These two aspects as the display of pride are seen in Galatians 5:26. See J. Piper, *Desiring God: Meditations of a Christian Hedonist* (Portland: Multnomah, 1986), 221-223, for his view that both boasting and self-pity are

manifestations of pride. "Boasting is the response of pride to success. Self-pity is the response of pride to suffering" (222).

7   Interestingly, in his sin man has condemned himself to being the source of his own identity. Whether he feels it or not, he is necessarily insecure as he is inadequate, by definition, as creature to provide his own identity. He is not God. He is not the source of truth. As he did not create himself, he did not in fact define himself. All people are fundamentally isolated, lonely, and insecure, no matter how arrogant they may feel and act.

8   This is in no way meant to minimize the fact that these same people are genuine victims to whom we are to give sincere aid and compassion. It is just recognizing that we will resort to anything for the purpose of pride.

9   R. Foster, *Prayer: Finding the Heart's True Home* (San Francisco: Harper, 1992), 60-61.

10 W. Hilton, *Toward a Perfect Love* (Portland: Multnomah, 1985), 88.

11 When it is done out of secret pride, it is sinful; there may well be cultural situations in which we should, out of love, follow the cultural practices and not give offense. "Ironically, pride in its positive sense [the product of identity] is compatible with true humility. On the other hand, false humility [the product of self-image] is a kind of pride. True humility is thinking of yourself neither too highly nor too lowly." D. Clark, "Philosophical Reflections on Self-Worth and Self-Love," *Journal of Psychology and Theology* 13 (Spring 1985): 9.

12 J. Edwards, *Religious Affections* (Portland: Multnomah, 1984), 108.

13 Ibid., 47

14 Hilton, *Perfect Love*, 79.

15 Ibid., 88.

16 Death is the logical consequence of sin. God is the only One who exists in Himself; all else exists because He gives them existence. God is our source of life. Sin separates us from God who gives us life. Death is the natural result. So also, when we are united with Christ, life is the natural result.

17 We are referring here to definitive sanctification in which, in our position before God, we are declared holy. Progressive sanctification refers to the process of becoming more like Christ in our daily lives.

18 We are not now both the old man and the new man simultaneously. Paul speaks of the full transaction as a past event: "Do not lie to one another, since you laid aside the old self with its evil practices, and have put on the new self who is being renewed to a true knowledge according to the image of the One who created him" (Colossians 3:9-10). This is speaking of the transfer from Adam to Christ and our death in Him that occurs at conversion.

19 The first two paragraphs dealing with the nature of this union with Christ contain ideas from J. Murray's *Redemption Accomplished and Applied* (Grand Rapids: Eerdmans, 1955), 169 ff. To these we added the third idea of "corporate."

We must not miss the additional observation that this passage actually speaks of the entire Trinity. The Holy Spirit is called the Spirit of God, with God perhaps referring to the Father, and He is called the Spirit of Him who raised Jesus from the dead. This seems in the context most certainly to be the Father. Thus, the Spirit is not only the Spirit of Christ, but the Spirit of the Father also. In some sense, the whole Trinitarian Godhead dwells within us! (See also John 14:16-17, 23, and 17:20-23.)

20 Ibid., 169.

21 See also 1 John 1:7 for this implication.

22 A. Hoekema, "The Reformed Perspective," in *Christian Spirituality: Five Views of Sanctification*, ed. D. Alexander (Downers Grove: InterVarsity, 1988), 81.

23 This is most apparent in Paul's pervasive pattern of indicative-imperative. First he says something is true, then he says to live it as true. We are united with Christ, so we are to live in union with Christ. We have been made holy, therefore we are to be holy. We have died to sin, therefore we are to stop sinning. Since we have the Spirit living within us, we are to "walk by the Spirit" (Galatians 5:16, 25). John is saying the same thing. This is also the key to understanding John's first epistle. When he writes of abiding, is he referring to salvation or to fellowship? The answer is both. Those who know God abide in Christ and He in them; they are to live it out. They are to love God and their brother and not sin. Those who sin and hate their brother do not abide in Him and are of the devil. John presents a black and white picture because God has designed us so that whatever we are, we manifest. Thus, those who are in Christ are to abide in Him.

24 Though we can know God directly through the Spirit, this is not our primary avenue for learning normative truth. This we learn first in Scripture. The Spirit convicts us of the truth of Scripture, and as we grow in the biblical truth world view, He enables us to perceive and apply truth in the people and the circumstances of our lives. The Spirit never contradicts Scripture and usually illuminates in the context of previously learned truth. Nevertheless, He is able to operate outside of Scripture, giving non-normative revelation (or communication, if one prefers) and enabling literal conversation with God.

25 Piper, *Desiring God*, 112.

26 O. Chambers, *My Utmost for His Highest* (Grand Rapids: Discovery House, 1963), 175.

27 This is Richard Foster's organization of the spiritual disciplines as found in his book *Celebration of Discipline: The Path to Spiritual Growth* (San Francisco: Harper & Row, 1988, rev.).

28 Likely, this is included in Foster's concept of submission.

29 Piper, *Desiring God*, 216.

30 Chambers, *Highest*, 219.

31 Having been saved by faith, we are sanctified by faith. Having begun by faith, we are made complete by faith (see Galatians 3:5).

32 Hilton, *Perfect Love*, 22.

33 This was true for the apostles also. The experience of the transfiguration made prophecy more sure. See 2 Peter 1:16-19.

34 Others also have made this point. See S. Grenz, *Theology for the Community of God* (Nashville: Broadman, 1994), 524.

NOTES - CHAPTER 8

1 David Fisher, pastor at Park Street Church, Boston, MA., has also called for a renewed theology of the Church along the same lines we are suggesting. See D. Fisher, "A Ministry for the 21st Century," Bueermann-Champion lectureship, January 26-29, 1993, Western Seminary, Portland, OR.

2 This is something of an oversimplification. This does not mean that Israel was not spiritual, but that God dealt with the nation as a whole as His people to whom He laid claim and over whom He ruled. The remnant

was the true Israel who was in relationship with Him.

3   See W. Bodine, "Power Ministry in the Epistles," ch. 6 in *The Kingdom and the Power*, ed. G. Greig and K. Springer (Ventura, CA: Regal Books, 1993), 197-206, for arguments against the cessationist view. J.I. Packer, in the following chapter, "The Empowered Christian Life," generally supports Christians practicing the miraculous gifts.

4   G. Cosby, "The Call to Community: Depending on God's Grace," pt. 2, *Sojourners* 15, no. 7 (July 1986): 37.

5   See Andres Tapia, "Reaching the First Post-Christian Generation," *Christianity Today*, September 12, 1994, 18-23, for a discussion of how the X generation is (or should be) affecting the ministry of the church, including the desire for real community.

6   For instance, if you ask troubling questions aloud in a Sunday school class, Bible college, seminary class, or even the lunchroom of a seminary faculty, you will probably get a defense of the accepted answer, if only out of concern for others who are listening. Speak with almost any professor or mature teacher alone, though, and you will most likely participate in an open, honest exploration of difficult questions.

7   For the impact of culture on our understanding of Scripture, see C. Kraft, *Christianity in Culture* (Maryknoll, N.Y.: Orbis, 1979). Challenging our traditional views of revelation and hermeneutics, the entire book is worth reading.

8   An ultimate concern repeated in Scripture is that peace and order prevail as much as possible in worship (see 1 Corinthians 11:16; 14:40).

9   Eugene H. Peterson, *The Message: The New Testament in Contemporary English* (Colorado Springs: NavPress, 1993).

10 It is clear that Jesus fulfilled all three significant offices from the Old Testament—namely Prophet (God spoke in Him, Deuteronomy 18:15-19; Hebrews 1:1-2); Priest (He offered the final sacrifice for sin, Hebrews 2:17-18; 4:14-16; 5:1-10; and most of chs. 7, 8, 9, and 10); and King (Hebrews 1:8-9).

Perhaps we do not make enough of Jesus' prophetic office in comparison to the other two. Yet in our controlling text in Matthew 11, John asked Jesus whether He was "the coming one"—a reference to the prophet Moses foretold (Deuteronomy 18:15). Even in Revelation 5 Jesus is not only the slain Lamb (corresponding to His office of priest) and Lion (the office of king), but also the One worthy to open the seven-sealed book and reveal its contents (the office of prophet). And the testimony of Jesus is the spirit of prophecy (19:10). The Revelation is the testimony of Jesus which God gave to Him to give to John (1:1-2).

11 K. Bockmuehl, *Listening to the God Who Speaks* (Colorado Springs: Helmers & Howard, 1990), 28, suggests that the prophetic experience has been democratized on the basis of such Old Testament passages as Isaiah 40:13-14; Jeremiah 31:31-34; and Ezekiel 36:25-27. So by His coming and bringing in the new covenant, Christ makes sovereignty an inward rule, the prophetic office universal, and the priesthood perfect. Thus writes E. Sauer, *The Triumph of the Crucified* (Grand Rapids: Eerdmans, 1966), 18, 92.

Since Jesus is our Brother (Hebrews 2:11-13, 17), and He fulfills the offices of Prophet, Priest, and King, we do also. By sending His Spirit, Jesus united Himself with His people and everything which He experienced is also their portion (Matthew 10:40; John 14:16-19, 26-28; 16:7-15). So by virtue of the believer's union with Christ, all believers fulfill all three offices. This is also the explicit witness of Scripture. We are designated priests (Revelation 1:6), a holy priesthood (1 Peter 2:5) who offer spiritual sacrifices (Hebrews 13:15-16). We are royalty, for we are a royal priesthood (1 Peter 2:9), and we will rule the nations with Him and sit on His throne (Revelation 2:26-27; 3:21). And we are also prophets, who proclaim His excellencies (1 Peter 2:9) as His witnesses (Acts 1:8).

That all should be prophets is not so strange when we consider the record of creation. There is a sense that this fulfills the original mission God had intended for humanity from the very beginning. For not only did God give a dominion mandate to man and woman as the working out of the Kingdom center of Scripture (Genesis 1), but a priestly and prophetic one as well within that larger theme.

Similarly, Sauer (91) writes that humanity has a prophetic status in creation as he investigates the nature of things and perceives spiritual ideas and eternal truths expressed in the world around him. By his understanding humankind "becomes the interpreter of the meaning of earthly nature, and by virtue of it exercises a prophetic task in his earthly kingdom." We concur wholeheartedly in his observation. This prophetic mandate reaches its greatest potential only as we uncover all the treasures of wisdom and knowledge hidden in Jesus Christ (Colossians 2:3).

All believers are prophets due to their union with Christ, the witness of Scripture, and the mandate of creation.

12 See the recent call to unity in R. Koivisto, *One Lord, One Faith* (Wheaton: Victor, 1993).

13 R. Hays, *Echoes of Scripture in the Letters of Paul* (New Haven: Yale, 1989), recognizes the importance of community. He asserts that Paul's is an ecclesiocentric hermeneutic: where Scripture speaks as a living Word, it "creates communities whose lives are hermeneutical testimonies, embodying the word, making its speech

palpable." Scripture continues to speak to "call into existence the community in which it can be heard rightly" (168). Paul also conceives of the community as an eschatological one. The end of the ages has come upon it (1 Corinthians 10:11) (168). Eschatological reversal has occurred (169); there are ironic reversals and temporal warps (170). M. Glodo, "The Bible in Stereo: New Opportunities for Biblical Interpretation in an A-Rational Age," ch. 9 in *The Challenge of Postmodernism: An Evangelical Engagement*, ed. D. Dockery (Wheaton: Victor, 1995), calls for the community to practice a "hermeneutic of imagination," wedding image to proposition in biblical exposition (12).

14 One concrete idea to demonstrate community is for pastors to learn to work together—not just to pray, to engage in mission or evangelism, but to share sermon notes, get input, socialize together, and truly love one another.

See also the prominence of community for theology in S. Grenz, *Theology for the Community of God* (Nashville: Broadman, 1994).

NOTES - CHAPTER 9

1 "Natural" is better understood as *creation* and the way it usually works according to our perception. God works equally all the time, and on occasion reveals His special (to us) working which we call miracle.

2 Millard Erickson, in *Where Is Theology Going?* (Grand Rapids: Baker, 1994), attempts to prognosticate theological development. Among the principles he acknowledges as guiding such prognostication is an understanding of the pattern of theological development (19-21). He sees a pendular or oscillating pattern in theological emphases between polar opposites, with the time growing shorter and shorter between reactions in the opposite direction. We agree with him in this

and have mentioned such pendulum swings more than once in this book.

At the same time, we also believe in the forward motion of theological development so that our biblical theology of the Kingdom center and our eschatology in particular are informing our understanding in a theology of theological change (see 25). In spite of our individual and collective sinfulness and constant penchant for falling away from the truth, God is nevertheless unfolding His truth in a kind of spiral that encompasses these pendulum swings and still moves forward. Erickson does not state such a view explicitly, in spite of addressing these issues head on. He seems basically to agree with us, though. It is implicit in his term *theological development*, and in his statement that "as theology moves onward, the agenda moves down to smaller details" (23).

3   He might do this by putting it in print, or teaching it and waiting for a response, or asking questions of the leaders in his local church. If it has merit, it slowly makes its way out into the broader church, to be tested by those from different cultures and traditions. The most helpful ideas are adopted widely and then subjected to the test of time.

4   A more commonly known example is the vowel-pointing of the Hebrew Bible. When the first parts of the Old Testament were composed, written Hebrew indicated only consonants. Since most Hebrew words are constructed from a root of only three consonants, there are a great many words that differ only by the vowels. But the written vowels were added later in Israel's history by nameless scribes. How do we know that they understood which word was to be indicated, hundreds of years after the original writing? The Spirit works quietly in usual human processes.

5   We say "core ideas in these doctrines" because there may be some minor details that do not change the

essence of the truth. For instance, regarding the Apostle's Creed, many of us would disagree that Christ descended into hell. This is a minor detail that has little effect on core truth. Our salvation is linked to His death and resurrection, core ideas in the creed that cannot be rejected without destroying the truth. So the Apostle's Creed can serve as a rule of faith for us, though this detail may be disregarded.

6   T. Oden, "Postmodern Evangelical Spirituality," paper presented to the Evangelical Theological Society, November 19, 1993, Washington, D.C. Both he and W. Pannenberg have addressed this matter.

7   Another aspect of this interconnectedness of all things is responsibility to and for community. Through speedy travel, incredible telecommunications capabilities, and economic interrelationships we are truly a global community, whether we like it or not. Now, more than ever, the starving orphan in drought-plagued northern Africa is our neighbor. We have the responsibility to think about how participation in our economic systems here affects that little girl there.

We need to seek a cosmic forgiveness, not just pardon for our individual sins. This is called *corporate solidarity*. It, too, is a biblical concept, and we should have been the leaders in corporate repentance and community action in rebuke to our individualistic culture.

8   This parallels the debate in biblical theology: Is the exegete supposed to recount as accurately as possible what the text says and the historical-cultural background that gave rise to it, or is she also supposed to interpret what it means and what it means for the Church in her day, which seems to be encroaching on the turf of systematic theology?

9   In making this suggestion, we mean to do more than just change the name or even the central idea.

Salvation history (*Heilsgeschichte*) is something of a technical term for a particular construct. We are addressing the formulation of salvation history by Oscar Cullmann, its latest major proponent. (Wolfhart Pannenberg can be considered to be in the tradition of salvation history in the largest sense, in that God reveals Himself and is accomplishing His salvific end in history. But he disavows salvation history, making some of the same criticisms we would make.)

We contend against salvation as God's purpose in history and against the suprahistorical nature of salvation history (as Cullmann formulated it). In suggesting Kingdom history (*Reichsgeschichte?*) we are suggesting a whole construct (including at least the biblical center and paradigm of reality in Chapters 4 and 5, and the understanding of God's work in history as expressed in this chapter). In proposing this construct, we want to affirm some elements of Cullmann's formulation, such as the proleptic end of history in Christ and the resulting tension of "already and not yet," the unfolding of revelation (which is what our hermeneutic is all about), and the necessity of divine revelation in addition to God's immanent historical acts in order to interpret those acts.

Wolfhart Pannenberg also dislikes the suprahistorical nature of salvation history, preferring an immanent working in all of history so that all of history is revelatory. But he confines revelation only to historical acts, disavowing divinely inspired interpretation of those acts. Instead, the interpretation arose naturally in the immediate experience of and subsequent reflection on those events. Scripture records that human interpretation, but it is not inspired or authoritative. We can't know if Scripture's interpretation or a different one is correct until it is all over. History can be interpreted and all truth and reality accounted for only from the perspective of the end. Then how can we interpret history? The end has come proleptically in Jesus Christ, so we can use the *Christ-event* as the end in order to interpret history. This means that God's revelation in history is entirely understandable through historical methodology, and there is no authoritative revelation to insult the sensibilities of modern man.

While we agree with Pannenberg that God reveals Himself in all of history, we disagree with him that God reveals Himself only in historical acts—which is a rather tricky thing to say anyway since a divine revelation (Spirit to spirit) can be considered a historical act since an historical person experiences and receives it.

We do not intend to throw out the baby with the bath water. It is quite possible to keep the name *salvation history* and offer another version of the idea that makes some of the corrections we suggest. In principle, this is what many evangelicals have done when they espouse the general idea of salvation history for understanding Scripture while dropping its troublesome elements. We have chosen to change the name for our suggested formulation because we also believe that Kingdom is the central theme.

10 Reading John Bright's *The Kingdom of God* (Nashville: Abingdon, 1953) is an interesting exercise. It explains the social, cultural, and political forces behind the development of events in Scripture. For those unaccustomed to thinking of biblical events as being truly historical, human, incarnational experiences, such a portrayal of the historical forces left out of Scripture can cause doubt about the divine aspect of the events. Reading Paul Johnson's *A History of Christianity* (New York: Macmillan, 1976) can have the same effect when one discovers facts such as the bribery that occurred to influence the results of the Council of Nicea, where the orthodox view of the nature of Christ was decided. Liturgy and worship and tradition tend to divest these events of their *human* causes so that they feel more

miraculous and supernatural. The Church in general needs a better understanding of both the transcendence and the immanence of God to view properly the mystery of God's acting in history. This would help to avoid a *de facto* suprahistorical view within the church.

11 Neither do some in our time, who are of Reconstructionist bent, understand this when they try to legislate the morality of the Old Testament in our own society.

NOTES - CHAPTER 10

1   R. Hays, *Echoes of Scripture in the Letters of Paul* (New Haven: Yale, 1989), 160. Whether we agree with Hays or not, he challenges us.

2   Ibid., 157.

3   Ibid., 156.

4   D. McCartney and C. Clayton, *Let the Reader Understand* (Wheaton: Victor Books, 1994), 158-159, suggest this fairly common example as one possible deeper meaning to be found by using restrained reader-response, as they believe the biblical writers did.

5   The author of Hebrews takes the current Roman idea requiring the death of the testator and reads this aspect back into the Old Testament concept of covenant. Can we take such modern concepts as requiring a testament to be written and witnessed, and find these in the concept of covenant? It seems that we can, at least in most instances.

6   This is what Sandra Schneiders professes she is willing to do if the Bible cannot be found to have meaning from her feminist perspective. See "Does the Bible Have a Postmodern Message?" in *Postmodern Theology: Christian Faith in a Pluralistic World*, ed. Frederic B. Burnham (New York: Harper, 1989), 71.

7   It is not the insidious subjectivism that results in the breakdown of shared meaning, written against by Erickson, *Evangelical Interpretation* (Grand Rapids: Baker, 1993), 31.

8   Ibid., 28.

9   "Christian Values in a Post-Christian Context," in *Postmodern Theology*, 26-31.

10 Remember that the existential meaning often includes the essential meaning since this meaning is also sometimes intended by the human author. See Chapter 5 for a review.

11 McKnight criticizes this canonical approach as anchoring meaning in the past in such a way that it limits the ability of finding/applying meaning in the modern religious context, *Postmodern Use of the Bible* (Nashville: Abingdon, 1988), 79.

12 This statement is complicated by the presence of other meanings in the text, which we can use to develop theology as above. Other meanings can be many and will vary according to the horizon of the reader. These other meanings and deeper meanings, divinely intended but unknown to the human author, are all objective in the text. Subjective meanings are essentially applications of these objective meanings to the particulars of our own lives (and are one way that Scripture is experienced as being more meaningful). This clarifies the deliberately simplified distinction in Chapter 5 between the objective deeper meaning and subjective deeper meanings. An example of deeper meaning in the sense of subjective meanings (or applications) would be the conviction to help the bag lady who stops in front of your house to ask you for a pot in which to cook her food. You would do it as an act of justice in recognition of her personhood (rather than an act of condescending mercy that is in some sense optional), according to meaning found objectively in the parable of the Good Samaritan.

13 Hirsch himself has qualified his own definition so much along these lines that it is hardly the same view expressed in *Validity in Interpretation*. See *The Aims of Interpretation* (Chicago: University of Chicago Press, 1976).

14 See McKnight, *Postmodern Use of the Bible*, 219-220, for such observations. See also his summary of Stulmacher's reconstituted historical method which recognized that "The biblical texts witness to a reality that the principles of historical study, as enunciated by Troeltsch, are not capable of perceiving: a witness of God that transcends particular historical periods" (82).

15 See W. Kaiser and M. Silva, *An Introduction to Biblical Hermeneutics* (Grand Rapids: Zondervan, 1994), 268.

16 G. Osborne, *The Hermeneutical Spiral* (Downers Grove: InterVarsity, 1991), 277.

17 On the issue of continuity versus discontinuity, see P. Verhoef, "The Relationships Between the Old and the New Testaments," in *New Perspectives on the Old Testament*, ed. J.B. Payne (Waco: Word, 1970), 293-295; K.L. Barker, "False Dichotomies Between the Testaments," *JETS* 25/1 (1982): 3-16; M. Karlberg, "Legitimate Discontinuities Between the Testaments," *JETS* 28/1 (1985): 9-20. The last two works seek to show the growing rapproachement between dispensationalists and covenant theologians. Karlberg, in particular, draws attention to a third view, which holds that promises to Israel will be realized in history prior to the consummation of history; how or when is unknown. The paradigm of reality accommodates both views and offers a compromise.

18 Osborne, *Spiral*, 287ff.

19 Ibid., 311. While we may say that our paradigm meets these various tests and criteria, we know that we will have to demonstrate this. That is a goal for our future study.

20 Yet this does not mean total abandonment of such phi-
    losophy, for some good is to be retained. Indeed, it is
    really not possible to do such.

21 Wm. Dyrness, *Learning about Theology from the Third
    World* (Grand Rapids: Zondervan, 1990).

22 Osborne, *Spiral*, 317. For a critique of narrative theolo-
    gy in the arena of apologetics, see D. Clark, "Narrative
    Theology and Apologetics," *JETS* 36/4 (Dec., 1993):
    499-515.

23 At first one might think that this paradigm is more
    compatible with amillennialism, especially with the
    idea that prophecy pertaining to events after the ascen-
    sion is to be fulfilled spiritually, as B. Waltke, "A
    Response," in *Dispensationalism, Israel and the Church*,
    C. Blaising and D. Bock, eds., (Grand Rapids:
    Zondervan, 1992), 355, asserts. Yet it need not be. The
    paradigm affirms both realities of meaning, the essential
    and the existential. God is working out the essential in
    the existential, the spiritual in the earthly (oversimpli-
    fied), so we personally tend to expect an eventual
    earthly and spiritual fulfillment of prophecies that
    Waltke spiritualizes.

24 The aspect of actualization in the paradigm of reality is
    related to the concept of horizons and the goal of the
    new hermeneutic or hermeneutical circle. The inter-
    preter is to enlarge his horizon until it fuses with the
    text's horizons. The goal is a "fusion of worlds" or
    "merging of horizons." See A.C. Thiselton, "The New
    Hermeneutic," in *New Testament Interpretation*, ed. I.H.
    Marshall (Grand Rapids: Eerdmans, 1977), 317.
    However, the paradigm affirms both realities, the exis-
    tential and essential, and upholds the integrity of the
    original intention. It is not so much a fusion of hori-
    zons, as though God's Kingdom or essential reality
    might change, as it is a subjection of one reality to
    another, with our world view being brought into con-
    formity with His. See R.G. Gruenler, "The New

Hermeneutic," *The Evangelical Dictionary of Theology*, ed. W. Elwell (Grand Rapids: Baker, 1984), 763-765.

25 D. Hesselgrave, "The Three Horizons: Cultural, Integration and Communication," *JETS* 28/4 (1985): 453. He projects the receptor audience as a third horizon. It seems good also to make the Kingdom a fourth horizon to help us interpret the other three. It is transcultural, appealing to all cultures to conform to the realm of God's Kingdom.

26 James B. De Young and Sarah L. Hurty, "Reproducing the Hermeneutic of Jesus: Kingdom Reality As a Biblical Hermeneutic," paper presented to the Evangelical Theological Society, Washington, D.C., November 18, 1993, 33ff. See our study for full bibliographic information about our sources for these matters.

27 See T. Tiessen, "Toward a Hermeneutic for Discerning Universal Moral Absolutes," *JETS* 36 (1993): 189-207. He sets forth five helpful principles.

28 The same may be said of Longenecker's "developmental hermeneutic" discussed by Tiessen (see note above) whereby Galatians 3:28 is made the heart of the gospel and emphasis is placed on redemption as exceeding creation. The Kingdom center is a more comprehensive concept than redemption.

29 Also B. Walsh and J. Middleton, *The Transforming Vision* (Downers Grove: InterVarsity, 1984), 37-39. The paradigm of reality also meets the four conditions of a Christian cultural vision, acknowledging the spiritual, the multidimensionality of life, God's norms for His creatures, and community.

NOTES - APPENDIX A

1 There are several such summaries available for reading. Here are a few listed in order of simplicity for understanding. For those who may find our necessarily

compact summaries a little difficult, we recommend the first three in the list as more basic and readable.

A. Tapia, "Reaching the First Post-Christian Generation," *Christianity Today* (September 12, 1994), 18-23.

J. Miller, "The Emerging Postmodern World," in *Postmodern Theology: Christian Faith in a Pluralistic World*, ed. F. Burnham (New York: Harper, 1989), 1-19.

M. Erickson, *Evangelical Interpretation* (Grand Rapids: Baker, 1993), 99-114.

D. Dockery, ed., *The Challenge of Postmodernism: An Evangelical Engagement* (Wheaton: Victor, 1995). See especially chapters 8-13.

E. V. McKnight, *Postmodern Use of the Bible* (Nashville: Abingdon Press, 1988), 27-62.

N. Murphy and J. McLendon, "Distinguishing Modern and Postmodern Theologies," *Modern Theology* 5:3 (April 1989):191-214.

We used these and several other sources for our own understanding of these three periods.

2   E. McKnight, *Postmodern Use*, 36. Much of this section is a summation of the material in McKnight, 27ff.

3   Ibid., 42.

4   Murphy and McLendon, "Distinguishing Theologies," 192.

5   McKnight, *Postmodern Use*, 42.

6   Ibid., 43.

7   Ibid., 43.

8   Murphy and McLendon, "Distinguishing Theologies," 192, 196-197. Yet at the same time, collectivism developed as "a powerful correlate of individualism" (197).

9   We draw here on the summary by S. Schneiders, "Does the Bible Have a Postmodern Message?" in *Postmodern Theology*, ed. F. Burnham (San Francisco: Harper & Row, 1989), 60-61.

10 As Schneiders, "Postmodern Message?", has written: "The scholars seemed to be caught in an infinite historical regress, tracing the ever more remote explanation of the ever more fragmented text into an ever receding antiquity that was ever less relevant to the concerns of the contemporary believer" (61).

The distinction between the interpretation of the text and its application has been clearly maintained, with the result that making application has come to be "an essentially extrinsic operation" often leaving the reader "alienated from the revelatory encounter which brought him or her to the text in the first place" (61).

11 For this summary and the representative figures of each period, we are indebted to S. Hayner, lectures given to the Review of Graduate Theological Education retreat, Salishan Lodge, Gleneden Beach, Oregon, October 28-30, 1994.

12 We use here the summary found in *Evangelical Interpretation* (Grand Rapids: Baker, 1993), 100-101. See also his nine-point summary of modernism, 105-107.

13 Murphy and McLendon, "Distinguishing Theologies," 202-203.

14 Ibid., 191, 199.

15 Schneiders, "Postmodern Message?" 62.

16 Ibid., 63.

17 From F. Burnham, ed., *Postmodern Theology* (San Francisco: Harper & Row, 1989), x-xi.

18 Ibid., xii.

19 We draw here on Erickson, *Evangelical Interpretation*, 102-103, who has drawn on others for this fourfold grouping. See D. Griffin, Wm. Beardslee, J. Holland, *Varieties of Postmodern Theology* (Albany: CUNY, 1989), 1-7.

20 Ibid.

21 References to his book in the following section will be included in parentheses.

22 These are found in full in his *Evangelical Interpretation*, 114-125.

23 See Chapter 5 where we distanced ourselves from Platonic dualism as far as the paradigm of reality is concerned. We affirm that our approach finds support in several passages of Scripture, particularly from the Book of Hebrews, where some have charged even that author with Platonic dualism (and they have been effectively refuted).

24 McKnight discusses the role of community in reading as a stop on the way to a radical reader-oriented approach, which he embraces. The individual eventually reigns supreme in the act of reading (16-17). We take the role of community in determining the legitimacy of a reading more seriously than he does, while recognizing that sometimes the individual is the one who is correct.

NOTES - APPENDIX B

1 See D. Moo, "The Problem of *Sensus Plenior*," *Hermeneutics, Authority, and Canon* (Grand Rapids: Zondervan, 1986), 202.

2 Validation of a hermenuetical approach may involve different criteria for us of the modern age. We should seek to understand the criteria of the biblical writers and let theirs become ours.

3 J. Sanders, *Canon and Community* (Philadelphia:

Fortress, 1984), 68.

4 Moo, "Problem," 199.

5 Ibid., 206, 210-211.

6 R. Longenecker, *Biblical Exegesis in the Apostolic Period* (Grand Rapids: Eerdmans, 1975), 214-220.

7 R. Hays, *Echoes of Scripture in the Letters of Paul* (New Haven: Yale, 1989), 181.

8 W. Kaiser and M. Silva, *An Introduction to Biblical Hermeneutics* (Grand Rapids: Zondervan, 1994), 246.

9 M. Silva, "New Testament Use of the Old Testament," in *Scripture and Truth*, ed. D.A. Carson and J. Woodbridge (Grand Rapids: Zondervan, 1983), 164. Yet Silva warns that "indiscriminate imitation is not called for; we need not reproduce the New Testament hermeneutic in all its features (any more than to do apostolic evangelism requires us to board ships instead of airplanes)."

10 Hays, *Echoes*, 181-182. Some additional comments from Hays on Paul's hermeneutic are worth repeating. Commenting on Longenecker's view he writes: "He places Paul on a theological pedestal. We are to believe and 'reproduce' his teachings but not to emulate the freedom with which he reads Scripture...the position recommended by Longenecker is inherently unstable: it commits us to a peculiar intellectual schizophrenia in which we arbitrarily grant privileged status to past interpretations that we deem unjustifiable with regard to normal, sober hermeneutical canons. (Let us not deceive ourselves about this: Paul would flunk our introductory exegesis courses.)...those who hold such views are strange successors to Paul, whose letters are models of hermeneutical freedom....Scripture interpretation is the theological matrix within which the kerygma took shape; removed from that matrix, it will die" (181-182).

11 S.L. Johnson, *The Old Testament in the New* (Grand Rapids: Zondervan, 1980), 93-94.

12 K. Snodgrass, "The Use of the Old Testament in the New," in *New Testament Criticism and Interpretation*, eds. D.A. Black and D.S. Dockery (Grand Rapids: Zondervan, 1991), 414, 427.

13 G.K. Beale, "Did Jesus and His Followers Preach the Right Doctrine from the Wrong Texts?" in *Right Doctrine from the Wrong Texts?* ed. G.K. Beale (Grand Rapids: Baker, 1994), 399-404.

14 See W. Klein, C. Blomberg, R. Hubbard, *Introduction to Biblical Interpretation* (Dallas: Word, 1993), 139-145.

15 D. McCartney and C. Clayton, *Let the Reader Understand* (Wheaton: Victor, 1994), 150-164. They seem to combine aspects of *sensus plenior*, *Heilsgeschichte*, Christology, canonical criticism, and others to discover this meaning. Their controls are four: the grammatical-historical meaning, the analogy of faith, God's redemptive history, and the Holy Spirit's directing of the Church (164). They view Kaiser's view as ridiculous and perverse (161).

16 D. Bock, "Use of the Old Testament in the New," in *Foundations for Biblical Interpretation* (Nashville: Broadman & Holman, 1994), 108-109.

17 B. Chilton, *A Galilean Rabbi and His Bible* (Wilmington: Michael Glazier, 1984), 191-192. He identifies this approach as the threefold process of analogy (discovering possible analogies to our circumstances); critical meditation, to decide to what extent a passage accords with our situation, where God speaks to us, and where He doesn't (we make a critical identification with a passage); and experience (the text describes our own experience in faith, at the point of the second feature. We move beyond our experience to where we experience God finally addressing us through the text).

The paradigm of reality, while similar to this, provides the avenue whereby to know God's present activity—actualization of essential reality—and provides parameters of control. The paradigm calls upon us to know God as essential reality reveals Him, in contrast to Chilton's process.

18 Ibid., 187. Another who calls for deriving our hermeneutic from Scripture is N. Gulley, "Reader-Response Theories in Postmodern Hermeneutics: A Challenge to Evangelical Theology," ch. 12 in *The Challenge of Postmodernism: An Evangelical Engagement*, ed. D. Dockery (Wheaton: Victor, 1995).

NOTES - APPENDIX D

1 Riots by slaves did occur in the Roman Empire under Eunus in Sicily and Spartacus in Italy. See H.P. Liddon, *Explanatory Analysis of St. Paul's First Epistle to Timothy* (Minneapolis: Klock and Klock, rep. 1978), 71.

2 Ibid., 72. Ignatius Polycarp 4.3 shows the early Church's view on the question: "Do not be haughty to slaves, either men or women; yet do not let them be puffed up, but let them rather endure slavery to the glory of God, that they may obtain a better freedom from God. Let them not desire to be set free at the Church's expense, that they be not found the slaves of lust." The concern for the gospel and its reputation is clear here. Concern for the faith of slaves is expressed in Didache 4.10-11. "Thou shalt not command in thy bitterness thy slave or thine handmaid, who hope in the same God, lest they cease to fear the God who is over you both; for he comes not to call men with respect of persons, but those whom the Spirit has prepared. But do you who are slaves be subject to your master, as to God's representative, in reverence and fear." Ignatius applies the figures of slave and free to himself, reflecting Paul's terminology (Ign. Rom. 4.3): "I do not order you as did Peter and

Paul; they were Apostles, I am a slave. But if I suffer I shall be Jesus Christ's freedman, and in him I shall rise free. Now I am learning in my bonds to give up all desires."

3   E. Elliot in *Passion and Purity* (Old Tappan, N.J.: Revell, 1984), 107ff., has an interesting discussion of patriarchy and believes that it is God-ordained.

4   Some may object to putting this reference here and instead would place it under essential reality. Yet whether "head" is defined as "representative," "prominent" or "eminent" part of the body, "authority over," "source," "responsibility for," "author" or "rulership," "head" appears to be an existential matter. See the survey of these ideas by Walter Liefeld, "Women, Submission and Ministry in 1 Corinthians," ch. 7, Alvera Mickelsen, *Women, Authority & The Bible* (Downers Grove: InterVarsity Press, 1986), 138-139. Man and woman are essentially the same, on the basis of their creation (Genesis 1:26-28) and their re-creation (Galatians 3:28). Therefore "head" appears to be an existential matter, or else it would necessitate an essential difference between them for all eternity.

5   1 Clement 21.8 seems to elevate the dignity of children as fellow believers in the following words, after addressing wives: "Let our children share (*metalambanetosan*) in the instruction which is in Christ, let them learn the strength of humility before God, the power of pure love before God, how beautiful and great is his fear and how it gives salvation to all who live holily in it with a pure mind."

6   See Mike Mason, *The Mystery of Marriage* (Portland: Multnomah Press, 1985), 153-154. The whole chapter on submission is worth reading. Similarly see Richard Foster, *The Celebration of Discipline* (San Francisco: Harper & Row, 1988), 117-121. The equation of submission and love obviously does not apply in difficult situations where true love requires us not to submit.

7   The earliest Church Fathers did not repeat such concepts as headship and the submission of wives to husbands. Interestingly, the relationship of wives to husbands is considered differently in the Apostolic Fathers.
(1) The term *head* is never used of the husband in relationship to the wife (nor is it used of Christ in any
way). (2) The term *submit* is never used of a wife's
responsibility to her husband. The term is used for sub-
mitting to one another (1 Clement 2.1; 57.2), to masters (Didache 4.11; Barnabas 19.7), to government (1
Clement 61.1), to generals (1 Clement 37.2), to church
officials (1 Clement 1.3; 57.1; Ignatius to Ephesians 2.2;
to Magnesians 2; 13.2), to God (1 Clement 20.1), to
Christ (1 Clement 34.5), to the will of God, the law (1
Clement 34.5), to one's neighbor (1 Clement 38.1) and
is used of appending one document to another
(Polycarp 13.2). The absence of a reference to wives is
conspicuous. (3) The command that is given to wives is
the command given to husbands in the New Testament,
namely "to love." Yet it is expanded to include love for
all believers. For example, 1 Clement 21.6-7 reads: "Let
us lead our wives to that which is good. Let them
exhibit the lovely habit of purity, let them show the
gentleness of their tongue manifest by their silence, let
them not give their affection by factious preference, but
in holiness to all equally who fear God." Polycarp to the
Philadelphians 4.2 reads: "Next teach our wives to
remain in the faith given to them, and in love and purity, tenderly loving their husbands in all truth, and loving all others equally in all chastity, and to educate
their children in the fear of God." It may be that the
Apostolic Fathers did not consider such concepts as the
headship of the husband and the submission of the wife
to her husband as lasting. The explicit statements
emphasize mutual submission (Ignatius to Ephesians
2.2; 1 Clement 1.3-2.1; 37.5). The closest a Father
comes to the idea of a wife being in submission comes
in 1 Clement 1.3: "and to the women you gave instruction that they should do all things with a blameless and

seemly and pure conscience, yielding (*stergousas*) a dutiful affection (*kathekontos*) to their husbands. And you taught them to remain in the rule of obedience (*hypotages*) and to manage their households with seemliness, in all circumspection." These last words are immediately followed by 2.1: "And you were all humble-minded and in no wise arrogant, yielding subjection rather than demanding it." Apparently, among later Church Fathers, the following do comment on a wife's subjection to her husband: Chrysostom (homily 20.1 in Ephesians; homily 26.2 in 1 Corinthians); Photius (1 Corinthians 11:3); Cyril, Arcad, and Pulch; and Theodore Mopsuestia (1 Corinthians 11:3).

8   Some may wish to place points 1-4 under essential reality, but it seems better to regard them as statements regarding existential reality. See n. 15.

9   Just what the woman's covering and authority are is disputed. A. Padgett, "Paul on Women in the Church," *JSNT* 20 (1984) 69-86, makes several suggestions on this passage in line with an egalitarian viewpoint. On v. 7 he suggests that glory means that the woman is the splendor, the grandeur, the succor of man. She is the last part of man to be created. She was created out of man (v. 8) because his situation was "not good" (Genesis 2:15). She was created because man needed her help ("because of the man," v. 9) (80-81). Because of these facts, woman ought to have the right ("authority") or ability or freedom to choose whatever hairstyle she chooses (71-72). She has such freedom because of the female messengers (not "angels") whom Paul would send to the Corinthian church and who should be free to adopt their own hairstyle (81-82). W. Liefeld ("Women, Submission & Ministry") suggests that the woman ought to have authority over her head to make decisions about her head, especially on the subject of veiling. Yet he prefers to see it as the right for women to pray and prophesy publicly (145-146), but not if they

bring shame to their husbands, caused by social offense. Hence he finds a double meaning. He does not believe that Paul writes in opposition to the pagan Corinthian practice of a ritual sex change (Kroeger) or maintains sexual distinctions that rampant homosexuality was blurring (cf. Romans 1:26-27). Liefeld, 146, believes that in this passage Paul uses the principle of headship to accommodate himself to Jewish and pagan standards of female decorum in order to avoid disgrace. The paradigm that this study presents is workable, however these problems are resolved, since it assumes that the context points to cultural patterns in which essential reality needs to be actualized.

10 The *de* of v. 3 may better mean *now* (so the NIV) rather than but (so the NASB).

11 Padgett ("Paul on Women in the Church") suggests that Paul is describing Corinthian custom in vv. 3-7b, and in vv. 7c-12 he corrects this custom on the basis of what it means to be *in Christ* (v. 11). The rest of the passage (vv. 13-16) reinforces Paul's egalitarian statements of vv. 10-12. Yet it seems more plausible that Paul is continuing his principle of not giving offense (last mentioned in the context immediately before, 10:31-34). He is the example, as is Christ.

12 "Nature," as Paul uses it, involves both the law of God and the informal laws of custom; it probably does not refer to the creation. Thus, nature does not represent something that is inviolable, just as the hair customs of Leviticus 19:27 were no longer standards for believers in Paul's day. So Liefeld ("Women, Submission & Ministry," 147-148) writes. See also J. De Young, "The Meaning of 'Nature' in Romans 1 and Its Implications for Biblical Proscriptions of Homosexual Behavior" *JETS* 31 (Dec. 1988) 429-441. Even the use of *synetheian* ("custom," "habit") in v. 16 puts the "emphasis on the principles behind the headcovering rather than on the headcovering itself" (Liefeld, 148). The

Corinthians should practice these customs, but a crucial doctrinal issue is not at stake. Even the terms describing the violations of custom or tradition are important to note. "Shame" (*kataischunei*, vv. 4-5; *aischron*, v. 6), not "proper" (*prepon*, v. 13), and "dishonor" (*atimia*, v. 14) do not seem to carry a moral or spiritual sense in the context.

13 So BAG, 675. It is "modifying what has gone before," so C.J. Ellicott, *St. Paul's First Epistle to the Corinthians; with a Critical and Grammatical Commentary* (Minneapolis: James Family, rep. of 1887 ed.), 1:206. Liefeld ("Women, Submission & Ministry") also sees it as a strong adversative that may range "from a complete reversal of the previous argument" to showing that "the freedom of the woman in verse 10 does not mean complete independence from her husband" (p. 146).

14 V.P. Furnish, *The Moral Teaching of Paul* (Nashville: Abingdon, 1979), 101.

15 See James B. De Young and Sarah L. Hurty, "Here, But Not Yet: A Paradigm Toward Understanding the Role of Women in Ministry," a paper presented to the Evangelical Theological Society, San Francisco, CA., Nov. 20, 1992, endnote 26, pp. 38-39, for fuller explanation. We suggest that views that solve the problem of this prohibition by saying that women may prophesy but not weigh or discern prophecy, and that prophecy in the Church may not have the same degree of authority as prophecy of the Old Testament, miss the mark. Implicit to vv. 26-30 is the participation of women. Instead, we suggest that the meaning is that Paul is simply reiterating the prohibitions or restrictions already given regarding tongues and prophecy. It is as though Paul is saying that women especially need to play by the rules. This finds support in the fact that when Paul summarizes the content of this chapter, he mentions prophecy and tongues but not the silence of women. We believe that this also explains the closely related

passage of 1 Timothy 2:12ff. Finally, violation of Paul's prohibitions is "shameful" (14:35)—a matter of disgrace but not sin (as in 11:6).

In addition, we observe that of these three uses (tongues, prophesying, women), the first two do not seem to be universal norms. (What would we do in a small gathering of five or six, or in a large one of five hundred? What if a culture allows for everyone to pray at the same time—such as in Korea? Could they also speak in tongues this way? What if the service went for five or six hours?) So if the first two cases are not universal, there seems to be no reason to believe that the third is.

16 That it is legitimate to consider Kingdom reality or history as a center for interpreting 1 Timothy is demonstrated by the references to Christ (or God) as the King. He is viewed as King in His transcendence here (1 Timothy 1:17; 6:15-16), as well as in 2 Timothy (2:12; 4:1,18; cf. 1:10; 4:8). Yet He is also as immanent as co-ruler: "we will reign with him" (2 Timothy 2:12) and a personal friend: "the Lord stood at my side and gave me strength" (2 Timothy 4:17).

17 Again, a much fuller treatment of this passage can be found in our paper, "Here But Not Yet: A Paradigm," 17-25.

NOTES - APPENDIX E

1 Dialectical Theology is a slippery term since the main leaders who shared certain common attitudes rather quickly developed them in diverse ways. Karl Barth is recognized as the first important leader, beginning with the publication of his *Römerbrief* in 1919 [English translation, *The Epistle to the Romans*, 6th ed., trans. E.C. Hoskyns (London: Oxford University, 1993)]. See "Barth, Karl" and "Neo-orthodoxy" in *Evangelical*

Dictionary of Theology, ed. Walter Elwell (Grand Rapids: Baker, 1984).

2   A full summary of Cullmann's development in this area can be found in Theodore Dorman's *The Hermeneutics of Oscar Cullmann* (San Francisco: Mellen Research University Press, 1991).

3   O. Cullmann, *Salvation in History*, trans. S. G. Sowers (London: SCM Press, 1967), 89.

4   Ibid., 88.

5   Ibid., 90.

6   Ibid., 88.

7   O. Cullmann, *The Christology of the New Testament*, trans. S. Guthrie and C. Hall (Philadelphia: Westminster, rev. 1963), xiv.

8   Actually, we don't usually encounter them first in Scripture, but in *kerygma*, which is someone preaching or telling these things. But ultimately they are telling what is in Scripture.

9   The preached gospel is also called "the Word" (Philippians 1, 2; Acts 13), but ultimately for us this is found recorded in Scripture.

10 See chapter 9 again for a review of this process.

11 It is true that our formulation of a biblical theology—the sense we make out of the bits of data yielded by the grammatical-historical hermeneutic—is done from our perspective. But we contend that this does not erase the distinction between the "causes" that produced the text and the "effects" the text has on us, as some in postmodernism believe. Meaning is made sense of in interaction between the text and the interpreter. This is a continuing spiral where the text and historical data from the horizon of the text continually empower the reader to more accurately distinguish between her horizon and that of the text and to understand the meaning

that the text has, independent of her. See Appendix A.

12 See E. McKnight, *Postmodern Use of the Bible* (Nashville: Abbingdon, 1988), 219-220. 219-220, regarding such ideas in reading non-literary texts and literary texts where the world to which the text refers is not the same world as that of the text itself, but is an extension of that world.

13 Ibid., 234, for this observation and its source.

NOTES - APPENDIX F

1 E. Johnson, "Author's Intention and Biblical Interpretation," in *Hermeneutics, Inerrancy, and the Bible* (Grand Rapids: Zondervan, 1984), 416.

2 Ibid., 427.

3 Ibid., 425-426. Such a distinction between sense and referent is commonly accepted. For example, see G. Osborne, The *Hermeneutical Spiral* (Downers Grove: InterVarsity, 1991), 76-78, who cites the work of M. Silva, *Biblical Words and Their Meaning: An Introduction to Lexical Semantics* (Grand Rapids: Zondervan, 1983), 103-107.

4 Therefore, some of the same criticisms can be made of Johnson. He is unwilling that "the enlarged context of progressive revelation" should change the defining sense of the original passage. Yet could not the divine Author have so inspired the human author to allow a canonical or essential meaning? Is this approach adequate to explain those instances where the later author will say that the earlier text means something different (as the "this is that" of Matthew 11:10) or that it is fulfilled in Christ (even granting the elasticity of "fulfill"), as many passages in Hebrews and elsewhere purport? How do we discern the additional narrow references? Are these authoritative, like the New Testament's

narrower references? What prevents total subjectivity in the delineating of the referents?

5   E. Radmacher, "A Response to Author's Intention and Biblical Interpretation," in *Hermeneutics, Inerrancy, and the Bible*, 435 (hereafter cited as *HIB*).

6   Ibid., 436-437.

7   W. Kaiser, "A Response to Author's Intention and Biblical Interpretation," in *HIB*, 444-445.

8   Ibid., 446. This seems like an unnecessary deduction, especially when many interpreters find that the New Testament itself finds such essential or deeper meaning.

9   For example, D. Moo, "The Problem of *Sensus Plenior*" in *Hermeneutics, Authority, and Canon*, ed. D.A. Carson and J. Woodbridge (Grand Rapids: Zondervan, 1986), 186-87, 201-203, 211. Moo explicitly examines the impact of finding additional meaning on the doctrine of the inspiration of Scripture and the authority of Scripture and finds the idea of additional meaning compatible with such theological concerns.

10 See *HIB*, 883-885. Yet in his commentary on this last article, N. Geisler clarifies it as opposing meaning "not based in a literal understanding," and should not be understood as eliminating typology or designated allegory or other literary forms (898).

11 Ibid., 899.

12 Ibid., 900-901.

13 R. Youngblood, "A Response to Patrick Fairbairn and Biblical Hermeneutics as Related to the Quotations of the Old Testament in the New," in *HIB*, 782. See J. Wenham, *Christ & the Bible* (Downers Grove: InterVarsity, 1977), 103.

14 Ibid. See S.L. Johnson, *The Old Testament in the New* (Grand Rapids: Zondervan, 1980), 51. Johnson is one of the most vocal advocates of reproducing the

hermeneutic of the New Testament (see Appendix B).

15 Ibid., 787. See G.von Rad, "Typological Interpretation of the Old Testament," in *Essays on Old Testament Hermeneutics* (Richmond: John Knox, 1963), 39.

16 S.L. Johnson, "A Response to Patrick Fairbairn and Biblical Hermeneutics as Related to the Quotations of the Old Testament in the New," in *HIB*, 796, quoting D. Steinmetz, "The Superiority of Pre-Critical Exegesis," *Theology Today*, 37 (April, 1980): 27, 38.